BRITISH SECRET PROJECTS 4

BRITISH SECRET PROJECTS 4

BOMBERS 1935 to 1950

TONY BUTTLER MA AMRAeS

Crécy Publishing Ltd

www.crecy.co.uk

British Secret Projects Volume 4
Bombers 1935 to 1950
Tony Buttler MA AMRAeS

Published in 2020 by Crécy Publishing

A CIP record for this book is available from the British Library

Printed by Pelikan Print in Turkey

ISBN 9781910809341

Crécy Publishing Ltd
1a Ringway Trading Estate, Shadowmoss Rd
Manchester M22 5LH
Tel (0044) 161 499 0024

www.crecy.co.uk

FRONT COVER ART **Front cover image is a specially commissioned artwork by Daniel Uhr showing the proposed Avro 684 Stratosphere Bomber development of the famous Lancaster.**

REAR COVER

TOP **Manufacturer's model of the Fairey O.21/44.**

MIDDLE **Photo of a manufacturer's model of the Supermarine 328 which would have been included in the project brochure.** *Ralph Pegram*

BOTTOM **Buckingham B.Mk.I KV335 taken on 20 April 1945.**

FRONT FLAP

TOP **The 'conventional' Handley Page '70 Ton Bomber' design (14.1.43).**

BOTTOM **The piston-powered Handley Page '70 Ton Bomber' design fitted with a canard or rider-plane (14.1.43).**

Contents

Introduction

This volume completes this author's revision and updating of his titles in the British Secret Projects series. It also completes the separation of the Second World War volume into individual fighters and bombers titles, which has permitted a considerable expansion to be made in terms of additional photos and illustrations. The bulk of the text is unchanged from the first edition, but a good number of newly discovered projects and drawings and some new information are now included for the first time, and as many of the photographs of real aircraft as possible have been changed. Some of the new images here have almost certainly never been published before.

One particular feature of this second edition is the expanded background to the de Havilland Mosquito. I had no idea that quite a number of other companies looked at the concept of a fast unarmed bomber during the late 1930s and I am very grateful to Ralph Pegram for opening my eyes to these studies. His contributions also appear in a new chapter covering composite ('piggy-back') Bombers, and elsewhere. When summing up Ralph adds "all in all when you look at which of these designs was supported and what was dropped the official decision making proved to be pretty sound. There are not many designs in here that look as if they were lost opportunities, and quite a few were clearly flawed."

The sub-title dates, 1935 to 1950, embrace the rearmament period right through to the debuts of the final types developed during the war, some of which then take us into the recently revised post-1950 books in this series. Finding demarcation lines for what to include here was difficult and some readers may disagree with the decision to omit, or discuss only briefly, several 1933/34 period designs. However, an official post-war report noted that 'even the pre-1936 heavy and medium bombers (such as the Whitley and Hampden) could only partially be adapted to 1938 standards.' The Whitley was depicted as being 'still too slow and lumbering,' so when the first edition was written I felt that a more thorough coverage of such aeroplanes really belonged to a review of 1920s and early 1930s developments. To date, a volume covering this earlier period has never been written.

Certain post-war flying boat projects proposed in the late 1940s for service in the 1950s are also discussed. Had any of these types been put into service then they would have carried 1950s weaponry, but when they were designed the concept of the large military flying boat had become out of date and so these projects (and their requirements) were omitted from the post-war fighter and bomber volumes, and held back for this work.

As for all of the titles in this series, extensive use has been made of previously unpublished primary source material held by museums and record offices and in company and private collections. And to keep in line with the earlier volumes, particular emphasis has been given to the design competitions between projects from different companies. The result is the most complete record yet written to show the extent of British bomber design and development undertaken before and during the war. Project data throughout is the manufacturer's estimates; if submitted to the Ministry, these figures would normally be re-assessed by specialists and often changed (weights in particular would regularly increase) but using company data as much as possible provides a common factor in presenting the figures.

The interest which has been generated by the British Secret Projects series, and the follow-on American and Soviet volumes on which I was so fortunate to work, has been quite wonderful and is very much appreciated. Producing second editions like this has enabled me to say a big 'thank you' to everyone who has bought my books, to those who have attended my lectures, and for everyone's support over a career as an aviation historian which, as I write, is approaching 25 years! When the first words of British Secret Projects: Jet Fighters were written in the late 1990s, I never imaged that they would send me along such a wonderful path. I have been very lucky!

Tony Buttler MA, AMRAeS
Bretforton, November 2019

Acknowledgements

So many people have helped to put this book together. As before the lists of unbuilt projects in the Putnam series of books on British aircraft manufacturers, and selected other titles listed in the bibliography, provided the framework from which to begin my own research. After that I must thank the following for allowing me to raid their archives for information, drawings and photographs and for permission to publish material. I hope I've not forgotten anyone. Sadly, some of these folk are now no longer with us.

Attempts have been made to try to confirm permission to use certain Saunders-Roe drawings, but without success. Should their use be a cause of upset than I sincerely apologise.

Peter Amos (Miles Aircraft archive); the late Fred Ballam (Westland archive); Michael J. F. Bowyer; Sir George Cox; Ken Ellis; Chris Farara and the late Albert Kitchenside of the Brooklands Museum archive; the late Harry Fraser-Mitchell (Handley Page Association); the late Peter Green; Duncan Greenman (Bristol AiRchive); Barry Guess (BAe Heritage, Farnborough); Bill Harrison; Bob Hercock (Rolls-Royce Heritage, Filton); George Jenks (Avro Heritage); Tim Kershaw (Jet Age Museum); Brian Kervell; Paul Lawson and the staff of the BAe Brough Heritage Centre; Gordon Leith (RAF Museum, Hendon); the late Roger Lindsay; Paul McMaster (Ulster Aviation Society); the late Eric Morgan; the late Jim Oughton; Ralph Pegram; Clive Richards; Brian Riddle (National Aerospace Library); the staff of the Science Museum at Wroughton; the late Ray Sturtivant (Air-Britain); Les Whitehouse (Boulton Paul archive); Ray Williams (Armstrong Whitworth archive), and the staff of the National Archives at Kew.

In addition I am particularly grateful to Phil Butler for supplying the contracts listing and for various photographs and other material, to Ralph Pegram for artworks, background information and a number of previously unknown drawings, and Joe Cherrie for making models that filled gaps in my illustrations. And I must thank yet again the team at Crécy for their support and for completing another splendid production. It is such a pleasure to work with you all.

Chapter One
Light Bombers and Ground Attack

ABOVE A model depicting possibly an early version of the Phillips & Powis (Miles) M.44. *Miles Aircraft via Peter Amos*

During the early 1930s Britain assumed that the most likely enemy in any future war would be France, and several new military aircraft were developed with this in mind. The aeroplanes most influenced by this theory were some new bomber designs intended to replace types already in service. These included the Handley Page Hampden and Vickers Wellington medium day bombers (both originally developed to Specification B.9/32 although they entered service in much modified form) and the Fairey Battle light day bomber. The Battle was produced to P.27/32 and by the beginning of the war was serving in quantity with the RAF. The day bomber was considered to be one of the prime elements of Britain's main striking force against France and (as Colin Sinnott notes in *The Royal Air Force and Aircraft Design 1923-1939*) the distance to Paris was taken as the criterion for its range.

After the outbreak of war some British forces, including squadrons of Battles, were sent to France but, when the Germans invaded in 1940, the Battles were found to be outclassed against the *Luftwaffe's* fighters and were shot down in large numbers. These events signalled the end of the light day bomber as a prime element in Britain's forces and so the type does not feature very much in this book. As the war progressed a new type appeared which partially filled the gap left by the light bomber: the ground attack aircraft. The conflict's 'fast moving' battles with tanks and armoured vehicles required specialist aircraft to deal with them and, from the RAF's point of view, the task was to be largely filled by variants of the Hawker Hurricane, Typhoon and Tempest fighters. However, in 1942 and 1943 the first efforts were made by industry to produce a dedicated ground attack aircraft and these feature later in this first chapter.

At the start of the Second World War, the RAF did not believe in ground attack; it felt that the battlefield was not the place for aeroplanes so specific types dedicated to the ground attack and close-support roles fell outside RAF doctrine. The Service did have some Army co-operation types, such as the Westland Lysander, but considered that combat aircraft were better used for interdiction, which is why the RAF used types like the Blenheim and Battle and not equivalents to the German Junkers Ju 87 dive bomber and Ju 88 multi role-aircraft. The British Army disagreed and put considerable pressure on the RAF to change and eventually, by the time of the D-Day landings, the RAF had moved on to close air support with aircraft like the Typhoon. The key to ground attack operations is air superiority, which basically allows the operation of any other type of aeroplane over the battlefield.

Fairey Battle Mk.1 (flown)	
Span	54ft 0in (16.46m)
Length	52ft 2in (15.90m)
Wing Area	422sq.ft (39.21sq.m)
All-Up-Weight	10,792lb (4,895kg)
Powerplant	1 × 1,035hp (772kW) Merlin I
Max Speed/Height	241mph (388km/h) at 13,000ft (3,962m)
Armament	2 × 0.303in (7.7mm) machine guns, 1,000lb (454kg) bombs

ABOVE Fairey Battle serial K7558.

BELOW Hawker Henley serial L3243.

Hawker Henley (flown)	
Span	47ft 10in (14.58m)
Length	36ft 0in (10.97m)
Wing Area	342sq.ft (31.77sq.m)
All-Up-Weight	9,400lb (4,264kg)
Powerplant	1 × 1,025hp (764kW) Merlin II
Max Speed	300mph (483km/h)
Armament	750lb (340kg) bombs

Specification B.20/40

After the Fairey Battle, the next major day bomber specification was P.4/34 which was issued to tender on 12 November 1934 and was met by two prototypes, the Fairey P.4/34 and the Hawker Henley. The former followed the Battle's basic form and first flew on 13 January 1937 but it remained a prototype, although one example, K5099, was modified in March 1938 with a smaller span and raised tailplane to act as a flying mock-up for the Fairey Fulmar fleet fighter. The Hawker Henley, another type closely related structurally to the Hurricane, flew on 10 April 1937 and was ordered into production, but the Air Ministry's already shifting philosophy towards the light bomber brought changes to the requirements and the type was eventually used as a target tug.

The final effort to produce a light bomber was Specification B.20/40 of 1940 although, signifying the changes in thinking that had been made, this document actually called for a Close Army Support Bomber. This document requested a high-speed (280mph [451km/h] at 5,000ft [1,524m]) using a Merlin engine, plus dive bombing and a photo reconnaissance capability. Boulton Paul, Fairey and Hawker are known to have responded and a design from Westland was prepared which also appears to have been produced against B.20/40, despite being rather later in time scale.

Boulton Paul P.95

This two-seat bomber was powered by a Bristol Hercules VI (HE.6.SM) or a Rolls-Royce Griffon. It had a low, straight wing with a parallel-chord centre section, but sweepback on the outer wing leading-edge to assist in dealing with wire barrages, and also featured twin fins and rudders to keep the field of fire clear to deal with an attack from astern. There was a long canopy over the pilot and his gunner, although the rear was left open for the latter's ring-mounted twin 0.303in (7.7mm) Browning machine guns. One fixed, forward-firing Hispano 20mm cannon and four more Brownings were housed in each wing, while the fuselage and wing bomb bays could each hold one 250lb (113kg) bomb; the aircraft had a tricycle undercarriage. The crew were seated close together but the brochure acknowledged that this arrangement was not so satisfactory, from the point of view of rear defence, as when placing the gunner in the tail. The gunner was also able to get shots vertically downwards to each side of the rear fuselage. With the Hercules maximum rate of climb was given as 1,620ft/min (494m/min) at 5,000ft (1,524m) and service ceiling

Boulton Paul P.95 (c11.40)	
Span	44ft 0in (13.41m)
Length	35ft 6in (10.82m)
Wing Area	?
All-Up-Weight	12,440lb (5,643kg)
Powerplant	1 × Hercules VI or Griffon
Max Speed/Height	323mph (520km/h) or 316mph (508km/h) at 16,000ft (4,876m)
Armament	10 × 0.303in (7.7mm) machine guns, 2 × 20mm cannon, bombs

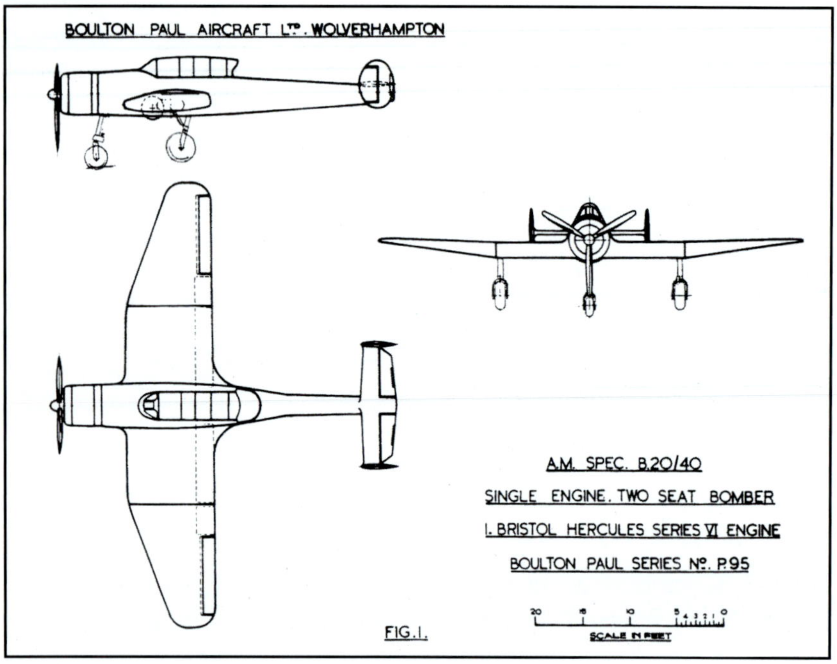

ABOVE Boulton Paul P.95 (c11.40). The wing guns (cannon inboard) were mounted either side of the leading-edge kink. *Les Whitehouse*

BELOW Artist's impressions of the Fairey B.20/40 (late 1940).

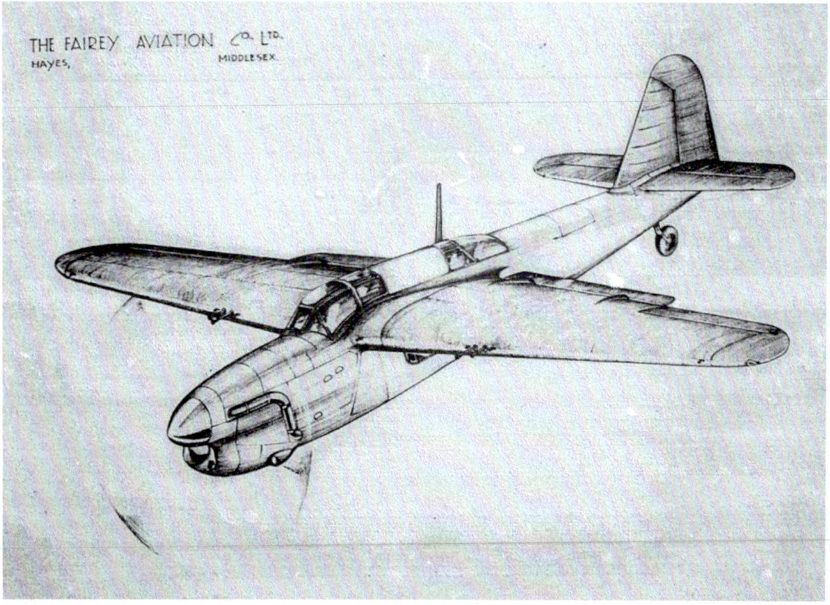

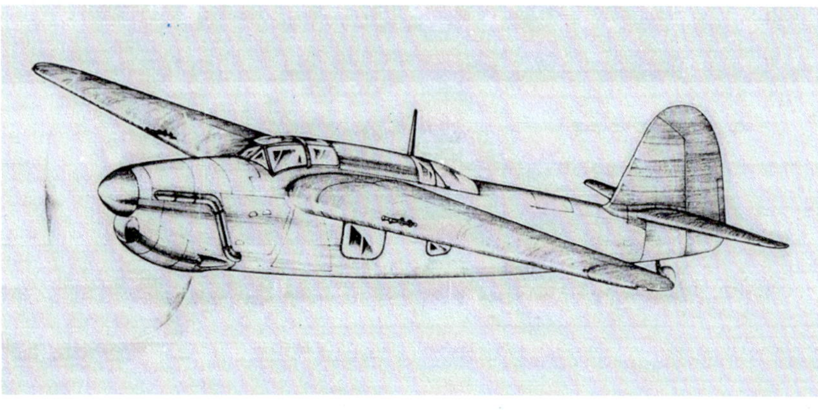

27,500ft (8,382m); equivalent figures for the Griffon were 1,825ft/min (556m/min) at 5,000ft and 30,000ft (9,144m). The aircraft's speed in a 60° dive, with flaps set at 90°, was not to exceed 300mph (483km/h).

Fairey B.20/40

Fairey stated that three main characteristics of B.20/40, high speed, good view (especially downwards) and dive bombing, were all met by the existing Barracuda (Chapter Seven) and so the tender offered that particular aeroplane suitably modified to meet the requirements. The requested 280mph (451km/h) speed was not thought possible with a Merlin (the most suitable powerplant) but this new design 'was small and as cleanly designed as possible' and its estimated 265mph (426km/h) was considered by Fairey to be a reasonable achievement. The high, mid wing gave an exceptionally wide field of view for the crew, both above and below, and it had external flaps which would be adjusted to positive angles for take-off and landing and to negative angles for braking in a dive bombing attack. This type of flap, developed full-scale on the Fairey P.4/34, had the advantage of comparatively light pitching moments in the dive and did not result in an excessively turbulent wake over the tail.

Except for the simplification brought by the removal of naval fittings, the B.20/40's structure was identical to the Barracuda's. Wing construction was light alloy throughout, a stressed skin reinforced with transverse stringers being used to cover two main spars and the ribs, but the ailerons would be fabric covered. The extreme forward and rear portions of the fuselage, including the engine mounting, used a tubular metal

Fairey B.20/40 (late 1940)	
Span	49ft 2in (14.99m)
Length	39ft 11in (12.17m)
Wing Area	?
All-Up-Weight	11,810lb (5,357kg)
Powerplant	1 × Merlin RM.5.SM
Max Speed/Height	265mph (426km/h) at 10,750ft (3,277m)
Armament	6 × 0.303in (7.7mm) machine guns, bombs

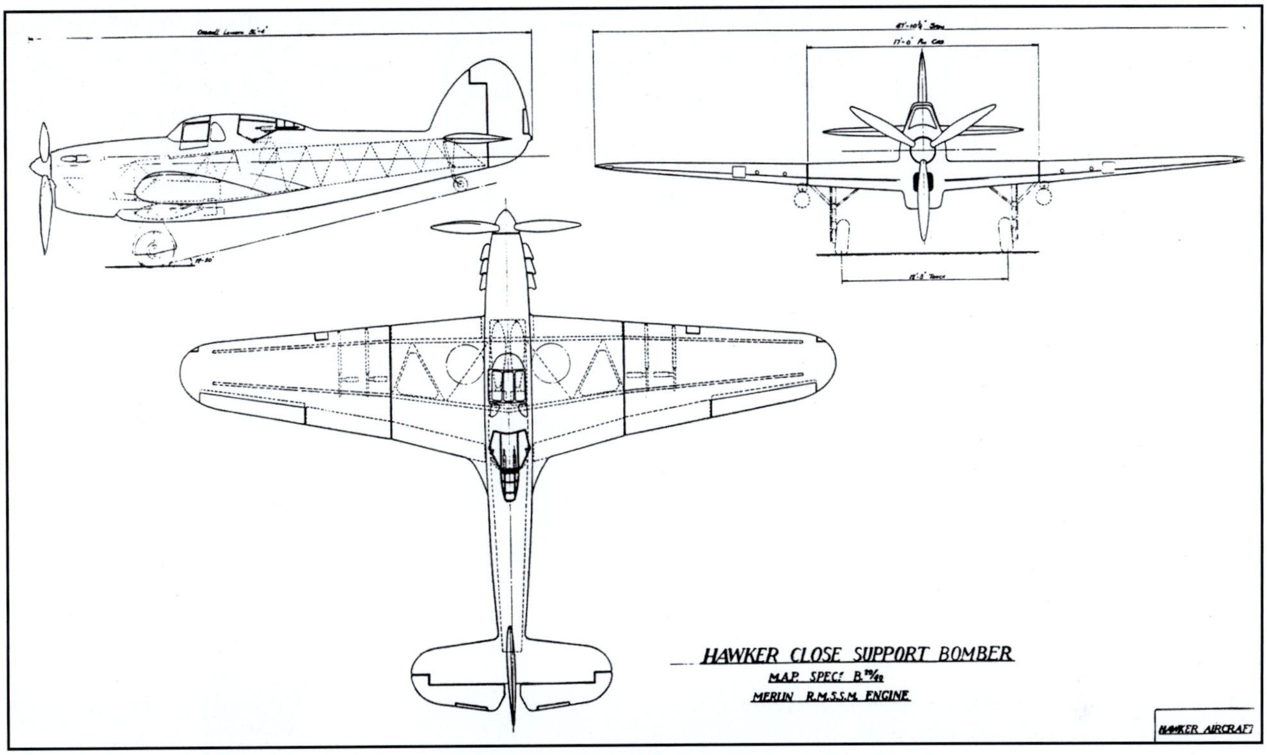

ABOVE The Hawker P.1006 close support bomber (late 1940). *Chris Farara*

structure but the remainder was composed of light alloy monocoque. The fin and tailplane were made of stressed skin built up on cantilever spars. Armament comprised four 0.303in (7.7mm) machine guns firing forward, two more facing rearwards plus bombs, and 195gal (886lit) of internal fuel were carried. The aircraft would take 3.5 minutes to reach 5,000ft (1,524m) and 17.83 minutes to 20,000ft (6,096m); service ceiling was 25,500ft (7,772m) and range with normal load 500 miles (805km).

Hawker P.1006

Hawker also offered a modification of an existing design, the Henley. No detailed information survives, but the drawing shows few changes from the original Henley except for a more powerful RM.5.SM Merlin; the span was unchanged and the length only slightly increased. Two 0.303in Brownings were housed in the rear cockpit and another pair in the middle of each wing, and two 250lb (113kg) bombs were carried in a fuselage bay beneath the pilot with one more under each wing.

Hawker P.1006 (late 1940)	
Span	47ft 10in (14.58m)
Length	36ft 4in (11.07m)
Wing Area	?
All-Up-Weight	?
Powerplant	1 × Merlin RM.5.SM
Max Speed/Height	?
Armament	6 × 0.303in (7.7mm) machine guns, 4 × 250lb (113kg) bombs

Westland B.20/40

This dive bomber project, a variant of Westland's B.7/40 design (Chapter Three) but without the Delanne wing, appears to have been created about six or seven months later than the above; some published sources credit it to B.20/40 but not Westland's own documents. It featured a Bristol Centaurus engine, a cannon under each wing and four machine guns in a rear cockpit turret.

BELOW Sketch of the Westland dive bomber (6.41). *Westland Archive*

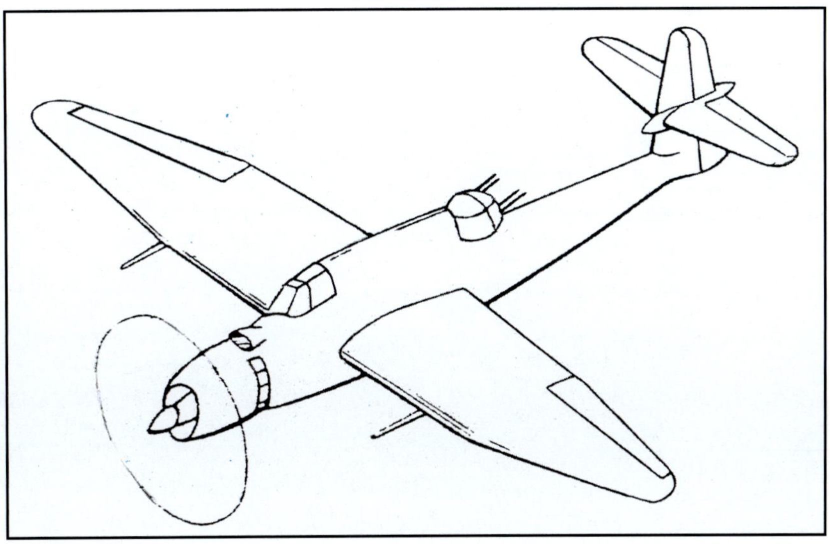

Westland B.20/40 (6.41)	
Span	53ft 0in (16.15m)
Length	?
Wing Area	400sq.ft (37.16sq.m)
All-Up-Weight	13,500lb (6,124kg)
Powerplant	1 × 2,150hp (1,603kW) Centaurus
Max Speed/Height	290mph (467km/h) at 5,000ft (1,524m)
Armament	2 × 20mm cannon, 4 × machine guns, bombs

Specification B.20/40 was not proceeded with and none of these designs was accepted for construction.

Ground Attack

On 7 March 1942 a draft specification, which never received a number, was raised for a 'highly manoeuvrable single-seat low attack aircraft for employment against military forces on the ground, aircraft, invasion craft and shipping.' The aircraft's primary role was to be the destruction of tanks and similar targets and it was to replace the Hurricane Mk.IID (the IID was armed with two 40mm cannon and served as a ground attack 'tank buster'). It was classed as an Army Direct Support Aircraft and was to carry more guns, of heavier calibre, than the Hurricane: the alternatives were three 40mm cannon; two 40mm cannon plus two 20mm cannon; four 20mm, two 20mm and six unguided rocket projectile (RP) racks; or two 20mm with one Vickers 47mm (3.5lb [1.6kg]) gun. Provision

ABOVE An unidentified ground-attack Hawker Hurricane displays its cannon armament in an excellent air-to-air photo.

BELOW Hurricane Mk.IID KZ320 fitted with 40mm Vickers S guns.

was also to be made for two 500lb (227kg) bombs. The maximum speed had to be at least 280mph (451km/h) at 3,000ft (914m) and an excellent forward view was considered essential. This new type of aeroplane had to be in full-scale production by January 1944.

On 25 March the Assistant Director, Research and Development (Technical), RD/ADT, at the Ministry of Aircraft Production, Capt R. N. Liptrot, completed an investigation identifying three possible types of aircraft that could fill this requirement – a twin-boom pusher with one Merlin 61 (top speed 195mph [314km/h], span 57ft [17.37m]); a twin-boom pusher with one Sabre III (223mph [359km/h], 65ft [19.81m]); or a normal twin-engine type with two Merlin 61 (225mph [362km/h], 70ft [21.34m]). Since this was a 'new' type of aircraft, there were various arguments suggesting what might actually be built – should the RAF continue with a Hurricane with 'heavy armament' or (as ACM Sir Wilfrid Freeman noted on 26 April) should it be an aircraft designed and built by one of the 'smaller' companies such as General Aircraft or Westland? A letter was sent to Airspeed, Armstrong Whitworth, Boulton Paul and Phillips & Powis on 15 August 1942 outlining the new requirement, but Boulton Paul delayed its submission because of a lack of information on both the rocket projectiles and the 47mm gun (which was not yet in existence). In the meantime a design was offered by Cunliffe-Owen.

Cunliffe-Owen Attack Aircraft

This brochure, submitted on 30 August 1942, outlined four versions of the same aircraft:

No 1 carried thirty *(sic)* 0.303in (7.7mm) machine guns mounted at a fixed angle of depression,

No 2 had nine 40mm cannon – seven in the aerofoil body at a fixed angle of depression and the other pair placed horizontally under the outer wings,

No 3 was a version with three banks of four RPs,

No 4 (to illustrate the design's versatility) was a dive bomber.

A big feature for 1 and 2 was that the pilot could fly straight across his target instead of diving onto it.

On 10 September 1942 R. S. Sorley commented that this design, from a sighting and technical point of view, was open to several objections, but the combination of loads within an all-up-weight of 18,000lb (8,165kg) was interesting, if it was possible. Five days later N. E. Rowe, DTD, reported that it was unsuitable for ground attack because the angled-down guns gave insuperable sighting problems and technical limitations. There was strong support elsewhere for the Hurricane IID rather than this nine-gun design which, at 68ft (20.73m) span, was too big to be satisfactory in the low attack role. Cunliffe-Owen was informed as such on 18 September but was also asked to produce a design for the latest updated requirements for a low attack aircraft. Three days later Airspeed, Armstrong Whitworth, Boulton Paul, Cunliffe-Owen and Phillips & Powis (which in October 1943 became Miles Aircraft) were officially invited to tender; only Airspeed did not.

Armstrong Whitworth AW.49

During the first years of the war the chief designer at AWA, John 'Jimmy' Lloyd, had become interested in low-drag aerofoils and in 1942 the company received a contract from the Directorate of Scientific Research to design and construct a full-scale wing section that would be used for laminar flow wind tunnel tests at the National Physical Laboratory. AWA's solution was to fit the wing's structure onto a relatively thick but accurately shaped outer skin – the reverse of usual contemporary practice, where the skin was fitted to the structure – and the wing gave good results in the tunnel. By the time the ground attack requirement appeared, AWA had sufficient confidence in this wing to consider putting it onto a real aeroplane and the specification gave Lloyd the opportunity to do so.

The AW.49 was actually submitted two days before the invitation to tender was sent out. It had twin booms and a pusher engine, either a Rolls Merlin X or Napier Sabre IV, which helped the pilot's view and removed the turbulent airflow over the wing that would have been present on a tractor arrangement. A retractable or fixed undercarriage could be used although AWA recommended the former because a fixed version would cut the top speed by around 25mph (40km/h). Three 40mm cannon were housed in the nose and two 20mm in the wing roots, and the two 500lb (227kg) bombs would be carried under the wings; alternative weapon options were three 20mm and two 40mm, or five 20mm. Maximum range for the Sabre variant on internal fuel (175gal [796lit]) was 1,010 miles (1,625km). After the AW.49 was rejected, AWA continued its work on laminar flow and adopted the flying wing arrangement to gain the maximum benefit from it. This resulted in the AW.52 research aeroplanes flown after the war and the AW.50 and AW.56 jet bomber projects.

Armstrong Whitworth AW.49 Version I (9.42)	
Span	48ft 0in (14.63m)
Length	36ft 2in (11.02m)
Wing Area	325sq.ft (30.19sq.m)
All-Up-Weight	10,316lb (4,679kg)
Powerplant	1 × 1,280hp (954kW) Merlin X
Max Speed/Height	291mph (468km/h) at 3,000ft (914m)
Armament	see text
Armstrong Whitworth AW.49 Version II (9.42)	
Span	48ft 0in (14.62m)
Length	36ft 2in (11.02m)
Wing Area	325sq.ft (30.19sq.m)
All-Up-Weight	12,129lb (5,502kg)
Powerplant	1 × 2,500hp (1,864kW) Sabre IV
Max Speed/Height	355mph (571km/h) at 3,000ft (914m)
Armament	see text

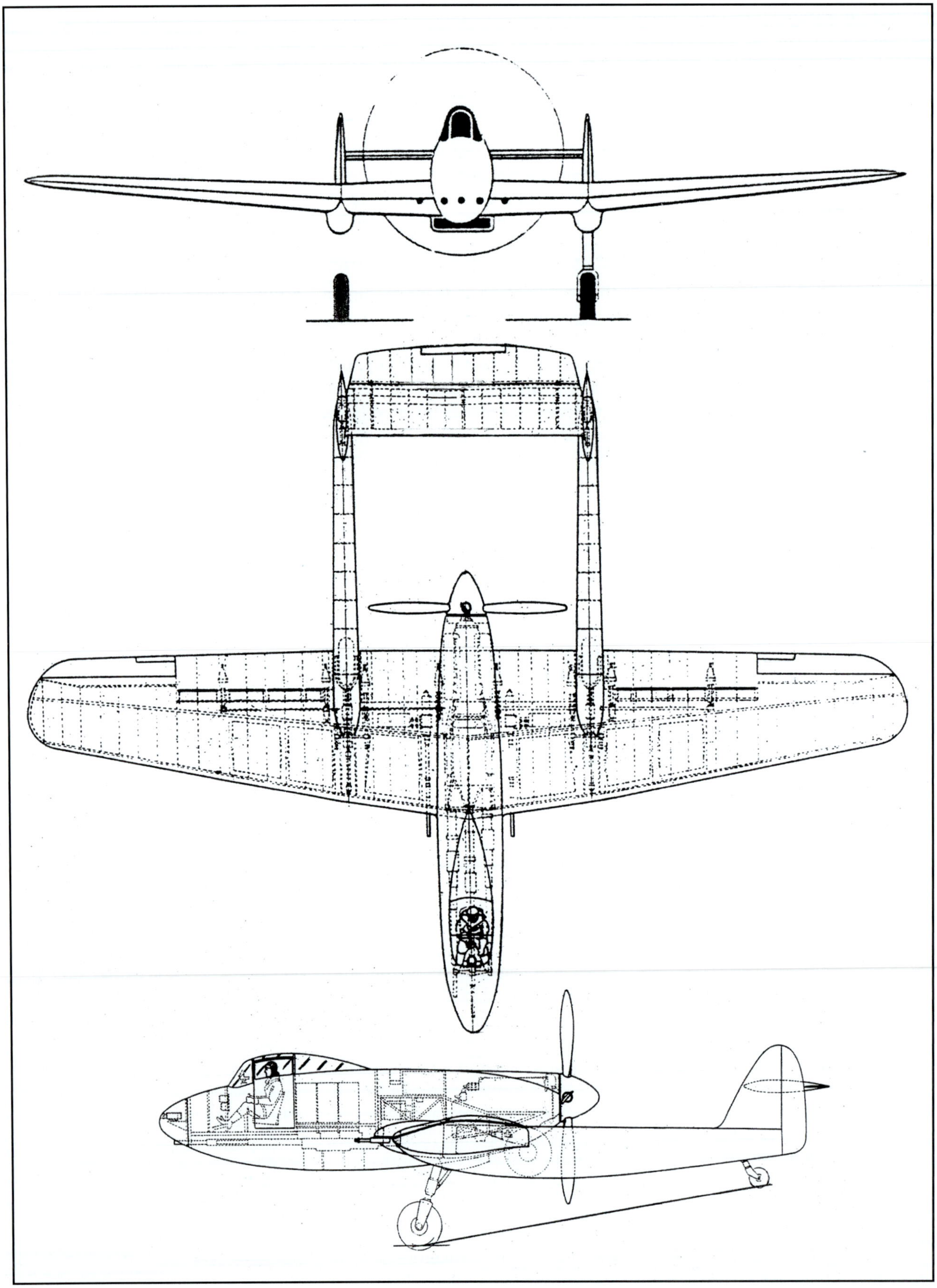

ABOVE Armstrong Whitworth AW.49 (11.9.42). *Ray Williams*

Boulton Paul P.99

A similar layout to the AW.49 was adopted here, but the P.99 used a Griffon engine and contra-rotating propellers and had a single fin and rudder in the centre of the horizontal tail; a tailwheel was also fitted under the fin. The major factors in choosing the twin booms were to give the pilot the best possible view while, at the same time, striving to meet the requirement that the aircraft should be capable of entering production in the minimum time (to satisfy this it would have to be ordered 'off the drawing board'). It was known that the American Lockheed P-38 Lightning fighter suffered from tail flutter at high speed which might produce some prejudice against the twin-boom configuration, but a careful study of the causes of the P-38's problems, including a breakdown of flow resulting in the tail being in a turbulent region or rotational component of the slipstream, indicated that the P.99 should be free of them; the second element, for example, would not exist with contra-rotating propellers.

A normal tailwheel undercarriage was chosen since it would be more suitable for operating from advanced bases. Two bombs or eight RP were carried under the wings and there were alternative cannon fittings in the lower front fuselage, a single 47mm flanked by two 20mm or the twin 20mm in the middle with one 40mm to each side. A total of 260gal (1,182lit) of internal fuel was carried. To avoid the propeller when baling out from the aircraft, the pilot had a downward escape mechanism in which the lower forward fuselage beneath his seat fell away. Maximum rate of climb (up to 2,000ft [610m]) was 2,140ft/min (652m/min) and range with normal load 785 miles (1,263km). The time allowed for preparing this project prevented its general construction from being determined satisfactorily (the issue was 'too important to be lightly treated') but Boulton Paul noted that very promising results had been obtained on the use of plastics, both for structural members and detail parts, and this knowledge and technique would be pressed into use wherever possible.

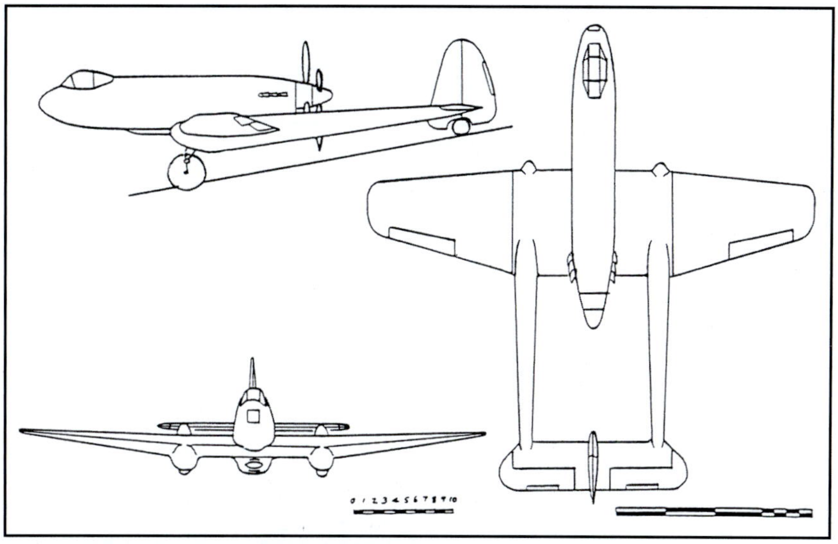

ABOVE Boulton Paul P.99 (6.10.42). *Les Whitehouse*
BELOW Artist's impression of the P.99. *Les Whitehouse*

Boulton Paul P.99 (6.10.42)	
Span	44ft 8in (13.61m)
Length	45ft 6in (13.87m)
Wing Area	360sq.ft (33.45sq.m)
All-Up-Weight	14,074lb (6,384kg)
Powerplant	1 × 1,760hp (1,312kW) Griffon II
Max Speed/Height	315mph (507km/h) at 17,000ft (5,182m)
Armament	see text

Boulton Paul P.100

This project, another pusher design with contra-rotating propellers, also featured a canard (foreplane) and had the wing, with tip fins and rudders, placed to the rear of the fuselage. Such a layout required a tricycle undercarriage and the gun options available to the P.99 were supplemented by the additional choice of four 20mm cannon. This unorthodox design was chosen as the logical solution to the problems set by the specification. The size and weight of the armament was such that it demanded primary consideration and so the fundamental problem was to arrange the guns and sights in the ideal positions for operation and maintenance; the structural and aerodynamic arrangements were of secondary importance.

The P.100's layout solved the first problem 'adequately' while the second issue could be resolved by either 1) a twin-engine tractor aircraft or 2) a single-engine pusher with either a) twin booms, b) a tail first, or c) pterodactyl arrangement. The twin tractor would be

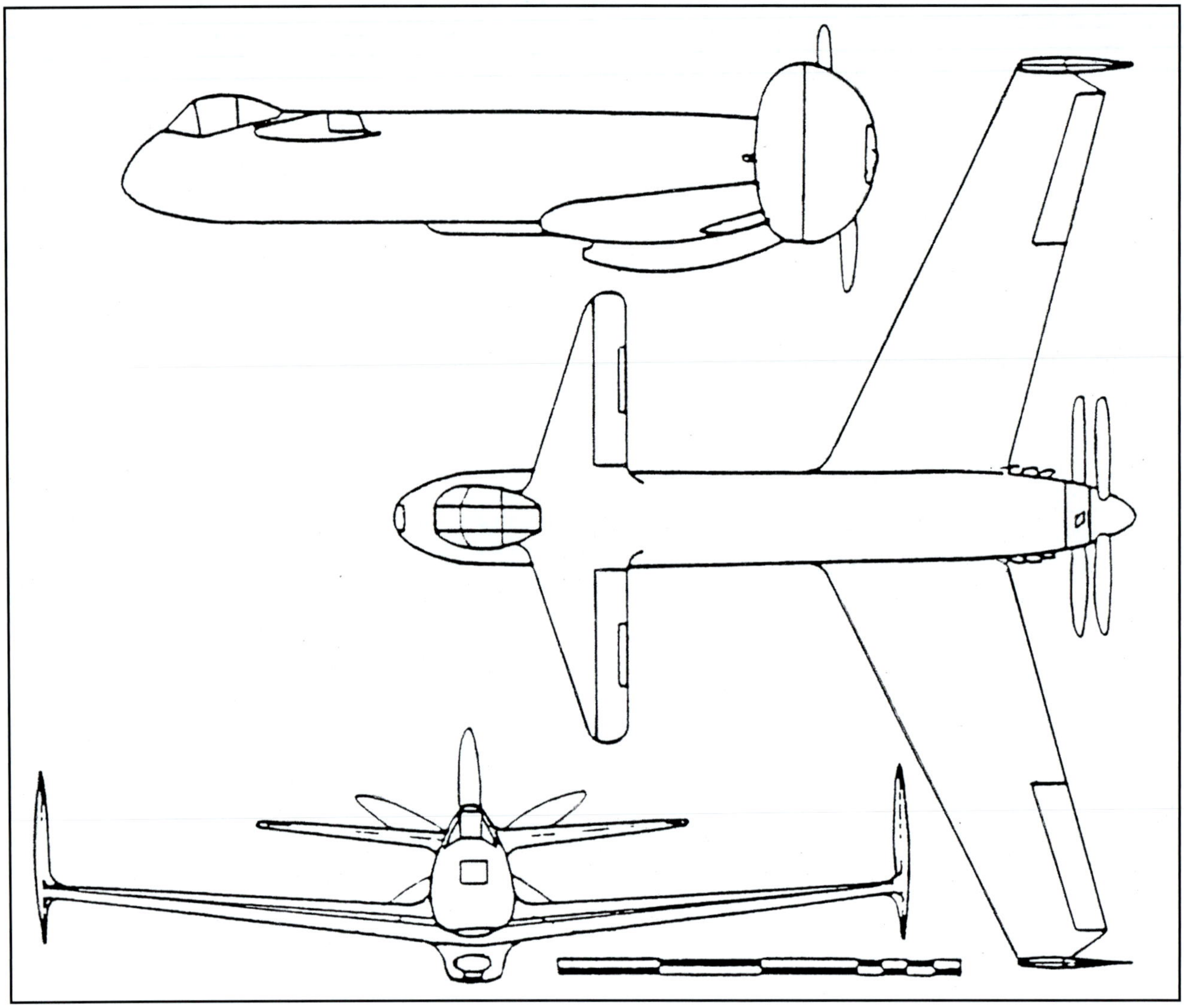

ABOVE Boulton Paul P.100 (6.10.42). *Les Whitehouse*

BELOW Artist's impression of the P.100. *Les Whitehouse*

a more complex aircraft to manufacture and would not be as manoeuvrable as 2a or 2b, especially in the rolling plane, while 2c was a reasonable solution but its control and stability in the pitching plane was inferior to all of the others. The twin boom was aerodynamically conventional but was not as clean or as light in weight as the tail first. In the tail-first machine both the stabiliser and main wings were lifting surfaces and it followed that for equal wing loadings the span of this aircraft would be smaller than for any other monoplane type. Consequently its rolling acceleration and velocity would be greater while the pitching stability would differ little from the conventional machine, since both the longitudinal disposition of the main and stabilising surfaces were not much different.

The greatest departure from a normal aircraft was in the yawing plane and in order to harmonise the three controls it was felt that some special design features would be necessary. For both stability and control it was desirable to place the fin and rudder surfaces as far aft as possible and, to achieve this without tail booms, the wings had been given considerable sweep-back. In the absence of wind tunnel tests, calculations had been made which indicated that two quite moderate fin surfaces would give the required feet-off stability. In order to ensure that the stabiliser would stall before the main wing it was given a slightly heavier wing loading, which would eliminate the sudden dropping of a main wing if the flying speed became too low. No tail also meant that there would be no tail buffet or flutter – the forward stabiliser would operate in undisturbed air and by placing it above the main wing the latter should also be clear of the stabiliser wake.

Boulton Paul P.100 (6.10.42)	
Span	40ft 2in (12.24m) Canard 20ft (6.10m)
Length	34ft 2in (10.42m)
Wing Area	270sq.ft (25.08sq.m) Canard 67sq.ft (6.22sq.m)
All-Up-Weight	13,450lb (6,101kg)
Powerplant	1 × 1,760hp (1,312kW) Griffon II
Max Speed/Height	335mph (539km/h) at 17,000ft (5,182m)
Armament	see text

This configuration offered a saving in weight and drag against the rear fuselage, normal tailplane and elevator of a conventional layout and resulted in a considerable increase in top speed, roughly 9mph (14.5km/h). The pilot used the same emergency system as the P.99 to depart the aircraft, while the bombs and rockets were carried under the middle of the main wing; internal fuel capacity was also the same as the P.99 as were the comments relating to the method of construction. The maximum rate of climb (up to 2,000ft [610m]) was 2,020ft/min (616m/min) and the range with a normal load 795 miles (1,279km). Contra-rotating propellers were more efficient than a single airscrew, especially in climb and take-off.

Boulton Paul P.101

Unusually for 1942 this project was a biplane but the basis for the proposal was the early 'in-service' date, Boulton Paul stating that 'nothing short of a stereotype design can hope to be in production by 1 January 1944.' Therefore the P.101 contained no unknown quantities, either aerodynamic or constructional, and could be 'ordered off the drawing board' with confidence. It lacked the excellent pilot's view of the previous designs but efforts had been made to fulfil all of the other requirements. The fixed undercarriage saved considerable weight but increased drag, although the requisite top speed could be achieved, and the aircraft's construction would adhere to standard Defiant fighter practice.

Two complete Defiant wings were used, staggered to give a better view for the pilot, while the guns were housed, along with the main wheels, in large spats. The options were four 20mm; three 40mm; two 20mm and two 40mm;

BELOW Boulton Paul P.101 (6.10.42). *Les Whitehouse*

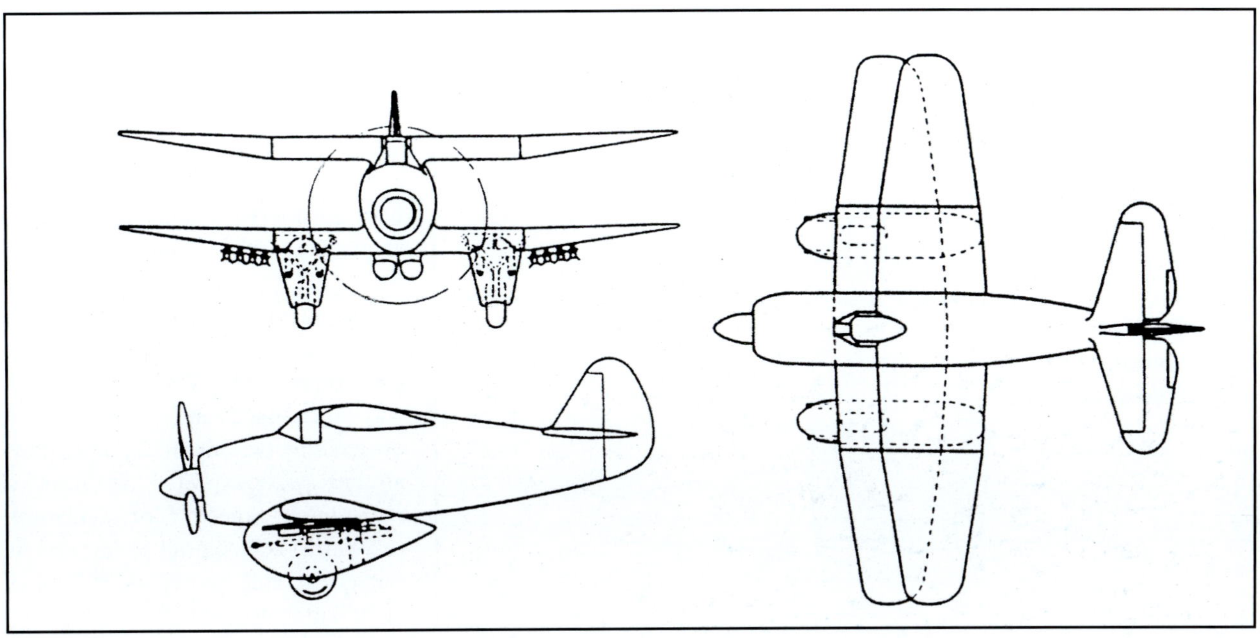

Boulton Paul P.101 (6.10.42)	
Span	36ft 7in (11.15m)
Length	33ft 7in (10.24m)
Wing Area	?
All-Up-Weight	15,210lb (6,899kg)
Powerplant	1 × Centaurus 12.SM
Max Speed/Height	317mph (510km/h) at 18,000ft (5,486m)
Armament	see text

Cunliffe-Owen 'Twin' (10.42)	
Span	62ft 0in (18.90m)
Length	?
Wing Area	530sq.ft (49.24sq.m)
All-Up-Weight	16,263lb (7,377kg)
Powerplant	2 × 1,645hp (1,227kW) Merlin 32
Max Speed/Height	315mph (507km/h) at 3,000ft (914m)
Armament	3 × 40mm plus alternatives

or two 20mm plus bombs or RPs. There was no provision for the 47mm but the required two 500lb (227kg) bombs were carried under the wing centre section and eight RPs were loaded under the outer wings. Maximum rate of climb (up to 3,000ft [914m]) was 2,200ft/min (671m/min) and range with normal load 750 miles (1,207km).

Cunliffe-Owen Attack Aircraft

This brochure actually described two aircraft, one single-engine and the other an orthodox twin-powerplant machine. No drawings have been traced for any of Cunliffe's ground attack designs but the twin was described as 'Mosquito-ish in general character' and carried 460gal (2,091lit) of internal fuel. Cunliffe considered the twin to be the really practical answer to the problem, in spite of objections to its size and the attendant reduced manoeuvrability. The small single-engine tractor design, only 42ft (12.80m) in span, was more unconventional and accommodated the pilot below the fuselage to give a better view out.

BELOW **Phillips & Powis (Miles) M.42 (8.42).** *Miles Aircraft via Peter Amos*

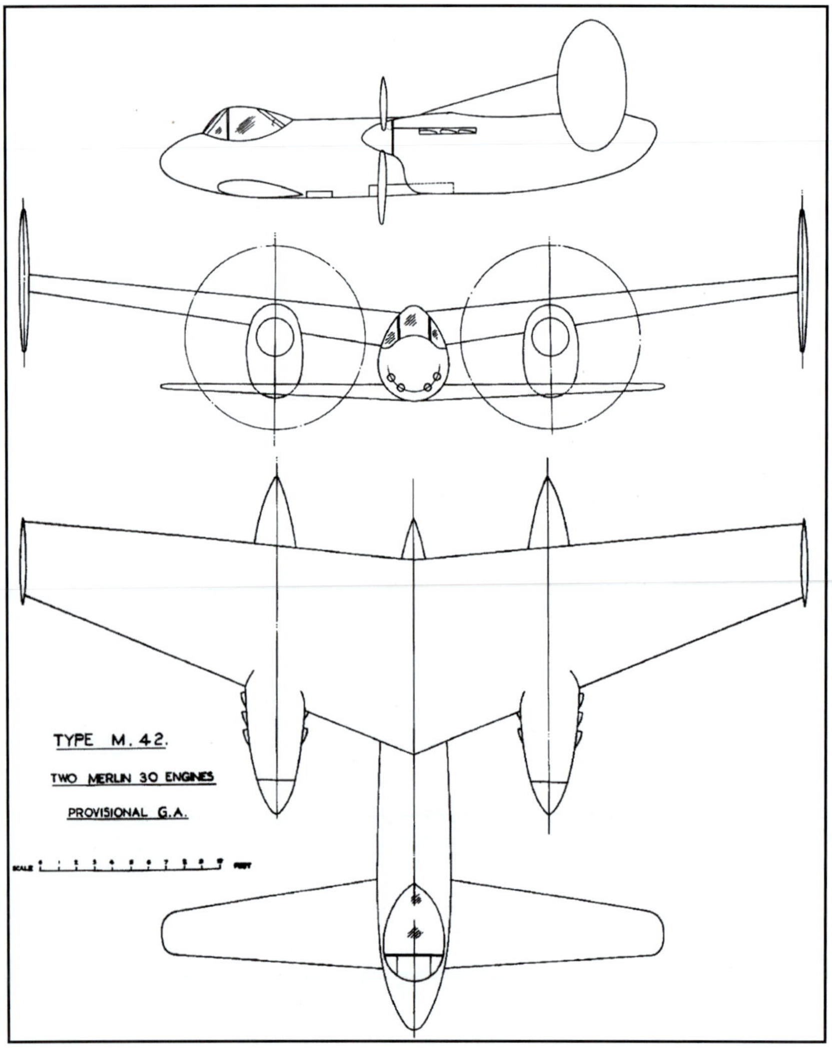

Phillips & Powis (Miles) M.42

The M.42 used the Libellula arrangement employed on several of the company's wartime designs, which here meant a large straight canard (foreplane) with a swept mainplane fitted to the rear fuselage. Small size was a major characteristic of the Libellula layout and contributed much to the high manoeuvrability of such designs, the design team considering that in this case it was 'almost ideal for the purpose specified.' The M.42 had two Merlin 30 engines mounted in nacelles on the main wing, yet it was only slightly larger than a Hurricane and had double the weight and power. There were five alternative armaments (besides two 500lb [227kg] bombs carried amidships) mounted in a group in the lower fuselage – three 40mm; two 40mm and two 20mm; four 20mm; two 20mm and six RP packs; or one 47mm and two 20mm. Normal range for all three of George Miles' attack designs was 750 miles (1,207km), but this could be doubled to 1,500 miles (2,414km) when carrying jettisonable tanks.

By January 1943 Phillips & Powis had considered a high-performance shipborne torpedo bomber version of the M.42, the only external change being a slightly smaller wing of 42ft 0in (12.80m) span and 390sq.ft (36.23sq.m) area. The all-up-weight was unchanged and it was to be powered by two Merlin 32 units. This aircraft was expected to have a maximum speed of 325mph (523km/h) at 5,000ft (1,524m) and its range was still quoted as 750 miles (1,207km).

Phillips & Powis (Miles) M.42 (8.42)	
Span	42ft 6in (12.95m) Canard 27ft 6in (8.38m)
Length	29ft 4in (8.94m)
Wing Area	393sq.ft (36.51sq.m)
All-Up-Weight	14,300lb (6,486kg)
Powerplant	2 × 1,600hp (1,193kW) Merlin 30
Max Speed/Height	?
Armament	see text

Phillips & Powis (Miles) M.43

The Libellula layout was used again for the M.43. In fact this design was similar to the M.42 but was a little smaller and used a single and more powerful Griffon mounted in the rear fuselage; the main wing was also swept at a greater angle. Both designs had tip fins on the main wings, both could use either metal or wood construction, and both were designed for rapid production and ease of maintenance. Again the M.43's guns were mounted in the lower fuselage, but on this design the recoil forces from the guns would be transmitted directly to the engine bearers and would, therefore, be absorbed by the inertia of the engine. Consequently, the severe structural problems involved with mounting guns in the wings of an orthodox single engine type were eliminated.

The M.42 and M.43 were in fact submitted together in a single brochure on 7 September 1942, ahead of the official invitation to tender. The M.43 had a slightly lower performance than the M.42 but both types were expected to be highly manoeuvrable. A mock-up of the M.43 'Tank Buster' was also built.

Like the M.42, by January 1943 (when they appeared in a Miles document) the M.43 had also been adapted for possible naval use, only this time as a shipborne fighter. This design would have been even smaller, with a span of 25ft (7.62m), wing area 225sq.ft (20.90sq.m) and all-up-weight 7,000lb (3,175kg), it would have been powered by a Merlin 32 and would be armed with 4 × 20mm or 2 × 40mm cannon. The estimated maximum speed was 330mph (531km/h) at 5,000ft (1,524m).

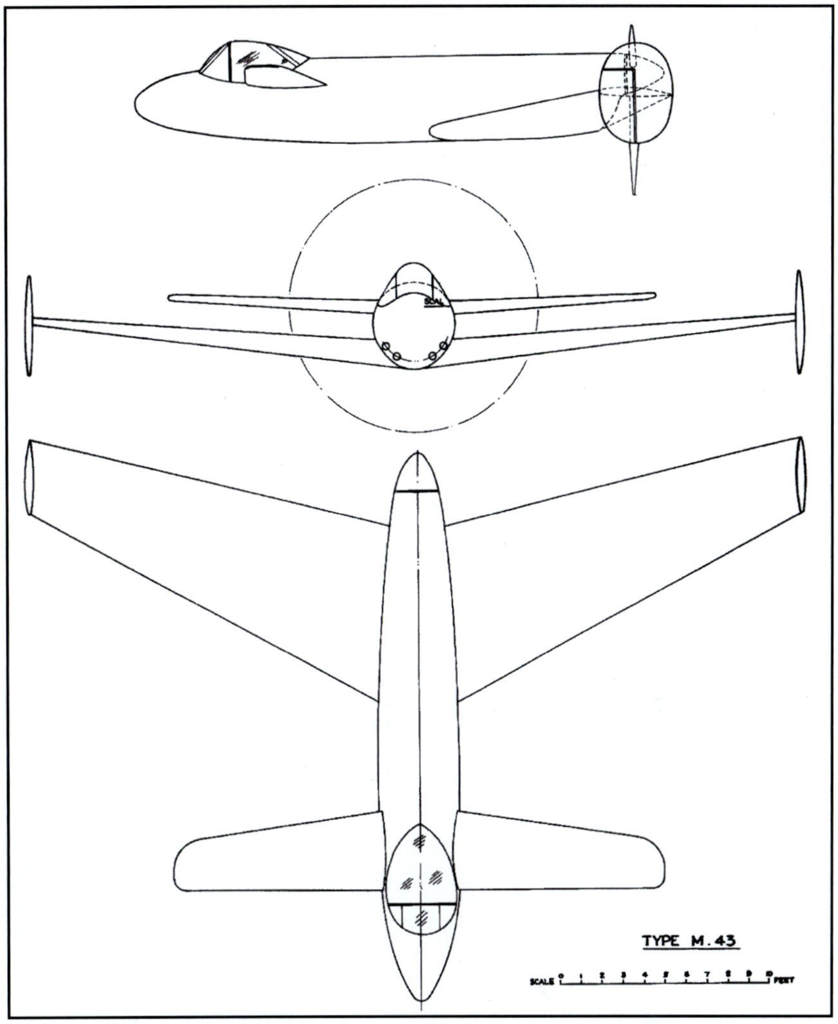

ABOVE Phillips & Powis (Miles) M.43 (8.42). *Miles Aircraft via Peter Amos*

Phillips & Powis (Miles) M.43 (8.42)	
Span	37ft 0in (11.28m) Canard 23ft 6in (7.16m)
Length	26ft 2in (7.98m)
Wing Area	300sq.ft (27.87sq.m)
All-Up-Weight	11,400lb (5,171kg)
Powerplant	1 × 2,000hp (1,491kW) Griffon
Max Speed/Height	?
Armament	see text

Phillips & Powis (Miles) M.44 (9.42)	
Span	48ft 0in (14.63m)
Length	37ft 8in (11.48m)
Wing Area	425sq.ft (39.48sq.m)
All-Up-Weight	14,700lb (6,668kg)
Powerplant	2 × 1,600hp (1,193kW) Merlin 30
Max Speed/Height	?
Armament	?

Phillips & Powis (Miles) M.44

Despite offering potential advantages for a low-level attack aircraft, the Libellula arrangement was as yet unproven and would take longer to develop than an orthodox type. Therefore on 19 September 1942 George Miles submitted an additional more orthodox twin-engine design called the M.44 which had two Merlin 30s in underslung wing nacelles along with twin fins and rudders. It carried the same armament as the M.42 and M.43 Libellula designs, and offered the same range performance.

The man who did much of the analysis and appraisal of new aircraft designs was Capt R. N. Liptrot and he completed his report on these ground

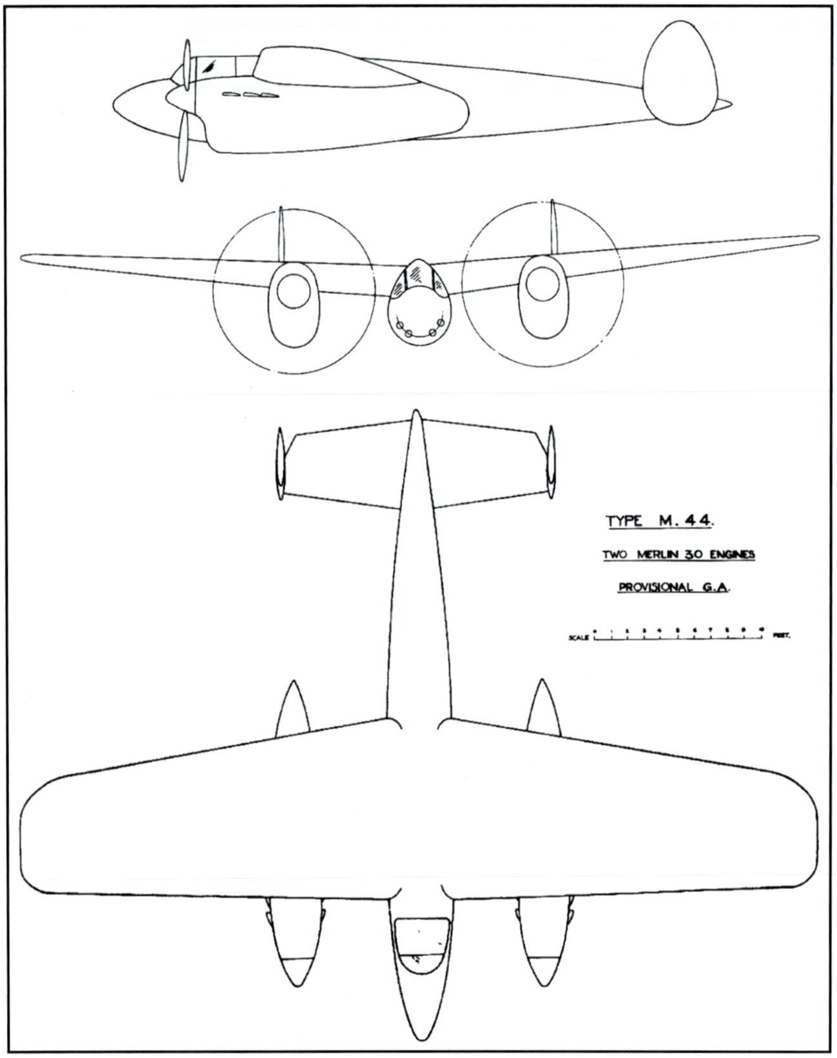

ABOVE Phillips & Powis (Miles) M.44 (9.42). *Miles Aircraft via Peter Amos*

BELOW Manufacturer's artwork for the Phillips & Powis (Miles) M.44 low attack aircraft.

attack types on 19 December 1942. He seemed disappointed that AWA had apparently not explored possible alternative layouts, but rather to have accepted from the very start that the twin-boom pusher was the most appropriate to a single-engine type to satisfy the requirements. Having accepted that, AWA had gone into the design far more thoroughly than any of the others. Quite apart from its laminar flow performance, the method of wing construction showed definite merit for a low-level attack aeroplane because it offered the desired simplicity and rapidity of construction. The AW.49 also carried more armament than the specification demanded.

Liptrot's biggest criticisms were that the AW.49's twin-boom arrangement was structurally difficult in regard to stiffness and that problems were anticipated in providing ground cooling for the engine – talks with Rolls-Royce had confirmed that the pusher arrangement was quite impracticable unless fan cooling was provided. He also felt that Lloyd had considerably underestimated the structure weight and had made a big mistake in choosing the Merlin X – the Merlin 32 would be better and could replace it.

In his analysis Liptrot ignored the Boulton Paul P.101 biplane because of its relatively poor view and

Chapter Three
Medium Bombers

ABOVE Mosquito B.Mk.XVI ML963.
Crown Copyright

This chapter has been revised considerably from the first edition. The main reason is Ralph Pegram's work revealing the level of study into high-speed unarmed bombers undertaken by industry as a whole, far more than previously thought and far from just de Havilland with its Mosquito. These designs were not linked by an official specification and so are described in turn in Part One, preceded by a review from Ralph. de Havilland's follow-on work is also described, before moving on to other medium bomber programmes in Part Two.

Part One: High-Speed Unarmed Bombers

The de Havilland Mosquito was to prove a highly successful aeroplane and become the RAF's first multi-role aircraft. Built mainly of wood and fitted with two Merlin engines, and no defensive armament to save weight, it was designed to fly so fast that no defensive fighters would be able to catch it. Many published sources state that the concept of the very fast unarmed bomber, as proposed by de Havilland in 1939 in a project which became the Mosquito, was a big surprise to the Air Staff and received vigorous opposition, except for the lone voice of the Air Member for Development and Production, Wilfrid Freeman. There was indeed much opposition to it, but far more support was forthcoming than has usually been recognised; in addition the concept of a fast unarmed bomber was not new because several other firms had put forward similar proposals during the late 1930s. In fact the idea interested some senior RAF officers as early as the late 1920s, and in 1935 a possible twin-Merlin type was examined by RAE. In some respects the concept of a high-speed unarmed bomber replaced the earlier proposals for Composite aircraft and 'Assisted Take-Off Projects' reviewed in Chapter Two.

Ralph Pegram writes:

"In the closing months of 1939, just as de Havilland was refining its Mosquito design, a number of broadly similar, and hence competing, two-seat, twin-engine, high-speed projects were prepared.

Light bombers with a performance similar to or little less than contemporaneous fighters had formed part of the RAF frontline since the First World War. They were two-seat machines with a rear gunner. By the early 1930s the speed of aircraft was reaching the point where a simple open cockpit for the gunner was no longer sufficient and a fundamental rethink was required if this class of bomber was to continue.

In late 1930 the Air Ministry was more than aware that aviation technology had advanced sufficiently to allow for more demanding specifications to be raised. Retractable undercarriages, flaps, slots, cantilever structures, etc, were all proven and should be employed on military aircraft. The push for 'something new' for the RAF commenced with fighter Specification F.7/30 and then moved on to discussions for bombers. Thoughts centred around the design of a high-speed two-seat bomber capable of carrying a 1,000lb (454kg) bomb load at over 200mph (322km/h) with a range of 1,000 miles (1,609km). Both twin and single engine types were considered with the single engine concept preferred in order to keep the size of the aircraft relatively small. Rolls-Royce's proposed 1,000hp (746kW) development of its Buzzard engine was suggested and some concept designs based around this were prepared by industry, notably a cantilever monoplane by Supermarine, which was by no means small. Around the same time Armstrong Whitworth suggested a twin-engine Kestrel-powered cantilever monoplane with pusher propellers and no rear gunner. This too was not small. Although no official specification was raised, not least because this class of bomber did not at that time meet any RAF requirement, elements of it were to reappear a year later in amended and watered-down form, as the two medium bomber specifications B.9/32 and P.27/32.

No further work was undertaken on light, high-speed bombers while the World Disarmament Conference at Geneva was in session but, after that had collapsed, the Fairey Battle design, which had started out as a two-seat medium bomber, grew in response to revised Air Ministry changes to the specification. This led some in the Ministry to raise concerns over the lack of a true high-speed, single-engine light bomber and RAE was requested to assess the potential performance that could be expected of the concept. This was generally positive and so Specification P.4/34 was issued in November 1934 for such an aircraft, broadly as a Hawker Hart replacement. Tenders came from Hawker (for the Hurricane-based Henley) and from Fairey, whose design was basically a downsized Battle. Both were constructed but no production contracts, as bombers, were awarded and the idea faded.

An RAE report on the possibility of a twin-Merlin bomber, capable of 330mph (531km/h) and with three machine guns in streamlined mountings, led to provision for such a type being included in the Experimental Programme for 1936, but this was also dropped to reduce the number of new types under development. There was high expectation in the Ministry that the twin-engine medium bomber type outlined in Specification P.13/36 (Chapter Four), for which high speed was a major requirement, would make the need for a dedicated high-speed type unnecessary, but the hoped-for performance began to look increasingly unlikely. The Air Staff then drafted a note on 'The possibility of dispensing with the armament in the light bomber class' which restarted the debate on the value of true high-speed bombers.

As Handley Page worked on its HP.56 project to meet P.13/36, chief designer George Volkert became increasingly of the opinion that a high-speed bomber should be fundamentally different, and in May 1937 he wrote up his thoughts as 'A Memorandum on Bombing Policy and its Influence on Design,' which was submitted to the Air Ministry. He believed that a high-speed bomber should be unarmed and rely on speed as its primary means of defence, and his proposal was for an aircraft of comparable dimensions and engines to the P.13/36 project but with a refined aerodynamic shape, no guns and hence a smaller crew, which would allow a cruising speed of up to 300mph (483km/h) when carrying a 3,000lb (1,361kg) load.

Prompted by this, Air Chief Marshal Edgar Ludlow-Hewitt wrote a memo in November 1937 in which he stated that he 'saw a place for a high-speed, unarmed bomber,' which appears, from subsequent events, to have been the catalyst for a change in Air Ministry thinking. He followed this up in April 1938 with a note to Wilfrid Freeman where he saw a role for a 'special bomber, not unarmed, for harassing attacks. New type of bomber – High Speed Bomber.'

[The relentless up-sizing of the main bomber force, Wellington to Manchester, Whitley to Warwick to Stirling, all within a period of just two years, and the subsequent focus on the ill-advised, all-things-to-all-men, heavily armed 'Ideal Bomber' (B.1/39 – all Chapter Four) left a huge gap at the lower end of the scale. However effective a large cannon-equipped powerful bomber could be, there was always going to be a role for something small, faster and more manoeuvrable. Types like the Beaufort and Botha (Chapter Seven) were not the answer.]

April 1938 also saw the submission to Freeman of a new composite bomber design from Shorts. As seen in Chapter Two, Shorts' composite design drew a negative reaction from the Air

Ministry which did not believe that it was reasonable for a single airman to act as pilot, navigator and bomb aimer on a long duration mission mostly over enemy territory. Ludlow-Hewitt, however, was still tabling ideas, and he wrote to the Under-Secretary of State describing a bomber with 1,000lb (454kg) bombs, four guns and a range of 1,500 miles (2,414km) that could also serve for reconnaissance purposes.

Sir Alan Cobham's Flight Refuelling company had now refined and proven a viable inflight refuelling system and employed Marcus Langley, a well-regarded aircraft designer, to propose some specific aircraft types to demonstrate the benefits. The design of the FR.5 bomber, roughly along the lines of P.13/36, was submitted to DDOR, Group Captain Robert Saundby, who indicated that the Air Ministry had a preference for an unarmed, high-speed bomber. Langley responded with the FR.7 design in January 1939.

Next, Folland's small design team had drawn up a number of speculative aircraft concepts to demonstrate its design capability and had won a contract to construct the Fo.108 testbed aircraft for engine development. Although his early designs for a composite bomber had come to nothing, Folland had maintained an interest in the idea for a small, unarmed, high-speed bomber and wrote an article for one such scheme for the newly-launched magazine *Aeronautics* in August 1939. This featured an unarmed, single-engine, one-man bomber with an unspecified engine that would give a top speed of 470mph (756km/h). It carried a single 500lb (227kg) bomb and was intended for precision dive bombing. Folland argued that with sufficient speed a bomber could not be intercepted unless detected at considerable distance from its target. A Folland company design, the Fo.111 unarmed composite bomber, was then submitted to the Air Ministry in November (Chapter Two). Folland's claims for speed were not accepted by the Ministry's technical staff and the design was rejected for the same reasons as for Shorts' the previous year, despite a vociferous campaign by Oliver Stewart.

The Air Ministry had by now rejected the composite bomber idea on at least three occasions. Although composite bombers were no longer a consideration, increasing interest at the Air Ministry in unarmed or lightly armed high-speed aircraft was apparent throughout 1939, although no Operational Requirement or Specification was raised, yet in the last quarter of the year more companies submitted broadly similar speculative designs along these lines. In October 1939 Armstrong Whitworth drew up its twin-Merlin, three-seat, unarmed AW.45. That same month General Aircraft submitted its two-seat GAL.46 project (reviewed in the sister volume on fighters). This was also a twin-Merlin design; it could carry 2,000lb (907kg) of bombs and/or four cannon and was pressurised for high altitude. Then in February 1940 Shorts submitted a twin-Merlin design as a formal tender.

The de Havilland Mosquito story, which runs in parallel with these speculative projects, is well known. It does seem likely that de Havilland secured the contract in preference to others because the Mosquito was a very good design, the firm's design department was not overworked and its works had plenty of spare capacity, and the design minimized the use of 'strategic' materials. All in all, it really does look as if the Mosquito was just one of several project designs submitted in late 1939 and early 1940, which raises the possibility that the initiative for a high-speed unarmed bomber might well have originated in the Air Ministry."

Some of the high-speed bomber designs prepared whilst the Mosquito was moving towards reality were as follows:

Airspeed AS.47

Airspeed produced a high-speed all-wood twin-boom bomber project in 1939/40. This was to be powered by two 2,200hp (1,641kW) Napier Sabre engines, one tractor unit, one pusher, with the pilot and navigator/bomb-aimer positioned in between in a slightly offset cockpit. Span was 58ft (17.68m), length 53ft 9in (16.38m), estimated top speed 470mph (756km/h) at 18,500ft (5,639m) and range 1,000 miles (1,609km) with 1,000lb (454kg) of bombs.

BELOW Airspeed AS.47 (1939/40). *Bob Beard*

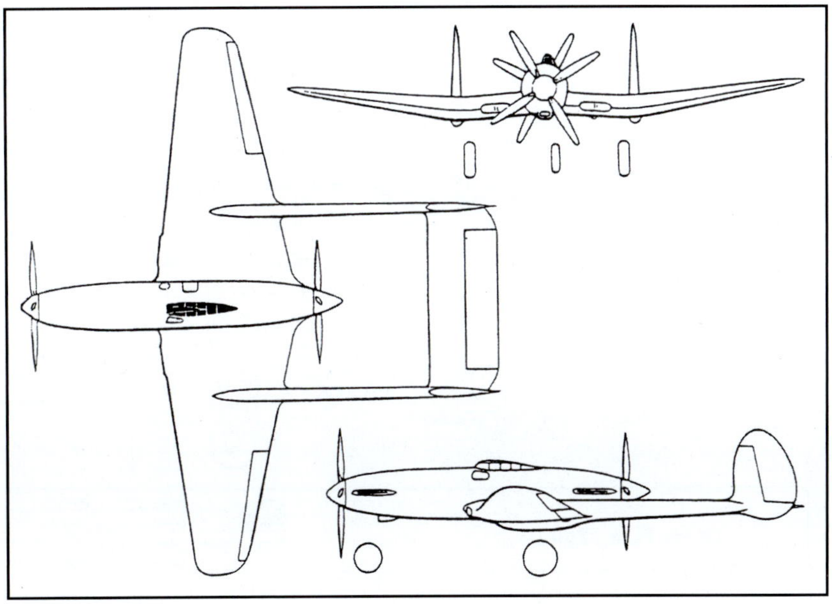

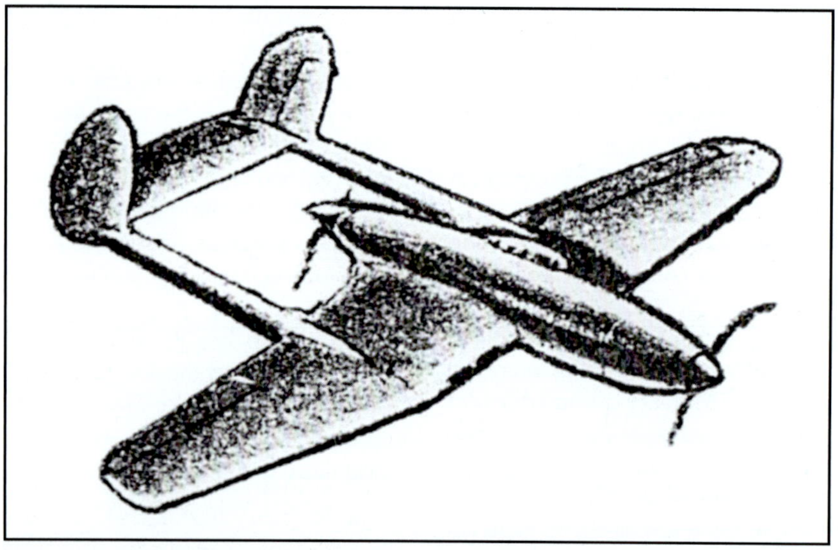

ABOVE Artist's impression of the AS.47.

OPPOSITE Armstrong Whitworth AW.46 (16.1.40).

Armstrong Whitworth AW.45

The AW.45 was a twin-Merlin-engine design from October 1939, probably for bomber or reconnaissance work, and had three crew with the front compartment pressurised for high-altitude operation. There appears to be no defensive armament and the design's large fuel tank volume (in the wings and fuselage) and recessed cooling system suggested long range and high speed. AWA's new long-travel tricycle undercarriage was fitted and the structure was to be light alloy monocoque. Span 43ft (13.11m), length 36ft 3in (11.05m), wing area 298sq.ft (27.69sq.m). Armstrong Whitworth's AW.46 project appears to have been an enlarged four-engine aircraft but similar in general design.

Flight Refuelling

In October 1938 Flight Refuelling submitted the unsolicited FR.5 design for a conventional medium bomber with in-flight refuelling capability, but was told that the Air Ministry had a preference for a high-speed unarmed bomber. Thus in January 1939 the firm submitted the FR.7 design to meet this requirement.

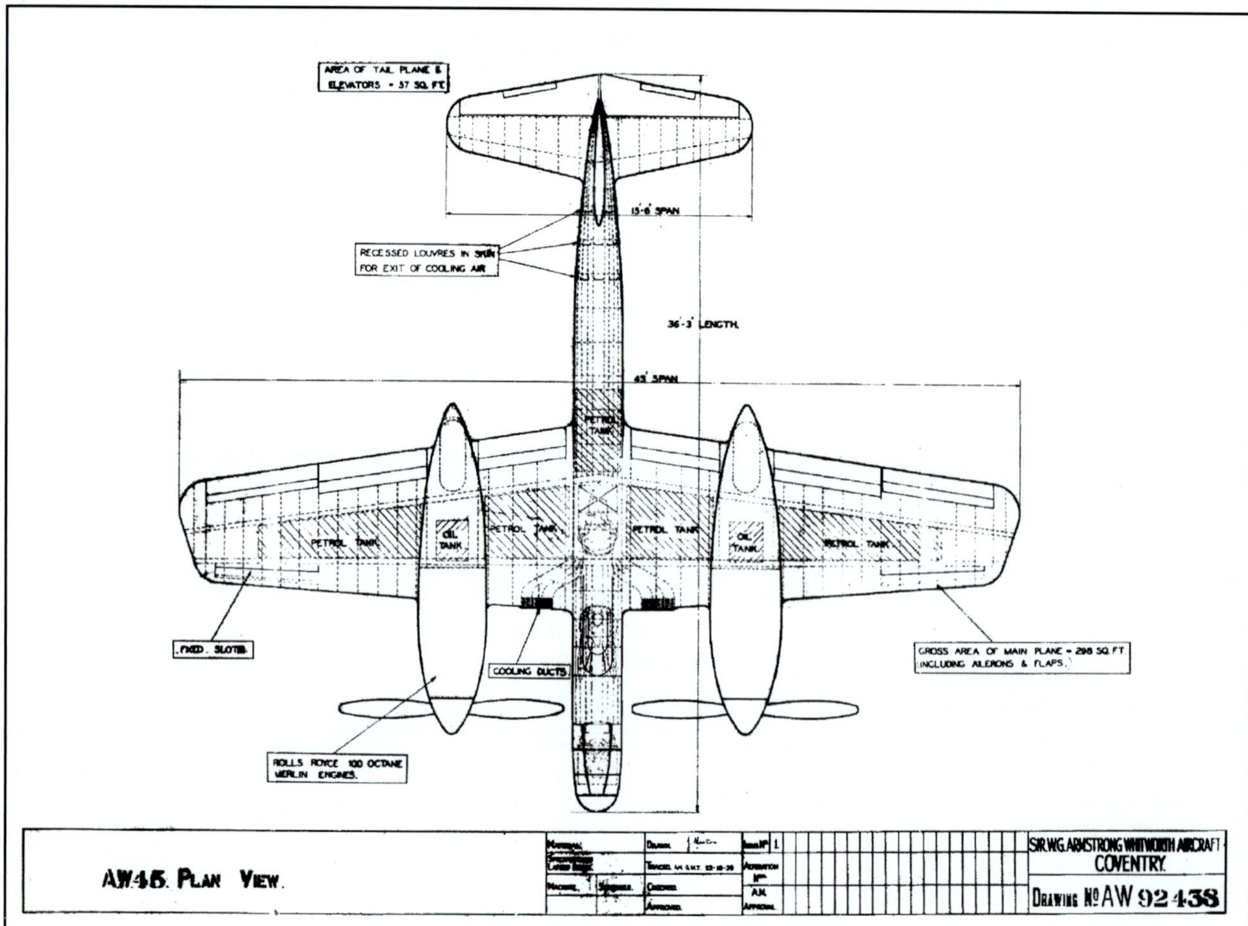

BELOW Only a plan view is available for AWA's AW.45 project (23.10.39).

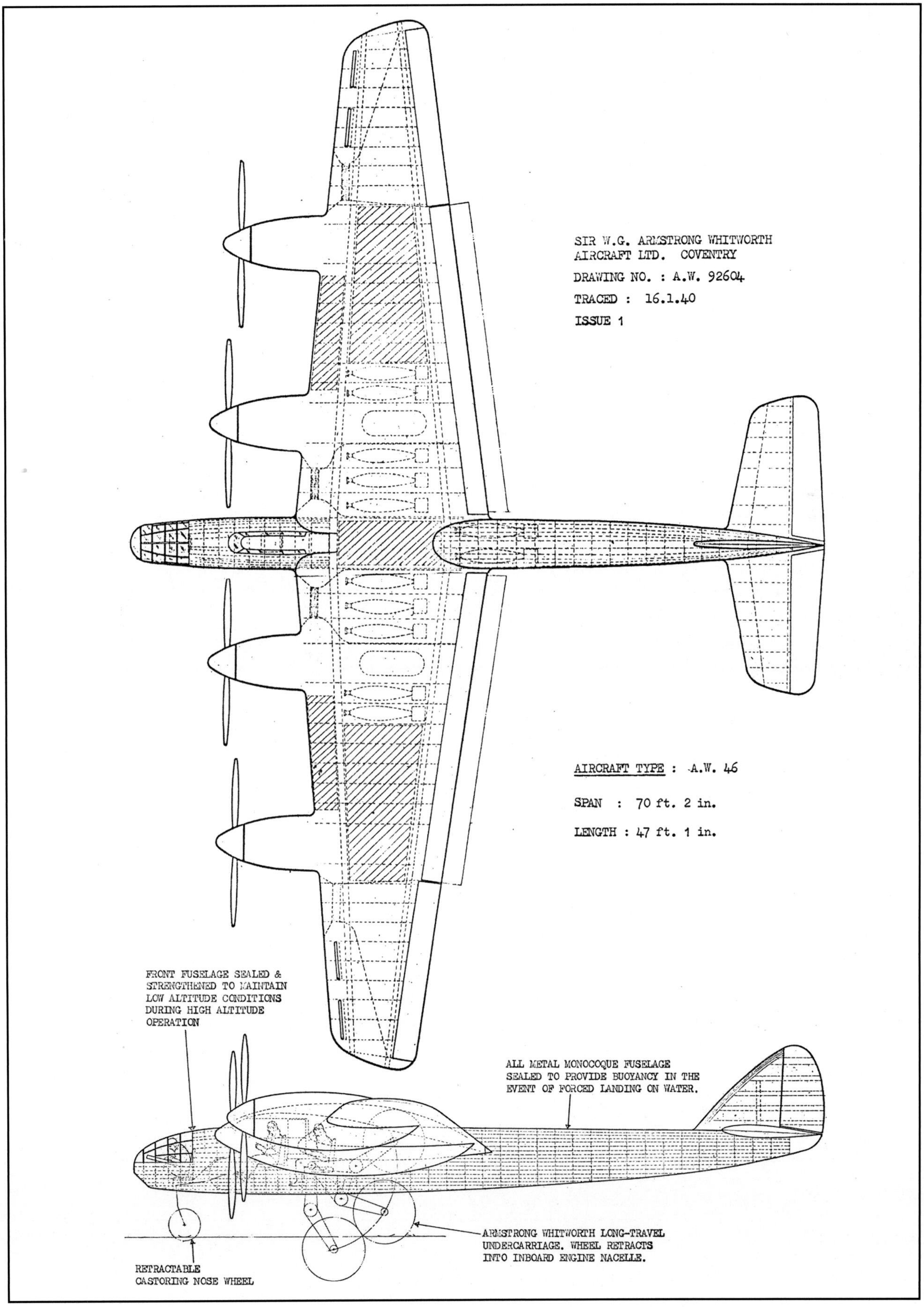
SIR W.G. ARMSTRONG WHITWORTH
AIRCRAFT LTD. COVENTRY
DRAWING NO. : A.W. 92604
TRACED : 16.1.40
ISSUE 1
AIRCRAFT TYPE : A.W. 46
SPAN : 70 ft. 2 in.
LENGTH : 47 ft. 1 in.
FRONT FUSELAGE SEALED & STRENGTHENED TO MAINTAIN LOW ALTITUDE CONDITIONS DURING HIGH ALTITUDE OPERATION
ALL METAL MONOCOQUE FUSELAGE SEALED TO PROVIDE BUOYANCY IN THE EVENT OF FORCED LANDING ON WATER.
ARMSTRONG WHITWORTH LONG-TRAVEL UNDERCARRIAGE. WHEEL RETRACTS INTO INBOARD ENGINE NACELLE.
RETRACTABLE CASTORING NOSE WHEEL

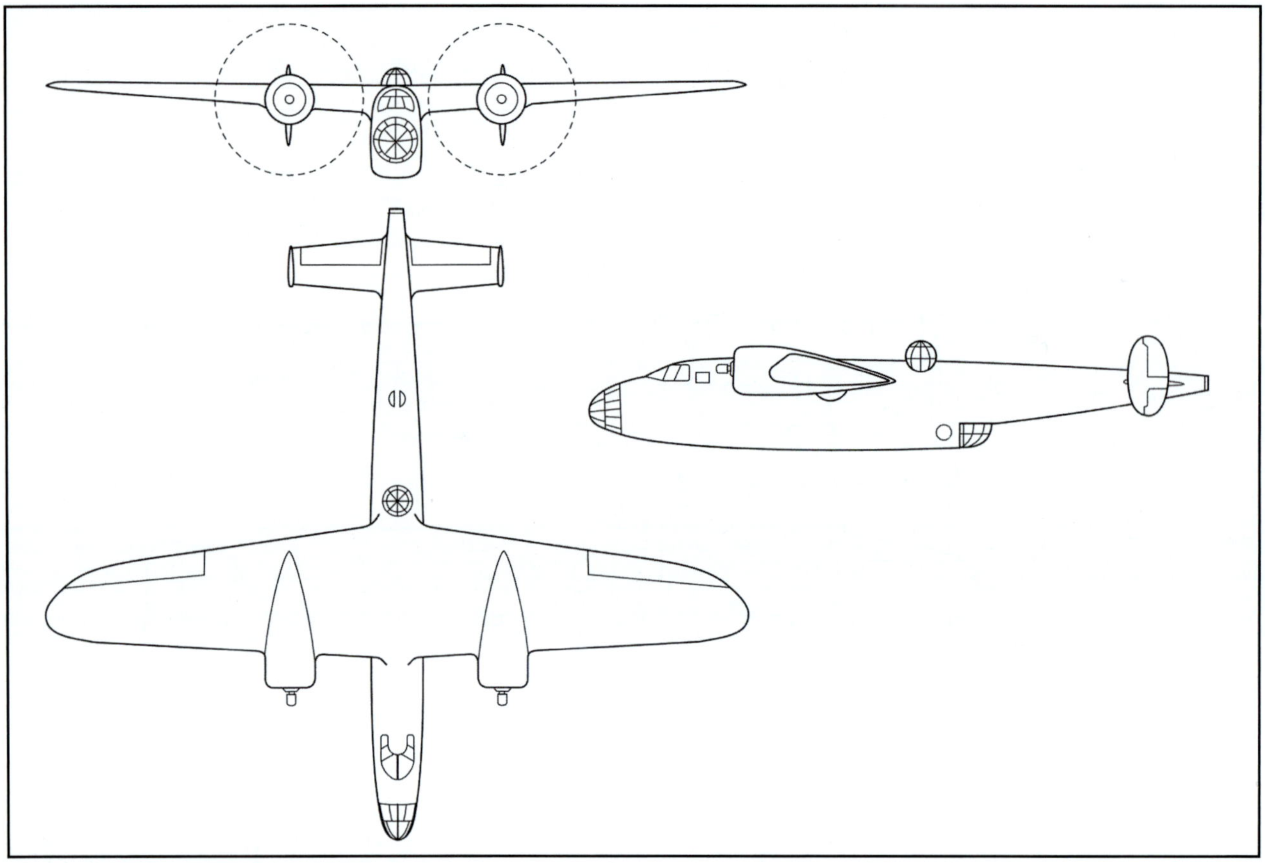

ABOVE Flight Refuelling FR.5 (10.38).

BELOW Flight Refuelling FR.7 (1.39).

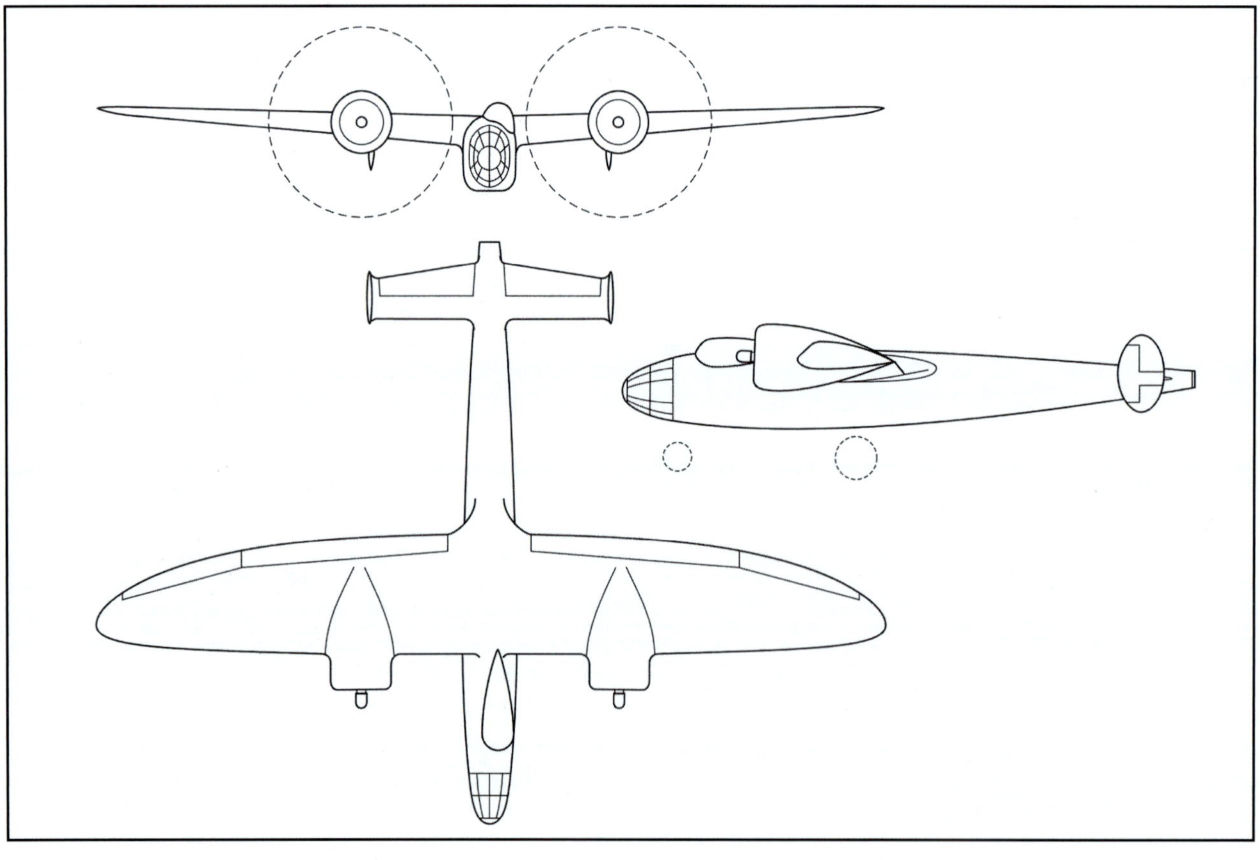

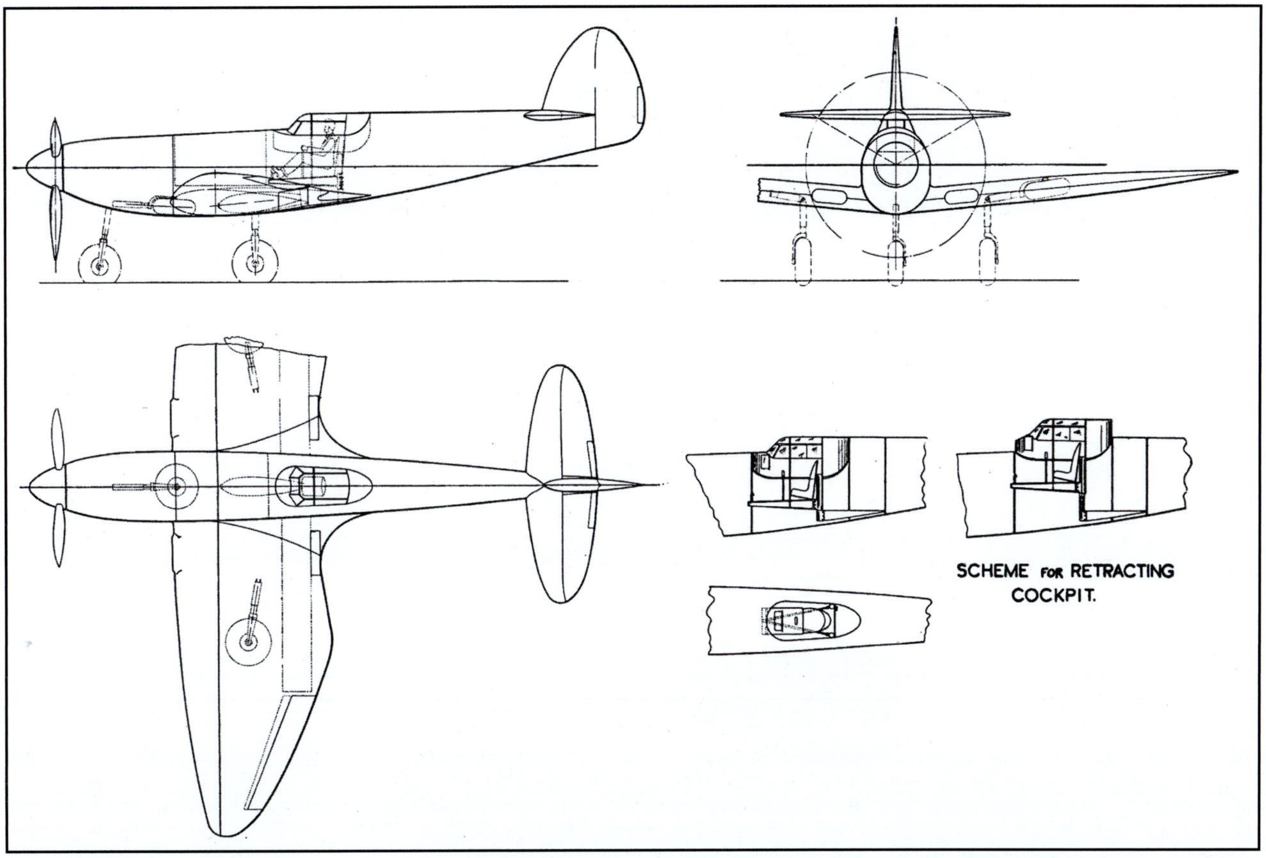

ABOVE **Folland single-engine design reproduced in *Aeronautics* for August 1939. This formed the basis of H. P. Folland's theories for a high-speed bomber.**

Folland High-Speed Bomber

Henry Folland's ideas for a single-seat, single-engine high-speed bomber appeared in *Aeronautics* for August 1939. The type described in the magazine was based on the assumption that speed would be better than defensive armament for certain types of bombing and a clean single-engine single-seat aircraft, designed on on fighter lines, seemed well suited for the task. Folland wrote that 'the difference in speed between existing types, single-engine fighters and multi-engine bombers, is approximately 70mph to 80mph [113km/h to 129km/h].....and new bombers are coming along which are considerably faster. There has been considerable controversy as to whether a bomber can be made at least as fast as the interceptor,' but he maintained that this could be done with this new type. Folland added that 'it is now well known that the major increase in performance has been brought about by aerodynamical cleanliness, rather than increased engine power, so that the cleaner the aeroplane the faster it becomes with a given weight per horsepower.'

This bomber would reach its objective in the shortest possible time using speed as its safeguard. No armament would be fitted, this saving in weight then contributing to the bomb load, and the aircraft would be capable of attacking a target 700 miles (1,126km) away. After discharging its bomb (probably a 500-pounder) the aeroplane would be in a relatively light condition,

BELOW AND OVERLEAF **This model of a high-speed light bomber is held by the Solent Sky Museum at Southampton. It shows an unbuilt Folland design but no information is known about the project (it may be the Fo.113 or Fo.114, the former of which was designed to B.1/40). The turret houses two machine guns.**

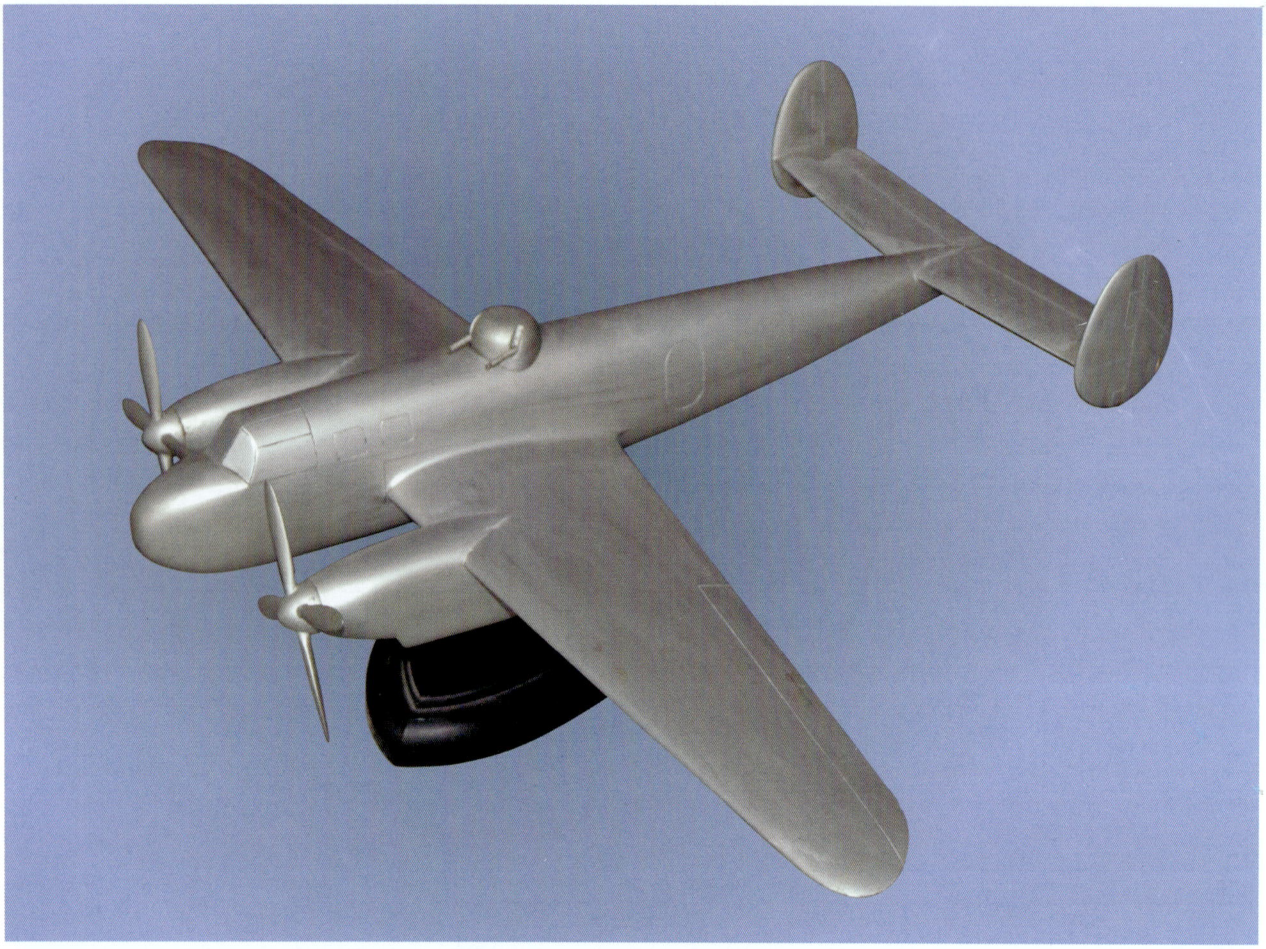

which in turn would provide a high rate of climb to get away from its pursuers; this, combined with a high forward speed, should give the pilot every chance of reaching base. This aircraft could also serve as an interceptor (with guns and no bombs) or as a photo-reconnaissance aircraft, it had a tricycle undercarriage (another advanced feature) and its maximum speed was 470mph (756km/h) at 15,000ft (4,572m). Gross weight at take-off as a bomber was 11,050lb (5,012kg) and as an interceptor with guns only and no bombs 9,675lb (4,389kg).

Handley Page Unarmed Bomber

The head of Handley Page's Experimental Department, Gustav Lachmann expressed misgivings regarding Specification P.13/36 (Chapter Four) and his HP.56 project submission to that document was subsequently reconfigured as the four-engine Halifax heavy bomber. In its place Handley Page proposed a radical new high-speed class of bomber carrying no defensive armament.

In May 1937 George Volkert, chief designer at Handley Page, completed a document called 'A Memorandum on Bombing Policy and Its Influence on Design.' This was prepared, possibly in response to an approach from the Air Ministry's Research & Development department, with a view to ascertaining the 'benefits' to a bomber if it did not have to carry defensive armament and crew, a subject about which Volkert felt most strongly. He opened by declaring that a 'drastic revision of present ideas is essential if the utmost performance and destructive power is to be obtained.'

Part 1 assessed the current state of modern airborne warfare and bomber design. From a bombing point of view, one of several points noted that 'the need for providing complete defence from attack from every possible direction .... has [in this country] led to the almost universal adoption of nose and tail turrets, and a crew of at least four or five.' Volkert observed that 'the most efficient bomber is the one which can carry out the greatest destruction with the smallest crew and the simplest equipment' and added that 'every other consideration will have to be sacrificed to the need for high speed, without which the maximum element of surprise is lost in any attack, as well as the greatest safeguard of the crew. Just as the bomber depends for its success on sudden attack and surprise, so for its defence it must rely on high speed and high altitude together with poor visibility.' He also felt that the fast unarmed bomber could 'closely approach the aerodynamic ideal' whereas 'the fighter must in this respect remain inferior due to the presence of guns, sights and the like and the need for a wide field of vision for the pilot.'

In Part 2 Volkert presented an unarmed bomber project in comparison with the existing P.13/36 medium bomber specification. One point to be raised was that the armed bomber required many extra fully trained aircrew to risk their lives to defend their pilots and navigators while the aircraft itself would fly at least 22mph (35km/h) slower than the unarmed machine and, as a consequence, would have to spend more time in the air. Volkert's project possessed a near perfect aerodynamic fuselage with a 'pointed' nose and tail, a smooth exterior surface and a fully retracting undercarriage. The elimination of guns, gun crews and turrets greatly increased its bomb carrying capacity and made the aircraft much more manoeuvrable and safer to fly. It had a much simpler structure than the equivalent P.13/36 and the entire bomb load was housed in the fuselage leaving the wing for the fuel and undercarriage; this allowed the wing thickness at the centre to be reduced from 21% to 18%. The aircraft would be quicker, cheaper and easier to produce than the P.13/36 with defensive armament.

The unarmed machine when carrying a normal load of 3,000lb (1,361kg) of bombs, instead of P.13/36's normal 1,000lb (454kg), would be 1,165lb (528kg) lighter in all-up-weight (24,608lb [11,162kg] against 25,773lb [11,691kg]), it would cruise at 300mph (483km/h) instead of 278mph (447km/h), take-off and landing runs were shorter and the time taken to cover 1,000 miles (1,609km) was cut by 7.5%. The figures for higher bomb loads were equally impressive.

On 15 July Captain Liptrot, then Research Director Aircraft 3 (RDA3), completed an appraisal and his calculations suggested that this bomber's top speed could eventually exceed that of the Spitfire, the fastest fighter of the day, which would make it quite immune from attack by any single-seat fighter. His and Volkert's arguments gave strong support to the view that 'the elimination of defensive armament ought to be given serious consideration.' Liptrot acknowledged the counter argument that in the ups and downs of aircraft development there would always be a stage when there was a fighter possessing higher performance than the bomber then in service. However, as he had been 'pointing out for years,' the maximum possible separation at any stage of development could not be expected to be more than 15% in favour of the fighter, so when a bomber in service had a top speed of 350mph (563km/h), the very best fighter within sight could not be expected to have a top speed of more than 400mph (644km/h). Other factors affected the fighter, such as time on patrol and endurance, and Liptrot deliberately continued his report in a provocative vein to start an argument within the service – he knew that the design of the RAF's future fighter and bomber aircraft would be critical to the country's survival.

The arguments did indeed follow. On 26 July 1937 R. H. Verney, DTD, gave the concept guarded support. CinC Bomber Command, Air Chief Marshal E. R. Ludlow-Hewitt, also supported the idea and gave his approval on 23 April 1938 but noted that 'the term 'unarmed' is, I think, a misnomer. It is not an unarmed bomber that we require but a speed bomber.' In August 1937 W. Sholto Douglas, ACAS, wrote to DCAS urging support for the development of a smaller type of bomber, but DDOR was against

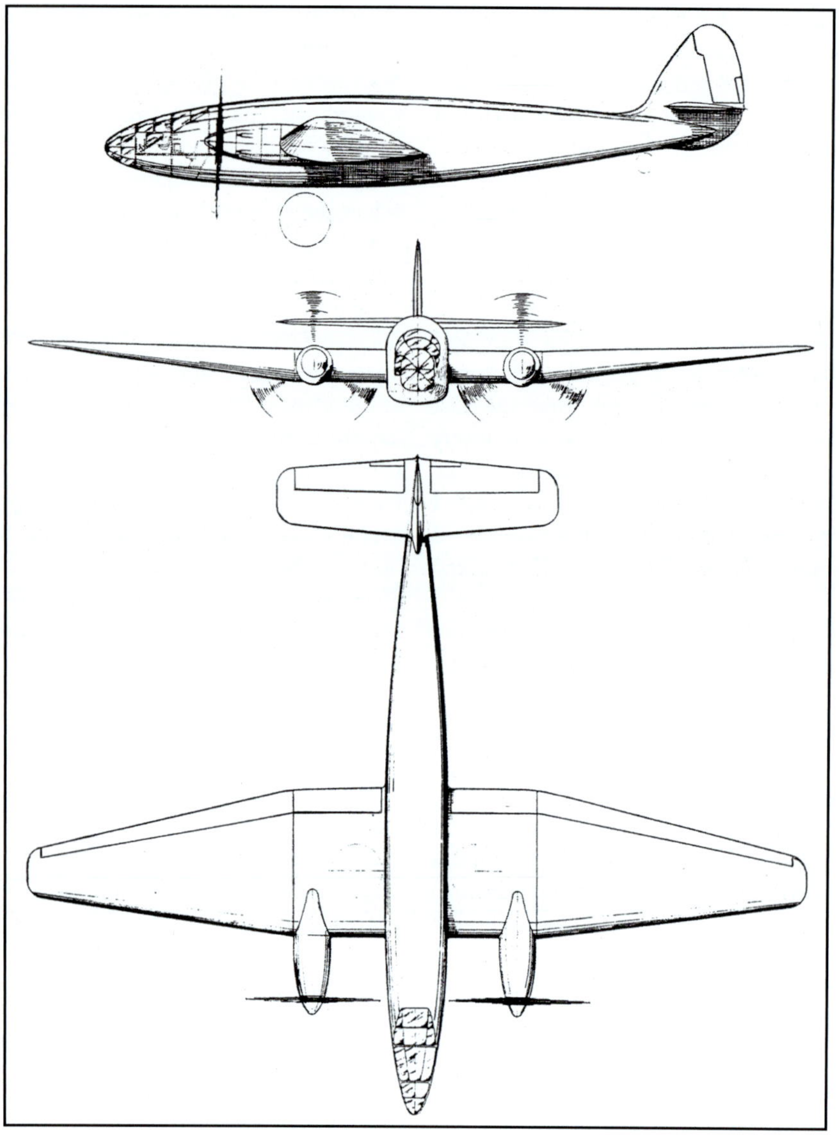

ABOVE Handley Page high-speed unarmed 'P.13/36' (5.37). *Handley Page Association*

the concept. CAS agreed on 5 December 1938 that a specification should be written and prototypes built. However, on the previous 7 August the Operational Requirements department declared that it was 'unsafe to assume that any great increase in the speed of a bomber can be obtained by the partial elimination of its defensive armament' and that 'the 'speed' bomber does not show over the 'standard' bomber any substantial economy in production, maintenance, operational effort, flying personnel or wastage in time of war.' It concluded that the 'speed' bomber did not enjoy a sufficient advantage over the 'standard' bomber, in any material respect, which could compensate for its limited operational role.

Handley Page 'High-Speed P.13/36' (5.37)	
Span	88ft 6in (26.97m)
Length	71ft 6in (21.79m)
Wing Area	988sq.ft (91.79sq.m)
All-Up-Weight	24,608lb (11,162kg) with 3,000lb (1,361kg) of bombs
Powerplant	2 × Vulture
Max Speed/Height	380mph (611km/h)
Armament	7,000lb (3,175kg) bombs maximum

On 7 August 1939 Ludlow-Hewitt wrote 'I am strongly of the opinion that the development of the fastest possible bomber, whatever its size, is a project which ought to be put in hand so that we should have available a prototype of this kind of bomber should the need arise.' He felt such a project should 'no longer be delayed and that it should now be given the highest possible priority.' A week later Sholto Douglas, as ACAS, declared that he did not like the idea of an unarmed bomber, however speedy, because he did not believe that it would remain speedy enough for very long. He did, however, think it would be a wise precaution to encourage DTD to go ahead with the production of a prototype of Blackburn's B.28, a new private venture high-speed bomber design (page 49).

During 1938 Handley Page analysed its unarmed scheme further and RAE Farnborough was asked to comment on Volkert's figures officially, which it judged to be reasonable. The data assessed by RAE, however, related to a different aircraft, possibly an update or revision of the original design, though no drawing is available. It was submitted in February 1938 and again had no defensive armament. The review observed that to achieve this performance would require a high degree of attention to the aircraft's surface finish and drag. Ralph Pegram adds 'It is worth noting that the RAE estimates of propeller performance appear to be flawed. By specifying Vultures and 17ft (5.18m) diameter three-blade propellers it would not have been possible to achieve 350mph (563km/h) at full throttle height or above. Tip speed was noted as Mach 0.85 at take-off but no account appears to have taken of the fact that at 15,000ft (4,572m) it would be well in excess of Mach 1.0, thereby reducing thrust dramatically.'

Handley Page High-Speed Bomber (2.38)	
Span	75ft 0in (22.86m)
Length	?
Wing Area	800sq.ft (74.32sq.m)
All-Up-Weight	27,000lb (12,247kg) with 2,500lb (1,134kg) of bombs
Weight (intermediate load)	22,000lb (9,979kg) with 1,000lb (454kg) bombs
Powerplant	2 × Vulture
Max Speed/Height (with the intermediate load)	356mph (573km/h)
Armament	?

Handley Page's projects were never likely to be built; Volkert's 'memo' concentrated more on the principles and ideas rather than any detail design, but his documents, and Handley Page and its designers, played their part in establishing this category of aircraft in the RAF inventory.

Shorts High-Speed Unarmed Bomber

Shorts' chief designer Arthur Gouge had been collaborating on composite aircraft projects with Robert Mayo of Imperial Airways (the Shorts Mayo programme, Chapter Two) and during 1938 presented concepts for a single-seat composite bomber, but these were rejected by the Air Ministry. In a letter to the Air Ministry on 18 November 1939 Gouge now conceded that the composite scheme was unlikely to allow a bomber to reach the kind of speeds that Folland had suggested. He wrote 'I am in agreement with your technical people that a large increase of speed cannot be obtained by the use of the composite scheme. At the most I should only put this at about 400mph (644km/h) due to certain savings in weight, with the consequent reduction in size which might be achieved. It seems fairly definite that with a twin-engined machine we could achieve a top speed of around 385mph (619km/h) carrying a load of four 500lb (227kg) bombs. This aircraft could also carry two 20mm cannons.'

Gouge had now effectively dropped the single-seat bomber idea in favour of a twin-Merlin two-seat unarmed type to be used either conventionally or configured as the upper component of a Mayo composite. The result was truly a Mosquito clone, in size, weight and performance, and also with Spitfire-style elliptical wings, and it was formally tendered to the Air Ministry in February 1940.

The brochure stated 'it is concluded that the best defence for a bomber is to have a speed equal to that of the interceptor fighter. The speed aimed at, 400mph (644km/h), is higher than that at present attained by interceptor fighters, and will be comparable to the speed likely to be obtained from future aeroplanes of this type. It is, therefore, proposed that no defensive armament be fitted, as it is most unlikely that the aeroplane could be successfully attacked by interceptor aircraft. It is proposed, however, to provide armour protection for the crew and to fit self-sealing fuel tanks.

In order to obtain a very high maximum speed it is necessary to employ a high wing loading at the start, with a consequent increase in take-off run. The ground performance may necessitate the aircraft operating only from aerodromes possessing prepared runways, but this limitation is considered outweighed by the speed increase made possible. Take-offs from normal aerodromes would be possible if the Mayo composite method of assisted take-off was employed.'

This bomber landplane could be made an upper component by incorporating the necessary support and release fittings in the airframe, whilst the lower component would be an obsolescent type of bomber. The advantages of this were that the loaded unarmed bomber could now take off from any normal aerodrome, and that the hazard due to any one engine cutting out during take-off was considerably reduced. The disadvantages were that a launching aircraft and crew were required, and the time lost in mounting the upper component onto the lower.

BELOW Shorts High-Speed Two-Seat Twin-Engine Bomber (2.40). *Ralph Pegram*

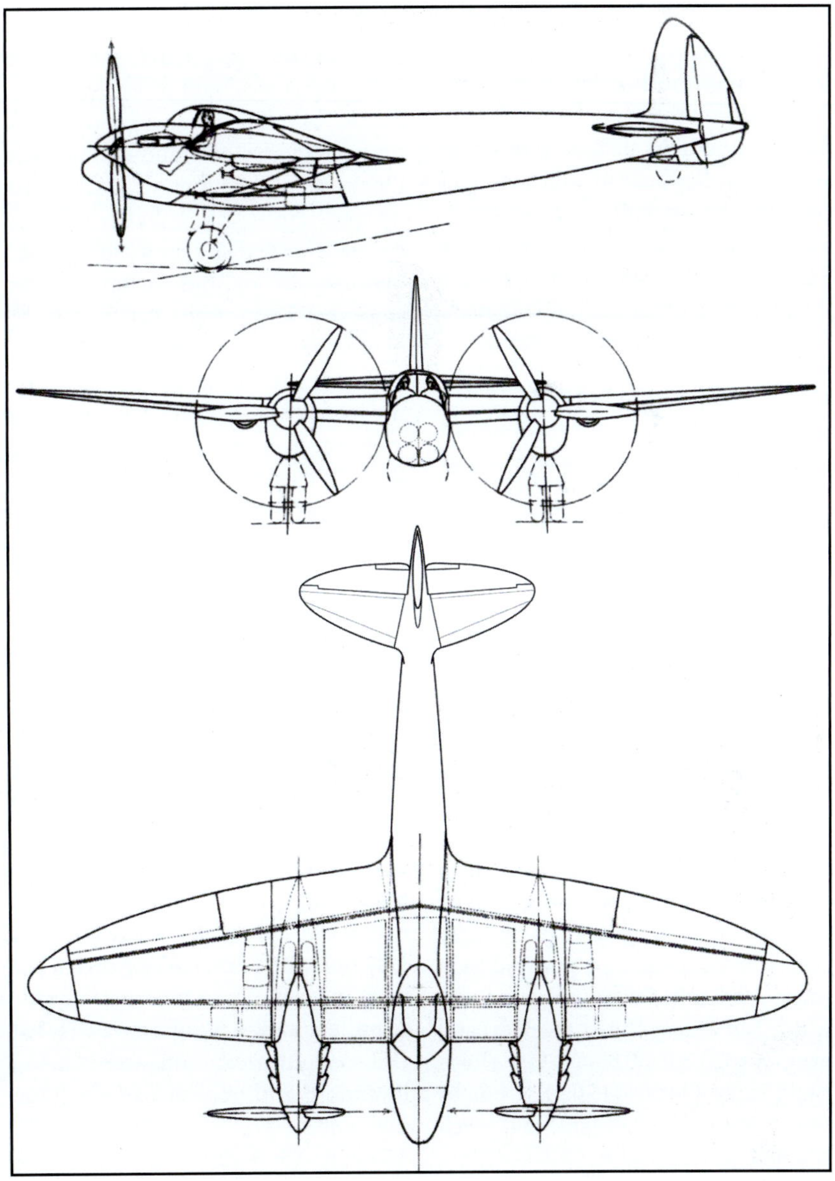

Shorts High-Speed Two-Seat Twin-Engine Bomber (2.40)	
Span	51ft 0in (15.54m)
Length (datum horizontal)	40ft 9in (12.42m)
Wing Area	430sq.ft (39.95sq.m)
All-Up-Weight	21,000lb (9,525kg)
Powerplant	2 × 1,350hp (1,007kW) Merlin RM.2.SM
Max Speed/Height	Full load 400mph (644km/h), half fuel and no bombs 407mph (655km/h), both at 21,000ft (6,401m)
Armament	4 × 500lb (227kg) bombs

The proposed aircraft had a two-spar wing and would be driven by twin Merlin units fitted with 12ft (3.66m) diameter three-blade Rotol constant-speed fully-feathering propellers. A total of 772gal (3,510lit) of fuel would be carried in self-sealing tanks in the inner wing, the fuselage behind the cockpit above the bomb bay, and in the nose. Four bombs stacked in two pairs went in the bay beneath and just to the rear of the cockpit, and the main undercarriage legs had twin wheels. The estimated range in still air when flying at maximum economic cruising power was 2,000 miles (3,219km).

de Havilland DH.98 Mosquito

Again contrary to many published sources, long before the outbreak of war the Air Ministry was well aware of the value of adopting wood for aircraft construction to save light alloys and forgings. Sir Geoffrey de Havilland (GdH) and his staff felt an unarmed wooden bomber would be smaller, lighter and much faster than the conventional Specification P.13/36, which called for a medium bomber with forward and rear defensive guns, but it would still be capable of taking an effective bomb load well into enemy territory. On 6 September 1939 his team completed preliminary estimates for an aircraft powered by a single 2,000hp (1,491kW) Napier Sabre which had a span of 47ft (14.33m) and wing area 330sq.ft (30.66sq.m) and which could carry 1,000lb (454kg) of bombs over 1,500 miles (2,414km) and reach 400mph (644km/h) at 16,000ft (4,877m).

Between 14 and 18 September comparisons were made between this and another design having two Merlins, a 55ft 6in (16.92m) span, 440sq.ft (40.88sq.m) wing area and 400mph (644km/h) top speed. The latter was then scaled up into two further designs and all three were compared against a layout with a single Sabre or two Napier Enlarged Dagger (E.112) engines. By 4 October work had progressed to an aircraft of 51ft 3in (15.62m) span and 410sq.ft (38.09sq.m) wing area with either two Merlins or two Griffons, the Merlin being the more favoured since the use of Griffons depended on the availability of that engine.

A letter to Sir Wilfrid Freeman, AMDP, on 20 September brought the first concrete proposals. Freeman was a supporter and GdH wrote 'we believe that we could produce a twin-engine bomber which would have a performance so outstanding that little defensive equipment would be needed.' He stressed that wood was specially suited to really high speeds because all of the surfaces were smooth and free from rivets, overlapped plates and undulations, while its use would not encroach on the labour and material (described as 'bottleneck' material) being used in the RAF's expansion programme.

The preliminary specification was two Merlins, 1,500 miles (2,414km) range, two 500lb (227kg) or six 250lb (113kg) bombs, a pilot and observer and a maximum speed of 405mph (652km/h) at 20,000ft (6,096m). If Sabres were available the same performance and range was possible with 4,000lb (1,814kg) of bombs, three crew and two guns. Freeman consulted R. N. Liptrot who felt the firm was optimistic in suggesting such a high maximum speed. Later Liptrot expressed annoyance saying it was 'ludicrous for a firm making such a far-reaching claim for a new aircraft type to present it in so meagre a way.' He felt DH's weight predictions were far too low and that the speed was much too high and he predicted a maximum of 350mph (563km/h) and 19,500lb weight (8,845kg), which forced DH to revise its figures to 386mph (621km/h) at 20,000ft (6,096m).

On 1 November 1939 AVMs Arthur Tedder and Sholto Douglas, DGRD and ACAS respectively, agreed that this type would only be of interest as a bomber if it had effective rear defence, despite being aware that this would bring a drop in performance, 'but the speed of opposing fighters … is such that we cannot hope to depend upon obtaining security by a margin of superior performance. If designed without effective rear defence, it could only be considered as a development aircraft for possible use on fast reconnaissance duties.' It was made clear to GdH that fitting this aircraft into future production plans was difficult, the supply of turrets would 'tax our resources' while producing the required additional engines was unlikely to be possible. They had 'regretfully' concluded that it would not be practicable to proceed with this type for production as a bomber, but if the company was willing to consider it as a machine to help develop high-performance in-service aircraft, they were glad to consider it further. It was generally felt that if a successful prototype bomber was produced, it would be impracticable to fit it into the production programme without displacing other types and causing general dislocation.

In fact on 16 October DH had begun to study what effects fitting a defensive armament of two guns on top and one underneath might have. This resulted in a streamlined and fairly simple two-gun tail turret on the Merlin version but the arrangement knocked 20mph to 30mph (32km/h to 48km/h) off the top speed, so on the Griffon aircraft GdH decided to make the rear defence first class with a full four-gun turret. The more powerful engines ensured that the high speed was retained but calculations suggested the turret added 2,400lb (1,089kg) in weight to give a maximum of 18,000lb (8,165kg) and also made the aircraft more complicated to build. On 2 November the initial studies were made towards a four-cannon fighter version. However, H. Grinsted, DDRD, noted that 'our experience of Messrs de

Havilland is that they are extremely slow in producing anything for the RAF' and added that most technical and production experts had grave doubts as to the company's ability to achieve its performance and production promises.

On 8 November 1939 Grinsted heard from C. C. Walker, DH's chief engineer, that the Griffon aircraft's size had been increased but, fitted with a Frazer-Nash four-gun tail turret, capacity for 1,000lb (454kg) bombs and a crew of three, it could still make 390mph to 400mph (628km/h to 644km/h) at 20,000ft (6,096m). Walker stressed how quickly this aircraft could enter production but acknowledged that the Air Ministry would not commit itself to large production on a type for which it had no experience. On the other hand, DH could not put all of its design effort towards producing a single prototype, so the idea of a small batch of aeroplanes was suggested as a solution.

At a conference held at Whitehall on 12 November it was decided to arrange ordering around fifty examples of the DH.98, as the project was called, with Merlin RM.2.SMs. Tedder informed GdH on 20 November that it had been decided to build two prototypes with the four-gun turret and asked him to construct a mock-up. At this point there were actually three high-speed bomber projects now under discussion, the DH.98, the Blackburn B.28 and a bomber conversion of the Bristol Beaufighter. The latter was not considered to be very promising but both Blackburn's and DH's designs did generally conform to the broad bomb load/range requirements that the Air Staff had in mind.

A meeting held at the Air Ministry on 22 November, which included W. S. Farren, Wilfrid Freeman and Liptrot plus Clarkson and Bishop of de Havilland, brought matters together. The two versions of the DH.98 were of similar size but the second had a rear turret that produced a difference of 30mph to 40mph (48km/h to 64km/h) in speed. Bishop reported that the first design would demonstrate the main features of the type whereas the second was a development adapted as a bomber for service use, but the main objective was to produce an aeroplane within about nine months without interfering with the production of other types; it was not the company's intention to produce both aircraft simultaneously. DH claimed that the design was four years ahead of the Spitfire, its wood construction was so perfected that the smooth skin would eliminate sources of drag and its ducted internal radiators added 10mph (16km/h) to the speed.

Freeman contended that introducing a turret tended to defeat DH's objective of producing a bomber which would outpace the contemporary fighter. The

BELOW de Havilland DH.98 Mosquito prototype E0234 is seen on the Hatfield runway (for the first time?) on 21 November 1940. This aircraft later received military serial W4050. *Phil Butler*

ABOVE AND TOP The Mosquito photo-reconnaissance prototype was W4051. *Crown Copyright*

question was speed versus armament and Freeman suggested that DH should concentrate on an aeroplane which could not be overtaken by any contemporary enemy aircraft. If the following programme could be guaranteed by the company, he would recommend it to the Air Council purely as a gamble:

a. Provide a Merlin aeroplane having the highest possible speed with a maximum 1,500 miles (2,414km) range within the next nine months;

b. Then immediately commence constructing a modified type with Griffons capable of the same range at 375mph (603km/h) and to be ready within another nine months;

c. Then commence a still further modified type with Sabre engines capable of greater speed over the same range.

Freeman got his way in having any guns deleted and a draft requirement was raised for a high-speed light reconnaissance aircraft capable of 400mph (644km/h) at 18,000ft (5,486m). An order for fifty was placed on 25 January 1940 and Specification B.1/40 was written around DH's proposals on 1 March. Within the Ministry, however, there was still some fierce opposition. Surprisingly Ludlow-Hewitt, considering his comments towards the Handley Page project above, insisted on the absolute necessity of rear defence. His objections were mainly based on the grounds of tactics. He wanted his fast bombers to penetrate individually heavily defended territory to reach selected targets and, for reasons of morale if nothing else, it was necessary for the aircraft to be able to defend itself. One convert, however, was AVM Tedder and, in addition, the broad idea that de Havilland should design and build an aircraft of its own was felt to be a good one.

DH submitted its detailed estimates for both Merlin and Griffon machines at the end of November 1939 and, thereafter, intensive work proceeded on the unarmed Merlin type or a fighter version with an alternative four cannon nose until year's end, when the design requirement was finalised. A mock-up was examined at Hatfield on 29 December and such was the pace of progress that when the specification was raised in January 1940 de Havilland was almost ready to start construction. For a period it looked as if one of the prototypes would have leading-edge ducted radiators and the other underslung Beaufighter style radiators, but the second arrangement was not actually flight tested until mid-1943 when it revealed a quite violent tendency to wing drop. It transpired that the Mosquito's leading-edge radiators produced an early, inboard stall and thus avoided any premature loss of lift at the tips.

GdH first proposed the alternative long-range fighter version in May 1940 and two months later further unease about the unarmed bomber helped in the authorisation for another prototype to be built as a fighter. Liptrot quickly requested a specification, which became F.21/40, for an aircraft armed with four 20mm and four 0.303 (7.7mm) nose-mounted guns. However, there was debate on whether this aeroplane should be primarily for day or night work, and be armed with fixed guns or a turret. Experience of regular German air raids meant that night fighting tactics were being modified almost nightly, while the new development of air interception radar was another factor. In the end a two-seat fixed-gun fighter was selected.

Another influence was the AS.48 night fighter from Airspeed, a project which was abandoned after its drawings, data and mock-up were destroyed during a bombing raid on Hatfield on 3 October 1940. It was clear that a variant of the Mosquito long-range fighter could undertake the night fighting role and this version eventually received a go-ahead, while the original long-range Mosquito was dropped. AVM Linnell wrote on 29 April 1941 'I am hopeful of great things of the Mosquito as a night fighter.' When this variant flew 17 days later it did not sport the nosewheel undercarriage which, at one stage, was thought to be needed.

The existence of the fighter variant certainly helped to keep the Mosquito alive because there was still plenty of criticism, even after the bomber prototype had flown in November 1940. On 2 December 1940 'Archie' (Sir Archibald Sinclair, Secretary of State for Air) wrote to 'Max' (Lord Beaverbrook) saying 'War experience tends to show that this bomber would be useless for the purposes for which it was designed. On the other hand I am inclined to think that it may be useful for photo recce and target towing if the equipment can be installed.' He did feel that it might be possible to use it for short-range bombing in suitable weather conditions but suggested that no more orders should be placed until satisfactory prototype trials were complete. Two weeks later 'Archie' added that he did feel better about the Mosquito fighter.

In early spring 1941 Sir Henry Tizard was asked to appraise all of the industry's new aircraft types currently in the design and development stage and to give views as to their future. His comments on the B.1/40 Mosquito were brief: 'This was originally a 'stunt' machine to be developed in small quantities. It has flown satisfactorily but I do not think it will be particularly useful for anything. I understand only a small order has been placed and a few of them may fill a useful purpose – e.g. long distance ocean fighter.' Freeman, now VCAS, wrote a typically vitriolic observation to Air Marshal Linnell on 29 April which embraced the whole subject of forthcoming types but clearly had the Mosquito in mind: 'Tizard's experience is negligible. He believes in figures and promises, both as regards delivery and performance, which have no basis for justification, and I will not agree to a sacrifice of a really good certainty for the doubtful Whittle [that is, the Meteor jet fighter] and the [Hawker] Typhoon/Tornado [fighter], which we know, without considerable alteration, will not be able to operate at great heights. I take it that this file will not go to Sir Henry Tizard.'

ABOVE The Mosquito was manufactured in many different versions. This is one of the fighter-bomber FB.Mk.VIIIs which had a 57mm Molins cannon under the nose. It also carries D-Day stripes.

The first Mosquito flew on 25 November 1940 with B Conditions marking E0234 (the name Mosquito had been bestowed by June 1940). A visit to A&AEE Boscombe Down from 19 February 1941 for brief handling and performance trials revealed that the aeroplane was pleasant to fly with its flying qualities considered generally good. Best rate of climb was 2,880ft/min (878m/min) at 11,400ft (3,475m) and top speed 388mph (624km/h) at 22,000ft (6,706m). The last figure brought general astonishment. Nobody, not even the de Havilland team, were sure it that would be faster than the Spitfire and many officials had poured scorn on the idea, yet here it was – 388mph. de Havilland's Richard Clarkson remembered Fred Rowarth, Boscombe's chief technical officer, taking his hat off to the Mosquito's speed after he had completed the calculations (the average maximum speed of early production aircraft proved to be 383mph [616km/h]). From now on many more took the aircraft seriously. On 16 January 1941 E0234 was flown at 6,000ft (1,829m) alongside a Spitfire and the Mosquito was able to fly away in 'a fairly convincing manner.'

Frequent design changes had still to be made due to the evolution of the fighter requirements and the failure of the Air Staff to decide i) whether it definitely did not require the unarmed bomber version and ii) what proportion of the total output was to be built as bombers, fighters or photo reconnaissance aircraft. The last pair always had precedence over the bomber but the bomber was never actually cancelled. As if in full and final acknowledgement to DH's thoughts on gun turrets, the suggestion to fit one in mid-1941 was rejected by the Ministry after flight testing. N. E. Rowe, DTD, wrote on 4 July that the turret 'must be kept in front of the rear spar to preserve the balance of the aeroplane.' The original position meant that it protruded into the middle of the bomb compartment which thus prevented any bombs from being carried. By moving the turret as far aft as possible towards the rear spar it was conceivable that two 250lb (113kg) bombs could be carried, but that position needed the fuel tanks to be redesigned while the CofG would then be at the limit for acceptable longitudinal stability.

Over and above these basic difficulties, however, flight testing showed that the turret resulted in a serious loss in speed and gave an increase in landing run. Rowe reported that at 22,000ft (6,706m) the optimum range speed dropped from 252mph to 220mph (405km/h to 354km/h) and maximum cruise from 335mph to 300mph (539km/h to 483km/h), while the maximum full throttle level flight speed at 23,000ft (7,010m) fell from 378mph to 340mph (608km/h to 547km/h). Rowe concluded that 'it is impractical to turn the Mosquito into a bomber with a four-gun turret and still retain a reasonable bomb load. Moreover, and bearing in mind that the top speed of the Spitfire V is only 385mph [619km/h] at 23,000ft [7,010m], it seems essential to retain the highest speed possible in the aeroplane.'

Eventually the Mosquito proved itself to be an outstanding aircraft in almost every role given to it, the list of which grew once its superb performance was acknowledged. As confirmation of the type's acceptance, on 24 July 1941 the Air Staff reported that it was 'very anxious to make the utmost use of the potentiality of the Mosquito' and it was pushing to increase production to 150 per month. A total of 7,781 was eventually built and production did not cease until 1950.

de Havilland Mosquito Mk.IV (flown)	
Span	54ft 2in (16.51m)
Length	40ft 9.5in (12.43m)
Wing Area	454sq.ft (42.18sq.m)
All-Up-Weight	21,462lb (9,735kg)
Powerplant	2 × 1,480hp (1,104kW) Merlin 21/23
Max Speed/Height	341mph (549km/h) at 20,000ft (6,096m) at 17,000lb (7,711kg) mean weight
Armament	4,000lb (1,814kg) bombs maximum

Specification B.3/40

Blackburn B.28

This private venture high-speed light bomber and reconnaissance design, first proposed in 1939 and mentioned briefly above, was based on the Botha torpedo bomber (Chapter Seven). It was powered by two Griffons and had a span of 54ft 9in (16.69m) and length (tail down) of 39ft 0in (11.89m). Specification B.3/40 was written around the project and indicated a maximum speed of at least 400mph (644km/h) at 18,000ft (5,486m), with the warload to include two 500lb (227kg) or four 250lb (113kg) bombs; there was also an allowance to fit a four-gun turret. This seems to have been a quite long-lived project and one prototype, X8500, was ordered in 1940; a mock-up was also built but the B.28 was eventually abandoned.

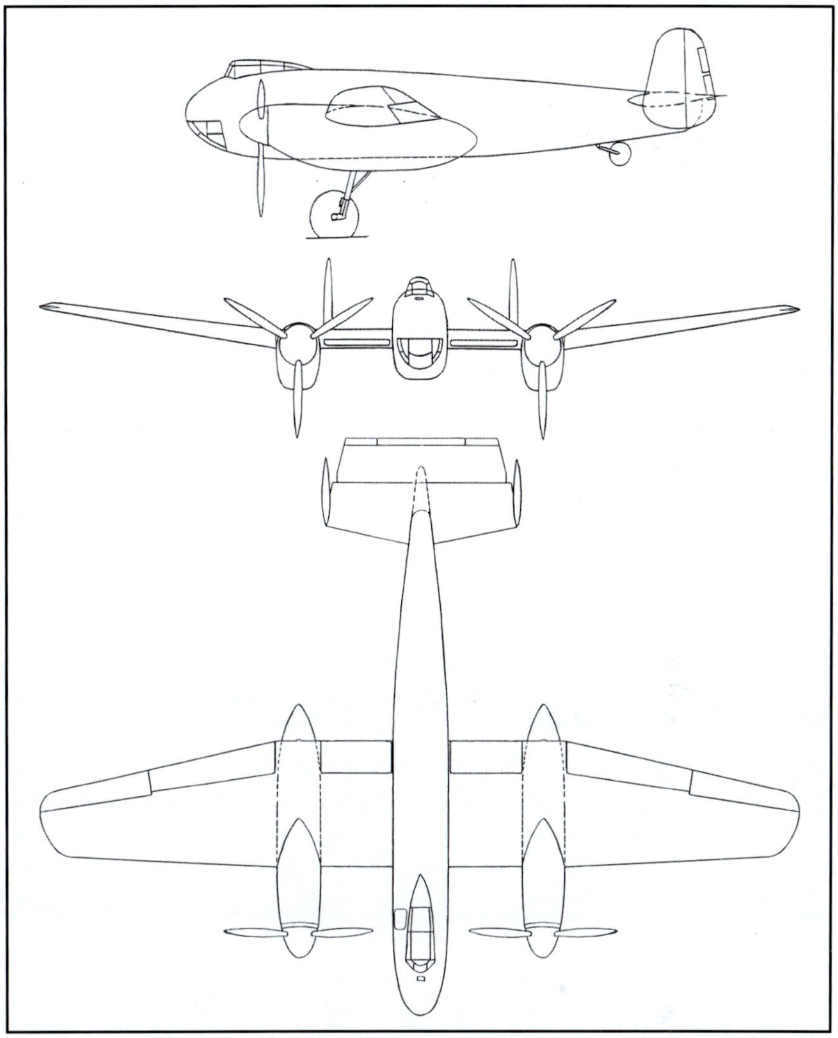

ABOVE Blackburn B.28 high-speed bomber. This updated drawing is dated 10 October 1940. *BAE Systems Brough Heritage Centre*

BELOW The B.28 mock-up pictured on 9 November 1940. *BAE Systems Brough Heritage Centre*

Specification B.11/41

Hawker P.1005

In late 1940 Hawker began scheming this project for a high-speed light bomber fitted with two Sabre IV engines. There was strong feeling that the RAF needed a new machine which could be either a high-speed bomber or a high-speed long-range fighter and it was felt that the production and maintenance benefits gained by using the same basic aircraft for the two types would be immense. Such a type offered less time over enemy territory, a high useful bomb load and less production hours than a heavy bomber but it would only be satisfactory if high speeds, in excess of 400mph (644km/h), were provided. Hawker felt that its experience in the techniques used in designing its Typhoon high-speed fighter could be most usefully employed here, rather than the techniques of heavy bomber design.

The P.1005 had three radiators per engine (one each side, in the wing, and one in the chin position under the propeller); fuel capacity of 1,100gal (5,001lit); and a main undercarriage hinged just inside the engine mountings

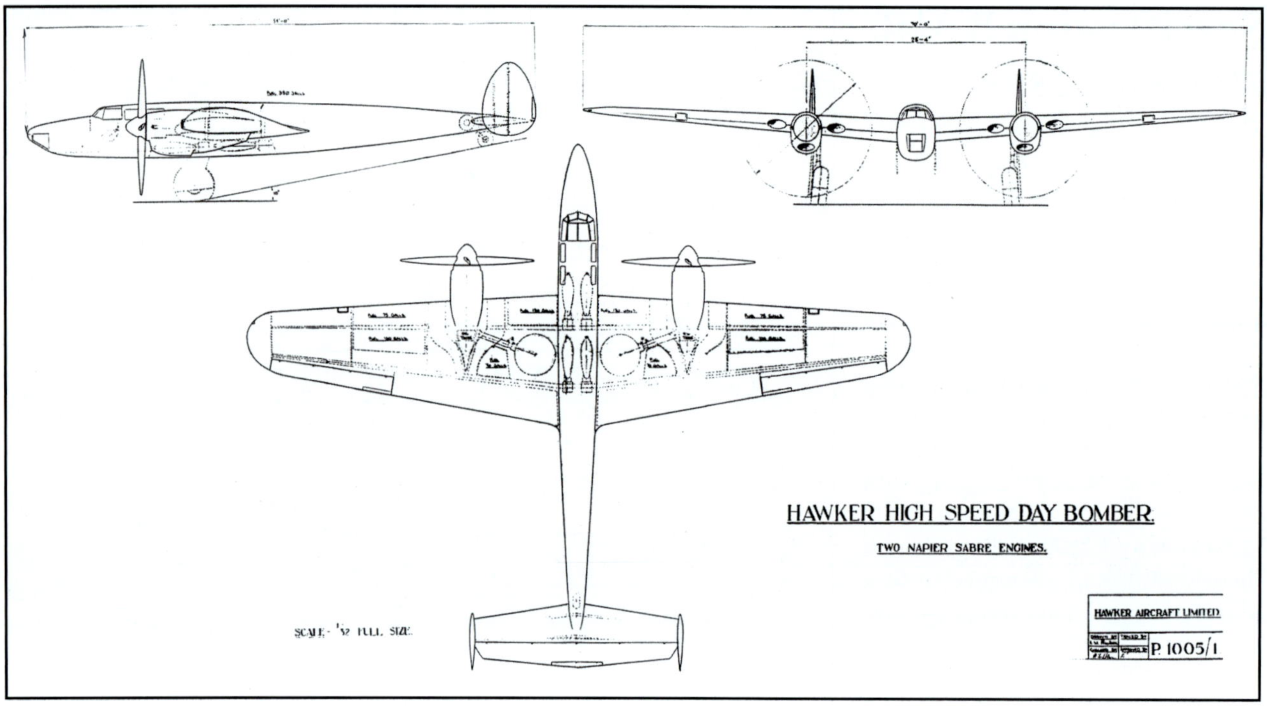

ABOVE Hawker P.1005 (12.40).

which retracted sideways into the thick centre-wing section. Flaps were provided and the ailerons were fitted along the outer wings while the choice of twin fins and rudders meant that a full length elevator was available (an alternative single central fin had been examined). Construction was all-metal and the aircraft had a comparatively narrow fuselage.

Originally, the objective was a bomb load of 2,000lb (907kg) but, after the requirements were increased, the internal weapon bay was eventually capable of taking up to 4,000lb (1,814kg) in the form of four 1,000lb (454kg) bombs, two 2,000lb or a single full 4,000lb bomb. Like the Mosquito, P.1005 had no defensive armament but provision was made for a circular 41in (104cm) diameter retractable turret in the dorsal position which would house four 0.303in (7.7mm) machine guns. The turret and its guns were designed to sink down into the fuselage on retraction, leaving just a small protrusion (shown on the fighter drawing) to disturb the streamlining; the turret's gunner raised the crew to four. The high-speed fighter variant was initially just a simple conversion that saw the introduction of a pair of forward-firing 20mm cannon to complement the turret's machine guns. However a more drastic modification was eventually completed with a shorter fuselage nose and six 20mm cannon beneath the cockpit.

Submission of the P.1005 to the Ministry was around the turn of the year and on 4 February 1941 Liptrot completed his appraisal in which he described the aircraft as a logical follow-on from the Mosquito. At this time a high-altitude version of the selected engine was under development which Liptrot stated would improve the climb and altitude performance. Operationally he gave the P.1005 merit over the Mosquito because it provided more normal equipment and a higher bomb load and did not attempt to rely solely on its speed and evasive power for safety, instead providing the four-gun turret for

BELOW The High-Speed Fighter version of the P.1005 with a shortened nose and six 20mm cannon. The small dorsal fairing indicates the position of the Wireless Operator's station or the alternative gun turret.

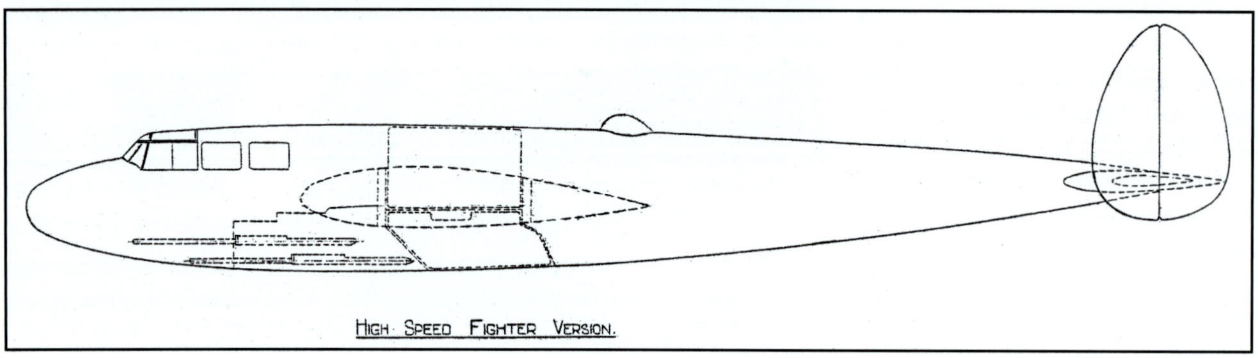

rear defence; the turret was also seen as an advantage over the Mosquito's fixed 0.303 (7.7mm) machine guns. Liptrot closed by saying the only major weakness was a slightly inadequate cruising range and he requested that Hawker should rectify this.

Rowe, however, expected an increase in weight as the design was developed and stated that only a product of the highest class was likely to be of value operationally. On 24 April he spoke to Sydney Camm and the designer chose not to push for a production order at once but instead settle for the aircraft solely as a prototype for the time being, with a review of the situation to follow in three to six months. He knew that the P.1005 would need two Typhoon engines and there would never be enough of these available, although perhaps in time a resource of engines would build up. Rowe reported this to Sir Henry Tizard who replied that they should push the aircraft forward saying 'we want to know what we can get from a really well designed twin-Sabred aircraft' – the P.1005 was felt to be the best proposal so far for a light bomber schemed around two Sabre engines.

In November 1941 draft Specification B.11/41 was written directly around the P.1005 and described a twin-engine high-performance bomber capable of being converted into a long-range fixed-gun fighter. As a bomber maximum speed was to be 400mph (644km/h) at 25,000ft (7,620m) (later increased to 430mph [692km/h]) and range with a 2,000lb (907kg) load 1,600 miles (2,575km) at 30,000ft (9,144m) (later raised to 1,750 miles [2,818km] with a 4,000lb [1,814kg] load); additional removable fuel tanks would be fitted for fighter operations to give a range of 2,100 miles (3,380km). B.11/41 was issued in early June 1942. The P.1005 brochure quoted a ceiling of 32,500ft (9,906m) and a time to 20,000ft (6,096m) of 10.5 minutes; with high-altitude versions of the Sabre fitted it was thought that a speed of 430mph (692km/h) would be possible at 36,500ft (11,125m).

On 22 October 1941 the Ministry declared that the P.1005 (also known as the Camm B.11/41) must come into production at the expense of the Hurricane and at a ratio of one Camm Bomber for two Hurricanes. However, this decision would be affected by the appearance of some competition in the shape of the Mosquito, whose value was at last receiving appreciation, and a new design from Bristol called the Type 163 Buckingham (see later). In addition a Sabre-engine Mosquito development called the DH.101 was prepared during the autumn of 1941 (described shortly).

Back in early August Air Marshal R. S. Sorley, ACAS(T), had compared these aircraft for CRD, Air Marshal F. J. Linnell. The Hawker gained in bomb load and speed at the expense of range and defence and, to a degree, poor navigation facilities. Its excess of speed over either was not great, while its armament was distinctly inferior to the Buckingham. Thus it seemed to Sorley that the Hawker B.11/41 fell into the category of a Mosquito replacement and in this the development possibilities of the Mosquito had to be taken into account because the Hawker was over a year further away from reaching production than the DH design. Sorley added that unless the B.11/41 had a development future that could be foreseen, it did not presently offer a sufficient advance to warrant large-scale production. He feared that the Air Staff would commit itself to the production of a design that in fact might already be at the end of its potential but then softened this comment by declaring that he had the greatest confidence in Sydney Camm, all of whose aircraft 'had astonishing developments in them.' He hoped that the P.1005 would show similarly good prospects.

On 18 November MAP requested 400 Bristol Buckinghams and 1,000 Camm bombers, but on 18 December the Aircraft Supply Council stated that development of the Buckingham, Hawker B.11/41 and an improved Mosquito might result in three types of fast day bomber being put into production, thereby repeating the state of affairs which had resulted in too many heavy bomber types. Linnell added that he had doubts about attempting the improved Mosquito. However, on 9 December, MAP's Research and Development department had written to RAE stating that 'a production order is about to be placed for the high-speed fighter-bomber which has been developed by Hawkers in a semi-private manner to date. A draft production specification has been drawn up to cover this order.'

On 22 December a meeting was held between Rowe, DOR, Camm and other Hawker and specialist staff. Camm said that Hawker would now design the aeroplane to carry the 4,000lb (1,814kg) bomb load but it was agreed that no steps were to be taken that would embarrass the project's primary function, its high speed. On 1 January 1942 Sorley noted that the P.1005's planning should proceed rather carefully. The project had been 'on and off for quite six months and it is only within the last two months that a final decision was taken to have it produced.' He felt that another change of mind would have a very bad effect upon Hawker, and probably MAP, but if DH were to do a Mosquito replacement, 'then there is not a good case for having both' and cancellation of the P.1005 would allow a greater concentration upon the Typhoon fighter. Three days later Camm asked Rowe about the prospects for using the P.1005 as a fighter and was told that this was entirely secondary to the main bomber role. As a fighter the agreed armament was now four 20mm, but Rowe wanted Hawker to concentrate on the design of the aeroplane as a day bomber.

Camm's redesign of the P.1005 was assessed by Liptrot in a minute dated 22 January, the main alteration being a 12% reduction in wing area but with the original span maintained. He expected an increase in top speed to 409mph (658km/h) at 25,000ft (7,620m) but other performance aspects were expected to suffer including a reduction in range by 70 miles (112km), an increase in weight of some 300lb (136kg) and a reduced ceiling of around 1,000ft to 1,500ft (305m to 457m).

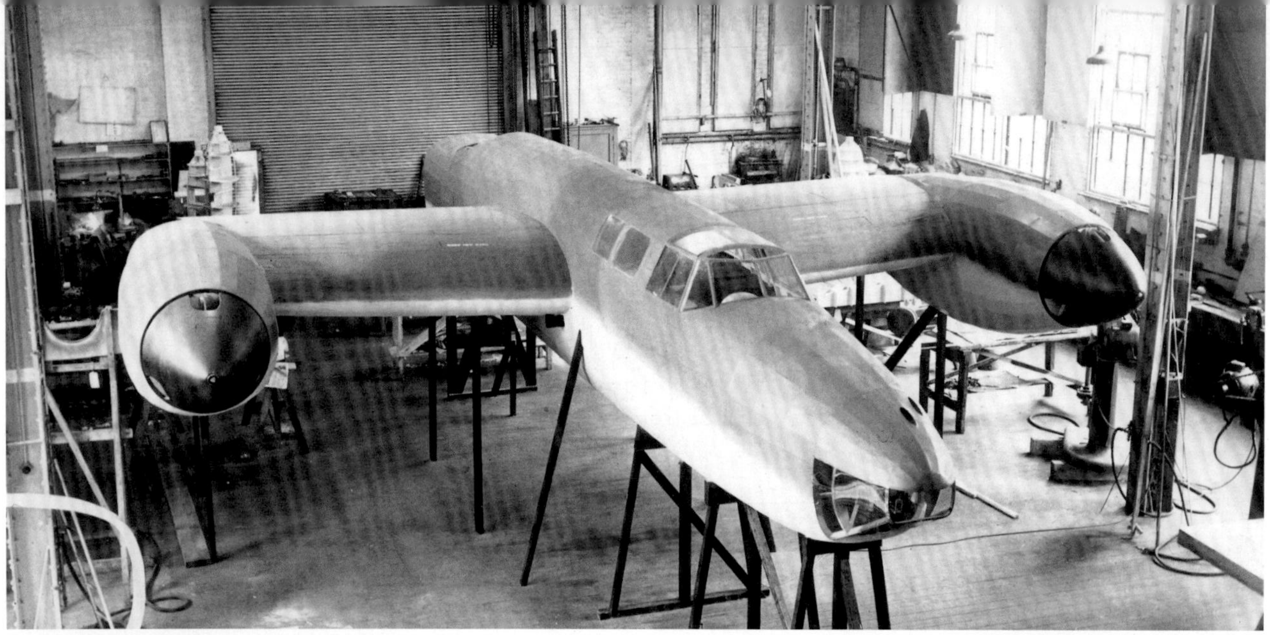

ABOVE Model by Joe Cherrie of the Hawker P.1005. *Joe Cherrie*

Liptrot had several objections to the revised wing – structurally it was difficult in regard to torsional stiffness while the poor lift distribution would probably produce tip stalling. He concluded that detailed investigations were needed before it could possibly be accepted; personally, he considered it quite unacceptable and felt some real risks had been introduced.

On 8 January a final decision to select the Hawker P.1005 or the de Havilland DH.101 (next page) had been delayed, in part because details of the latter had only just been supplied. But a week later the Air Staff felt it would be unwise to produce both and suggested dropping the P.1005. Early in the following month Liptrot reported that the position of this aircraft had become ill-defined since his department had been informed that its production was cancelled while the provision of a four-gun turret was, apparently, only an insurance against the P.1005's performance comparing unfavourably with contemporary enemy aircraft. In fact a note had circulated in the Ministry on 4 February saying that the requisition for the purchase of 1,000 Hawker bombers had been withdrawn and, therefore, there was no necessity to prepare a production specification.

Two P.1005 prototypes were ordered with serials HV266 and HV270. A mock-up was built which included the engine installations, inner wings and forward fuselage, and the Mock-Up Conference was held on 27 February 1942. On 17 March a final decision on the P.1005 was deferred for six months and one reason for this was that cancellation would upset Hawker because the company understood that orders for 1,000 aeroplanes were likely. These production plans had foreseen the replacement of the original Merlin Mosquito at a rate of 50 per month, although the changeover at Hawker would cost an estimated 700 Typhoons. Just two days later, at an Aircraft Supply Council Meeting, it was agreed that Buckingham production should be 25 a month, as already planned, but no production should be ordered for the Hawker Sabre bomber or the Super Mosquito with Griffons. In both cases prototypes only would suffice and it was felt that the Air Ministry would be ready to abandon the P.1005 because the company's fighter production was not to be prejudiced.

This was the end for the P.1005. Although the fully approved specification finally came through at the end of May, on 10 June the Deputy Controller of Research and Development gave verbal instructions that the order for the type was to be cancelled. A minute on 9 June explained that the P.1005's history was unfortunate and fraught with continual delays and vacillations of policy. In truth, no production capacity appeared to be available before about the end of 1944 and so the company was recommended to cease work on the two prototypes.

OPPOSITE PAGE The manufacturer's mock-up of the forward fuselage and inner wings of the Hawker P.1105.

The project was considered to be very promising but was abandoned because of the hopeless production prospects brought about by a shortage of capacity, not through any shortcomings in the design. Much later, in February 1944, Air Marshal Sorley explained that B.11/41 had been planned before the Mosquito had been accepted. Preparing early replacement types was normal practice and a probable reason for the Hawker project not going ahead was uncertainty at the time as to whether the Mosquito would be a success. During the period it had seemed sensible to encourage progress of the Hawker bomber.

No information has been traced detailing the level of progress made on building the two prototypes, but it seems likely that very little was actually done. The P.1005 was also offered (prior to April 1942) with Bristol Centaurus radials as the P.1015, which reduced the estimated maximum speed to 390mph (628km/h).

Armament: 4,000lb (1,814kg) bombs maximum, some documents indicate 2 × 0.303in (7.7mm) machine guns in nose. Fighter 6 × 20mm cannon, both versions 4 × 0.303in (7.7mm) machine guns in optional turret

Hawker P.1005 (12.40 onwards)	
Span	70ft 0in (21.34m)
Length	54ft 0in (16.46m) (as fighter approx. 51ft 0in [15.54m])
Wing Area	677sq.ft (62.90sq.m)
All-Up-Weight	31,225lb (14,163kg) normal, 34,000lb (15,422kg) overload
Powerplant	2 × 2,180hp (1,626kW) NS.8SM Sabre IV (alternative 2 × Centaurus)
Max Speed/Height	Sabre 415mph (668km/h) at 24,000 ft (7,315m), Centaurus 390mph (628km/h), high-altitude Sabre 430mph (692km/h) at 36,500ft (11,125m)
Armament	4,000lb (1,814kg) bombs maximum, some documents indicate 2 × 0.303in (7.7mm) machine guns in nose. Fighter 6 × 20mm cannon, both versions 4 × 0.303in (7.7mm) machine guns in optional turret

de Havilland DH.99/DH.101

The P.1005's competitors were the Bristol Buckingham (discussed shortly), the only type to reach production, and de Havilland's DH.101/DH.102. B.11/41 was written around the P.1005 but in the autumn of 1941 DH wanted a more powerful Mosquito and this specification became the design team's target. The result was a modified Mosquito with two Sabres which was initially called the DH.99 but then renumbered DH.101; together with the later DH.102 this was known as the Super Mosquito or 'hotted-up Mossie.' Estimated top speed was 417mph (671km/h) at 26,000ft (7,925m) (more powerful 2,180hp [1,626kW] Sabre NS.8.SMs offered 430mph [692km/h]), 4,000lb (1,814kg) of bombs were carried internally (though not the single 4,000 pounder) together with another 2,000lb (907kg) under the wings, and a new third crewman would act as a navigator. The required 1,750 miles (2,816km) range could be reached by carrying small external tanks – without these but with 6,000lb (2,722kg) of bombs aboard the range was 1,460 miles (2,350km), maximum speed 406mph (653km/h) and ceiling 27,300ft (8,321m) (with NS.8.SMs ceiling would be 35,000ft [10,668m]).

The DH.101 fitted with Sabres allowed the Mosquito's high-speed characteristics to be maintained, but with an increase in dimensions to permit sufficient crew accommodation for accurate bombing. However, on 4 April 1942 the company was notified of the unavailability of Sabre engines for this project and it was advised to use Griffon 61s instead, but the expected lower performance from the latter

BELOW de Havilland (DH.101) 'Twin-Sabre Bomber' (1942).

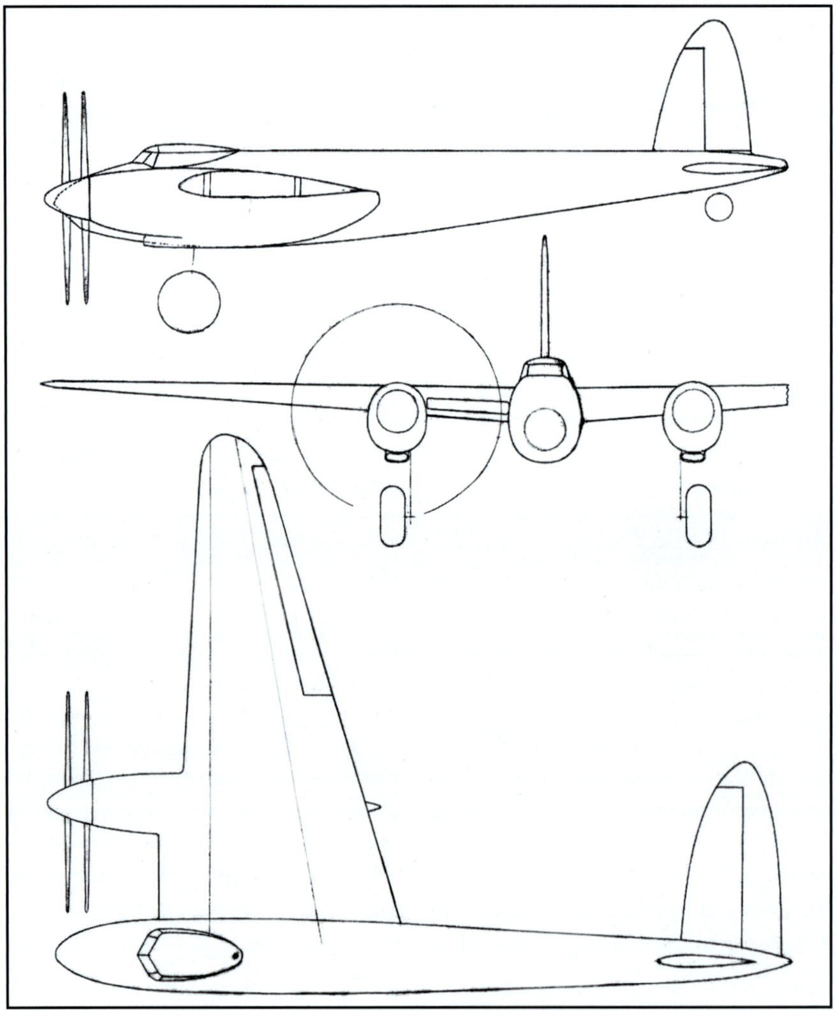

de Havilland DH.101 (early 1942)	
Span	70ft 0in (21.34m)
Length	?
Wing Area	710sq.ft (65.96sq.m)
All-Up-Weight	MAP Estimate 33,650lb (15,263kg)
Powerplant	2 × 2,180hp (1,626kW) Sabre IV NS.8SM
Max Speed/Height	417mph (671km/h) at 26,000ft (7,925m)
Armament	6,000lb (2,722kg) bombs maximum. Fighter conversion 4 × 20mm cannon, 4 × 40mm cannon

meant that the project was quickly dropped. In truth the planned production levels for the Sabre were insufficient to make the NS.8.SM available to this new project (or the P.1005) while DH added that it could not employ the Centaurus on the DH.101. The company had also been put off by the talk of fitting the turret onto the P.1005 which was entirely against company philosophy. Work now moved on to the DH.102 bomber.

Another undated de Havilland report has been found which compared the 'Twin-Sabre Bomber' with the Jet Mosquito described in Chapter Eight. This document, which does not quote DH.101, provided the data given in the second table. It also listed an internal fuel capacity of 6,110gal (27,776lit), an initial rate of climb of 1,950ft/min (594m/min), operational ceiling (500ft/min/152m/min rate of climb) 36,100ft (11,003m), dive speed 500mph (805km/h) IAS and a still air range of 1,468 miles (2,363km). It is hoped that the drawing reproduced here shows how the DH.101 would have looked.

As an aside, this report also made comparisons against a Mosquito fitted with Merlin 61 engines and counter-rotating airscrews and with 2,000lb (907kg) bombs on board. This aircraft's all-up-weight was 21,840lb (9,906kg) and, at this weight, it had a maximum speed of 426mph (686km/h) at 25,900ft (7,894m), initial rate of climb 1,670ft/min (509m/min), operational ceiling 34,000ft (10,363m) and still air range 1,340 miles (2,157km).

de Havilland 'Twin-Sabre Bomber' (1942)	
Span	66ft 0in (20.12m)
Length	48ft 6in (14.78m)
Wing Area	656sq.ft (60.94sq.m)
All-Up-Weight	(2,000lb/907kg bombs) 31,710lb (14,383kg)
Overload weight	(4,000lb/1,814kg bombs) 33,710lb (15,291kg)
Powerplant	2 × Sabre NS.20SIM
Max Speed/Height	337mph (542km/h) at sea level, 456mph (734km/h) at 36,700ft (11,186m)
Armament	Internal provision for 4,000lb (1,814kg) bombs

de Havilland DH.102

On 2 July 1941 Wilfrid Freeman told Linnell 'it was always my intention that the Mosquito should be followed by the Mosquito II built along the same lines but fitted with a Griffon engine.' Linnell replied that 'de Havillands are too full up with getting the original Mosquito going for us to worry them with the II;' nevertheless the DH.99 (DH.101) 'blown up Mossie' project was offered in mid-November 1941. Since neither the Griffon nor Centaurus were suited to the DH.101, DH withdrew from the B.11/41 specification and replaced the project with an alternative Merlin 61-powered aircraft, of slightly smaller dimensions, which used the present Mosquito as a basis. This was to be a high-speed night and day bomber and was called the DH.102 – it was similar to the DH.101 in appearance and had a pressure cabin and three crew, but less power. The project was described as a 'Mosquito Replacement' and designated the Mosquito Series II yet, with 5,000lb (2,268kg) of bombs on board and either Griffon or Merlin powerplants, it was expected to be slightly slower than its predecessor. Specification B.4/42 was allocated to the project and the

BELOW de Havilland DH.102 (5.42).

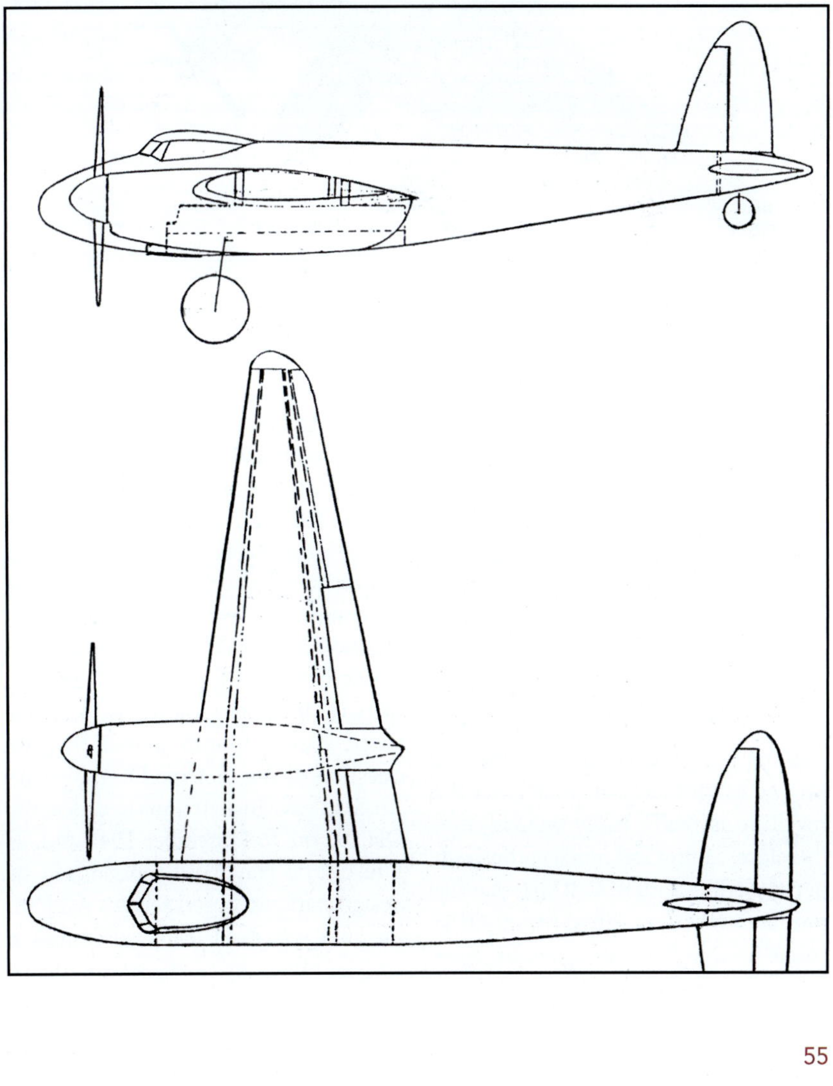

ABOVE AND LEFT Model of the DH.102 shown carrying serial MP478. *Joe Cherrie*

de Havilland DH.102 (5.42)	
Dimensions and weights unknown	
Powerplant	2 × Merlin 61
Max Speed/Height	c400mph (644km/h)?
Armament	5,000lb (2,268kg) bombs

construction of two prototypes, MP478 and MP481, was begun. By October 1942 these were reasonably well advanced but little enthusiasm was felt for the DH.102 either at de Havilland or within the Air Staff.

On 6 November GdH told Linnell that no mention had been made for any production of the '102.' There did not seem to be too much interest shown in the type and GdH added that 'tooling and generally preparing for production might have started months ago, but nothing has yet been done. In view of this we cannot feel convinced that the machine is really badly wanted and, therefore, cannot feel much enthusiasm in proceeding with it.' GdH felt that the production of a modified Mosquito in place of the '102' would save time which was important since his company now had the DH.100 jet fighter on its hands (later the Vampire) and was also considering a single-seat fighter with twin-Merlin 61s (which became the DH.103 Hornet).

The Air Staff was interested in the twin-Merlin fighter but DH could not undertake that and all of its other commitments, while the company's unease with the DH.102, after sensing doubt in the minds of the Air Staff as to the wisdom of proceeding with it, was noted. After a month deliberating the question of the unarmed bomber, the Air Staff gave instructions to cancel the DH.102 on 26 December 1942 and, as a result, de Havilland reorganised its design staff and began serious work on the more valuable Hornet and Vampire.

Miles M.39

Miles Aircraft also produced a design to B.11/41, in the form of its M.39 Libellula, and this was the only B.11/41 project to generate any flight testing. In 1941 Miles became aware of the high accident rates associated with deck landings on carriers and it was evident that many of the risks were due to the poor forward view in types like the Seafire. The company therefore began some private venture work to investigate the possibilities of evolving an unorthodox layout with the objectives of both improving the pilot's view and eliminating the complications and time wasting brought about by wing folding. After examining several possible layouts the solution appeared to be a tandem-wing arrangement, provided that it was aerodynamically feasible.

Miles was reluctant to submit a questionable design for official consideration and so decided to build and fly a rough mock-up which became the M.35; this was designed and completed in just six weeks. The first flight was made on 1 May 1942 and, although demonstrating that the tandem-wing arrangement was feasible, because of CofG problems it was difficult to get the M.35 into the air and it proved seriously unstable in flight. The layout was christened Libellula (after the entomological title for the dragonfly family) and proposals for a naval fighter were now submitted to the Admiralty and MAP, while Miles continued its research and moved on to a bomber.

A Libellula project called the M.39 was now prepared to the requirements of B.11/41 and submitted to MAP in July 1942 (after cancellation of the P.1005). In the meantime work also began on the M.39B, a 5/8ths scale flying model which flew on 22 July 1943. Registered U-0244, the M.39B was powered by two 140hp (104kW) de Havilland Gipsy Major engines, its front wing had a span of 25ft (7.62m) and the rear 37ft 6in (11.43m), length was 22ft 4in (6.81m) all-up-weight 3,200lb (1,451kg) and maximum speed 164mph (264km/h). In the air the M.39B apparently showed no disadvantages or undesirable handling characteristics; the CofG problems had been solved and the machine proved to be stable and controllable in all phases of flight, but it also did not appear to offer some of the main advantages claimed for the Libellula configuration.

Briefly the Libellula concept consisted of two wings mounted in tandem and interconnected by a short fuselage. The forward wing had less area than the rear wing (the proportions for the M.39 bomber were 1:3) and both were fitted with high-lift devices. Some of the expected benefits of the Libellula form were the attainment of a much greater permissible range of CofG movement than was possible with any orthodox layout; the ability to use high-lift devices to maximum effect on both wings; a reduction in structure weight of a large-span single wing compared with two wings of equivalent total area (this was particularly marked on very large aeroplanes); the elimination of weight and drag from tailplanes, elevators and their necessary long fuselage; and the improved view for the pilots of single-engine aircraft. There were also other aerodynamic benefits.

The forward wing was used for longitudinal control and could be combined with Miles' retractable auxiliary aerofoil high-lift flap-cum-elevator, a feature which helped the exceptionally large range of CofG movement. This not only provided a big range of lift coefficient for the front wing but also allowed the pilot to alter the available wing area with no variation in lift coefficient – in this way the wing area could be varied at will to correspond with the optimum value for any given load condition. It also provided a means of varying the area of elevator available for longitudinal control, which could be altered at will to correspond with any given flight speed – the arrangement was made up of elevators inboard and flaps outboard, both mounted as trailing-edge flaps. The rear wing carried the means of lateral control and could also carry, at its tips, fins and rudders for directional control; the CofG always lay between the two wings. On the M.39 the rear wing carried the flaps inboard and ailerons outboard and it had the tip fins and rudders. (Note: the forward wing on a Libellula design was not a canard chosen instead of a tailplane; here both wings acted as lifting surfaces.)

The M.39 had a low forward wing and a high rear wing so that the rear surface was clear of the forward wing's downwash effect and provided ground clearance for the propellers. It was intended that the M.39 should eventually be powered by three Power Jets W.2/500 units giving a speed of 500mph (805km/h) at 36,000ft (10,973m), but in 1942 these were not yet available and so the alternatives were two high-altitude Merlin 60 or Hercules VIII piston engines (the latter never went into production); the Libellula arrangement made substituting jets for pistons a fairly straightforward operation. The bomber's structure would be all-metal and the three crew were housed in a pressurised cockpit with a bomb bay placed amidships. A tricycle undercarriage was used and two 20mm cannon were mounted in the forward wing roots.

On 16 September 1943 MAP agreed to award a development contract which included the purchase of the M.39B with allotted serial SR392. An order for a full-scale M.39 prototype, RR910, was placed in November but this was never built. Miles continued to test the M.39B and, armed with the additional flight data that this provided, George Miles resubmitted the project in January 1944 with an improved performance, but again to no avail. The M.39C drawn in October 1943 was a version to be powered by two Merlin 68 engines.

Miles M.39 (7.42)	
Span	forward wing 37ft 6in (11.43m), rear wing 55ft 9in (16.99m)
Length	35ft 10in (10.92m)
Wing Area	forward wing 139sq.ft (12.91sq.m), rear 417sq.ft (38.74sq.m)
All-Up-Weight	26,750lb (12,134kg)
Powerplant	2 × Merlin 61
Max Speed/Height	'cruise' 360mph (579km/h)
Armament	6,000lb (2,722kg) bombs, 2 × 20mm cannon

BELOW The Miles M.39B with its original U0244 number. *Peter Amos*

ABOVE The M.39B seen on a test flight after the allocation of military serial SR392.

BELOW The M.39B in its final form wearing number U4. This view is thought to have been taken on 1 June 1946 during a Garden Party held at Woodley. *Peter Amos*

BELOW The Miles M.39 bomber. This particular drawing is not dated but shows the aircraft with three fins and two rudders. It also has a tricycle undercarriage with twin main wheels. *Peter Amos*

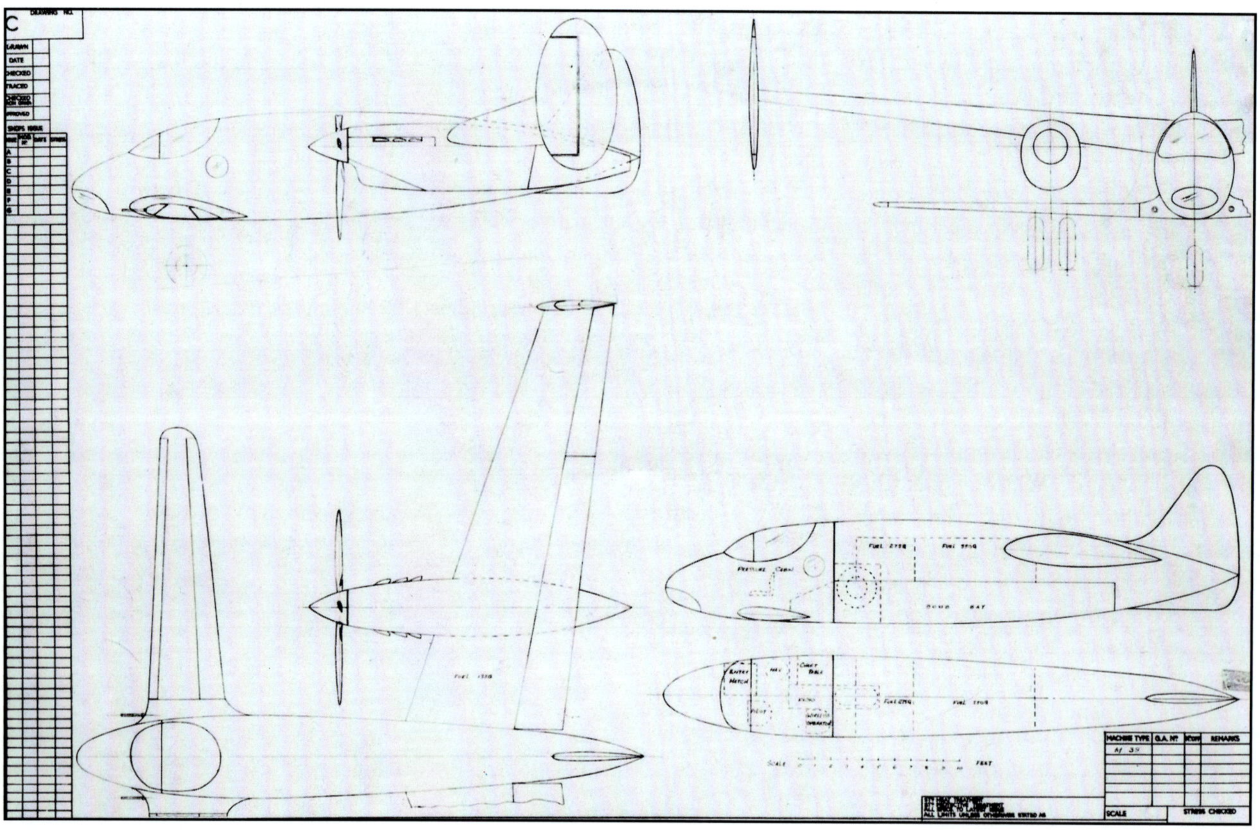

ABOVE Manufacturer's model of the M.39 high-speed bomber project. *Peter Amos*

BELOW The Miles M.39C (8.10.43). *Peter Amos*

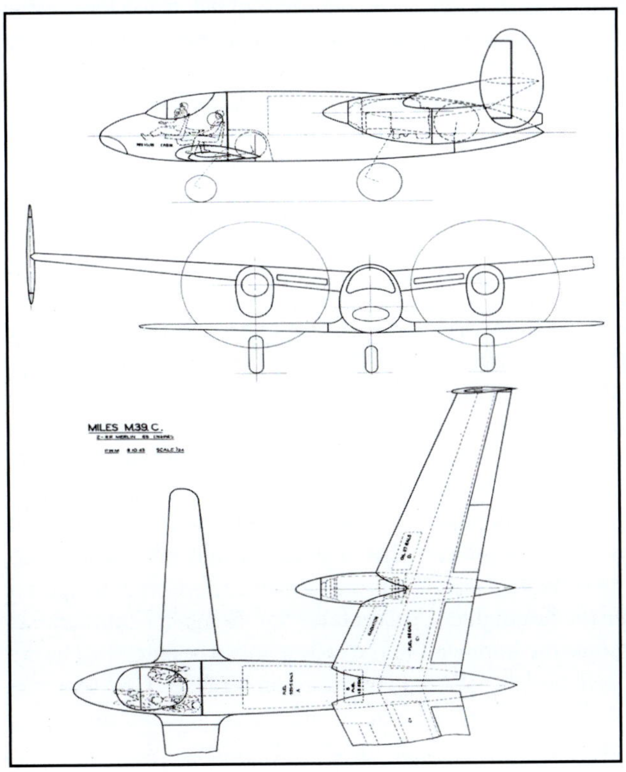

BELOW It was intended that the M.39 should in due course be powered by three Power Jets W.2/500 units.

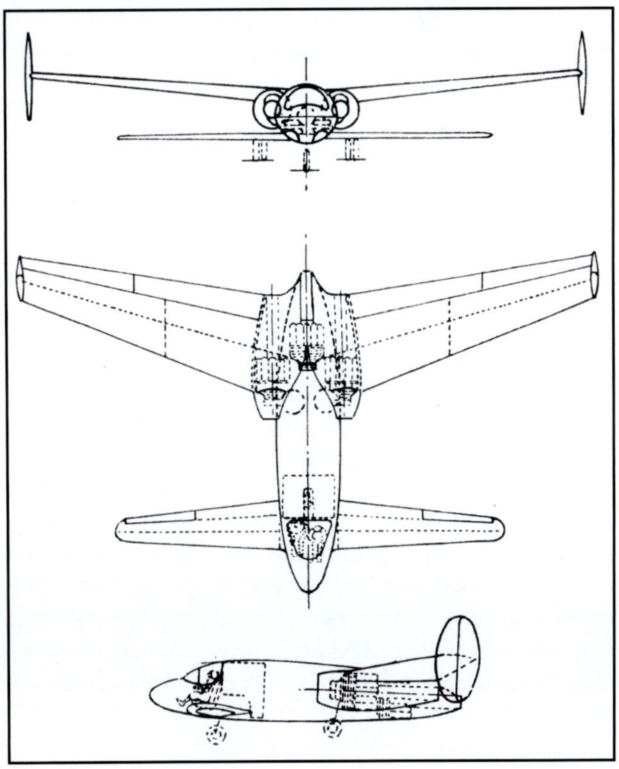

Part Two: Other Programmes

Specification B.9/38 Armstrong Whitworth Albemarle

In early 1938 the Air Ministry was expressing anxiety that, should war break out, the supply of light alloys for aircraft manufacture could be affected. In fact the supply position was considered to be so uncertain that the Air Ministry wanted an aircraft built of alternative materials just in case there was a breakdown in the production of heavy bombers. Thus it turned to Armstrong Whitworth, Bristol and de Havilland to provide designs for a composite aircraft type which would not use any materials that were already being employed for aircraft construction – in other words their aeroplanes would be built mainly from wood and steel tubes which would not encroach on the available light alloy capacity. As a consequence the majority of the fabrication could also be done in the woodworking industry while the metal portions were confined almost entirely to steel tube factories. Specification B.9/38 was prepared to cover the type and designs were forthcoming from AWA and Bristol, both of which were chosen for manufacture.

Armstrong Whitworth AW.41

Between the two World Wars AWA had had limited experience of designing and constructing in wood, most of its work had been in steel, but the 'ban' on the use of normal aircraft materials meant AWA used both alternatives in its design. This twin-engine study was submitted in February 1938 and could carry a normal bomb load of 1,500lb (680kg) over a range of 1,500 miles (2,414km), which could be increased to 3,500lb (1,588kg) over 2,000 miles (3,219km) in the overload condition. Despite AWA being instructed not to use any experimental techniques, the AW.41 did feature a tricycle undercarriage, an item which had been much used in America and offered possibilities that impressed AWA's chief designer John Lloyd. The aircraft was designed on the divided component principle where parts could be sub-contracted to firms and labour with little or no experience in aircraft work. Initially it included Rolls-Royce Merlin engines but, because the Air Ministry intended it to be a 'wartime' aircraft, it had to have a 'shadow' engine and the chosen alternative was the Bristol Hercules X. An AW.41 Mock-Up Conference was held on 22 June.

Bristol 155

Few details survive for Bristol's proposals but there were two versions of the design. The first had a conventional tail-down undercarriage, two Hercules engines, a span of 80ft (24.38m) and was expected to reach a top speed of 302mph (486km/h); the second featured a tricycle undercarriage, it had a span of 70ft (21.34m) and with the same powerplant offered a maximum 319mph (513km/h). The normal bomb load would be 1,000lb (454kg) carried over 1,500 miles (2,414km) but these figures could be increased to 4,000lb (1,814kg) and 2,000 miles (3,218km). A Mock-Up Conference to assess the project was held at Bristol on 15 June 1938.

After the respective Mock-Up Conferences, B.9/38 was replaced by two new documents, B.17/38 and B.18/38, which covered the individual Bristol and AWA designs respectively. Both called for a minimum 250mph (402km/h) at 5,000ft (1,524m) at maximum economic cruising power and a maximum bomb load of 4,000lb (1,814kg). However, Bristol was busy with the Blenheim and Beaufort bombers and in late 1938 made a start on what was to become the Beaufighter, so work on its 155 composite bomber was discontinued. This move left AWA alone to work on its AW.41 which was a home-grown design and not, as so many published sources have stated, the Bristol 155 transferred to the company for completion.

However, by June 1938 changes in policy had revealed that the projected bomber fell short of the Air Staff's ideal for a machine of this type and it was therefore decided to proceed with the design on the lines of an aircraft primarily equipped for reconnaissance but with provision for bombing. This change meant that extra navigation equipment was needed together with more fuel to extend the range to 4,000 miles (6,437km). Hercules engines were selected as the power units and, after the necessary changes to the design had been made, a final Mock-Up Conference was held in September. Two defensive turrets were specified, one behind the wing spar to cover an attack from above and the second a retractable turret at the bottom of the rear fuselage to cover the downward field of fire. Instructions to Proceed with 200 aircraft, straight off the drawing board, were given on 15 October, well ahead of the type's first flight. It was emphasised, however, that the scheme was first and foremost an insurance and it was always realised that this form of construction would result in a 'second-best aircraft.' In fact the original intention had just been to fit engines to the first few airframes for trials and to keep the rest in storage without engines, for use only if the necessity arose.

The new aircraft was named Albemarle and the prototype, P1360, made its maiden flight on 20 March 1940. However, it was found to require a very long take-off run and the span was subsequently increased, from the ninth production aircraft onwards, from 67ft (20.42m) to 77ft (23.47m). The new wing was first flown on the first production machine but there were other delays in getting the Albemarle into service and it was soon apparent that the type would not show much advantage over current types to make it acceptable for Bomber Command; it was clearly going to be outclassed by the new Stirling and Halifax (Chapter Four) and eventually all plans to use it as a bomber were dropped.

ABOVE The second Armstrong Whitworth Albemarle prototype P1361 photographed at Brockworth in April 1941. *Phil Butler*

To establish the price that had been paid for its 'special form of construction', A&AEE's report on the Albemarle, completed in August 1941, compared the type to a Vickers Wellington Mk.III, an aeroplane with a similar bomb load and engines. The Wellington's tare weight (that is, no equipment fitted) was 20,600lb (9,344kg) while the Albemarle's minimum was 24,000lb (10,886kg), which was considered to be the cause of many of the aircraft's indifferent characteristics. The Wellington also exhibited a superior performance – 270mph (434km/h) at 14,300ft (4,359m) rather than the Albemarle's 264mph (425km/h) at 14,000ft (4,267m) – and had the ability to carry 4,300lb (1,950kg) of bombs, as against 3,850lb (1,746kg), over 1,500 miles (2,414km).

Nevertheless, in spite of these deficiencies, it was considered that the Albemarle offered a satisfactory performance and was capable of being used as a general reconnaissance aircraft. Eventually 602 were delivered, mostly to the RAF to serve as transports and glider tugs but others were despatched to the Soviet Union where they achieved some popularity as freighters; an attempt to convert the Albemarle into a torpedo bomber was a failure. In a review written on 17 April 1943 Lloyd declared that he had never shown very much interest in this composite design and it was clear that, had it not been for the Air Ministry's demand for a machine that could be built without impinging on the usual resources of the aircraft industry, AWA would never have considered building such a peculiar and experimental aeroplane. He added that 'the whole idea was for an aircraft that could be built by the tinker, tailor and candlestick maker outside the industry.'

AWA AW.41 Albemarle (flown)	
Span	77ft 0in (23.47m)
Length	59ft 11in (18.26m)
Wing Area	803.5sq.ft (74.65sq.m)
All-Up-Weight	36,500lb (16,556kg)
Powerplant	2 × 1,590hp (1,186kW) Hercules XI
Max Speed/Height	264mph (425km/h) at 14,000ft (4,267m)
Armament	4,500lb (2,041kg) bombs, 4 × 0.303in (7.7mm) machine guns

BELOW AND OVERLEAF These views of Armstrong Whitworth Albemarle V1599 were taken on 28 April 1944 when the aircraft was serving as a prototype for the ST.Mk.I 'Special Transport' variant.

Specification B.7/40 and Bristol Buckingham

In May 1940 Specification B.7/40 was issued for a medium bomber with defensive armament which was intended to replace the Bristol Blenheim. It called for a maximum speed of at least 300mph (483km/h) at 5,000ft (1,524m), a normal load of 1,000lb (454kg) of bombs and a centre turret with at least two 0.5in (13.7mm) calibre machine guns. The following projects were produced after the Issue to Tender was made on 10 July to Armstrong Whitworth, Hawker and Westland, but only AWA actually tendered and its design did not attract the Air Staff. A project produced by Fairey in mid-1940 with twin Merlins may also have been prepared to B.7/40. The requirement was not proceeded with.

BELOW Armstrong Whitworth B.7/40 (11.9.40). *Ray Williams*

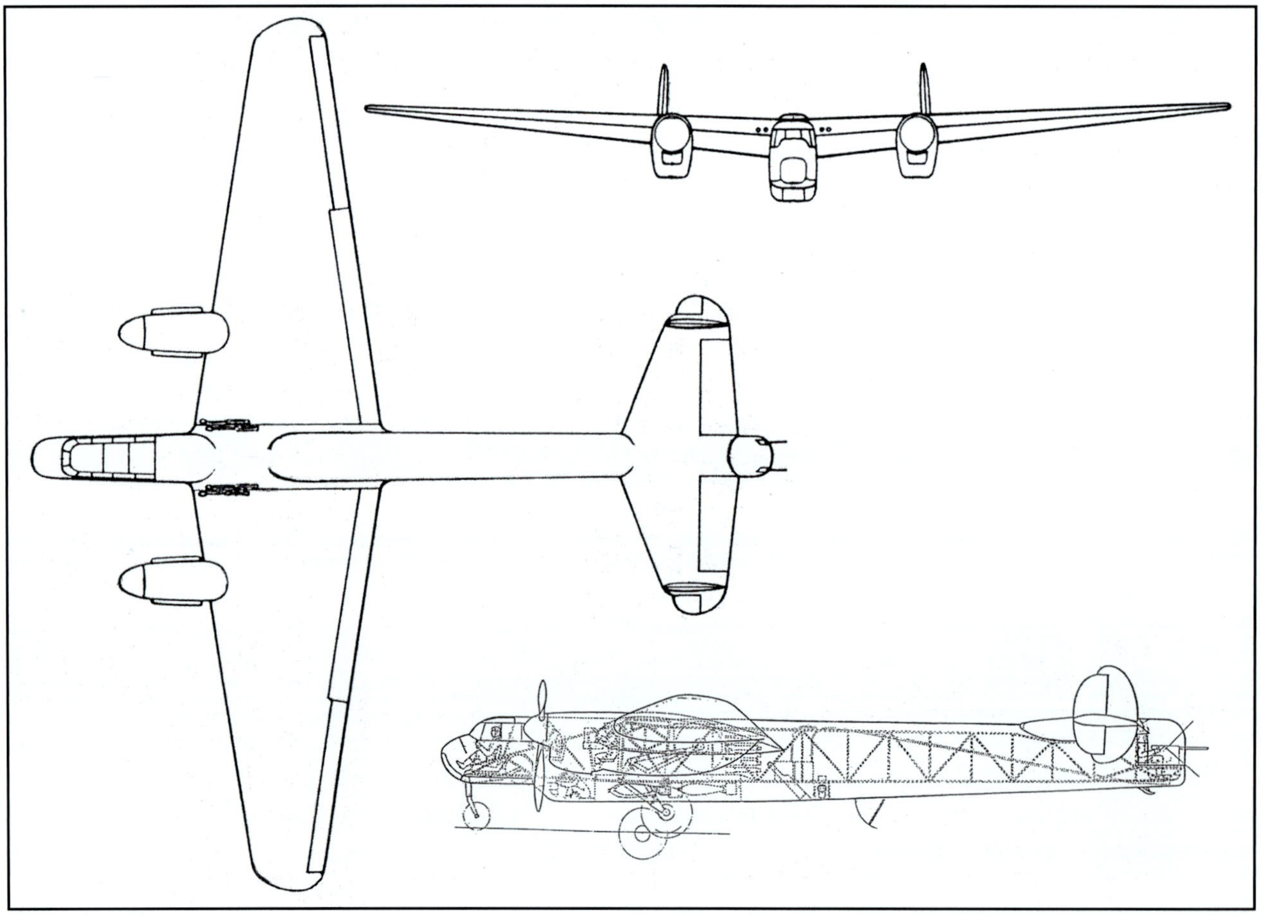

Armstrong Whitworth B.7/40

AWA found that it could not meet all of the requirements together without reaching an estimated weight of 26,000lb (11,793kg), which was thought to be excessive to carry such a small bomb load. However the design team's compromise still weighed 24,000lb (10,886kg) and used two Merlins and a mix of steel tube and wood construction similar to the Albemarle. The required 1,000lb (454kg) of bombs was housed in a fuselage bomb bay placed level with the wing roots but another 1,000lb could be loaded externally under the wings. For defensive purposes there were four 0.303in (7.7mm) machine guns in the upper wing roots and a twin 0.5in (13.7mm) tail turret; four crew were carried.

AWA B.7/40 (9.40)	
Span	72ft 0in (21.95m)
Length	61ft 3in (18.67m)
Wing Area	?
All-Up-Weight	24,154lb (10,956kg)
Powerplant	2 × Merlin
Max Speed/Height	300mph (483km/h)
Armament	2,000lb (907kg) bombs, 4 × 0.303in (7.7mm) plus 2 × 0.5in (12.7mm) machine guns

Hawker P.1001

This was a design based on the Henley close-support bomber.

Westland B.7/40

A Delanne type powered by a single Bristol Centaurus which was described by the company as a light bomber. The bombs were carried internally and there were four crew. A rear defensive turret housed four machine guns and, unusually, the sketch suggests that two more were housed in the leading edge of each rear wing.

Westland B.7/40 (8.40)	
Span	52ft 0in (15.85m)
Length	?
Wing Area	360sq.ft (33.45sq.m)
All-Up-Weight	16,200lb (7,348kg)
Powerplant	1 × 2,150hp (1,603kW) Centaurus
Max Speed/Height	290mph (467km/h) at 5,000ft (1,524m)
Armament	1,000lb (454kg) bombs, 8 x machine guns

Bristol 161 and Bristol 162

In January 1939 Bristol proposed a Beaufighter bomber with Hercules engines. In general, Air Staff policy had been to concentrate British production on heavy bombers because American close-support medium bombers were expected to be available in large numbers. Nevertheless a twin-engine machine was requested with development of an existing type the favoured option. The Blenheim had reached its developmental limit so Bristol was left with only the Beaufort torpedo bomber (Chapter Seven) and Beaufighter as suitable starting points; the latter being the clear favourite through its performance and versatility. However, the Beaubomber was not well received by the Air Staff and was turned down because it would involve a complete redesign of the internal layout and would also give no advance in comparison with contemporary bombers.

Bristol gradually developed its 1939 ideas through the Type 161 of mid-1940 into the Type 162. The 161 was proposed in two versions, a high-altitude medium bomber with a dorsal turret and four 0.303in (7.7mm) plus two more rearward-facing machine guns beneath the forward fuselage, and an army support aircraft in which the bomb load and the lower guns were replaced by two 20mm cannon. However, constant changes of requirements led to the design maturing into the 162 which was tentatively named Beaumont. By autumn 1940 B.7/40 had failed to bring forward any design that was considered suitable for construction and so when Bristol sent in its new proposals for the Type 162 Beaumont on 2 October, which fitted B.7/40's requirements closely, the Air Staff was ready to discuss them. The 162 had the rear fuselage, tailplane, fin and rudder of the Beaufighter Mk.III, but an entirely new front and centre fuselage for which a mock-up was built (the prototype Type 158 slim-fuselage Beaufighter Mk.III was never completed). An alternative drawing showed a straightforward way of making use of the majority of the existing tooling from the Beaufort and Beaufighter on a design that was identical to the Beaufighter Mk.III and IV.

Capt Liptrot's assessment, completed on 17 October 1940, noted that operationally the 162 was by far the better layout since the crew was grouped compactly, but it had the disadvantage that the wings would not remain standard and a new undercarriage was required. Liptrot concluded that the proposal could result in a very useful bomber but he did feel that its landing distance was too long for a type which would have to operate in support of the Army from poor quality advanced aerodromes.

BELOW Sketch of Westland's B.7/40 project (8.40). *Westland Archive*

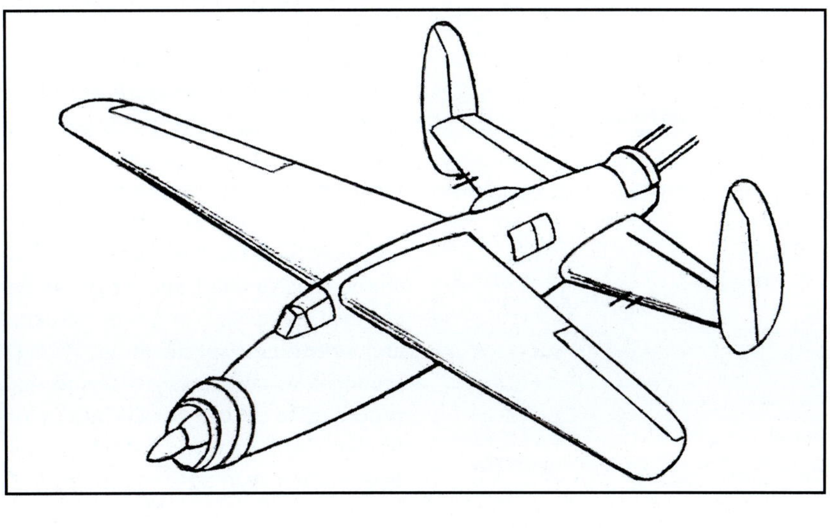

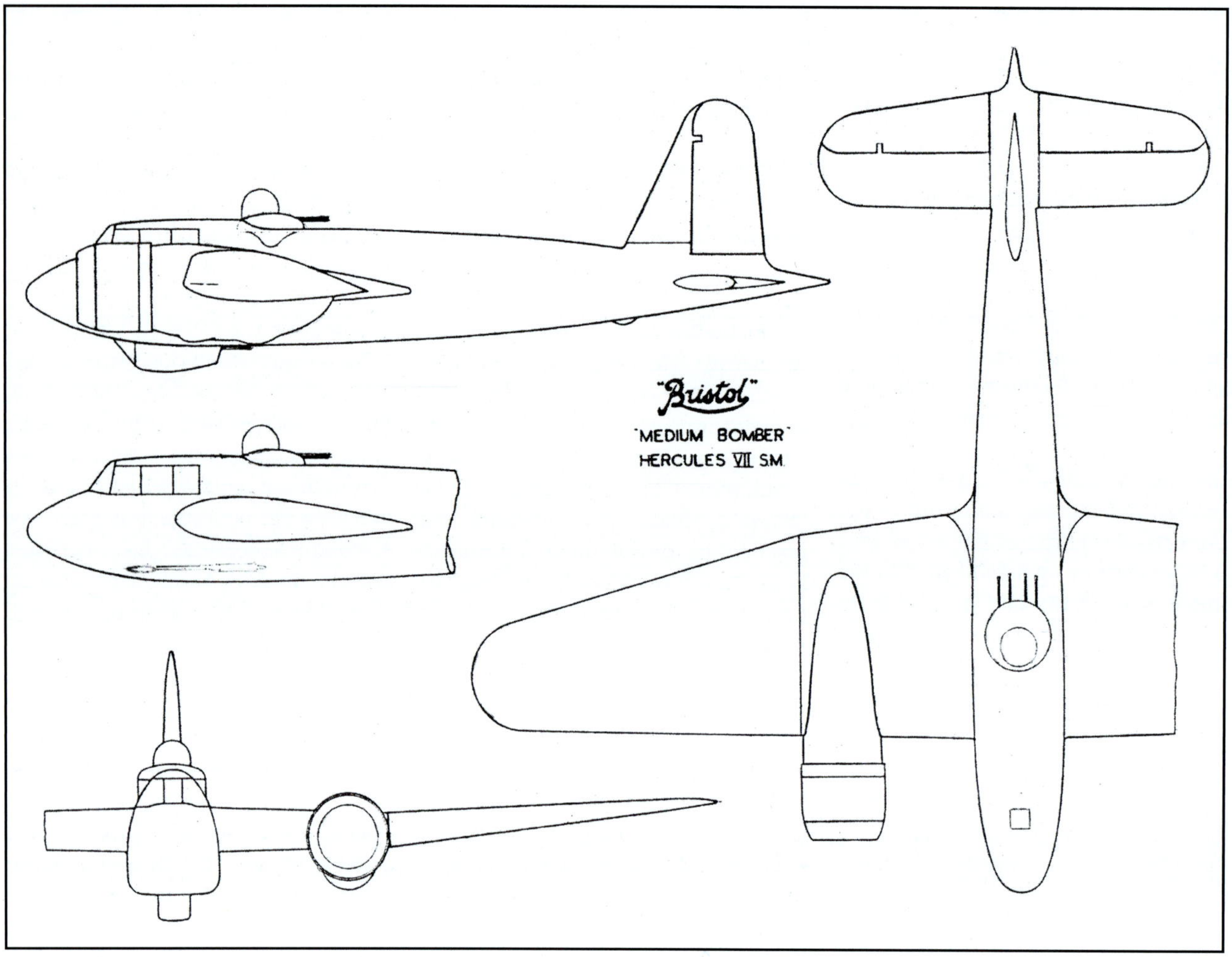

ABOVE Bristol Type 161 (mid-1940). The main view shows the high-altitude version, the additional nose view details the army support version. *Duncan Greenman Bristol AiRchive*

The Beaumont had four 0.303in (7.7mm) machine guns in a mid-upper turret, two more facing rearwards under the fuselage and four more in a fixed forward turret. A crew of three was specified and Merlin 5.SMs were an alternative engine which Liptrot calculated would give a maximum 305mph (491km/h) at 15,000ft (4,572m). Following a meeting between the Air Staff, MAP and Bristol in November, this development of the Beaufighter into a medium and direct support bomber received a go ahead together with a request to complete the mock-up. Another Air Ministry meeting, held on 3 January 1941, decided that twin rudders would be satisfactory while on 2 February Sir Henry Tizard gave authority for a formal contract for three prototypes.

Bristol 162 Beaumont (2.10.40)	
Span	?
Length	?
Wing Area	503sq.ft (46.73sq.m)
All-Up-Weight	21,800lb (9,888kg)
Powerplant	2 × Hercules VII
Max Speed/Height	315mph (507km/h) at 15,000ft (4,572m)
Armament	1,000lb (454kg) bombs, 10 × 0.303in (7.7mm) machine guns; for close support 2 × 20mm cannon plus 6 × 0.303in (7.7mm) machine guns

The decision to ask Bristol to complete the Beaumont mock-up after which the Air Staff and MAP would confirm the design as a requirement, and write a new specification (B.2/41) around it, was the reverse of the normal procedure to circulate specifications for tender. Construction of the Hercules Beaumont began in November 1940 with the first flight expected in summer or autumn 1941 but many requirement and design changes interfered with the aircraft's progress. The initial demands had covered bombing, dive bombing and direct army support but the last pair were cancelled in March 1941 since the Air Staff felt the American Brewster Bermuda and Vultee Vengeance would fill these roles. At the same time there was anxiety to improve the performance because full production was two years away and current estimates would then have been bettered by new American products. Increases in speed (to 360mph [579km/h]), bomb load (4,000lb [1,814kg]) and range (1,600 miles [2,574km]) needed more power than the Hercules could provide and Bristol was asked to redesign the project with the Centaurus.

Bristol 163 Buckingham

A new layout with a larger wing called the Type 163 Buckingham was accepted in March 1941 with a planned first flight in May or June 1942; all trace of the aircraft's Beaufighter origins were gone and Bristol was thinking of an aircraft weighing 29,000lb (13,154kg). The capability to carry a torpedo was introduced as a secondary requirement but in January 1942 this aroused much controversy at Cabinet level. The idea was raised that the near obsolescent Beaufort could be replaced by the Buckingham, but this was strongly opposed by the Admiralty who felt adapting a bomber for this task was always considered second best while the machine's comparative high speed made it unsuitable for such an adaptation. This plan was dropped six months later. B.2/41 was approved in August 1941 but more design and requirement changes led to its abandonment in spring 1942 to be replaced by B.P/41 (later I/P1) which covered both prototype and production machines. On 25 November 1941 Bristol began building the Buckingham prototype and the first flight date was set at November 1942, which displeased N. E. Rowe who wanted it in the air two months earlier.

A fourth prototype was confirmed on 12 May 1941 but no decision was taken on production. Discussions at the highest level dragged on through 1941 and 1942 as to whether a medium bomber was still required operationally and to how its production would fit into existing programmes; any loss in production of heavy bombers for example was considered unacceptable. At one stage this indecision forced Bristol to complain that it was losing interest in the project and to request more 'practical' interest from MAP. On 18 September 1941 VCAS told CAS that he 'should like to place an order for 400 Buckinghams now. Unless we introduce a new type of medium bomber into the production system without delay the lack of such an aircraft will be a serious gap in our forces in 1943/44. MAP will, of course, attempt to choke us off by depressing estimates of the effect on present production. Every time this problem has been put to them in the past they have done the same thing and it is about time they faced up to the vital necessity for planning new, as well as continuing existing, production. If they do not, there is a great danger that in the future we shall have quantity without quality.'

In November an order was placed for 400 Buckinghams with the first delivery due in March 1943 (this target was missed by nearly a year) but the initial planned production rate of 50 or 60 a month was then lowered to 25, a step that caused Bristol to express further discontent. The company felt that if the Buckingham was a worthwhile aircraft, this was insufficient to maintain a reasonable scale of operations; on the other hand, if the aeroplane was just an interesting development, this was far too expensive. Bristol complained of 'half-hearted planning, the inadequacy of which is realised too late.' However, delays to the prototype's completion were also partly due to the manufacturers and to technical problems.

The first Buckingham prototype, DX249, became airborne on 4 February 1943. One task earmarked for the type, in company with the Mosquito, was to press home daylight attacks on the enemy's heavy industry. However, the night bombing offensive against Germany was made effective by the use of radar navigational aids and with the US VIII Bomber Command (later Eighth Army Air Force) taking on the daytime work, the need for an additional day bomber fell away. It was felt that the Buckingham's armament and speed did not qualify it for use on unescorted day operations in North West Europe and at the beginning of 1944 it was decided that all Service aircraft would go overseas to replace Vickers Wellingtons; none was to equip home based squadrons except for a proposed operational trials unit to get the bugs out of the system.

When a report was submitted that detailed some severe problems uncovered during flight testing at A&AEE, with criticism extending to nearly every feature of the bomber's layout from an operational point of view, the programme was seriously reconsidered. The potential value of the aircraft and the need for its production was questioned and in August 1944 it was decided that there was no operational use for the type in the RAF in either bomber or PR versions; DCAS, N. H. Bottomley, recommended that production should be stopped at the earliest practicable stage. As a tactical bomber the Buckingham was unusable and pressure was to be directed at obtaining alternative American types to meet No2 Group's requirements.

Following the cancellation an assessment of the repercussions to the overall production programme found that a minimum of 119 Buckingham bombers would still have to be manufactured to keep the labour force together to produce, later, both the Brigand torpedo bomber (Chapter Seven) and Hawker Tempest fighter. It was realised that these Buckinghams would be virtually useless aircraft and, as soon as they were released by CRD, every effort was to be made to find them employment in miscellaneous units. Fitting equipment, and even engines, was seen as wasteful and it was decreed that the aircraft were to be stored until employed or authorisation was given to reduce them to produce.

Consequently much thought went into making something from what was now a worthless programme and the result was a high-speed transport or 'courier aircraft' conversion. Rowe told Bristol that the Air Ministry wanted bombers turned out as communications aircraft with space for four passengers behind a crew of three. Combat equipment, armour and turrets were stripped out with the seating fitted by hand, the fuel load was increased to 1,500gal (6,819lit) by putting long-range tanks in the bomb bay and the prototype conversion, KV338, first flew on 21 October 1944. Only 54 Buckinghams were delivered as B.Mk.I bombers, the remainder appearing as C.Mk.I transports.

ABOVE **View of the second prototype Bristol Buckingham DX255 taken during a flight from Boscombe Down in July 1944. This was the first aircraft to receive full armament and it was scrapped in November of that year.** *Crown Copyright*

BELOW AND BOTTOM OF PAGE 68 **These shots of Buckingham B.Mk.I KV335 were taken on 20 April 1945.**

ABOVE Bristol Buckmaster RP185 pictured in 1949/50.

Most series aircraft were flown direct to store at RAF Maintenance Units where they survived only a few years before being broken up. None saw squadron service and almost all had short flying lives, although a select few did find employment on test duties. One result was the realisation that service pilots would find it quite taxing to convert to the bomber, so a special trainer variant was prepared called the Type 166 Buckmaster. This involved removing the Buckingham's front fuselage and substituting a new one with full dual control and side-by-side seating; the rest of the structure was near identical to the Buckingham. Two prototypes, TJ714 and TJ717, were converted from partially complete Buckinghams, the first flew on 27 October 1944 and 110 were built as trainers for the Brigand.

As a postscript, it is interesting to look at some notes from an interview made on 18 February 1944 with J. E. Serby, CRD. The Buckingham originated when forward thinking was allowed to restart in 1941 (following the 'hold' on new designs introduced by Lord Beaverbrook at MAP during the Battle of Britain) but also when the four-engine bomber, a type considered better operationally, was being introduced. He noted that Air Marshal Sorley felt the day of the medium bomber was over and Serby had only forced the Buckingham forward because no other replacement was in sight for the 1945/46 period; rejecting this aircraft would have been tantamount to a decision to cancel the entire class of medium bomber. Sorley considered the medium class had reached its limit and had no further use, but the general view was that it could still fill some squadrons overseas. For close-support work he now favoured the fighter-bomber. Although Air Marshal Tedder had used medium bombers in big numbers in the Mediterranean theatre, their results when compared to those of fighter-bombers were inferior.

The Buckingham fulfilled expectations as to bomb load and range but it was down on speed when compared with fighter-bombers and could never achieve a high performance (the long gestation period meant that it was rather overtaken by the Mosquito). One Ministry memo described it as something of a hybrid – it was too small to carry either adequate defensive armament for daylight operations or suitable equipment for accurate bombing at night, so it was limited to daylight work in formation under strong fighter cover.

The great advances made in the Second World War to the capability of aircraft and weaponry forced operators to redefine the categories of the aircraft that they used. At the start of the conflict the medium bomber was typified by the Wellington which was capable of medium range but with the capacity to operate elaborate equipment for accurate day and night navigation and target location; by the mid-war years the Wellington was considered to have merged into the 'heavy' bomber category. Types such as the Buckingham were also classed as medium bombers but later on they could be more accurately described as tactical bombers. The Americans built aircraft of this class in large numbers and many examples of the Martin B-26 Marauder and North American B-25 Mitchell were also supplied to the RAF.

Bristol 163 Buckingham B.Mk.I (flown)	
Span	71ft 10in (21.89m)
Length	46ft 10in (14.27m)
Wing Area	708sq.ft (65.76sq.m)
All-Up-Weight	38,920lb (17,654kg)
Powerplant	2 x 2,400hp (1,790kW) Centaurus VII
Max Speed/Height	337mph (542km/h) at 14,400ft (4,389m)
Armament	4,000lb (1,814kg) bombs, 10 × 0.303in (7.7mm) machine guns

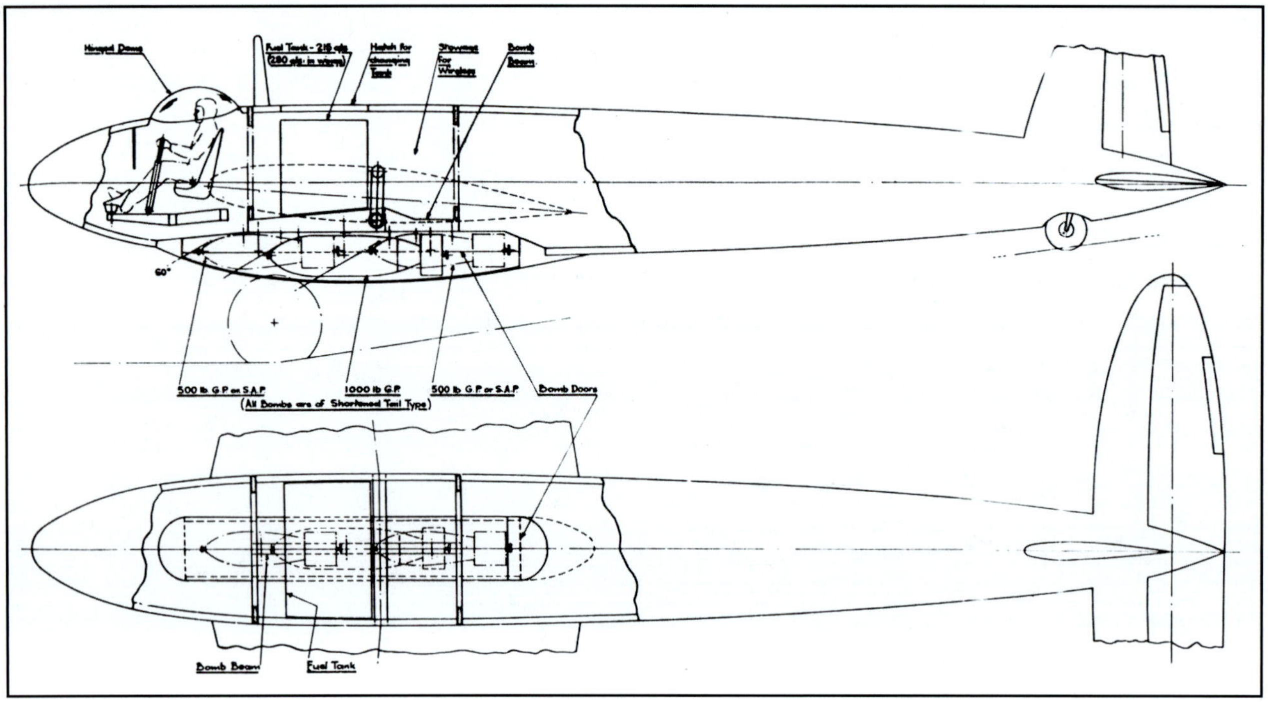

ABOVE Drawing showing the modifications made to the Vickers 432 fighter to turn it into an unarmed bomber.

Vickers Unarmed Day Bomber

Vickers also produced a proposal for an unarmed bomber development of its Type 432 twin-engine fighter which first flew in December 1942. This brochure was dated 6 May 1942 and showed a design that was very similar to the 432 then still under construction and stated that it was 'suitable for diving attack.' However, the fighter's pressure cabin had been replaced by a normal fuselage of the same external shape and size but with provision for bombs and a large fuel tank. The wings, powerplant, undercarriages and tail unit remained the same as the fighter and bombs were carried in a 'longitudinal tunnel' in the bottom of the fuselage structure. Maximum rate of climb at full load was given as 2,725ft/min (831m/min) and then 'over the target' 3,250ft/min (991m/min), both at 13,000ft (3,962m) altitude. Service ceiling was 40,300ft (12,283m) and range 1,250 miles (2,011km).

Vickers Unarmed Day Bomber (6.5.42)	
Span	56ft 10.5in (17.34m)
Length (on ground)	39ft 3in (11.96m)
Wing Area	464sq.ft (43.11sq.m)
All-Up-Weight	18,900lb (8,573kg)
Powerplant	2 × 1,530hp (1,141kW) Merlin 61 with 11ft 6in (3.51m) diameter 4-blade propellers
Max Speed/Height	318mph (512km/h) at sea level, 430mph (692km/h) at 28,000ft (8,534m)
Armament	1 × 1,000lb (454kg) and 2 × 500lb (227kg) bombs

Chapter Four
Heavy Bombers Part I

ABOVE Shorts Stirling Mk.III BK649 pictured during flight testing in the hands of A&AEE Boscombe Down. *Crown Copyright*

During the Second World War the heavy bomber was to become the RAF's main offensive weapon and by the end of the conflict its bomber force was incredibly powerful and capable. As a weapon of war this was of immense strategic value but it had taken years of effort and pain, and casualties, to put together. The first seeds were sown by two specifications laid down in 1936 for medium and heavy bombers, P.13/36 and B.12/36 respectively, at a time when the heavy bomber category was represented by the Handley Page Heyford and Fairey Hendon, the latter just entering service. What constituted a heavy bomber in 1936 was rather smaller than its equivalent in 1945; both the size and destructive power of such beasts was to grow enormously in the intervening and very eventful years. Prior to those two requirements, however, there is an earlier specification to examine briefly, B.1/35.

The World Disarmament Conference, convened by the League of Nations and held at Geneva between 1932 and 1934, failed to achieve disarmament worldwide. However, whilst it was in progress there was considerable uncertainty as to whether restrictions might be applied to offensive bomber types, or indeed whether this class of aircraft might be abolished altogether. With potential limitations on the size and/or number of bombers that it could procure, Britain could not commit to developing any new large bomber types, although design work was still ongoing. Once the Conference was over, however, all restrictions had gone and the Air Ministry began its Expansion Plans immediately, the first of which gained Parliamentary approval in July 1934. When war broke out in 1939 the frontline bombers which Britain had on strength all came from this period – the Battle, Blenheim, Hampden, Wellington and Whitley.

Specification B.1/35 Vickers Warwick

Vickers Wellington and Armstrong Whitworth Whitley

The ancestor of the Warwick was the very successful Wellington, whose story goes back to Specification B.9/32 for which an Issue to Tender was made on 17 September 1932. That programme falls outside the scope of this book, but the requirement was won by the Handley Page HP.52 (later to enter service as the Hampden) and the Vickers 271; the single Type 271 prototype, K4049, flew on 15 June 1936, though the production Type 285 was a much updated machine, making the Wellington emphatically a post-1935 bomber. Then in July 1934, following the lapse during the previous month of the weight limit imposed on heavy bombers by the Geneva Convention, the heavy bomber Specification B.3/34 was issued. This was won by the Armstrong Whitworth AW.38, which first flew on 17 March 1936 and entered service as the Whitley.

Vickers was also asked to tender to B.3/34 but the company felt that there was no point in doing so since, at the time, it was engaged on redesigning the B.9/32 to scale it up to a size which embraced practically all of the requirements of the new document. The first production Wellington was flown in December 1937 and manufacture of this type was maintained throughout the duration of hostilities up to October 1945, by which time 11,461 had been completed. The Wellington proved to be a most adaptable type and was the subject of a stream of evolutionary modifications, but a key feature of its success was its geodetic structure, which was also used on the Warwick and on the Windsor (Chapter Five).

The geodetic method of construction had been developed by Barnes Wallis for the R.100 airship and had also been used on the Vickers Wellesley bomber first flown on 19 June 1935. It comprised a framework of spirally crossing members that formed a latticework structure, the members being in tension or compression, to give a very strong and light airframe which was then fabric covered. The design was based on the principle that two geodetic arcs could be drawn to intersect on a streamlined surface in such a way that the torsional loads on each arc would cancel out that of the other. Wallis was involved with the design of the Wellington, Warwick and Windsor bombers and created the famous 'bouncing bomb' used to break the Ruhr dams in 1943.

In January 1935, on the recommendation of DTD, a new twin-engine heavy bomber specification B.1/35 was drafted. Like many British aircraft designers, DTD had recently visited America and was determined that the latest engineering techniques should be incorporated in new aircraft. In particular he wished to take advantage of new more powerful engines currently under development (such as the Bristol Twin-Aquila or Rolls-Royce Vulture) and these factors combined to make possible an increase in speed from B.3/34's 205mph (330km/h) up to 230mph (370km/h), together with a heavier bomb load – 2,000lb (907kg) normal and 4,000lb (1,814kg) maximum. B.1/35 was formally issued to industry on 29 May 1935 and on 30 July a Tender Design Conference was held to analyse eight projects. Information is not currently available for the Fairey and Gloster proposals.

Armstrong Whitworth AW.39

The Armstrong Whitworth AW.39 was a development of the Whitley with twin Merlins in streamlined nacelles or, alternatively, two of the new Armstrong Siddeley Deerhound power units. Its span was 84ft (25.60m), length 71ft 6in (21.79m), all-up-weight 23,950lb (10,864kg) and top speed 260mph (418km/h).

Boulton Paul P.79

Boulton Paul submitted a version of its P.79, which had originally been offered to B.3/34, and the proposal could have any of three different Bristol powerplants – the Taurus, Pegasus and Hercules. Its fuselage and tail structure was stressed skin entirely, whilst the wings had an all-metal box spar with the leading edge also all-metal but with the trailing section fabric covered. There were four defensive gun positions, three in power-operated turrets with the mid-upper made retractable to lie flush with the fuselage contours.

A remarkably advanced feature of this design was the six rotating weapon dispensers inside an internal bomb bay, the front four to carry four 250lb (113kg) or 500lb (227kg) bombs each as the main load, with the smaller aft pair used for light bombs or flares only. A mock-up of this bomb bay was built and each main dispenser could also carry, in a fixed position, a 'B' type bomb, at the time a still 'Secret' and quite bulky anti-battleship weapon; six more 'B' bombs could go under the wings in faired racks, three per side outboard of the engines. However, the rotating dispensers dropped their bombs through relatively small

Boulton Paul P.79 (6.35)	
Span	87ft 0in (26.52m)
Length	61ft 3in (18.67m)
Wing Area	954sq.ft (88.63sq.m)
All-Up-Weight	Taurus 23,500lb (10,659kg), Pegasus 24,250lb (11,000kg), Hercules 25,500lb (11,567kg)
Powerplant	2 × 1,050hp (783kW) Taurus TE.1.S, 900hp (671kW) Pegasus 5.SM or 1,300hp (969kW) Hercules 1.S
Max Speed/Height	Taurus 247mph (398km/h), Pegasus 234mph (377km/h), Hercules 261mph (420km/h) all at 15,000ft (4,572m)
Armament	16 × 500lb (227kg) or 250lb (113kg) bombs or 4 × 'B' bombs internally, 6 × 'B' bombs under wings, 4 defensive gun positions

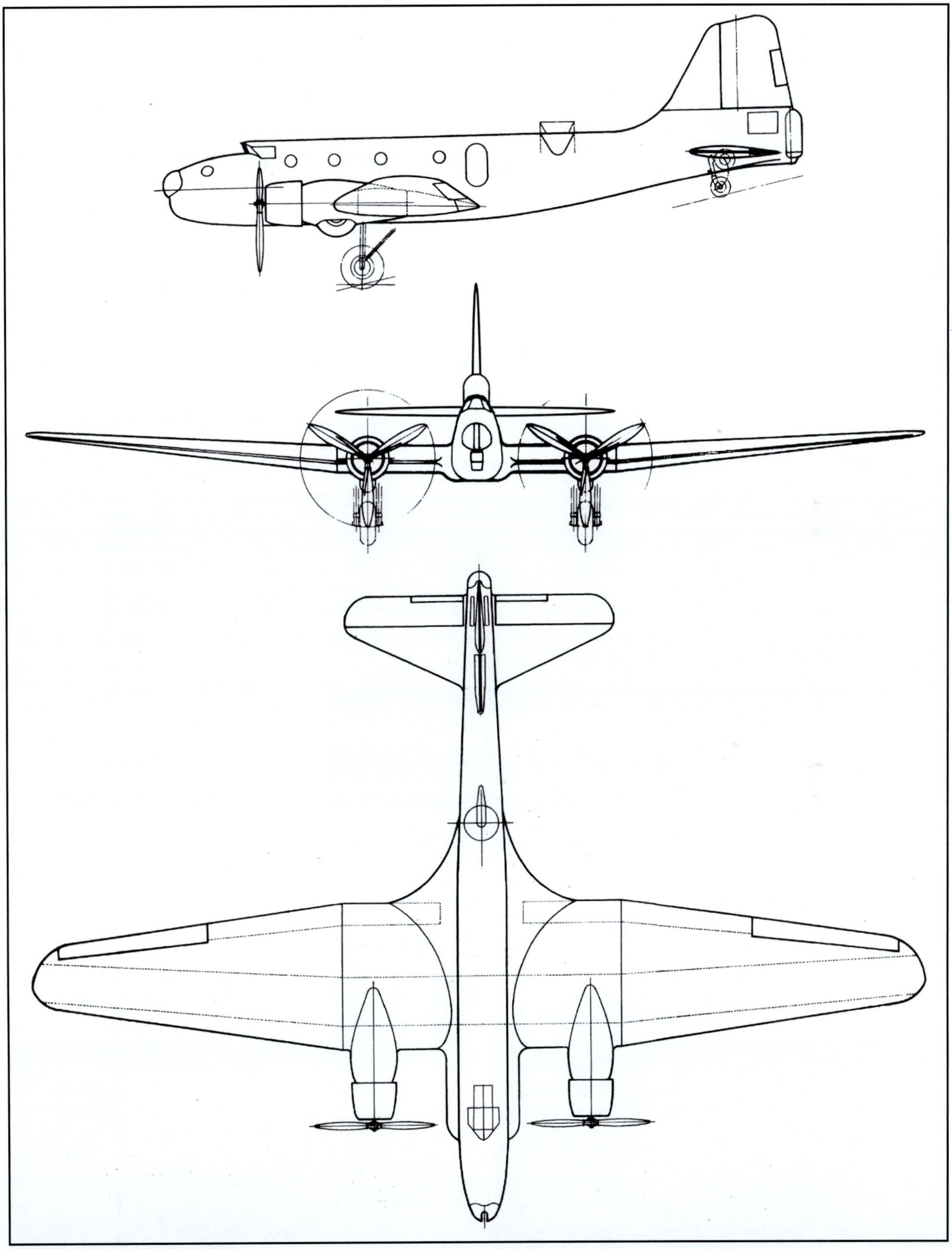

ABOVE Boulton Paul P.79 (6.35). The front-on view has the upper turret retracted. *Les Whitehouse, Boulton Paul Archive*

apertures, which meant that the P.79 would be incapable of delivering larger stores should they be developed – one reason why the design was rejected by the Air Ministry. A dual-control trainer version of the P.79 was also proposed.

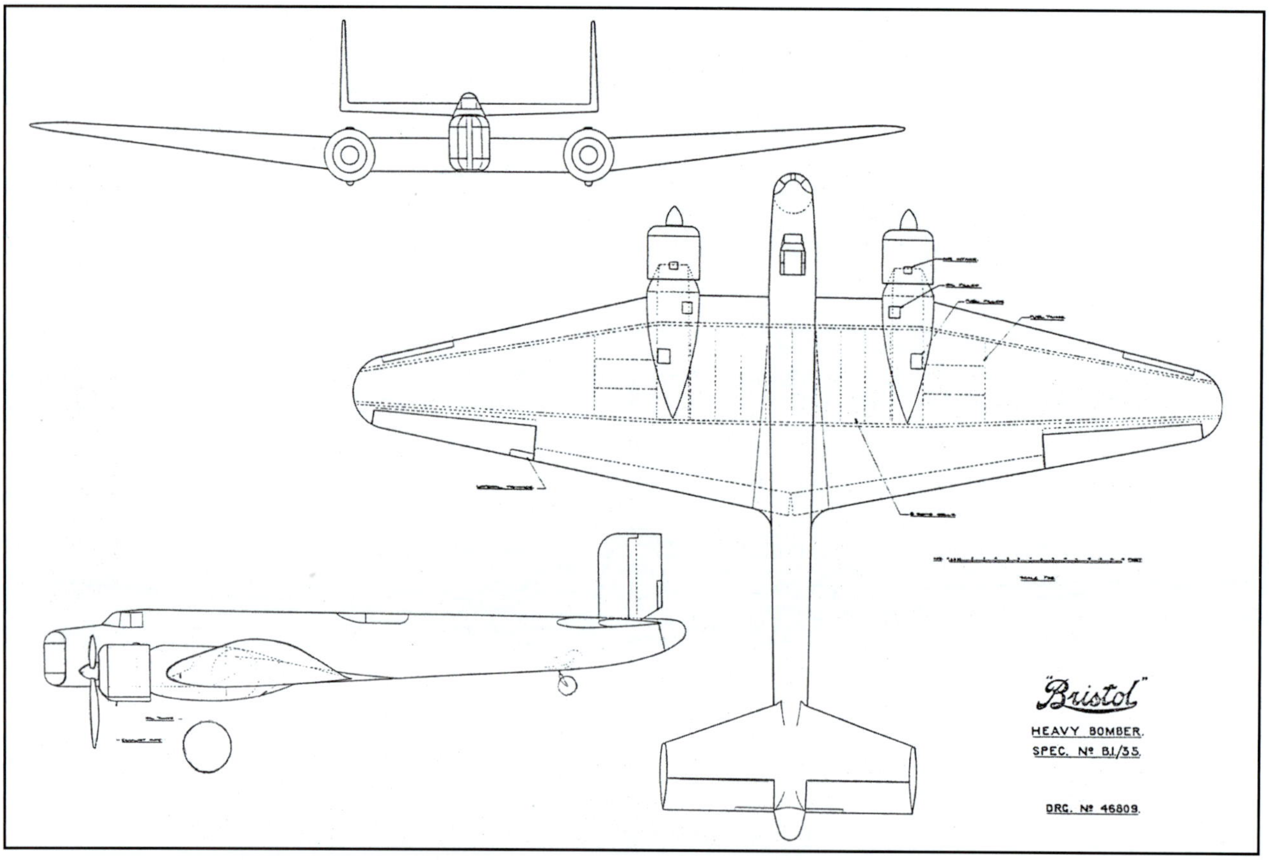

ABOVE Bristol B.1/35 (3.7.35). *Rolls-Royce Heritage Filton*

Bristol B.1/35 (3.7.35)	
Wing Area	910sq.ft (84.54sq.m)
All-Up-Weight	(734gal/3,337lit fuel) 22,850lb (10,365kg)
Powerplant	2 × Bristol Hercules SM engines
Max Speed/Height	?
Armament	8 × 500lb (227kg) or 16 × 250lb (113kg) bombs

LEFT AND BELOW A 1/32nd manufacturer's scale model of the Bristol B.1/35.

Bristol B.1/35

This design was in every way considered to be a development of Bristol practice. For example the wing used the firm's standard two-spar, steel flange, Alclad web-type structure, the covering and all of the ribs in Alclad also. The disposition of the crew and the arrangement of the equipment within the body was based on Bristol's recent transport bomber layout, the whole body having been reduced in size as much as was practical. The centre section of the wing between the engine nacelles was fitted with eight bomb cells which could carry the whole of any of the alternative bomb loads. Each cell could take one 'B' bomb or one 500lb (227kg) bomb completely internally, or alternatively two 250lb (113kg) bombs. All bombs were carried in a single layer, not in tiers, salvoes could be released in any required number, and the nose turret was used as the bomb aiming position. The section just outside each engine nacelle and between the spars was made into a fuel tank and sufficient fuel (948gal/4,310lit) was available to meet the 2,000 mile (3,219km) range requirement.

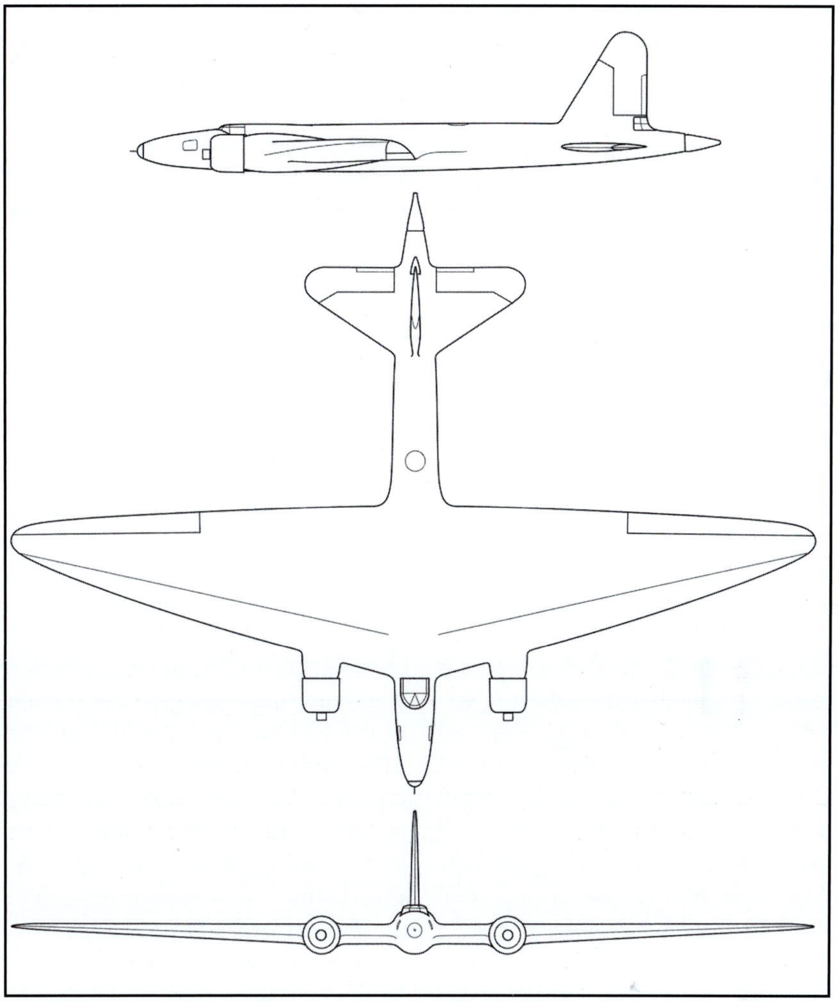

ABOVE Supermarine Scheme '4' to B.1/35 (1935). *Ralph Pegram*

Handley Page HP.55

The four-crew HP.55 was to have either two 1,000hp (746kW) Hercules or 1,200hp (895kW) Merlin XXs, a span of 95ft (28.96m), length 65ft 3in (19.89m) and estimated top speed 251mph (404km/h). The estimated range was 2,000 miles (3,219km).

Supermarine B.1/35

Reginald Mitchell's team at Supermarine prepared several conceptual designs to B.1/35, but none of them received a Type project number because they never became full status projects for submission to the design competition. However, the one drawing that survives, known as Scheme 4, did show elements in its design which later found their way into the Type 316 (page 79). Scheme 4 had a considerable degree of sweep on its wing and horizontal tail leading edges, with the trailing edges remaining essentially straight, and it was to have been powered by two Bristol Twin-Aquila units (an engine which in fact never left the drawing board). Defensive guns were mounted in a streamlined nose and remote-controlled tail turret. Scheme 4 was designed by Roger Dickson, who later in 1935 left Supermarine to join Saunders-Roe.

Vickers 284

The Vickers 284 was derived from the B.9/32 Wellington on a slightly larger scale and fitted with two Bristol Hercules HE.1.SM engines. It used Wallis's geodetic lattice light alloy structure with fabric covering.

Airspeed AS.29

In February 1936 Airspeed submitted a four-engine bomber called the AS.29 which had been prepared to B.1/35 but was too late to be part of the official competition. It was to be powered by four Bristol Aquila or Rolls-Royce (RR) Goshawk engines.

The Tender Design Conference gave first place to the Vickers 284 whose construction was simplified through its close similarity to the Wellington. DTD also recommended ordering one prototype each from Handley Page and Boulton Paul, whose designs had reached a high standard. CAS, however, was particularly anxious that AWA's project should be given a chance and the final choice, of which single prototypes of each were ordered on 7 October 1935, was Vickers (serial K8178), AWA (K8179) and Handley Page (K8180). The orders for the last pair were, however, cancelled on 4 March 1937 before the prototypes were complete.

The reason for their cancellation was essentially the appearance of specifications B.12/36 (heavy) and P.13/36 (medium bomber) in 1936 (both described shortly); AWA tendered the AW.42 to the former and Handley Page the HP.56 to P.13/36. On 31 August 1936 AWA's Mr Spriggs visited Wilfrid Freeman, AMRD, to discuss his company's workload, which included prototypes of the F.9/35 fighter and B.1/35 bomber. The latter's delivery was promised for April 1937, but in fact it was still in the design stage and unlikely to be flying before December 1937. Spriggs added that unless one of these contracts was cancelled, AWA would be unable to undertake the design of the B.12/36. Freeman added that the F.9/35 was unlikely to be flying until June 1938 which meant that it might be out of date before it was delivered. However, he felt disinclined to cancel either of the contracts 'as there is a tendency amongst aircraft manufacturers to take on more work than they can possibly compete with, then to get the order cancelled as soon as it suits them to do so.' He told DCAS that he wished to tell Spriggs that he must deliver these two aeroplanes and strengthen his design staff so that he could make the fullest possible use of John Lloyd's designing capacity.

Soon afterwards, on 22 September, Handley Page wrote to DTD, J. S. Buchanan, to report how investigations had shown 'that an aircraft built to meet P.13/36 as regards overall dimensions and general arrangement would be similar to the B.1/35 type.' Handley Page proposed to redesign the present B.1/35 (the HP.55) to conform to P.13/36 and to stop work on the B.1/35. On 12 October Buchanan wrote 'this is very disconcerting; the B.1/35 was first started nearly two years ago and very little has been done in spite of the promises of the constructors that they could, and would, accelerate the production of experimental aeroplanes.'

Buchanan had spoken to Rex Pierson at Vickers and he wished to continue his B.1/35 bomber. However, at this time the Wellington had still not been tested by A&AEE and should the AWA and Handley Page B.1/35s be dropped, the future of the heavy bomber would depend on the success of the Wellington and Wallis' geodetic construction. In addition, because of the planned tender competitions, AWA and Handley Page were not guaranteed orders for their modified designs. In the end the two B.1/35 projects were dropped, AWA and Handley Page having both concluded that it might be a very good thing to abandon them and proceed with more modern aeroplanes.

The construction of the Vickers 284, afterwards known as the Warwick, was to prove very protracted, partly through Vickers' work on the B.9/32; partly through the engine supply situation; and partly through the official view that this project, as a heavy bomber, tended to be eclipsed by other subsequent designs. During 1936 the fuel and bomb carrying requirements were raised and in January 1937 alternative Rolls-Royce Vulture power units were discussed; later the Napier Sabre was to join the possible engine list. The switch to Vultures in lieu of Hercules was made the following December and K8178 made its first flight on 13 August 1939 with these engines; the second Warwick, L9704, followed on 7 April 1940 with Bristol Centaurus units and, at this time, the decision was also taken to discontinue work on the Sabre mounting since insufficient engines would be available. In March 1939 Vickers had quoted for the Hercules Warwick a maximum speed of 288mph (463km/h), for the Vulture 332mph (534km/h) and for the Sabre 340mph (547km/h), each with an overload weight of 36,000lb (16,329kg).

BELOW **Vickers Warwick B.Mk.I BV214 photographed in May 1942.**

ABOVE LM818 was a Vickers Warwick Mk.V powered by Bristol Centaurus engines.

BELOW In 1944 L9704, originally the second Warwick prototype, was used to test some remotely-sighted twin barbette defensive guns mounted in the rear of the engine nacelles and which were intended for the four-engine Windsor bomber. The tail turret was replaced by the sighting position.

On 16 February 1939 the decision was taken not to take the aircraft beyond the prototype stage, specifically because of the high level of man-hours needed for the Vulture, but the move was reversed in January 1940. A switch was then made to the Centaurus but this too was in short supply. Finally, in July 1941, L9704 made another maiden flight, this time with American Pratt & Whitney Double Wasp units which completed the aircraft's fifth alternative engine installation; however in this form its performance was inferior to the Centaurus. Nevertheless a contract for 250 Double Wasp-powered aircraft was placed in December 1940 and 57 were built as bombers while later examples were equipped for air sea rescue duties. As finally delivered the Warwick was a great disappointment and, as a bomber, A&AEE classed it as a failure. A switch to service as a transport and in the air sea rescue role in part became necessary because of the type's shortcomings as a bomber. Later production Warwicks reverted to the Centaurus.

When K8178 had first flown the aircraft was two years late and, because the later heavy bomber designs had surpassed the Warwick in performance, B.1/35's requirements were by then redundant and obsolescent. The Air Ministry only permitted the type's development to proceed because it wished to have a larger version of the Wellington while considerable production advantages were expected to accrue from the use of common parts (the number proved to be much lower than hoped for). On 14 December 1942 R. S. Sorley, ACAS(T), told the Secretary of State for Air that 'the Warwick is of no operational value because it has such an unsatisfactory power to weight ratio that it has no ability to fly on one engine with any useful load. This is a basic failing of heavy twin-engined aircraft and is no more attributable to the fact that it is the Warwick than in any other similar sized aircraft. In summary the Warwick fails because it is an old design founded on an unsound basis, i.e. heavy twin-engined aircraft.'

Originally intended as a replacement for the Wellington, when fitted with Vultures the Warwick became a more satisfactory replacement, but it also competed with the Avro Manchester (discussed shortly) and was inferior to the four-engine types that followed; in truth it was a carry-over from the earlier generation of bombers. The Warwick did not enter production until 1942 having lingered on as an extra heavy bomber until other roles were found for it.

Vickers Warwick B.Mk.I (flown)	
Span	96ft 9in (29.49m)
Length	72ft 3in (22.02m)
Wing Area	1,006sq.ft (93.46sq.m)
All-Up-Weight	45,000lb (20,412kg)
Powerplant	2 × 1,850hp (1,380kW) Pratt & Whitney R-2800 Double Wasp
Max Speed/Height	224mph (360km/h)
Armament	6,000lb (2,722kg) bombs, 8 × 0.303in (7.7mm) machine guns

Specification B.12/36

Shorts Stirling

During the mid-1930s the Air Staff developed the concept that the heavy bomber would be its best weapon for both offensive and defensive operations. However, if such aircraft were to be used as an independent striking weapon they would require a greater range and carrying power than the medium and heavy bombers then under development. Fortunately recent advances in aero engines and aircraft engineering brought these objectives within reach and in 1936 two new specifications were produced, B.12/36 and P.13/36, the former calling for a bomb load of 8,000lb (3,629kg) and a range of 3,000 miles (4,828km) or a maximum load of 14,000lb (6,350kg) coupled with a 2,000 mile (3,219km) range. This bomber's cruise speed at 15,000ft (4,572m) had to be at least 230mph (370km/h) and defensive guns were to be carried in nose, amidships and rear turrets. Both specifications also called for catapult equipment to allow their aircraft to take off with heavy bomb and fuel loads when using existing engines.

In July 1936 B.12/36 was forwarded to AWA, Boulton Paul, Handley Page and Vickers, and the companies were told that in due course they would be invited to tender. Shorts was not on the original list but it was recommended that this company should also be invited to tender because it had a design on the drawing board which met most of B.12/36's limits. In addition, after its amalgamation with Harland and Wolff in Belfast, Shorts had ample drawing office staff and production facilities. B.12/36 was issued to industry in August.

Armstrong Whitworth AW.42

This project was offered with various alternative powerplants including the Merlin or Vulture from Rolls-Royce or the Armstrong Siddeley Deerhound. A total of forty-one 500lb (227kg) bombs could be carried, twenty in side-by-side wing cells between the outboard engines and another twenty-one in the fuselage; two 0.303in (7.7mm) machine guns were mounted in a nose turret, four more in a tail turret and another two in a retractable ventral 'dustbin' turret.

AWA AW.42 (9.36)	
Span	98ft 0in (29.87m)
Length	90ft 0in (27.43m)
Wing Area	?
All-Up-Weight	74,990lb (34,015kg)
Powerplant	4 × RR Merlin or Vulture or AS Deerhound
Max Speed/Height	370mph (595km/h)
Armament	41 × 250lb (113kg) or 500lb (227kg) or (probable) 7 × 2,000lb (907kg) bombs, 8 × 0.303in (7.7mm) machine guns

OPPOSITE The Armstrong Whitworth AW.42 with Merlin installation (9.36). Note the retractable ventral 'dustbin' turret. *Ray Williams*

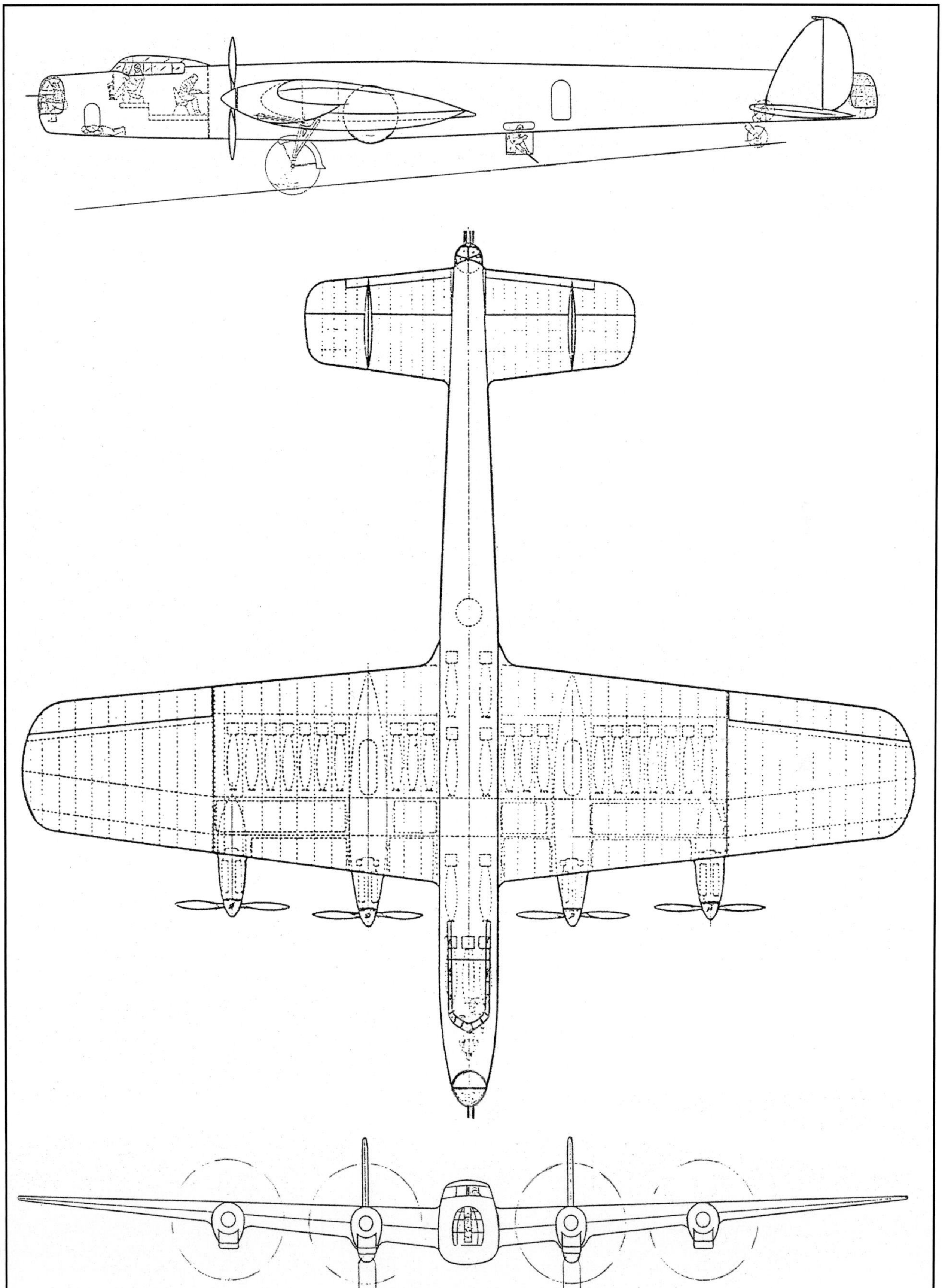

Boulton Paul P.90

This used an all-metal and mainly light alloy skin structure of the type successfully developed for the P.82 Defiant fighter. The fuselage was monocoque and the tailplane was rigidly bolted to the rear fuselage so that, from the point of view of stiffness and strength, it was virtually integral with the fuselage. The wing was constructed throughout in light alloy and had Frise ailerons and split flaps, the latter extending from the body side to the inboard end of the aileron. Its construction consisted principally of two box-type spars, the former also forming the leading edge, plus top and bottom connecting plates and rib formers connecting the spars together. Both flaps and ailerons were expected to be all-metal but, for ease of mass balancing, the latter could be fabric covered. The tail and fins were all-metal light alloy multi-cellular construction while the elevators and rudders would be fabric covered and fitted with trimming tabs.

The front turret carried two Browning machine guns, an amidships retractable turret housed two more while the tail defence consisted of Boulton Paul's patented 'Dumb-bell' type mounting which housed two Brownings to each side (total four) with the gunner housed in the rear fuselage. This arrangement, which was produced as a mock-up, placed the guns in stub winglet fairings in an attempt to reduce the drag penalties of a completely moving turret, while also eliminating the need for a massive cylindrical mounting as previously used on Boulton Paul's Overstrand bomber.

Provision was made to carry twenty-eight 500lb (227kg) or 250lb (113kg) bombs on the manufacturer's own rotating magazine carriers. These were housed in the lower fuselage, two magazines followed by three followed by two, and were interchangeable with normal RAF bomb beams and other carriers that held seven 2,000lb (907kg) bombs. A total of 1,812gal (8,237lit) of fuel could be carried in six wing tanks; cruise speed at 15,000ft (4,572m) was 248mph (399km/h) and service ceiling 35,000ft (10,668m). An alternative scheme had four Napier Daggers with the all-up-weight, fuel and performance all very similar to those of the Kestrel machine; the general layout was exactly similar except for changes to the engine installation.

BELOW Boulton Paul P.90 (1.10.36). *Les Whitehouse, Boulton Paul Archive*

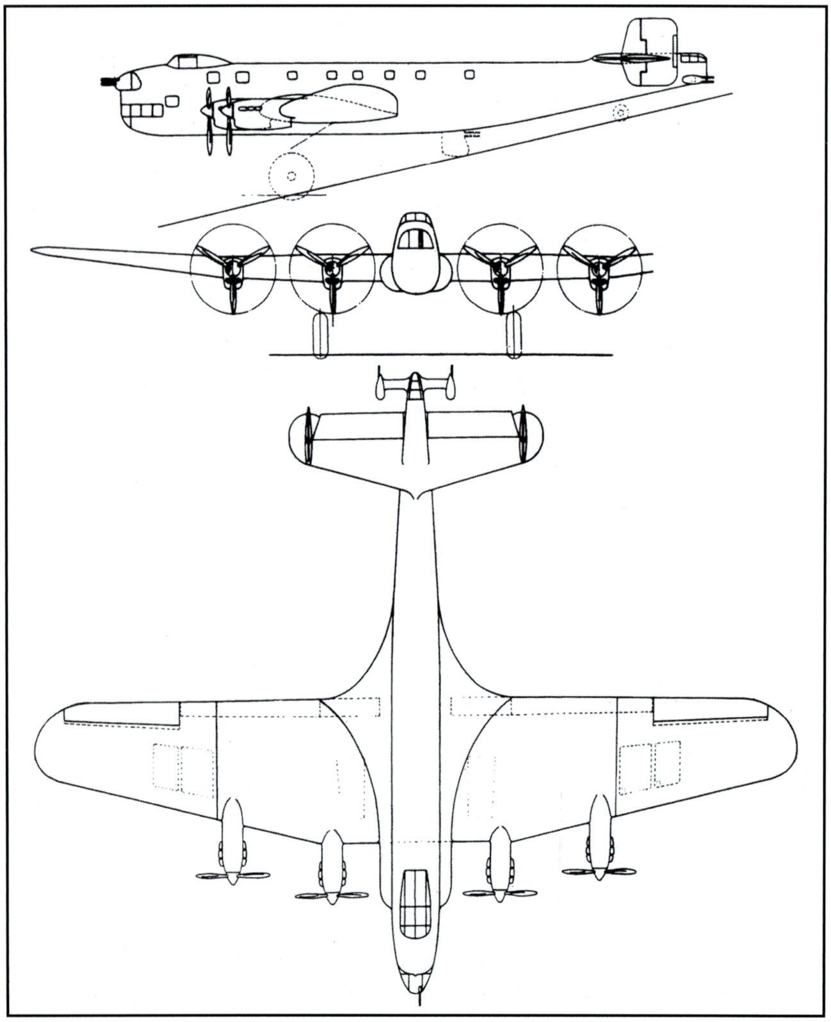

Boulton Paul P.90 (1.10.36)	
Span	100ft 0in (30.48m)
Length	77ft 3in (23.55m)
Wing Area	1,450sq.ft (134.71sq.m)
All-Up-Weight	47,922lb (21,737kg)
Powerplant	4 × RR Kestrel KV.26 or Napier Dagger
Max Speed/Height	290mph (467km/h) at 15,000ft (4,572m)
Armament	28 × 250lb (113kg) or 500lb (227kg) or 7 × 2,000lb (907kg) bombs, 8 × 0.303in (7.7mm) machine guns

Shorts S.29

No brochure is available for Shorts' original submission to B.12/36, principally because many of the company's papers and archives were lost during the war. However, the company's design office commenced work on the project in June 1936 and the design had four compartments placed astride the spar frames to carry twenty bombs in four tiers of five.

Shorts S.29 (mid-1936)	
Span	102ft 0in (31.09m)
Length	86ft 6in (26.37m)
Wing Area	1,300sq.ft (120.77sq.m) net
All-Up-Weight	53,100lb (24,086kg)
Powerplant	4 × Dagger E.108
Max Speed/Height	?
Armament	20 × 250lb (113kg) or 500lb (227kg) or (probable) 7 × 2,000lb (907kg) bombs, 8 × 0.303in (7.7mm) machine guns

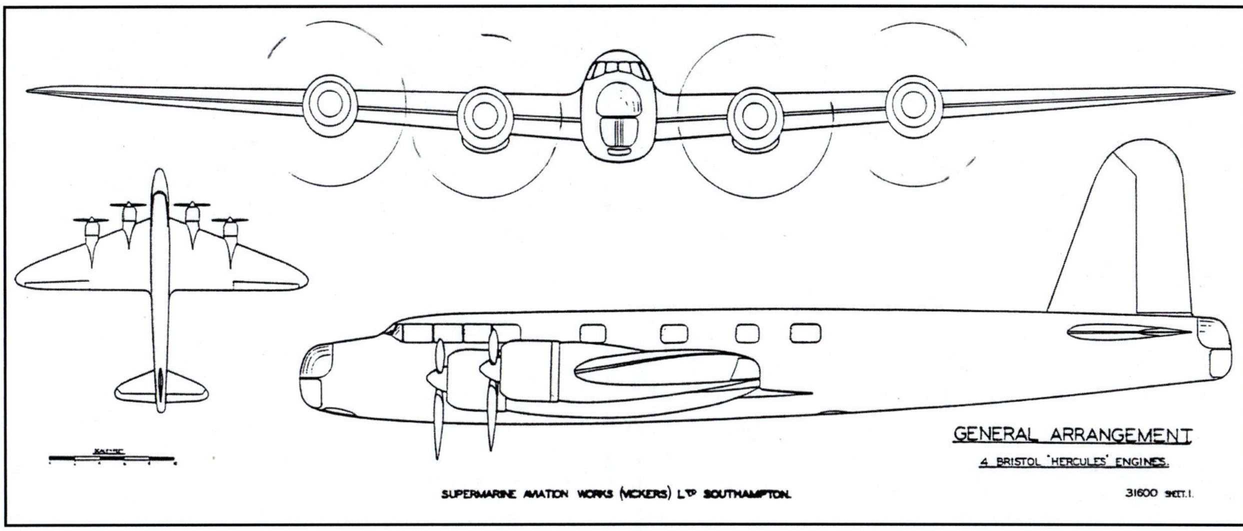

ABOVE The Supermarine 316 as originally designed by R. J. Mitchell, here with Hercules powerplant (29.9.36).

Supermarine 316 (30.9.36)	
Span	93ft 0in (28.35m)
Length	71ft 0in (21.64m)
Wing Area	1,240sq.ft (115.20sq.m)
All-Up-Weight	Merlin 51,855lb (23,521kg), Kestrel 47,460lb (21,528kg), Hercules 54,715lb (24,818kg), Pegasus 49,792lb (22,585kg), Dagger 49,364lb (22,391kg)
Powerplant	4 × 1,035hp (772kW) Merlin F, 855hp (638kW) Kestrel KV.26, 1,300hp (969kW) Hercules HE.1.SM, 900hp (671kW) Pegasus XVIII or 900hp (671kW) Dagger E.108
Max Speed/Height	Merlin 355mph (571km/h) at 18,000ft (5,486m), Kestrel 330mph (531km/h) at 17,000ft (5,182m), Hercules 370mph (595km/h) at 14,500ft (4,420m), Pegasus 330mph (531km/h) at 17,000ft (5,182m), Dagger 330mph (531km/h) at 15,000ft (4,572m)
Armament	29 × 250lb (113kg) or 500lb (227kg) or 7 × 2,000lb (907kg) bombs, 8 × 0.303in (7.7mm) machine guns

Supermarine 316

This aircraft's single-spar wing made the tier storage of bombs unnecessary; instead they could be slung in a single layer in the fuselage and in the wing aft of the spar. Wing bomb storage also had the advantage of distributing the load over the span thus cutting down the wing bending moments in flight and thereby the weight of the wing itself. The single spar was near the maximum thickness of the wing, was made in light alloy and employed stressed skin covering. No fabric was used except on the control surfaces while the metal surface, with flush riveting, enabled not only a perfectly smooth surface to be established but one which was perfectly faired, something that was impossible when using fabric. Fuel tanks were incorporated in the wing structure as portions of the metal leading edge while the chassis used four wheels in pairs side-by-side to reduce the space needed for retraction (in its final form this project carried 2,500gal [11,365lit] of internal fuel).

The fuselage comprised an all-metal streamlined shell with a structure of main frames between the bomb bays and secondary frames in between, all covered with Alclad sheet; the fuselage aft of the bombs became more truly monocoque. A single fin was chosen to help improve the tail gunner's field of view; while the nose and tail turrets, with fixed transparent cupolas and the guns mounted underneath the gunner, were interchangeable and could accommodate two or four Brownings; there was also a retractable mid-lower turret. The tail was as clean as it was aerodynamically possible to make it, while the rudder was long and narrow in order to reduce foot loads to a minimum. Both air and liquid-cooled engines could be used without alteration, except to the nacelles and cowling. The options were Bristol Hercules HE.1.SM or Pegasus XVIII, Rolls-Royce Merlin F or Kestrel KV.26, or Napier Dagger E.108, respective ceilings being 34,000ft (10,363m), 30,000ft (9,144m), 36,000ft (10,973m), 32,000ft (9,754m) and 32,000ft, and cruise at 15,000ft (4,572m) 300mph (483km/h), 258mph (415km/h), 275mph (443km/h), 258mph and 265mph (426km/h).

Vickers 293

This design employed geodetic construction (Duralumin with fabric covering throughout) and also offered a choice of engines – Bristol Taurus, Napier Dagger or Rolls Kestrel. The wing was elliptical and the undercarriage consisted of four separate units each retracting into an engine nacelle. All bombs were carried in the fuselage in superimposed layers (in an installation similar to the Wellington and Warwick) and all fuel (1,282gal [5,828lit]) was housed in the wings. The load comprised thirty 250lb (113kg) or 500lb (227kg) bombs, or eighteen 1,000lb (454kg) or seven 2,000lb (907kg) on special carriers. Respective service ceilings with these engines were 31,800ft (9,693m), 31,000ft (9,449m) and 33,000ft (10,058m); absolute ceilings 33,000ft, 32,300ft (9,845m) and 34,850ft

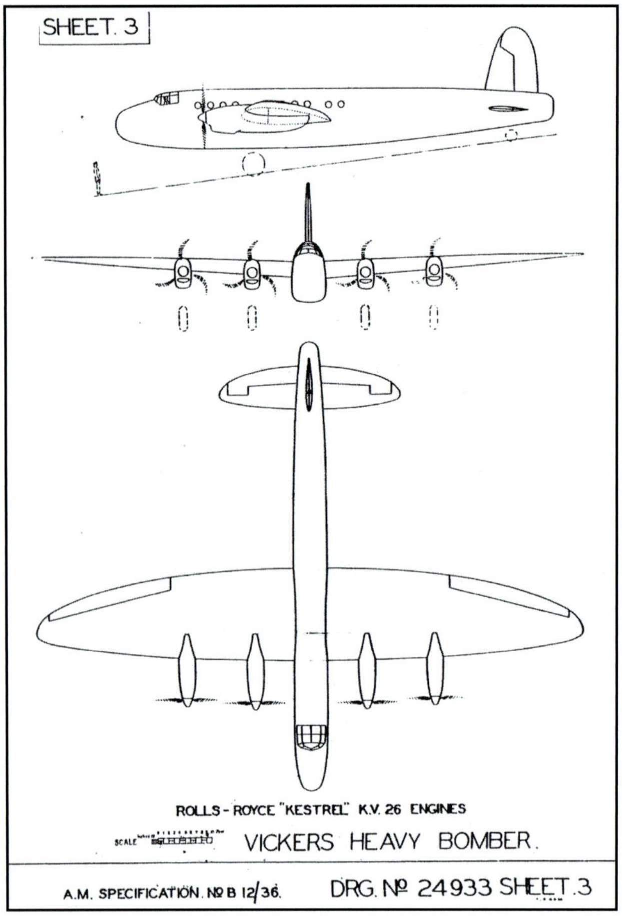

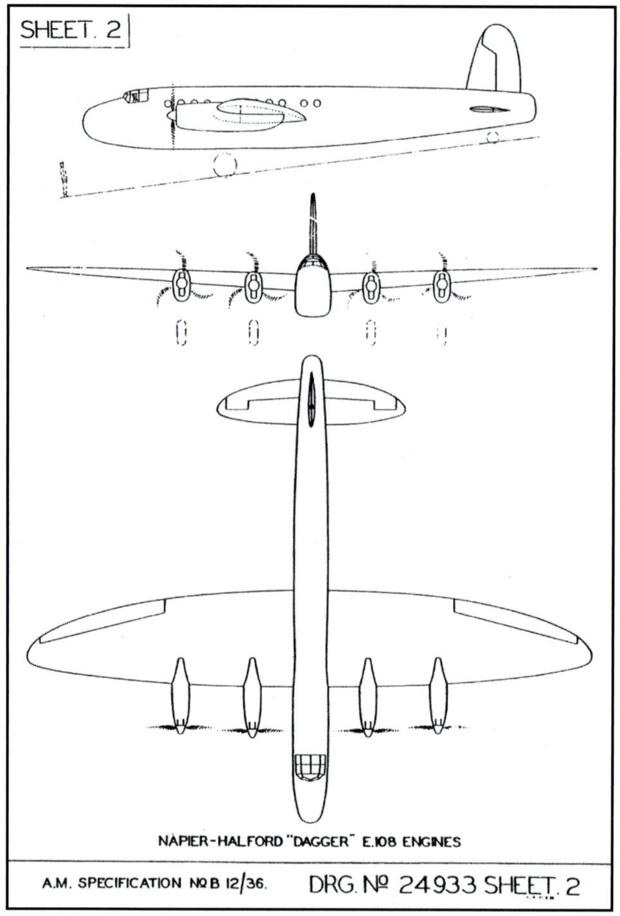

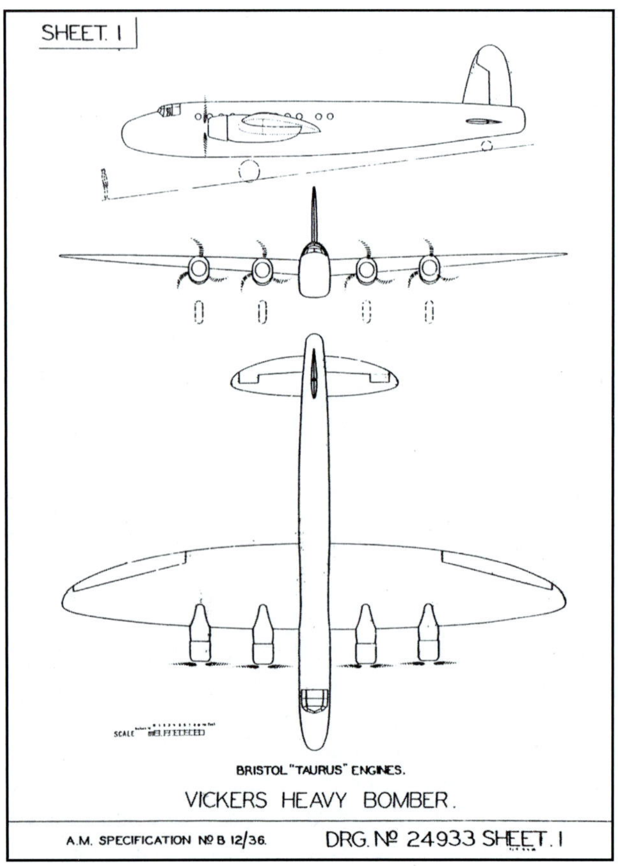

ABOVE AND LEFT **The Vickers 293 project to B.12/36 shown with Kestrel, Dagger and Taurus respectively powerplants respectively (9/36). Note the four-leg main undercarriage.**

(10,622m); maximum rate-of-climb 1,500ft/min (457m/min) up to 10,000ft (3,038m), 1,750ft/min (533m/min) at 5,000ft (1,524m) and 1,600ft/min (488m/min) at 15,000ft (4,572m); and cruise speeds at 15,000ft (4,572m) 245mph (394km/h), 233mph (375km/h) and 250mph (402km/h).

The standard Taurus had too much power and fuel consumption to be suitable for the specification so it was proposed to de-rate it by reducing the rpm from 3,225 to 2,975. The Taurus had been chosen ahead of the Bristol Perseus because of its extreme reliability in de-rated form and better performance; the Perseus gave not only a greater frontal area and fuel consumption but in fact hardly supplied enough power to meet B.12/36. There were three turrets – nose and amidships with two machine guns each and the rear with four.

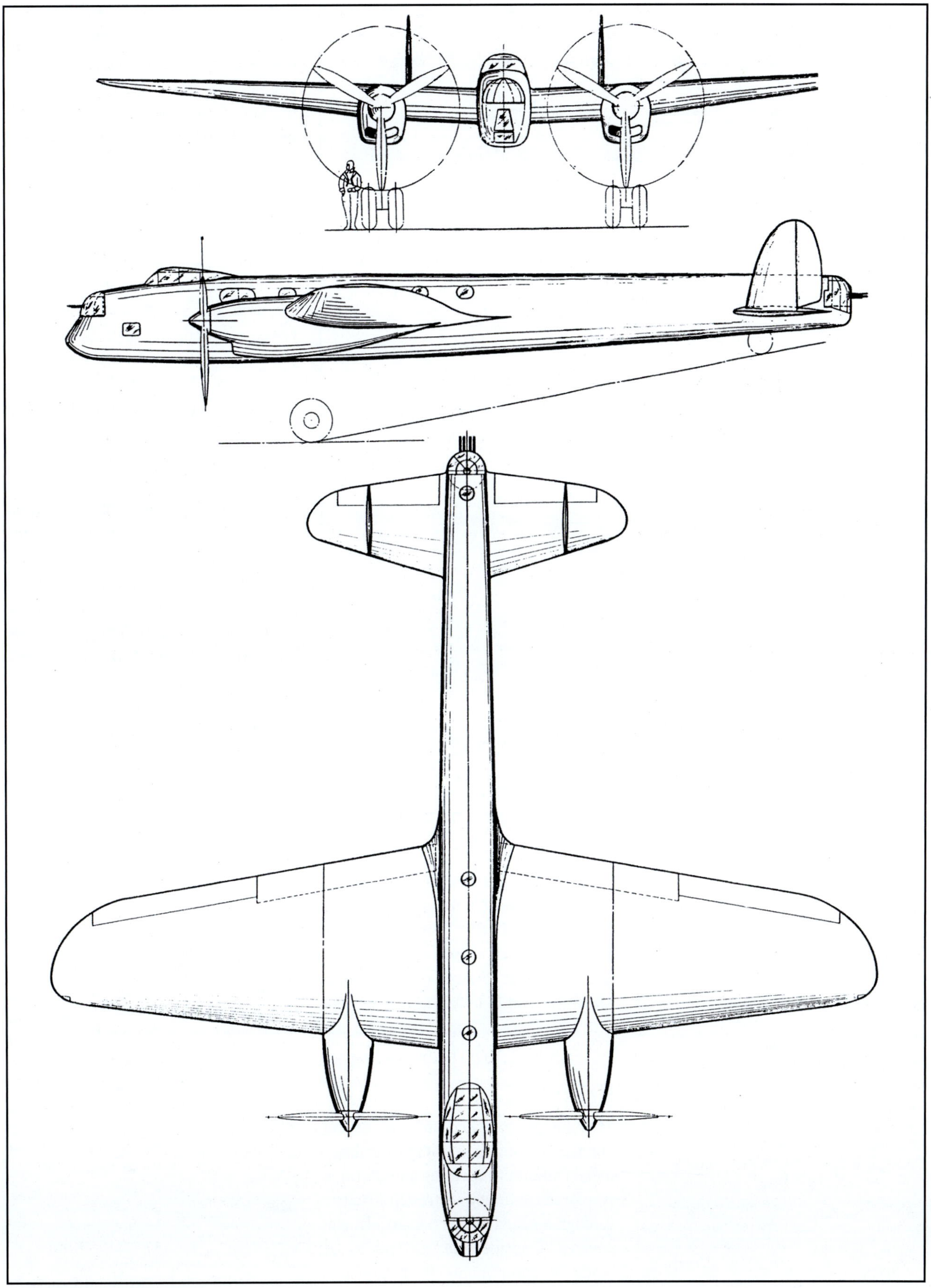

ABOVE Avro 679 (23.9.36).

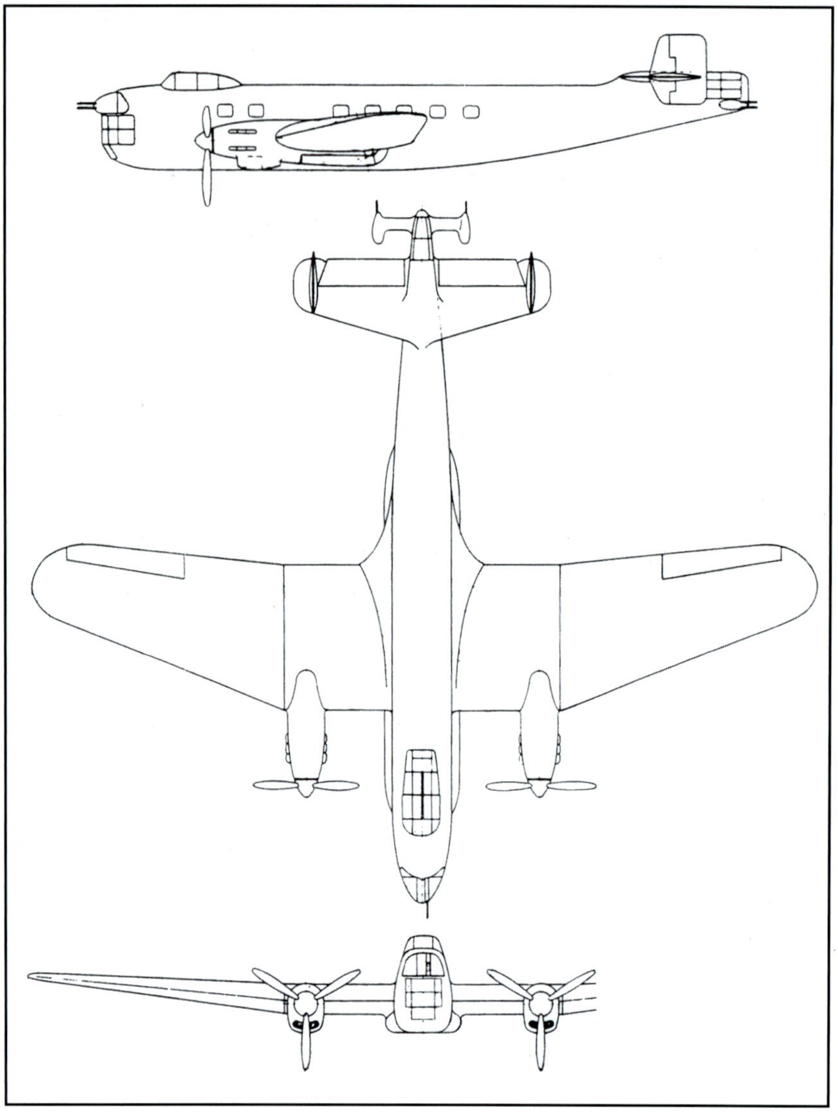

ABOVE Boulton Paul P.91 (6.1.37). *Les Whitehouse, Boulton Paul Archive*

Boulton Paul P.91

This aircraft used the same layout as the P.90 to B.12/36 and the same turret and rotating bomb bay arrangement, but it also offered as an alternative a much lower bay for normal bombs, though this was still wider than the rest of the fuselage. The P.91 employed two Vultures which gave an estimated maximum rate of climb of 2,240ft/min (683m/min) at 15,000ft (4,572m), cruise at that height of 277mph (446km/h) and service ceiling 38,000ft (11,582m).

Boulton Paul P.91 (6.1.37)	
Span	83ft 0in (25.30m)
Length	71ft 3in (21.72m)
Wing Area	950sq.ft (88.26sq.m)
All-Up-Weight	35,734lb (16,209kg)
Powerplant	2 × Vulture
Max Speed/Height	321mph (517km/h) at 15,000ft (4,572m)
Armament	16 × 250lb (113kg) or 500lb (227kg) or 4 × 2,000lb (907kg) bombs, 6 × 0.303in (7.7mm) machine guns

Bristol P.13/36

This design followed normal Bristol practice. Its wings had two spars with all-metal Duralumin covering and the body employed continuous extruded stringers through notched formers, again all metal covered. Considerable use was to be made of components from previous Bristol designs (the Blenheim and Types 149 and 152) where the drawings and jigs were in existence, such as a large number of the controls, the seating, engine components, fuel and oil systems, hydraulic systems, and details for the undercarriage, flaps and turrets. To assist manufacture it was proposed to make the main floor of the body as a separate chassis. The Hercules were to drive three-blade 13ft 9in (4.19m) diameter infinitely variable airscrews.

The designers noted that the size of this type of aircraft when fitted with Hercules radials was such that the wing was too small to accommodate the large bomb load. Therefore all of the sixteen smaller bombs up to 500lb (227kg) in size were to be carried in one tier in the bottom of the body, in four cells of four arranged one behind the other; the four 2,000lb (907kg) bombs were slung in the same position but would occupy two cells each. All of the fuel (1,320gal [6,001lit]) was housed in the centre plane and gave sufficient capacity for the maximum required range; and the rear defence comprised four 0.303in (7.7mm) machine guns housed in a fairing underneath the gunner, who aimed with a mechanically-operated sight. The estimated maximum cruise speed was 261mph (420km/h), rate of climb 2,600ft/min (792m/min) at sea level, time needed to reach 30,000ft (9,144m) 16.5 minutes, service ceiling 36,600ft (11,156m) and absolute ceiling 37,600ft (11,460m).

Bristol P.13/36 (6.1.37)	
Span	79ft 0in (24.08m)
Length	55ft 9in (16.99m)
Wing Area	800sq.ft (74.32sq.m)
All-Up-Weight (with 2,500lb/1,134kg bombs)	27,487lb (12,468kg) (Ministry 32,137lb [14,577kg])
Powerplant	2 × 1,450hp (1,081kW) Bristol Hercules HE.3.SM
Max Speed/Height	273mph (439km/h) at ground level, 315mph (507km/h) at 15,000ft (4,572m)
Armament	16 × 250lb (113kg) or 500lb (227kg) or 4 × 2,000lb (907kg) bombs, 6 × 0.303in (7.7mm) machine guns

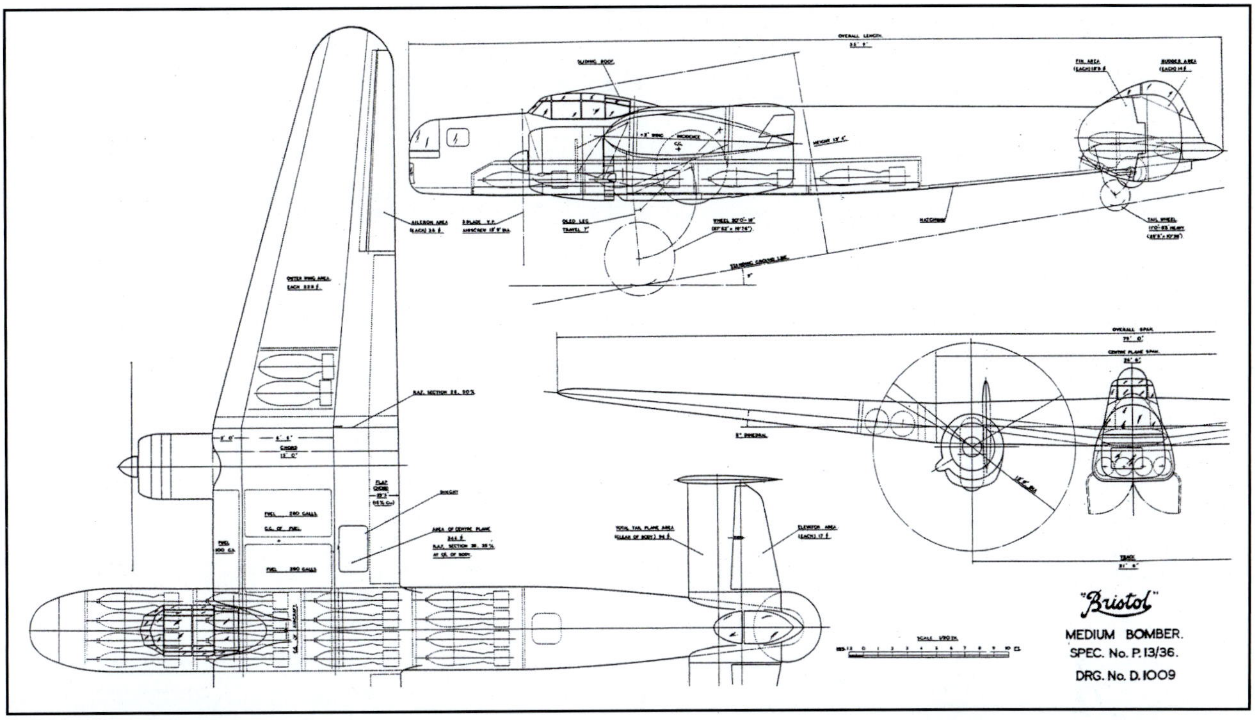

ABOVE Bristol P.13/36 (6.1.37).

Fairey P.13/36

Powered by two of Fairey's own P.24 engines with radiators in the wing centre section leading edge (Vultures or Sabres were alternatives), this streamlined design had an all-metal structure based on the P.4/34 light bomber and fabric-covered control surfaces. Bombs were carried in eight enclosed cells in the fuselage and six in the centre section; the former could be replaced by torpedo carriers. The nose turret had two 0.303in (7.7mm) Brownings and the tail turret four more; for improved streamlining the latter could be removed and replaced by retractable dorsal and ventral turrets aft of the bomb cells. Estimated time to 25,000ft (7,620m) was 13 minutes and service ceiling 34,500ft (10,516m).

Fairey P.13/36 (late 1936)	
Span	85ft 0in (25.91m)
Length	55ft 0in (16.76m)
Wing Area	?
All-Up-Weight	38,678lb (17,544kg)
Powerplant	2 × 1,750hp (1,305kW) Fairey P.24
Max Speed/Height	327mph (526km/h) at 15,000ft (4,572m)
Armament	4,000lb (1,814kg) bombs, 6 × 0.303in (7.7mm) machine guns

ABOVE Manufacturer's impression of the Fairey P.13/36 design (late 1936). *Bill Harrison*

Handley Page HP.56

This was to be powered by two Rolls-Royce Vultures, but chief designer George Volkert also assessed an alternative installation with a new 2,000hp (1,491kW) engine proposed by Napier (which later became the Sabre). The HP.56 had twin fins, large main wheels and a two-spar wing which employed a combination of corrugated and flat sheet covering in the most highly stressed areas; this was a break from normal Handley Page practice and the wing also contained all of the fuel (1,650gal [7,501lit]) in cells built integral to it. The monocoque fuselage, flaps, ailerons and tail assembly followed more recent Handley Page practice.

Handley Page HP.56 (1.1.37)	
Span	88ft 0in (26.82m)
Length	66ft 6in (20.27m)
Wing Area	975sq.ft (90.58sq.m)
All-Up-Weight	c39,000lb (17,690kg)
Powerplant	2 × Vulture X
Max Speed/Height	320mph (515km/h)
Armament	8,000lb (3,629kg) bombs, 6 × 0.303in (7.7mm) machine guns

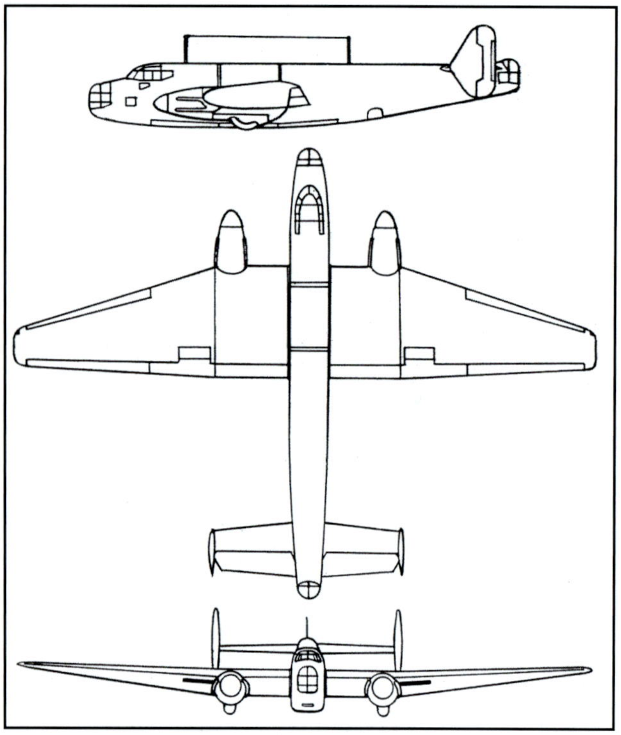

ABOVE **Handley Page HP.56 (1.1.37).**

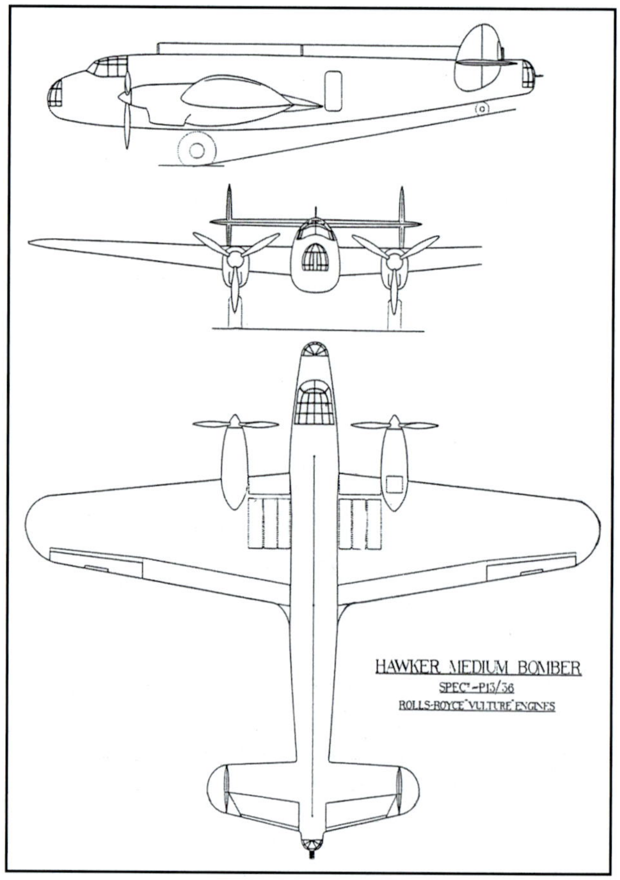

RIGHT **Hawker P.13/36 (1.1.37).**

Hawker P.13/36 (1.1.37)	
Span	87ft 0in (26.52m)
Length	72ft 8in (22.15m)
Wing Area	1,285sq.ft (119.38sq.m)
All-Up-Weight	?
Powerplant	2 × Vulture
Max Speed/Height	?
Armament	8,000lb (3,629kg) bombs, 6 × 0.303in (7.7mm) machine guns

Hawker P.13/36

Another design to use twin fins and two Vultures, this carried 1,820gal (8,274lit) of fuel in tanks placed in the inner wings between the nacelles and body.

Shorts P.13/36

No drawing of this project is known to exist but a photograph of the company's display model is available. It shows a design with twin Vultures and a single large fin.

BELOW **Model of the Shorts P.13/36 (1.37).** *Short Bros.*

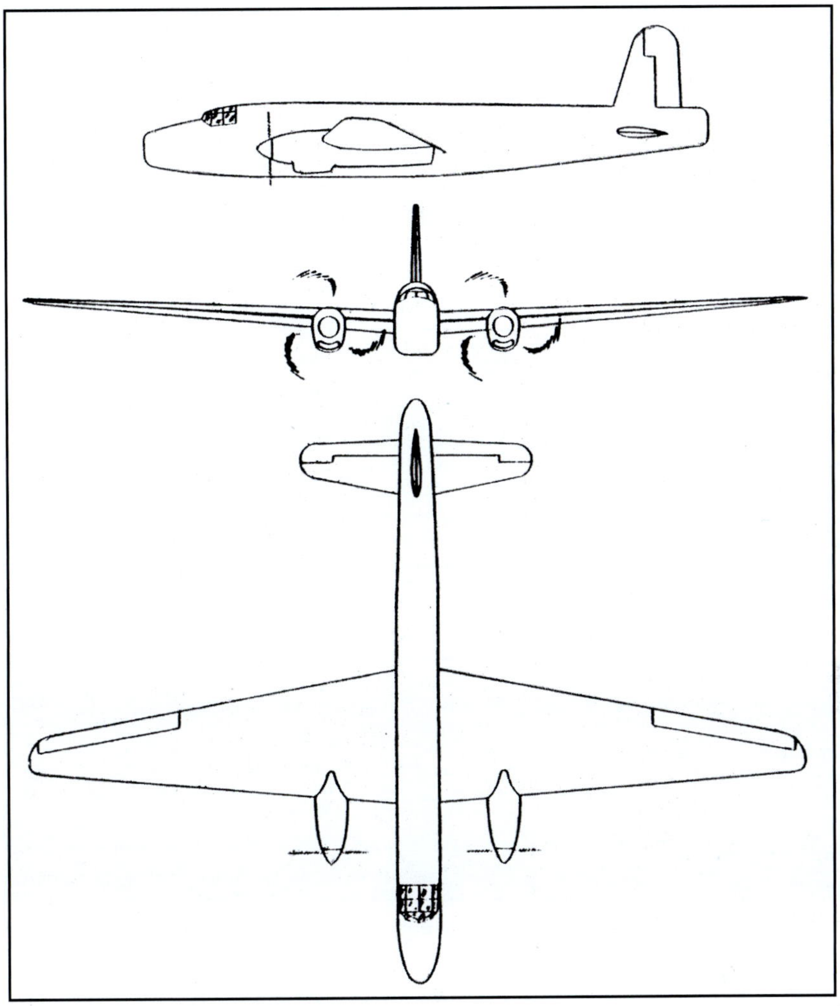

ABOVE Vickers P.13/36 (late 1936).

Vickers P.13/36

This project was derived from the B.1/35 Warwick and was powered by two Vultures. Span was about 97ft (29.57m) and length 72ft (21.95m). It was not tendered.

The Tender Design Conference was held on 10 February 1937 and Avro's 679 was placed first with Handley Page second. The HP.56 was chosen as the second string to Avro's project and DTD recommended that two prototypes of each should be ordered. Ordering duplicate prototypes had only become an accepted principle over the last decade or so because it helped to reduce the development period; hitherto this had been considered too expensive but the urgency generated by the prospect of war had drastically altered this situation. Avro and Handley Page received their formal prototype contracts in April.

Avro 679 Manchester

The Air Ministry was anxious that the 679's development should proceed as quickly as possible and on 1 July 1937 a production order was placed 'off the drawing board.' At this time the job of enlarging the RAF in readiness for war (the expansion programme) was in full swing and the Air Staff could not afford to wait, as previously, up to six years for a new aircraft to reach production. In 1935 the government granted permission to put a new type into production direct from the contractor's drawings and the Air Staff proceeded to use this discretion to the full. Both Avro's and Handley Page's designs had been analysed by DTD's department and it was their promise in the role of the RAF's new striking force that saw both ordered 'off the board.'

BELOW Model of the Avro 679 as it looked in March 1938. *Avro Heritage Centre*

ABOVE The second Avro Manchester prototype L7247. The third central fin is just visible.
BELOW Production Manchester Mk.I L7427.

ABOVE **The Manchester Mk.IA dispensed with the central fin and introduced larger tip fins. This picture was taken on 20 September 1941.** *Phil Butler*

In March 1937 it was decided that all medium bombers not delivered by 1 April 1939 should be replaced by P.13/36 types, preferably the Avro 679 but alternatively the HP.56, and the Chancellor of the Exchequer approved this scheme in April 1937.

The Mock-Up Conference was held on 4 May 1937 (two mock-up noses had to be scrapped before final approval was given) and on 4 August it was decided that the first prototype should be fitted with Hercules engines and the second with the Vulture (in the end no Manchester ever used the Hercules). Over the next year the torpedo and catapult launch requirements were dropped and the prototype L7246, now called Manchester, flew on 25 July 1939. The cumulative effect of these changes retarded the prototype's progress, particularly dropping the catapult in July 1938 when the structures for the first batch had been completed with the required fittings in place. These added weight but would be expensive to remove (£50,000 was quoted for new jigging), while such a step would also bring more delay.

Flight trials revealed that the Manchester exhibited poor take-off performance, especially at 40,000lb (18,144kg) weight, and was directionally extremely unstable; the second problem was solved by fitting a third central fin but weight was always an issue. During development both the fixed and military load rose considerably so that when the aircraft's weight was finalised it was found to be much heavier than expected. In May 1940 DGRD reported to AMDP that, since February 1939, the equipped weight had risen by 4,485lb (2,034kg) and a further 550lb (249kg) was about to be added. An unassisted take-off at more than 45,000lb (20,412kg) was not assured and the increases in equipment meant that the bomb load was being reduced to a negligible figure. Measures proposed by Avro to lighten the structure included reducing the thickness of the covering skin; wooden bomb doors; increasing the span from 80ft to 90ft (24.38m to 27.43m); and other changes in design and equipment, which gave a net saving of 1,550lb (703kg) – even so Avro was forced to restress the aircraft six times. The new wingtips were fitted to the prototypes in July 1940 and successful take-offs at 45,000lb were achieved, but the maximum fuel and bomb loads could still not be carried together.

This situation was compounded by development problems with the Vulture (failures were frequent and the aircraft struggled to maintain height on one engine – there were numerous forced landings). In 1940 Rolls-Royce abandoned the engine and this decision, together with the technical position of the Manchester itself, meant that the future of the type was extremely uncertain, just at the point when production was about to get going. Production of the Manchester gradually faded out until it ceased altogether in 1941 after just 200 had been built. There were proposals for alternative engines – a twin Centaurus arrangement was drawn in 1938 and there were plans to fit the Napier Sabre.

There was also a more radical Manchester development that had a dorsal and ventral double turret with four cannon in each and the nose and stern turrets faired over. In 1939 contracts were apparently placed with Shorts, Handley Page and Avro for versions of the Stirling, Halifax and Manchester fitted with cannon turrets, the three prototypes being R2659, R2665 and R2671. As the drawing shows, the Manchester redesign was quite extensive. The four 20mm turret was quite popular during the late 1930s being earmarked for the B.1/39 bomber (described shortly) and the Boulton Paul P.92 fighter, but none of these designs ever flew.

Avro 679 Manchester B.Mk.I (flown)	
Span	90ft 1in (27.46m)
Length	68ft 10in (20.98m)
Wing Area	1,131sq.ft (105.07sq.m)
All-Up-Weight	45,000lb (20,412kg)
Powerplant	2 × 1,760hp (1,312kW) Vulture I
Max Speed/Height	265mph (426km/h) at 17,000ft (5,182m)
Armament	normal 8,000lb (3,629kg), maximum 10,350lb (4,695kg) bombs, 8 × 0.303in (7.7mm) machine guns

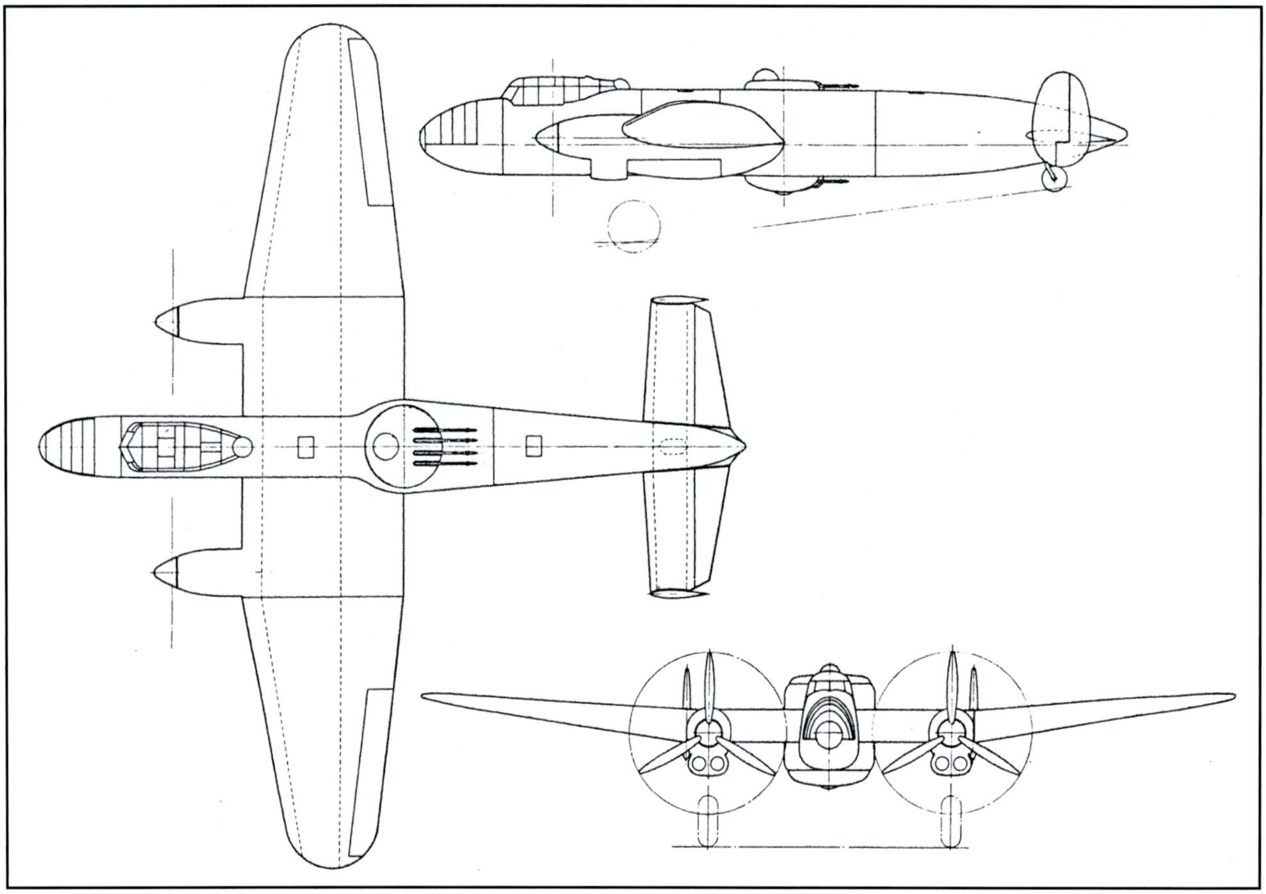

ABOVE This unbuilt Manchester variant fitted with cannon turrets was designed to be used as an armament development aircraft (1939).

Handley Page HP.57 Halifax

The HP.56 Mock-up Conference was held on 8 July 1937 and the serials allocated to the prototypes were L7244 and L7245. However, on 24 July CAS decided that the aircraft should be refitted with four engines. The new Vulture was already suffering from various technical difficulties, it was not going to give enough power and the Air Ministry was anxious not to have to rely on it too much. Its eventual failure was ultimately responsible for the redesign of both the Manchester and the HP.56, but the latter was modified well before first flight.

The Air Staff's discussions leading to the change in the type's powerplant were all-embracing but a choice of four Merlins was eventually made ahead of a twin Hercules installation since the Merlin was the only engine likely to be available in sufficient numbers. A version showing four Bristol Taurus radials had also been requested by Air Marshal Freeman on 19 July 1937. The Merlin produced less power than the Vulture, which meant four units were needed instead of two and, at first, Volkert was very unwilling to alter his project because the wings would have to be completely redesigned to take two units each. At that time a wing mounting two engines was highly experimental and had to be submitted for stringent strength tests at RAE, while the weight of the wing and the whole aeroplane rose by a large margin which necessitated the strengthening of the structural members. The span was increased from 88ft to 99ft (26.82m to 30.18m) and the weight went up from 39,000lb (17,690kg) to 52,000lb (23,587kg).

Work on the HP.56 was abandoned on 18 August and the design effort was switched to the new four-engine HP.57, which was essentially a new aircraft. Volkert admitted that the change was a terrible blow but he very quickly realised that advantages were going to accrue. On 3 September Handley Page was officially notified of the decision to switch to four Merlins and the work eventually delayed the prototype by about six months. However, the catapult requirement could now be deleted since enough power was available for a take-off at maximum overload, albeit with a long take-off run; the torpedo requirement was also dropped in July 1937. A revised Mock-up Conference was held in December, the hand-building of both prototypes began in March 1938 and by July most of the design work was complete with construction of the fuselage and other items of equipment well under way.

The prototype made its maiden flight on 25 October 1939. When the Avro Manchester became the first P.13/36 bomber to be chosen for production it was considered to show the greater promise. However, after Handley Page's

ABOVE **The second prototype Handley Page Halifax L7245.** *Crown Copyright*
BELOW **Halifax B.Mk.II W7773.**

ABOVE Serial LV833 seen here was a Halifax B.Mk.III.

project had been redesigned with four engines, it assumed a much greater importance in the Air Ministry's re-equipment plans. The first production order was placed on 7 January 1938 and these aeroplanes were to use the serials originally allocated to production HP.56s. Soon afterwards the type received its official name, Halifax, and it was to serve throughout the war in many roles. Later, following complaints made at the highest level about the aircraft's poor performance, it was re-engined with four Hercules – despite being perhaps the most successful of all British piston engines, the Merlin never really suited Handley Page's bomber. Over 6,170 examples of the Halifax were produced.

Handley Page HP.57 Halifax B.Mk.I (flown)	
Span	98ft 8in (30.07m)
Length	70ft 1in (21.36m)
Wing Area	1,250sq.ft (116.13sq.m)
All-Up-Weight	55,000lb (24,948kg)
Powerplant	4 × 1,130hp (843kW) Merlin X
Max Speed/Height	262mph (422km/h) at 18,000ft (5,486m)
Armament	13,000lb (5,897kg) bombs maximum, 8 × 0.303in (7.7mm) machine guns

Avro 683 Lancaster

As early as April 1937, before the HP.56 was modified with four engines, Roy Chadwick, chief designer at Avro, was giving thought to fitting four Hercules onto the Manchester. Air Marshal Sir Wilfrid Freeman (AMDP) also mentioned such a scheme and the first drawings were produced in 1939. Thus, when the Manchester's future came into question Avro had proposals ready to convert it into a four-engine aircraft. However, during August and September 1940 there was caution over the project – was this the correct step to take because the Halifax was currently the most favoured heavy bomber (and was to be used throughout as a yardstick)?

Initially Avro's project generated no enthusiasm at MAP, which thought that the Manchester was incapable of further development and felt that the company's optimistic promises were ill-founded. The main argument for proceeding was that, because the Manchester's jigs and tooling could be used, it was the best way to produce the greatest number of aircraft in a given time. Freeman supported Avro throughout the whole controversy and persuaded the Minister of Aircraft Production, Lord Beaverbrook, to give the company his permission to go ahead. A contract for one prototype, BT308 (a Manchester removed from the production line and rebuilt), was placed in September 1940. Patrick Hennessey however, who under Beaverbrook had much influence over the choice of new

ABOVE **Avro Lancaster prototype BT308 in January 1941. Hardly visible is the central Manchester-style third fin.** *Phil Butler*

BELOW **The second Lancaster prototype, DG595, was the first to be fitted with the standard tailplane with twin fins.**

RIGHT **Lovely study of Lancaster PD235, which was lost on 25 September 1944.**

Avro 683 Lancaster B.Mk.I (flown)	
Span	102ft 0in (31.09m)
Length	68ft 10in (20.98m)
Wing Area	1,300sq.ft (120.77sq.m)
All-Up-Weight	68,000lb (30,844kg)
Powerplant	4 × 1,460hp (1,089kW) Merlin XX
Max Speed/Height	281mph (452km/h) at 11,000ft (3,353m)
Armament	14,000lb (6,350kg) bombs maximum, 8 × 0.303in (7.7mm) machine guns

projects, was not helpful and even went so far as to refuse Avro the raw materials needed for the prototype's construction. Avro's Managing Director remembered Hennessey's final reply was 'to go and dig for it' (later Hennessey became more favourably inclined towards the aircraft).

Fortunately for Avro the distribution system for light alloys was imperfect and the company was able to obtain enough materials to build the aircraft, and work on BT308 began in August 1940. By late November the controversy was virtually over and the new type, named Lancaster on 29 October, was allowed to go ahead. This result was achieved through the initiative and perseverance of Avro and in spite of MAP, who only half-heartedly admitted that it might achieve a performance as good as the Halifax. By the end of the year, however, the design was showing sufficient promise for enough support to be gained within MAP to permit a sizeable order to be placed. The prototype, which first flew on 9 January 1941, was not built to a formal specification but the Air Ministry did formulate an Operational Requirement.

The initial proposals had only envisaged switching the engines and stretching the span to 100ft (30.48m) but Ministry requests for an operating weight of 57,000lb (25,855kg) eventually made it necessary to redesign the wing and most of the undercarriage. Nevertheless Chadwick described the differences in structure between the Manchester and Lancaster as 'small.' The production programme was accelerated and the Lancaster eventually became the premier aircraft, both in numbers and performance, in the British bomber offensive against Germany. Over 7,370 were built with a small number (300) powered by Hercules engines as an insurance against a possible shortage of Merlins (a situation which never came about).

Avro 684

In July 1941 Avro suggested a high-altitude Lancaster which had Merlin 60s and a nose similar to the experimental Vickers high-altitude Wellington flown in September 1940. A year or so later it drew a high-speed version with a streamlined nose, engine nacelles and rear fuselage, no nose turret and 0.5in (12.7mm) machine guns in dorsal and rear turrets.

In August 1941 Avro completed a brochure for its Type 684 Stratosphere Bomber. This all-metal aeroplane was designed to operate at a height that made it immune from fighter or anti-aircraft interference and, with the exception of the nose portion of the fuselage, was still identical to the Lancaster. The nose contained a pressure cabin, as designed for the high-altitude Wellington, which, in

BELOW Avro 684 Stratosphere Bomber as redrawn by George Jenks in 1990 (16.8.41). *George Jenks, Avro Heritage Centre*

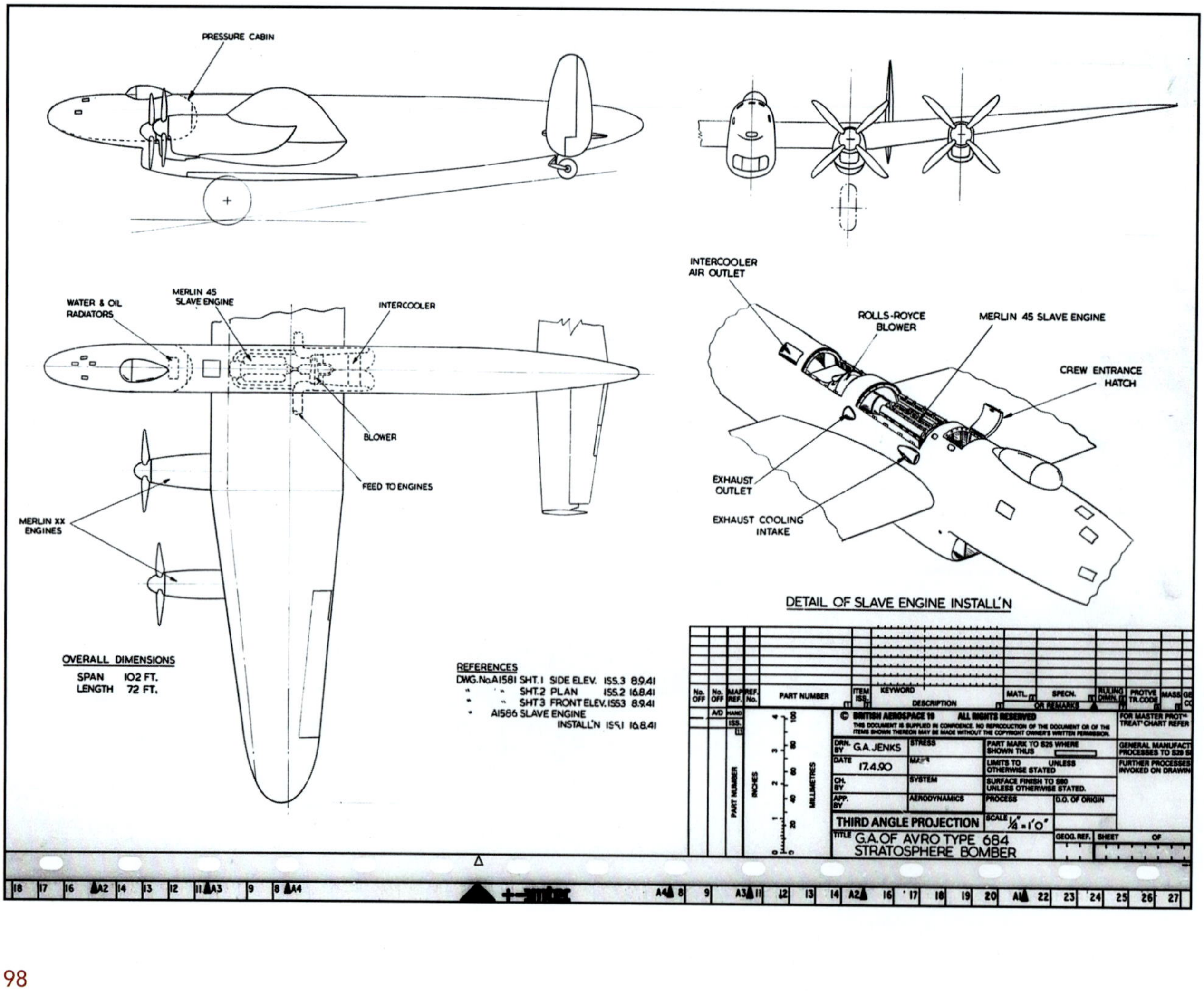

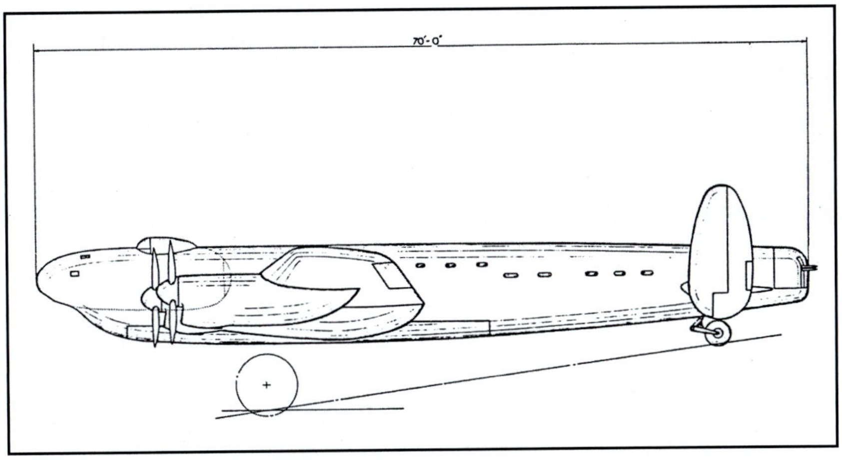

ABOVE This drawing of a modified Avro 683 Lancaster appears to be the first showing the bomber with a pressure cabin. It is dated 29 July 1941 and was quickly replaced by the 684 Stratosphere Bomber with its more streamlined fuselage. The length here is 70ft 0in (21.34m).

conjunction with a Rotol blower, would maintain air conditions corresponding to 10,000ft (3,048m) when flying at an altitude of 40,000ft (12,192m). To achieve this high-altitude flight the air flowing to the carburettors of the four wing-mounted Merlins would be increased in pressure by a 'slave' Merlin 45 housed within the fuselage between and above the wing spars (the blower was placed behind the rear spar). By regulating the rpm of the slave blower to suit the prevailing conditions its discharge pressure could be made to correspond to 20,000ft (6,096m) conditions at all heights between 20,000ft and 40,000ft (12,192m).

The 684 could carry either 4,000lb (1,814kg), 8,000lb (3,629kg) or 12,000lb (5,443kg) bombs, average cruise would be about 320mph (515km/h) and range 2,300 miles (3,701km). The service ceiling at the start of a mission (60,000lb [27,216kg] weight) was 42,000ft (12,802m) and at the end of a flight (at 38,492lb [17,460kg] weight) 49,600ft (15,118m). The absolute ceiling at the latter weight was 50,300ft (15,331m), sea level rate of climb at 60,000lb was 940ft/min (287m/min) and at 38,492lb 1,910ft/min (582m/min), time to 40,000ft (12,192m) was 57 minutes. A total of 2,130gal (9,683lit) of fuel was carried in the wings. The development workload needed for the standard Lancaster and its variants, and the new Avro 685 York transport which used the same mainplane, power eggs, tail and undercarriage, led to design work on the 684 being suspended.

Avro 684 (16.8.41)	
Span	102ft 0in (31.09m)
Length	72ft 0in (21.95m)
Wing Area	1,297sq.ft (120.49sq.m)
All-Up-Weight	60,000lb (27,216kg)
Powerplant	4 × Merlin XX, plus 1 × Merlin 45 (slave)
Max Speed/Height	410mph (660km/h) at 42,500ft (12,954m)
Armament	12,000lb (5,443kg) bombs, no defensive armament carried

Specification B.1/39 The Ideal Bomber

Despite the arguments for and against defensive armament, by 1938 the Air Ministry was fearful of the performance and armament of Germany's latest fighters and so the heavy bomber's protection had to be improved. Countering the fighter's machine guns or cannon would need up to six machine guns in turrets firing backwards and downwards but this alone would be insufficient – protective armour was also needed. In 1937 and 1938 experiments were made with thin sheets of armour plate and bullet-proof glass but there was a limit because of their effects on the aircraft's CofG. Self-sealing petrol tanks would also soon be available but, although good, they were twice as heavy as ordinary tanks. A good ceiling would help to avoid flak but this brought with it extra equipment such as oxygen and heating for both crew and guns (Browning machine guns froze at –10°C, the summer equivalent of 15,000ft [4,572m]). Each of these steps made a bomber larger, heavier and more complex.

In March 1938, partly from work done by the 'Bombing Committee' during 1937 and 1938, a paper was produced that detailed an Ideal Bomber for the RAF. It suggested an 'optimum size' standard type for all squadrons both at home and overseas and five sizes were considered from Type A (18,000lb [8,165kg] gross weight, 58ft [17.68m] span, 4,000lb [1,814kg] bomb load) to Type E (160,000lb [72,575kg], 172ft [52.43m], 44,000lb [19,958kg]), which was the largest possible aircraft capable of being developed within six or seven years. The Ideal Bomber had to have a defensive armament 'capable of developing a volume of fire sufficient to engage the maximum number of fighters which can attack simultaneously' while both experimentation and Spanish Civil War experience had revealed that 'the modern high-performance fixed-gun fighter can only operate successfully in the astern attack;' therefore the bomber would need a four-gun tail turret.

After considerable further study the Air Staff recommended that Type B (35,000lb [15,876kg], 80ft [24.38m], 8,000lb [3,629kg]) should be produced and the outcome was specification B.19/38 of mid-1938 which called for eight 20mm cannon mounted in two turrets amidships, one above and one below the fuselage, to give protection above, below and to the rear (it was considered that 0.303in [7.7mm] machine gun fire would be largely useless by the time the B.19/38 took to the air). By September it was clear that the aircraft would be substantially larger than first thought and on 28th December B.19/38 became B.1/39. This document requested a 280mph (451km/h) cruise and 2,500 miles (4,023km) minimum range at 15,000ft

(4,572m) with 9,000lb (4,082kg) bombs, four engines and a maximum weight of 50,000lb (22,680kg).

In January 1939 it was decided to invite industry to tender. Despite the decision to concentrate on the Halifax as the standard production bomber for the striking force, it was agreed in April that this in no way lessened the need to press on with advances in design. Sholto Douglas, ACAS, felt that the B.1/39's development should proceed on the highest priority and he declared that he would be prepared, if necessary, to visit the Treasury to explain the Air Staff point of view on the matter.

Meanwhile Boulton Paul, as part of the development work for its P.92 fighter, had successfully demonstrated the mounting and firing of a single 20mm Hispano cannon in a powered turret. This company had also developed a method for installing circular low profile multi-cannon turrets with a high degree of aerodynamic efficiency, where the loss in speed compared to an unarmed version was just 5%. It appears that industry was given sufficient information about this for tendering, with an agreement that the successful firm would then be supplied with all of the available information. Frazer-Nash developed a rival turret and it was acknowledged that the weight of such mountings would reduce the bomb load by 4,000lb (1,814kg). The response from industry to B.1/39 was substantial but information on the following projects is relatively sparse.

Armstrong Whitworth AW.48

A design which used semi-monocoque construction and AWA's usual conventional box-spar wing. The extensive fairing of the wings and fuselage made blending the two Boulton Paul turrets relatively simple, while a new feature was a long-travel undercarriage which gave the AW.48 the ability to fly directly onto a runway without a round-out before landing. A good deal of experimentation was made on this new landing gear which included sliding a model down a cable to demonstrate the approach angle and the response of the wheels on touching the ground. The AW.48 could carry nine 500lb (227kg) bombs internally and twelve more in underwing cells, giving a full load of 10,500lb (4,763kg) which was 1,500lb (680kg) over B.1/39's stated load. Internal fuel totalled 2,300gal (10,456lit), cruise speed was 302mph (486km/h) at 15,000ft (4,572m) and service ceiling 26,000ft (7,925m).

Armstrong Whitworth AW.48 (17.4.39)	
Span	104ft 0in (31.70m)
Length	85ft 0in (25.91m)
Wing Area	1,660sq.ft (154.22sq.m)
All-Up-Weight	73,060lb (33,140kg)
Powerplant	4 × 1,560hp (1,163kW) Griffon
Max Speed/Height	342mph (550km/h) at 15,000ft (4,572m), (Top 351mph [565km/h] at 17,000ft [5,182m])
Armament	10,500lb (4,763kg) bombs, 8 × 20mm cannon

(Note: for all B.1/39 design proposals weight and top speed are for 2,500 miles [4,023km] range.)

Avro 680

Avro's project used a conventional two-spar stressed-skin wing which, together with the tail, had plenty in common with the Manchester (although the brochure did not supply much detail). The two Frazer-Nash turrets projected outside the lines of the fuselage while four Hercules or Griffon, or a combination of two

BELOW Model of the AW.48. The fittings above the inner engines were probably for sliding the model down a cable to assess the AW.48's landing characteristics. This model actually features a tail wheel undercarriage which was not part of the design as tendered. *Ray Williams*

ABOVE Armstrong Whitworth AW.48 (17.4.39). *Ray Williams*

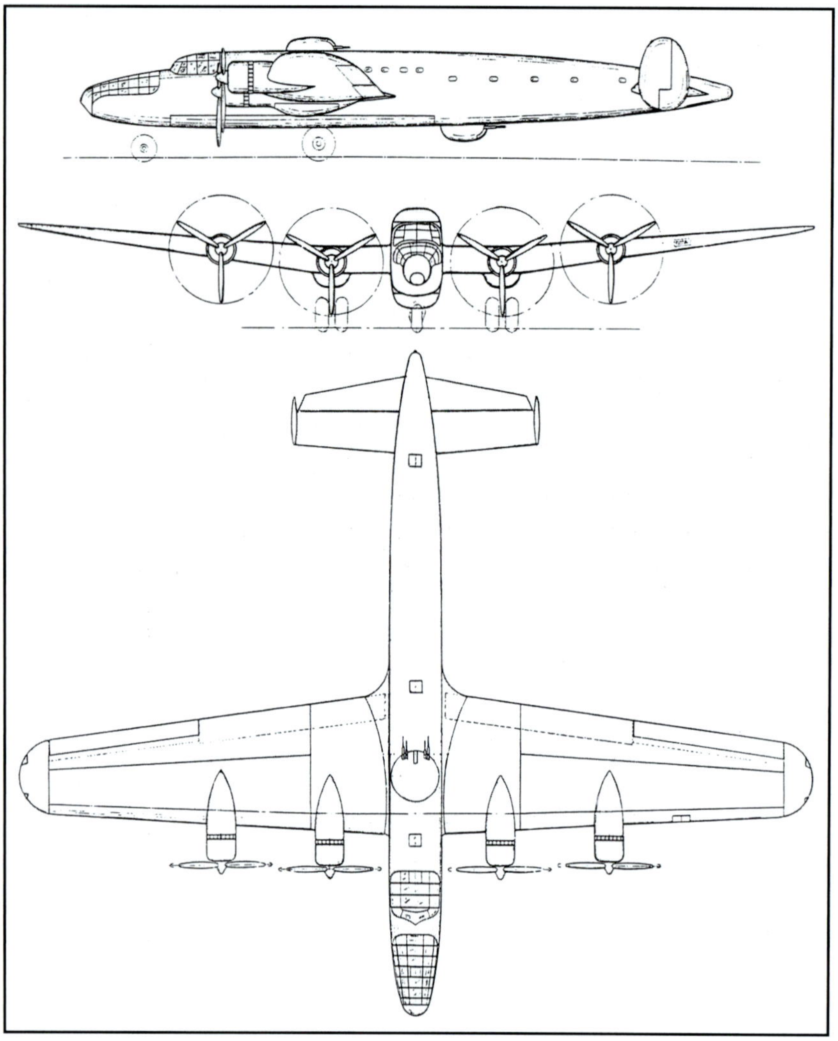

LEFT Avro Type 680 powered by Bristol Hercules engines (4.39).
George Jenks, Avro Heritage Centre

Avro 680 (4.39)	
Span	120ft 0in (36.58m)
Length	95ft 6in (29.11m)
Wing Area	1,835sq.ft (170.48sq.m)
All-Up-Weight	76,230lb (34,577kg)
Powerplant	4 × Hercules HE.6.SM or Griffon or 2 Vulture + 2 Merlin
Max Speed/Height	With Hercules 324mph (521km/h) at 15,000ft (4,572m)
Armament	9,000lb (4,082kg) plus bombs, 8 × 20mm cannon

The engine choice was four Griffons, standard Hercules or ducted radiator-cooled Hercules, which offered a cruise at 15,000ft of 272mph (438km/h), 261mph (420km/h) or 265mph (426km/h) respectively. Internal fuel was 2,650gal (12,047lit) and the service ceiling (Griffon) 24,000ft (7,315m).

Vulture and two Merlins, would form the powerplant. The cruise speed at 15,000ft (4,572m) with the Hercules was estimated to be 280mph (451km/h), with Vulture/Merlins this became 271mph (436km/h), and the service ceiling with the Hercules was 26,200ft (7,986m).

Blackburn B.30

This design had its two-spar stressed skin wings faired into the fuselage to assist with the installation of either Boulton Paul or Frazer-Nash turrets.

Blackburn B.30 (4.39)	
Span	104ft 0in (31.70m)
Length	83ft 6in (25.45m)
Wing Area	1,814sq.ft (168.53sq.m)
All-Up-Weight	Hercules 76,350lb (34,632kg), Griffon 74,750lb (33,906kg)
Powerplant	4 × Hercules HE.7.SM or ducted radiator cooled Hercules or Griffon
Max Speed/Height	Hercules 296mph (476km/h), Griffon 303mph (488km/h) both at 15,000ft (4,572m)
Armament	9,000lb (4,082kg) plus bombs, 8 × 20mm cannon

BELOW Model of the Blackburn B.30 with Hercules engines (4.39).

Bristol 159

Bristol's Type 159 was a development of the company's 'Standard Bomber' design of December 1935. Except for a single bomb cell placed outside each outer engine, the 159 carried all of its bombs, 15,000lb (6,804kg) maximum, in the inner wing and fuselage between the spars (in fact most of the B.1/39s had their bombs in the wings to enable the heavy turrets to be placed near the CofG). The fuel tanks, which held 2,580gal (11,729lit), were placed between the engines. The 159 used orthodox wing construction while its small diameter streamlined Bristol designed turrets, projecting from the fuselage, were housed mid-fuselage in an armoured monocoque structure. Bristol favoured the Hercules engine, although Griffons could also be installed. Type 159 would cruise at 282mph (454km/h) at 15,000ft (4,572m) and its service ceiling with the Hercules was 25,300ft (7,711m) and with the Griffon 23,700ft (7,224m).

Bristol 159 (4.39)	
Span	114ft 6in (34.90m)
Length	80ft 3in (24.46m)
Wing Area	1,800sq.ft (167.23sq.m)
All-Up-Weight	Hercules 77,860lb (35,317kg), Griffon 76,270lb (34,596kg)
Powerplant	4 × Hercules HE.7.SM or Griffon
Max Speed/Height	Hercules 302mph (486km/h), Griffon 303mph (488km/h), both at 15,000ft (4,572m)
Armament	15,000lb (6,804kg) bombs, 8 × 20mm cannon

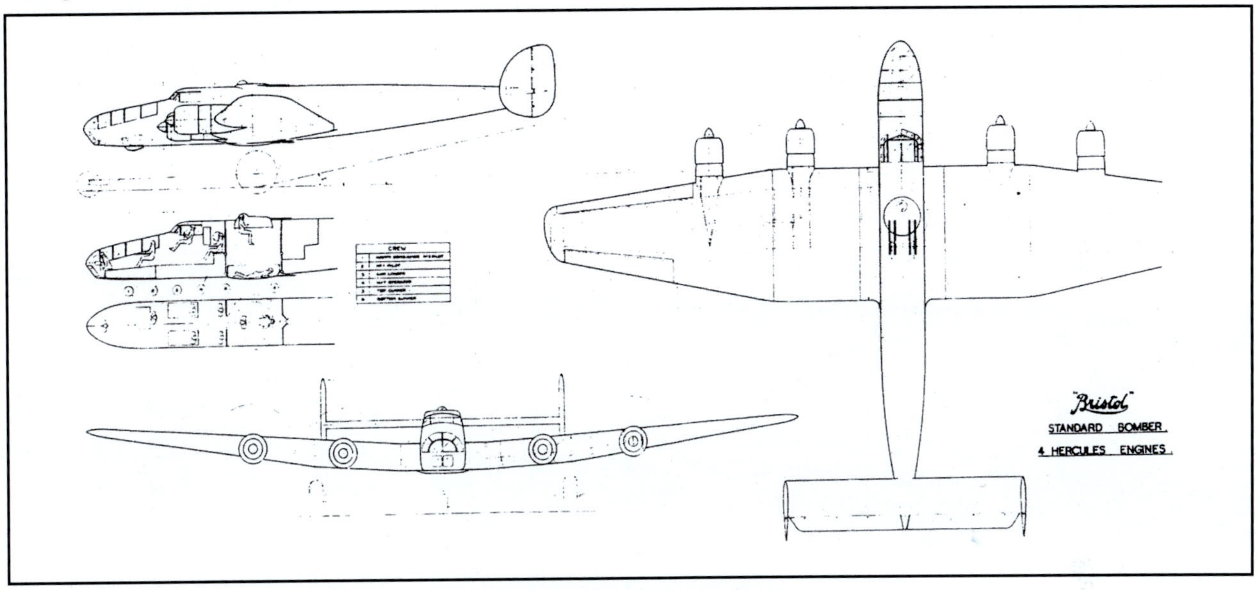

ABOVE **Early form of the Bristol Type 159 prior to the final layout being settled. At this stage the design was still described as the 'Standard Bomber', though it has heavy turrets fitted.** *Duncan Greenman*

BELOW **Bristol 159 with Hercules engines (4.39).** *Jim Oughton*

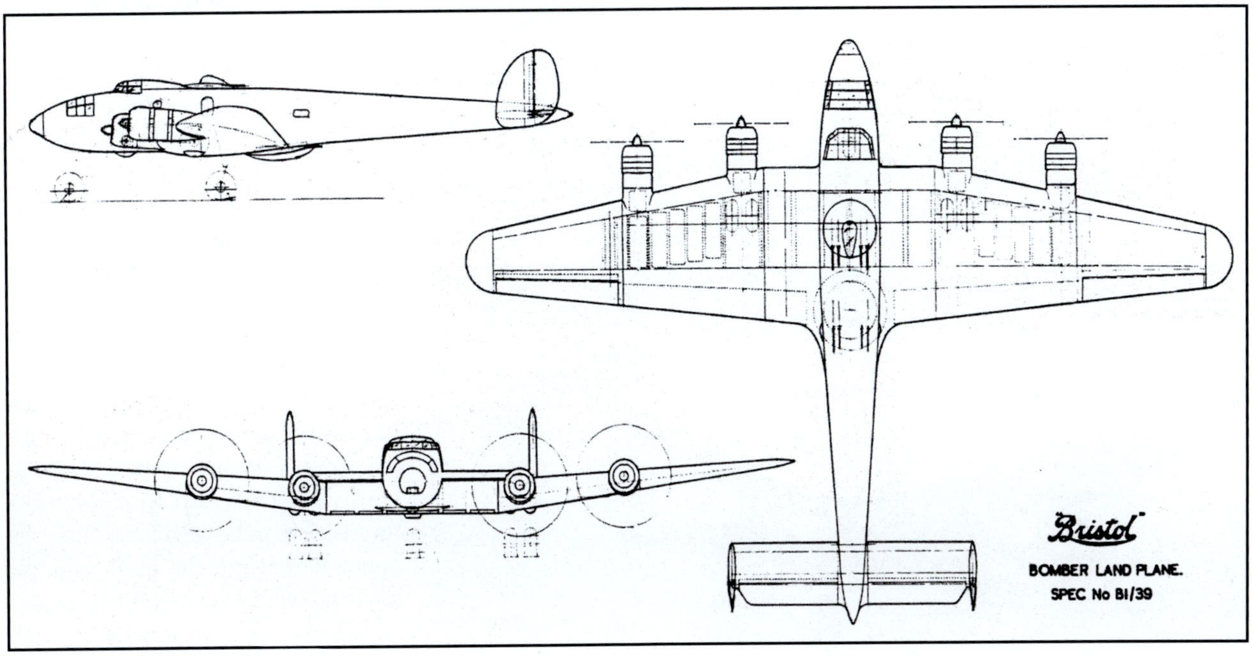

ABOVE Model of the Bristol 159. *Jim Oughton*

Fairey B.1/39

This was also Hercules-powered but it did offer an alternative using two of Fairey's own P.24 units, each of which were essentially two engines coupled together through a common gearbox and driving a contra-rotating propeller. Cruise at 15,000ft would be alternatively 267mph (430km/h) and 280mph (451km/h) and, to extend the range, either of the coupled Fairey engines could be shut down with its own propeller feathered; service ceiling for the Hercules was 21,400ft (6,523m) and the P.24 25,000ft (7,620m). Wing construction was orthodox and the turrets were merged into the wing and fuselage; 2,500gal (11,365lit) of fuel were carried.

BELOW Model of the Fairey B.1/39 proposal powered by Hercules engines (4.39).

Fairey B.1/39 (4.39)	
Span	Hercules 115ft 0in (35.05m), P.24 124ft 0in (37.80m)
Length	Hercules 93ft 6in (28.50m), P.24 90ft 0in (27.43m)
Wing Area	Hercules 2,090sq.ft (194.17sq.m), P.24 2,390sq.ft (222.04sq.m)
All-Up-Weight	Hercules 79,400lb (36,015kg), P.24 90,130lb (40,882kg)
Powerplant	4 × Hercules HE.7.SM or 2 × Fairey P.24
Max Speed/Height	Hercules 285mph (459km/h), P.24 315mph (507km/h) both at 15,000ft (4,572m)
Armament	9,000lb (4,082kg)+ bombs, 8 × 20mm cannon

Gloster B.1/39

Gloster's project had a deep wing of conventional structure which allowed all of the normal bomb loads to be housed internally, except for two 500lb (227kg) carried under the outer planes (maximum load was 9,400lb [4,264kg]). For high-altitude flight its Hercules HE.7.SMs could be replaced by turbo-blower variants but, alternatively, to improve performance the inner units could be replaced by the Centaurus. The brochure stated that, for the period, this project was planned on very progressive lines, geometrically expressing an exceptionally high standard of aerodynamic design with the front elevation approaching the ideal 'all-wing' arrangement. The turrets were positioned amidships, the upper faired into the cabin and the lower projecting from the fuselage, and the bomber would cruise at 279mph

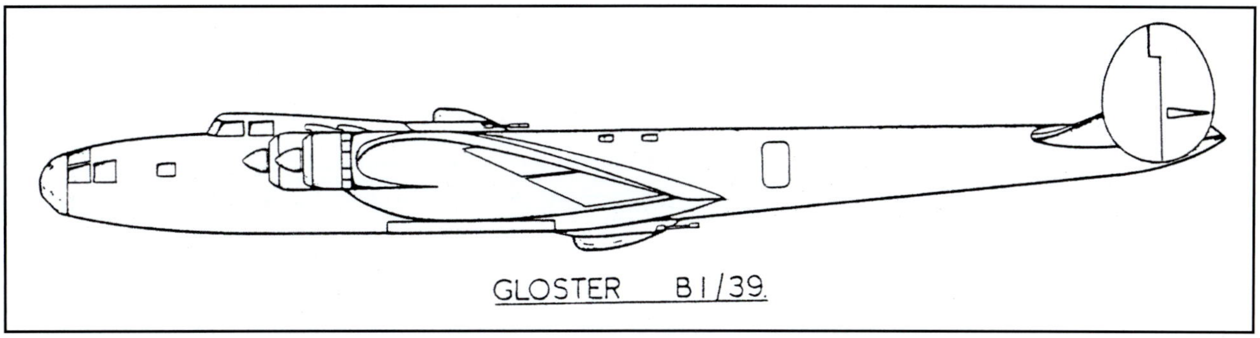

ABOVE The only known illustration of the Gloster B.1/39. *Jet Age Museum*

Gloster B.1/39 (4.39)	
Span	115ft 6in (35.20m)
Length	91ft 6in (27.90m)
Wing Area	2,040sq.ft (189.52sq.m)
All-Up-Weight	78,690lb (35,693kg)
Powerplant	4 × Hercules HE.7.SM
Max Speed/Height	289mph (465km/h) at 15,000ft (4,572m), (Top 301mph [484km/h] at 16,000ft [4,877m])
Armament	9,400lb (4,264kg) bombs, 8 × 20mm cannon

(449km/h) at 16,000ft (4,877m). Service ceiling with the Hercules was 22,700ft (6,919m) and 2,400gal (10,910lit) of fuel was carried.

Handley Page HP.60

Compared with the Halifax from which it was developed, the HP.60 used a high wing which helped blend in the upper Boulton Paul turret while the lower turret projected outside the fuselage. The wing employed wide box-spar construction and a long tricycle undercarriage and a twin tail was fitted. Power came from either Hercules or Griffon which gave a respective cruise at 15,000ft (4,572m) of 280mph (451km/h) and 277mph (446km/h), service ceiling for the Hercules was 23,500ft (7,163m) and the Griffon 25,700ft (7,833m), and 2,600gal (11,820lit) of internal fuel was carried.

Handley Page HP.60 (4.39)	
Span	115ft 0in (35.05m)
Length	92ft 6in (28.19m)
Wing Area	1,815sq.ft (168.62sq.m)
All-Up-Weight	Hercules 77,090lb (34,967kg), Griffon 75,350lb (34,178kg)
Powerplant	4 × Hercules HE.7.SM or Griffon
Max Speed/Height	Hercules 300mph (483km/h), Griffon 315mph (507km/h) both at 15,000ft (4,572m)
Armament	9,000lb (4,082kg)+ bombs, 8 × 20mm cannon

Shorts S.34

This was a mid-wing design based on the Stirling and was the only B.1/39 to feature a single fin (when fitted with Hercules engines) and a conventional tail undercarriage. Both turrets, placed one behind the other, were faired into the stressed skin box girder wing but when Griffons were fitted the S.34 reverted to twin fins and had the lower turret projecting from the fuselage. (At this stage the benefits of fully-faired turrets were unclear; in cases where they were merged into the wing surface the interference drag would be small but there might be considerable drag from the resulting thick wings.) Respective cruise at 15,000ft (4,572m) was 278mph (447km/h) (Hercules) and 268mph (431km/h) (Griffon), service ceiling 23,500ft (7,163m) and 26,400ft (8,047m), internal fuel 2,600gal (11,820lit).

Shorts S.34 (4.39)	
Span	113ft 8in (34.65m)
Length	93ft 9in (28.57m)
Wing Area	1,746sq.ft (162.21sq.m)
All-Up-Weight	Hercules 77,500lb (35,153kg), Griffon 75,850lb (34,405kg)
Powerplant	4 × Hercules HE.7.SM or Griffon
Max Speed/Height	Hercules 298mph (480km/h), Griffon 306mph (492km/h) both at 15,000ft (4,572m)
Armament	9,000lb (4,082kg)+ bombs, 8 × 20mm cannon

Vickers 405

B.1/39 requested metal wing skins with no fabric covering but for its Type 405 Vickers employed a special skin of Alclad and plywood bonded with synthetic rubber. For the fuselage the company drew on its experience of geodetic construction with fabric covering but also offered an alternative all-metal project which needed a 143ft (43.59m) span to maintain the landing and take-off performance; the extra 5,000lb (2,268kg) of structure weight that this generated cut the cruise speed by 7mph (11km/h). The 405's Frazer-Nash turrets, projecting from the fuselage, were placed more to the rear than on any other design, an arrangement which for balance needed the engines to be set well ahead of the wing. Once again power was supplied by either Hercules or Griffon to give a respective cruise at 15,000ft (4,572m) of 284mph (457km/h) and 278mph (447km/h), and service ceiling 27,500ft

Vickers 405 (4.39)	
Span	133ft 0in (40.54m)
Length	84ft 6in (25.76m)
Wing Area	1,770sq.ft (164.44sq.m)
All-Up-Weight	Hercules 82,500lb (37,421kg), Griffon 80,710lb (36,609kg)
Powerplant	4 × Hercules HE.7.SM or Griffon
Max Speed/Height	Hercules 300mph (483km/h), Griffon 319mph (513km/h) both at 15,000ft (4,572m), (Top 312mph [502km/h] at 17,500ft [5,334m] Hercules, 332mph [534km/h] at 18,000ft [5,486m] Griffon)
Armament	9,000lb (4,082kg)+ bombs, 8 × 20mm cannon

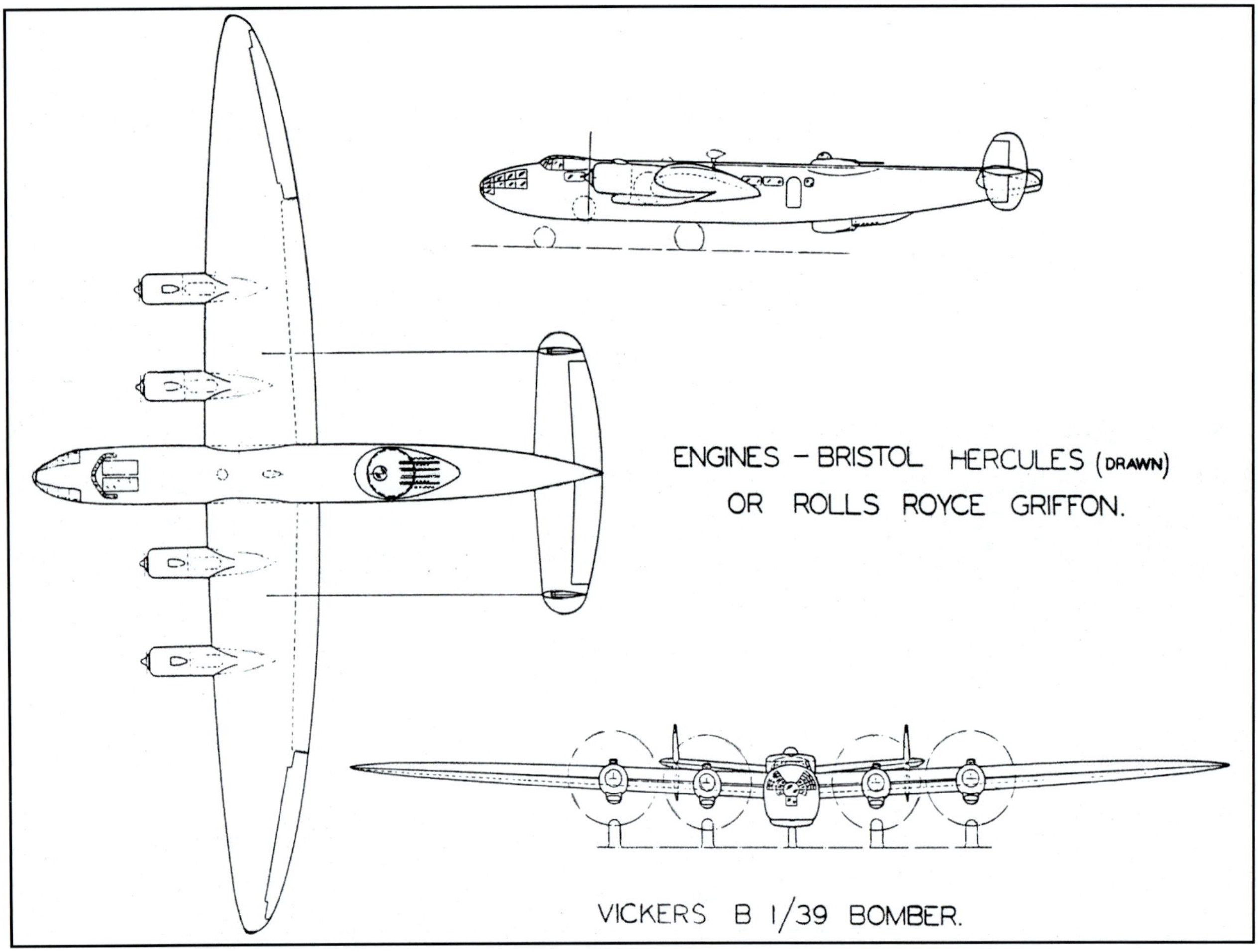

ABOVE Vickers 405 with Hercules powerplants and the unusual four-wheel main undercarriage.

(8,382m) and 30,000ft (9,144m). Internal fuel totalled 2,544gal (11,565lit) and the unusual main gears, with a main wheel housed in each of the four engine nacelles, also appeared on the company's Windsor bomber (Chapter Five).

The Air Staff's assessment of these designs showed that Fairey's B.1/39 was popular, with its superimposed turrets near the CofG and single tier bomb stowage considered to be good features, but Fairey's statement that the bombs should be dropped in a given sequence to maintain trim needed checking. Bristol's 159 had a good layout and the turrets, although not superimposed, were close enough together to provide a satisfactory layout, but the two-tier bomb stowage was a drawback. The single fin Shorts S.34 was disliked since the fin restricted the rear arcs of fire, but the alternative with twin fins and superimposed turrets was good. The chief fault of Gloster's project was a large blind area for the guns in the forward hemisphere.

The HP.60's turrets, which were not superimposed, had good arcs of fire but there were problems with crew communication. The AW.48 also suffered from cramped crew conditions but its armament layout was near equal to the HP.60 and the undercarriage design showed originality. However, positioning of the 405's turrets, well along the fuselage, was thought to be a weakness because they brought a degree of vulnerability and also needed a means of conveying their ammunition from its stowage position near the CofG. This project's stern field of fire was excellent but the close proximity of the rudders gave a blind area to the beam and its structure appeared to be complicated. After the tendering stage, Blackburn produced a revised forward fuselage for its B.30 that improved the crew arrangements but not the overall design, which was seen as not entirely satisfactory because the lower gunner's view and the forward arcs of fire of the bottom guns were restricted by the undercarriage housing.

The Tender Design Conference took place on 14 June 1939. The submitted designs were, in many respects, very similar which made it difficult to arrive at a final order of priority, so instead each design was placed in one of three groups:

1. Bristol, Fairey and Handley Page – most promising,
2. AWA, Avro and Shorts – nearly as good,
3. Blackburn, Vickers and Gloster – unworthy of further consideration and rejected.

It was felt that the web-less spar and geodetic 'pea-pod' of the Vickers 405's wing were novel but the structure appeared complex. The design was unacceptable but its remarkably low structure weight, due to its wide spaced geodetic construction, was of great interest and further investigations were requested for other uses including a revised Warwick; however, Vickers' estimates that a stressed-skin structure would be much heavier were not understood. In fact, none of the designs had kept within the gross weight requirement and it was recommended that this should be raised to 70,000lb (31,752kg).

In July 1939 Air Cdre Saundby, DOR, expressed his concern over proceeding with such an advanced project at this time. Originally it had not been planned to issue the Ideal Bomber requirement until experience with the Stirling, Halifax and Manchester was available for guidance, but the need to occupy industry had brought the project forward. CAS reported on 13 July that the tenders indicated that B.1/39 could not be met with the powerplants, materials, structural methods and standard of aerodynamics available now or expected within two years, the chief reasons being the high cruise speed and long range but the turrets were also a source of difficulty. There were fears that an immediate go-ahead for a B.1/39 type would only result in 'fruitless work' and 'wasteful expenditure.' Roderic Hill, DTD, felt that the chances of meeting B.1/39 within two years were 'insignificant' and so developing this as a standard bomber was seen only as a long-term possibility.

On 31 July, however, DTD instructed that Handley Page and Bristol should be invited to develop their proposals, plus some half-scale flight test models, as full technical investigations; if any satisfactory results were achieved from this then prototypes of the full-scale aircraft would follow. It was also suggested that Shorts should be contacted as a source of flying model experience. AWA's promising tricycle undercarriage was to be embodied into the Albemarle and possibly the B.1/39s later (its long travel and high energy absorption was considered to be a solution to the now serious problem of landing very heavy aeroplanes) but Avro's and Fairey's projects, despite being comparatively well placed, would not be continued; neither was Shorts' since that company was so heavily committed in other directions. On 16 September Vickers was informed that it had been unsuccessful in obtaining an order but the Air Ministry wished the company to continue developing the 'wide spaced geodetic construction for which a great saving in weight is claimed.'

BELOW AND OVERLEAF The mock-up of the Bristol 159's forward fuselage, depicting the design as it was to have been built, is seen in photographs dated 14 January 1941. By the spring of 1940 the bomber's structural design was well advanced and a rear fuselage section was completed for testing; wind tunnel results revealed that the type had excellent stability and low drag. The fuselage mock-up in the foreground is the Type 162 light bomber (tentatively named Beaumont – Chapter Three) for which no known drawing exists. *Jim Oughton*

This was followed in February 1940 by a request to proceed with the supply of an example of the main structure of the 405's proposed outer wing.

The scale models were dropped on 1 December 1939 but four full-size B.1/39 prototypes were ordered late in the month with serials X2871 and X2875 allocated to Bristol and X2880 and X2885 to Handley Page. As regards turrets and other major components, both the 159 and HP.60 were to be operationally interchangeable and detailed mock-ups of the aircraft were completed by the end of the year, at which point B.1/39 was enjoying a high priority. The Air Ministry had stipulated that Bristol and Handley Page should work in collaboration and specify the same components for their aircraft.

However on 25 May 1940, AVM Tedder, DAMDP, wrote 'in the present circumstances, we should suspend all construction activities in connection with these types' and added that staff would be better employed on more urgent needs. In mid-June the two companies were informed that all design work would cease, although none of the completed work was to be scrapped. Thus, although not killed outright by the German advance into France and MAP's consequent concentration on producing only certain types of aircraft, the Ideal Bomber was retired to obscurity, though in April 1944 it did come under consideration once more. In fact, during the design work that was completed, it was found that the aircraft's total structure weight, including the desired armament, would be too high relative to the available weight capacity left over for bombs and fuel. This problem too contributed to the prototypes being dropped. The two mock-ups were finally cleared for dismantling in January 1941.

An official post-war history notes that 'the most striking impression of the Ideal Bomber was the extraordinary ambition of the whole project, and had it reached fruition and proved successful in action this would probably have been among the most outstanding achievements in the history of aircraft design. On the other hand had the machine entered mass production and then proved to be inadequate, or even a total failure, then the results would have been catastrophic.' In the event the Halifax and Lancaster filled the gap and were to perform feats that could scarcely have been imagined in 1937 when the 'Ideal' discussions began. Perhaps the greatest value of the concept was in summarising what was known about the problems of bomber design at that time.

Chapter Five
Heavy Bombers Part II

ABOVE Vickers Armstrong Windsor prototype NK136. *Crown Copyright*

Specification B.8/41

Shorts 'Super Stirling'

In 1941 the growing strength of the Halifax and Lancaster ahead of the Stirling forced Shorts to consider a major development of its bomber; the result was a project often called the 'Super Stirling.'

Shorts S.36

The key element was the introduction of Centaurus CE.3.SM radials instead of the Hercules. The S.36 had redesigned wings and a longer fuselage which featured a large central bomb bay for various loads, including one 8,000lb (3,629kg) weapon; this represented a big improvement over the Stirling's individual bomb cells while six more wing cells could each take a 1,000lb (454kg) bomb. There were also changes to the empennage but a large proportion of the 'bits and pieces' used in the fuselage were retained. CRD described the new type as 'a typical night bomber having high useful load at a comparatively slow, economical cruising speed' (214mph [344km/h] at 15,000ft [4,572m], just 6mph [10km/h] more than the Stirling) but he recommended that a production order should be placed.

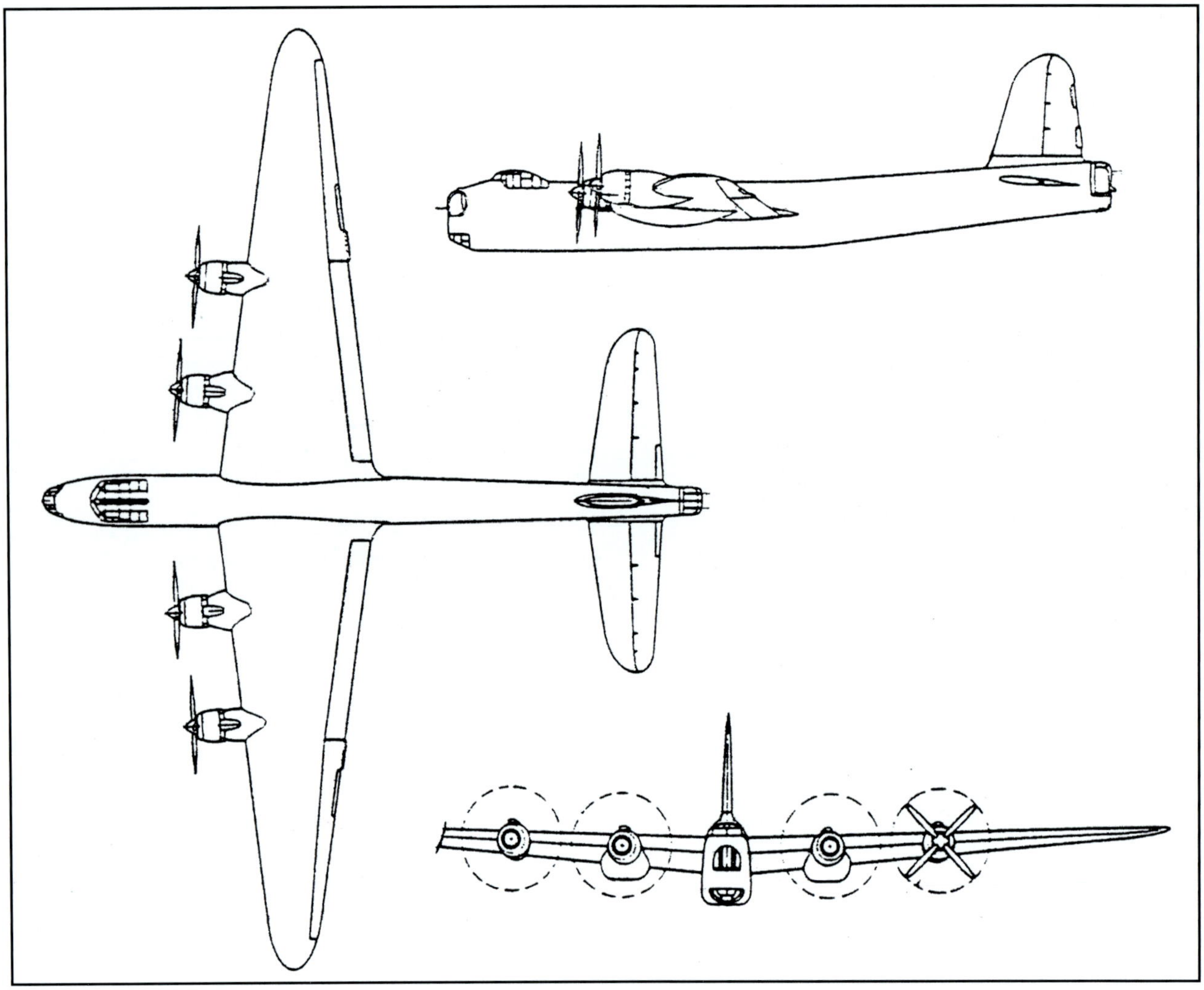

ABOVE **Shorts S.36 'Super Stirling' (15.7.41).**

The S.36 had a defensive armament of two 0.5in (12.7mm) machine guns in the nose, four more in both mid-upper and tail turrets plus an under turret with two 0.303in (7.7mm) machine guns. It was not seen as an all-new type, but shared a 'general similarity' to the Stirling.

The first estimates for what the designers called the 'Stirling III' were completed on 15 July 1941 and gave an all-up-weight of 103,100lb (46,765kg), and at 80,000lb (36,287kg) weight a top speed of 311mph (500km/h) at 20,000ft (6,096m) and a service ceiling of 29,300ft (8,931m). A month later Liptrot revised this to 105,000lb (47,627kg) and 295mph (475km/h) at 20,000ft (against 70,000lb [31,752kg] and 282mph [454km/h] at 12,500ft [3,810m] for the Stirling), but he considered the project 'to be well conceived and to be a logical next stage in the development of the heavy bomber.' The project was seen to have a similar take-off and flight performance to the Stirling but with much increased bomb load/range characteristics. Over 1,000 miles (1,609km) the S.36 could carry 23,500lb (10,659kg) of bombs against the Stirling's 14,000lb (6,350kg), and for 2,300 miles (3,701km) range it could take 10,000lb (4,536kg) against 4,500lb (2,041kg).

On 19 November Specification B.8/41 was raised to cover the project but, from the point of view of heavy bomber production, some within the Ministry were apprehensive about introducing the new type. The Controller General stated that the present Stirling was not designed for larger scale production as efficiently as the Halifax or Lancaster and it would be better to ask Handley Page or Avro to design a super bomber. However, on 27 December CRD declared that he wanted to order two B.8/41 prototypes as soon as possible, and on 9 January 1942 discussions between Messrs Gouge and McPhie of Shorts, DTD and CRD led to the decision to order two prototypes, the first without certain operational equipment but the second complete. Serials JR540 and JR543 were allotted to them and it was estimated that the first would fly in autumn 1943. Shorts was also told that it could prepare jigs for building twenty aircraft a month and an initial order for 150 was discussed.

On 11 May 1942 CinC Bomber Command, Air Marshal Sir Arthur

Harris, wrote that the B.8/41 was expected 'to eradicate the weakness of the present Stirling and with much bigger span wings should be a better aircraft. But the new potential given does not justify the change over – the switch will cost 126 Stirlings at Rochester plus a build ratio of two B.8/41s for three Stirlings. The best course is to concentrate on the Hercules VI Stirling which will go a long way to improving the really weak feature – its operating ceiling at weak mixture. The Hercules VI should push this up to 19,000ft [5,791m] from 16,000ft [4,877m] which is superior to the B.8/41.'

Two weeks later Shorts was told to cease work on the project, the Air Ministry having decided not to proceed with it. Four days later Gouge was told that the project was dead, the Air Staff having estimated that by the time the B.8/41 was in service, and taking into account the increases in additional weight that inevitably go on a new aircraft, the gain in performance and bomb load that it offered would be insufficient to justify the losses of standard production Stirlings. A further argument was that the Minister wanted the replacement for the RAF's contemporary heavy bombers to be limited to a single type. On 5 August 1942, after further consideration, Shorts decided not to proceed with the investigation, but it would continue with the addition of the split flap to the Gouge flap to minimise drag for landing. Quite an amount of work had already been done on this feature using the S.31 half-scale Stirling and the results were very promising.

Shorts S.36 'Super Stirling' (7.41 onwards)	
Span	135ft 9in (41.38m)
Length	101ft 0in (30.78m)
Wing Area	2,145sq.ft (199.27sq.m)
All-Up-Weight	104,000lb (47,174kg)
Powerplant	2 × 2,000+hp (1,491kW) Centaurus CE.3.SM
Max Speed/Height	311mph (500km/h) at 20,000ft (6,096m)
Armament	23,500lb (10,659kg) bombs, 10 × 0.5in (12.7mm) plus 2 × 0.303in (7.7mm) machine guns

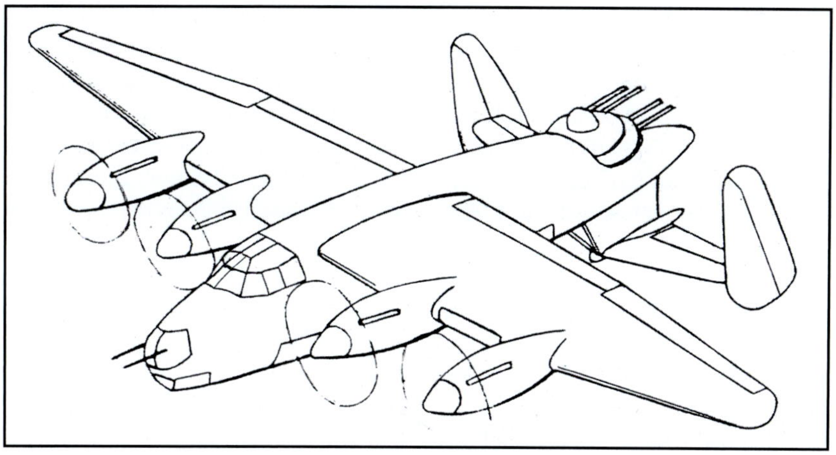

ABOVE Sketch of the Westland Delanne bomber possibly prepared to B.8/41 (10.41). *Westland Archive*

Westland 'B.8/41'

It is thought that a heavy bomber design produced by Westland in October 1941 was also drawn to Specification B.8/41. This was one of the company's Delanne efforts and was powered by four 1,500hp (1,119kW) Griffons. Span was 113ft (34.44m), all-up-weight 70,000lb (31,752kg), wing area 1,275sq.ft (118.45sq.m) and cruise speed 300mph (483km/h) at 20,000ft (6,096m), and the defensive armament included a nose turret with two machine guns and a four-cannon rear turret. The Delanne wing arrangement featured on a number of Westland's wartime projects, the rear wing having an area of 50% of the mainplane. Both acted as lifting surfaces and the idea was to give the aircraft a large range of CofG.

Vickers-Armstrongs Windsor

The final piston-engine bomber to be built and flown by Vickers was also the company's last bomber to use geodetic construction. This story of this aircraft, however, the Windsor, begins with a twin-engine medium bomber design.

Vickers Medium Bomber

Between April and June 1942, following discussions with DTD on a proposed replacement for the Wellington Mk.X, Vickers chief designer Rex Pierson produced a set of brochures for a twin-engine slim-fuselage high-speed medium bomber. These were based on the requirements of both B.11/41 and the Bristol Buckingham production specification (Chapter Three) and the first brochure was completed on 22 April. It defined a project (Scheme 'A') with five crew, a 4,000lb (1,814kg) bomb load, 1,600 miles (2,575km) range, a single fin and, for defence, a twin 0.5in (12.7mm) remotely-controlled turret placed in the rear of each engine nacelle. Rate of climb at sea level was 1,950ft/min (594m/min), time to 25,000ft (7,620m) 22.0 minutes and service ceiling 33,400ft (10,180m). Geodetic construction would have been used and 955gal (4,341lit) of fuel carried. The primary powerplant was the Bristol Centaurus VII, but the 1,640bhp (1,223kW) Rolls-Royce Griffon 61 was an alternative which gave a total weight of 33,510lb (15,200kg), a maximum speed (at mean weight) of 390mph (628km/h) at 26,500ft (8,077m), sea level rate of climb 1,700ft/min (518m/min), 27 minutes to 26,500ft and service ceiling 33,000ft (10,058m).

This brochure was never issued because on 6 May 1942 the design was refined for MAP's Capt Liptrot; Scheme 'B' was essentially the same design but had extra defence in the form of four more guns in a solid nose. On 26 May DOR declared that the proposal was unacceptable because it had neither the speed required for an unarmed bomber nor adequate armament as an armed bomber. Shortly afterwards Scheme 'C' was drawn which was a heavy bomber version powered by four Merlin 61s. The all-up-weight of this project was 55,000lb (24,948kg), maximum load 8,000lb (3,629kg) of bombs, maximum speed 385mph (620km/h) and cruise 330mph (531km/h), both at 23,000ft (7,010m), and range with a 4,000lb (1,814kg) load 1,600 miles (2,575km). MAP suggested that four Merlins fitted to a larger airframe might give a higher speed and allow a bigger bomb load, which would be attractive if it was operated primarily in Europe.

On 2 June Wilfrid Freeman appraised these projects and also observed that Vickers must not go on building the Wellington forever. In 1944 the Mk.X would be obsolete but Vickers was committed to geodetics and was, therefore, unable to build any other design but its own. Vickers' factories were laid out for geodetic construction and it was felt essential that a new type should be suited to this form in order to avoid a great loss of productive effort. Scheme 'A' was only a small step forward in bomb load and defence over the Wellington while Scheme 'B' had an improved defence but much the same bomb load. In performance, 'A' was much better than the Wellington and roughly equivalent to the Buckingham but was inferior to both in armament – the four 0.5in (12.7mm) remotely-controlled guns behind the engines were 'a most conspicuous disadvantage' which, owing to the size of the fuselage and the balance of the aircraft, would preclude any additional guns being added later.

Scheme 'B' had started as a heavy twin but could soon become overloaded by additions to its weight during building and in service, while 'C' showed a considerable improvement over the Lancaster in speed and had a tail turret with four 0.5in guns, but it was a little down in bomb load and range. Freeman felt the balance of advantage seemed to lie with 'C' which had a better bomb load and potential range than either 'A' or 'B', coupled with a greater reserve to allow for development and additional weight. The four-engine model resulted in a heavy instead of a medium bomber and would be a logical line of progress and he recommended that the Wellington X should be replaced by a heavy along the lines of Scheme 'C'.

Vickers' final twin-engine proposal was formulated and submitted on 9 June 1942. The basic layout was still the original design but it now had twin fins, plus dorsal and ventral turrets to replace the nacelle guns; Scheme 'D' had the original glass nose, 'E' the four extra nose guns. The same engines were used and the Centaurus variant weighed 37,300lb (16,919kg), carried a maximum 8,000lb (3,629kg) of bombs, and with a 4,000lb (1,814kg) load had a range of 1,550 miles (2,494km). The project was seen in some eyes as a geodetic version of the Bristol Buckingham. Pierson visited Filton to look at the Buckingham mock-up and

BELOW Vickers High-Speed Medium Bomber 'Scheme A' with defensive guns in the engine nacelles (4.42). *Eric Morgan*

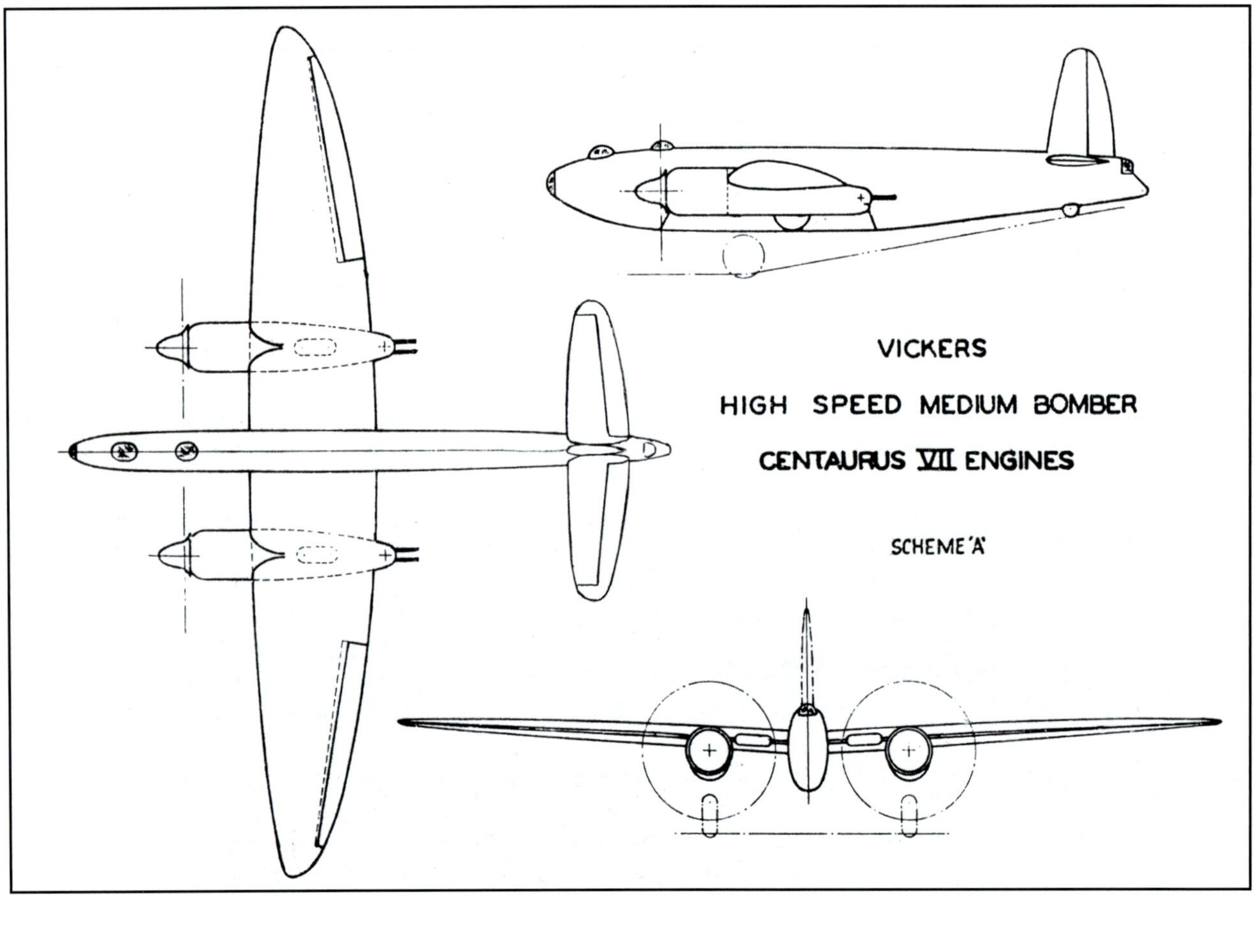

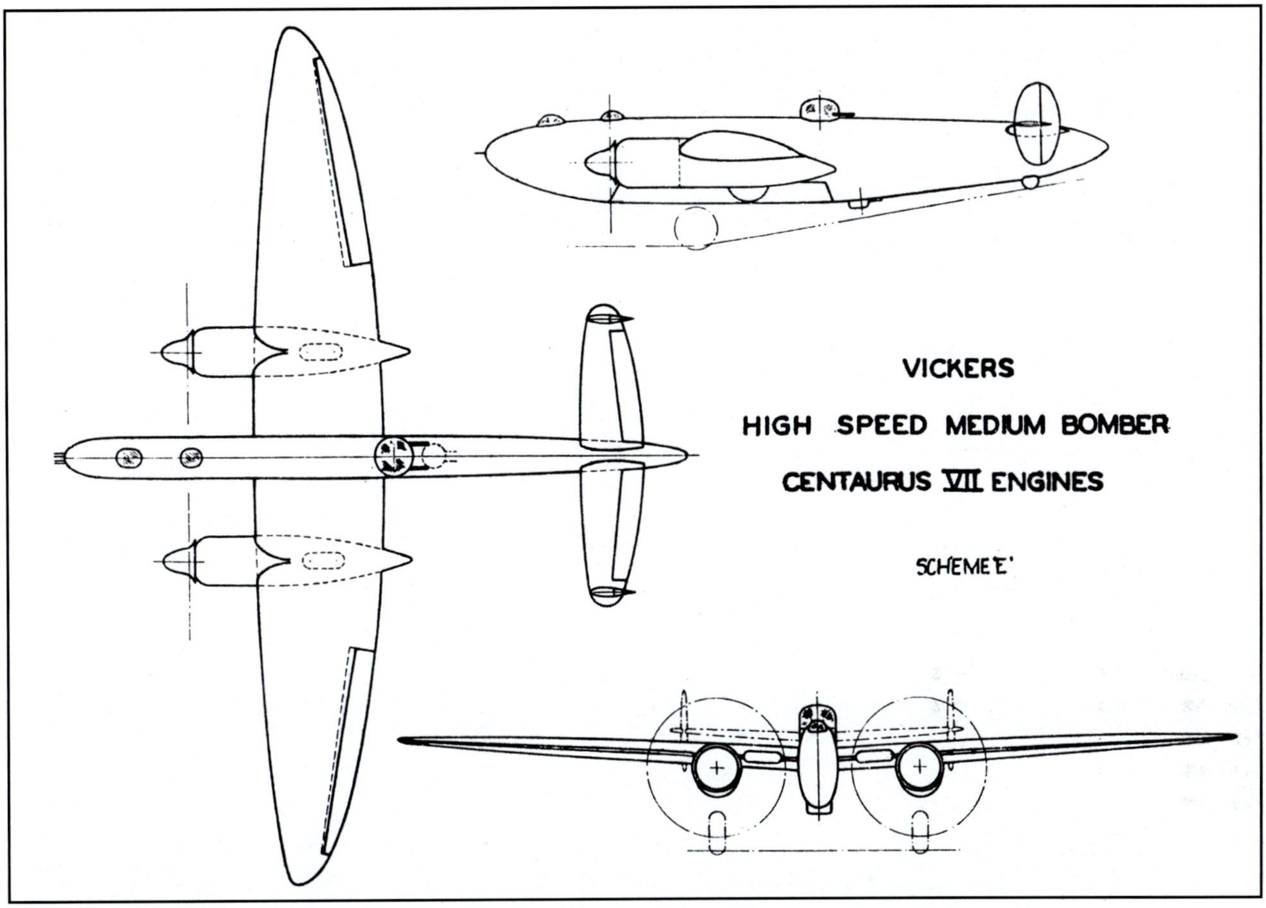

ABOVE Vickers High-Speed Medium Bomber 'Scheme E' with defensive guns in dorsal and ventral turrets and in the nose (3.5.42). *Eric Morgan*

the Centaurus installation while Bristol also supplied some Buckingham data, but no orders were forthcoming. The Air Ministry had quite liked the Wellington replacement but suddenly changed its requirements to a four-engine type. However, Vickers was already working on a high-altitude bomber with four Merlins to B.5/41 and the draft drawings indicated that the basic layout of its twin-engine medium bomber could be incorporated into the larger aircraft.

Vickers Medium Bomber (22.4.42)	
Span	80ft 0in (24.38m)
Length	59ft 0in (17.98m)
Wing Area	790sq.ft (73.39sq.m)
All-Up-Weight	35,500lb (16,103kg)
Powerplant	2 × 2,150hp (1,603kW) Centaurus VII
Max Speed/Height	392mph (631km/h) at 25,000ft (7,620m)
Armament	4,000lb (1,814kg) bombs, 4 × 0.5in (12.7mm) machine guns

Vickers 433 Warwick III

The Wellington Mk.V was an experimental variant of Vickers' successful medium bomber fitted with a pressure cabin and, as the development work on it matured in late 1940, the Air Staff became interested in a comparable pressurised version of the Warwick. Draft proposals from Vickers were prepared and discussed at the Ministry and on 9 January 1941 Lord Beaverbrook wrote 'High altitude bombers are to be developed intensively. I wish you to undertake this work. The Wellington V is to be fully developed with Hercules and Merlin engines (with the Merlin to take precedence) [and] the B.1/35 [Warwick] is to have a pressure cabin; the work is to be pursued urgently.' Detailed proposals were submitted to the Ministry in May and during the initial stages the project was known as the Warwick Mk.III. The fuselage was very similar to the Mk.V Wellington but the standard Warwick wings were replaced by an elliptical wing and four Merlin LX engines with ducted wing radiators. The cabin accommodated three crew and there was also a separate pressurised tail turret containing four 0.303in (7.7mm) machine guns and its gunner. The aircraft was predicted to have a range of 2,000 miles (3,219km) with 8,000lb (3,629kg) of bombs; at the end of its mission the service ceiling would be 43,500ft (13,259m).

Vickers Medium Bomber (9.6.42)	
Span	c80ft 0in (24.38m)
Length	c59ft 0in (17.98m)
Wing Area	c790sq.ft (73.39sq.m)
All-Up-Weight	37,300lb (16,919kg)
Powerplant	2 × 2,150hp (1,603kW) Centaurus VII
Max Speed/Height	353mph (568km/h) at 23,500ft (7,163m)
Armament	8,000lb (3,629kg) bombs, 4 × 0.5in (12.7mm) machine guns

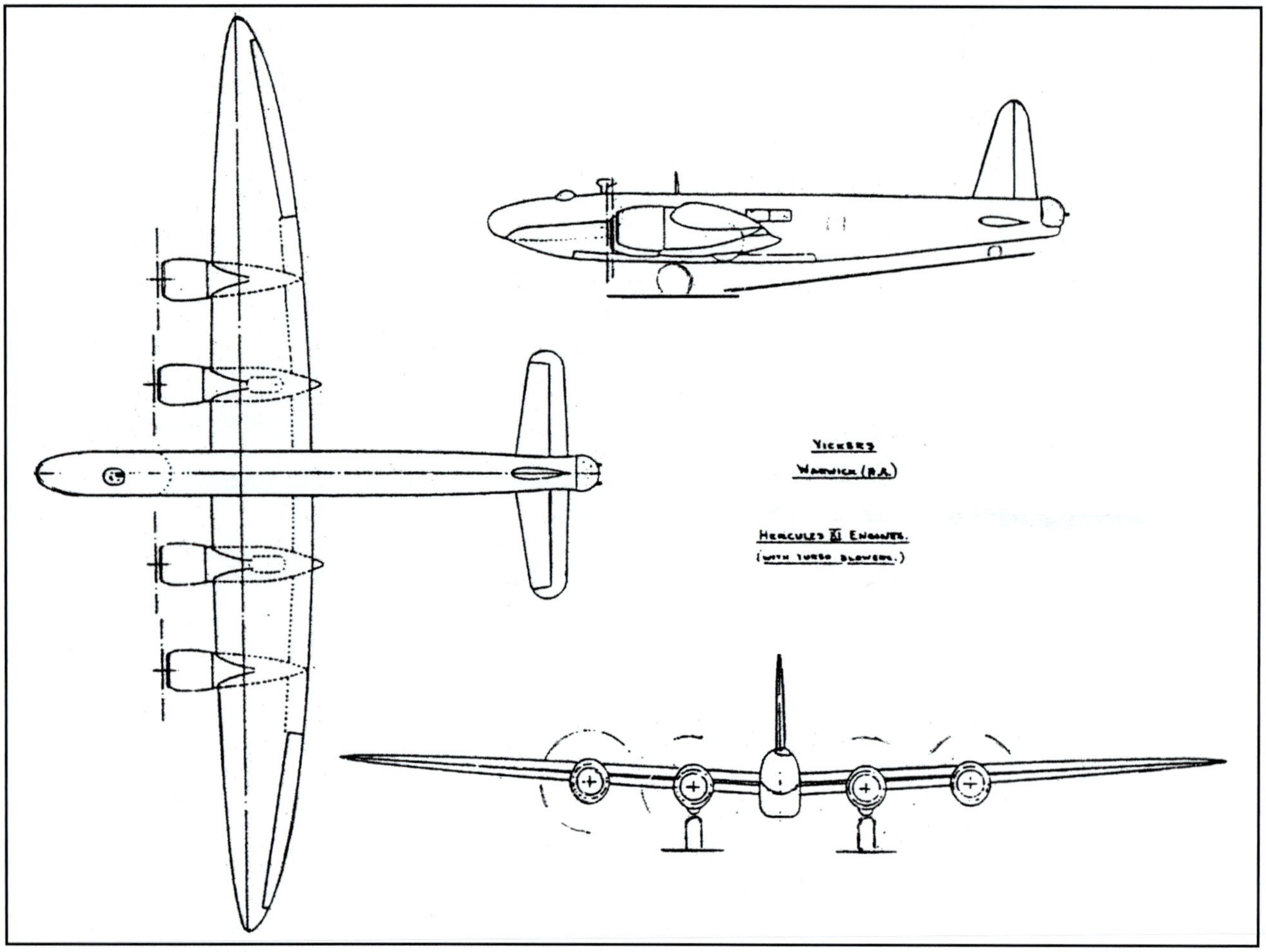

ABOVE The first Vickers Warwick Mk.III proposal, with four Merlins, was dated 3 May 1941. This version with Hercules XIs and turbo-blowers was drawn on 21 July 1941. *Eric Morgan*

In July a contract was placed for two prototypes, DW506 and DW512 both with four Merlin 60s, and in October Specification B.5/41 was drafted to cover the design. This called for a pressure cabin bomber with a maximum speed of not less than 345mph (555km/h) at 31,000ft (9,449m) and service ceiling of not less than 38,500ft (11,735m); the bomb load was to be 8,000lb (3,629kg). The B.5/41 had a much larger pressure cabin than the Wellington and on 13 July DTD wrote 'the immediate objective is to introduce this new type as a high-speed bomber, at oxygen heights and without pressure, into production as rapidly as possible.' A Design Conference was held on 8 October and the project continued with mock-up work and model experiments until 16 September 1942, when it was axed because of the appearance of a new bomber design to Specification B.3/42 and a consequent rearrangement of contracts. This later design was described as a Lancaster replacement and removed the high-altitude performance requirements.

Vickers 433 Warwick Mk.III (3.5.41)	
Span	117ft 0in (35.66m)
Length	76ft 1in (23.19m)
Wing Area	1,245sq.ft (115.66sq.m)
All-Up-Weight	52,500lb (23,814kg)
Powerplant	4 × 1,200hp (895kW) Merlin LX
Max Speed/Height	366mph (589km/h) at 31,000ft (9,449m)
Armament	8,000lb (3,629kg) bombs, 4 × 0.303in (7.7mm) machine guns

Vickers 447 Windsor

The B.3/42 resulted from the merger of the B.5/41 and the twin-engine Wellington replacement project. Vickers declared that it could not do the four-engine type at the required weight, so the weight limitations were dropped and it then became possible to combine the two designs. It was also possible to 'lift' most of Vickers' work on the B.5/41 into the B.3/42 since the new design had the same engines and wings but a different fuselage (for example a great deal of the calculations could be applied); however, all of the work on the pressure cabin was wasted. Vickers called the project its Type 447 and, for stressing purposes, B.3/42 requested a maximum speed of 350mph (563km/h) EAS.

The two prototypes, which retained the original serials, were to be joined by two more, MP829 and MP832 ordered on 4 July 1942 (in fact these were never built). The B.3/42 Mock-Up Conference took place on 29 and 30 October; another prototype, NK136, was ordered on 10 December; and on 1 January 1943 J. E. Serby

ABOVE W5798 was a Mk.VI Vickers Wellington fitted with a pressure cabin in the nose for flight at high altitude. *Phil Butler*

BELOW DR484 was another high-altitude Mk.VI Wellington. This particular aircraft had its tail turret removed. *Phil Butler*

notified Vickers of the extension of the contract to include the prototypes plus two pre-production aircraft (NN670 and NN673). This was followed on 21 April by a production order for 300 aeroplanes to be built at Weybridge and in the autumn the new bomber was called the Windsor B.Mk.I. The first prototype DW506 made its maiden flight on 23 October 1943, but the first two machines had to be limited to 55,000lb (24,948kg) all-up-weight because they had been too far advanced in construction for the additional strengthening to be incorporated that would take them up to B.3/42 standards.

The bomber's defensive armament was the subject of extensive investigation and controversy. In August 1942 a combination was established of two fixed 0.303in (7.7mm) machine guns in the nose plus two 20mm cannon in a turret at the extreme rear of the fuselage. In due course, however, the tail turret was dispensed with and the vacant position used as a sighting and control station for two barbettes, one at the rear of each outer engine nacelle, which each contained two rearward-firing 20mm guns. This later arrangement was officially adopted on 15 February 1943 and in 1944 the second Warwick prototype, L9704, was used to test it, but with 0.5in (12.7mm) machine guns fitted in lieu of the 20mm. In April 1944 it was also decided to provide stations for amidships beam guns as supplementary armament.

Initially the barbettes were to be fitted to the fourth Windsor but these were brought forward to go on NK136, which had now become the third prototype. This aircraft, known as the Type 461 and powered by Merlin 65s, was to be the only other Windsor to fly after DW406 and DW412 (on 11 July 1944) and it was much closer to the production standard; the remotely-controlled guns were not fitted until 1945 but they were used in firing tests until 1946. The weight of the barbettes raised problems over the aeroplane's CofG and the favoured solution was an extended nose. The single pilot cockpit also caused controversy because, in an emergency, access to the pilot's station by another crew member was near impossible. As a result on 16 August 1944 a drawing was produced showing the Windsor with a new nose based on an RAE 'Lancaster' design; here a seated bomb aimer controlled a twin 0.5in (12.7mm) turret behind which came the pilot's cockpit with side-by-side seating. All-up-weight was now 80,000lb (36,288kg).

ABOVE **The Vickers Type 447 Windsor prototype was DW506 seen here. It was powered by four Merlin 65 engines.**

BELOW AND OPPOSITE **The third Windsor prototype NK136 featured different engine cowlings and carried defensive guns in the rear of the outer nacelles.** *David O'Neill*

It was expected that the Windsor, starting at some 75,000lb (34,019kg) all-up-weight, would be capable of development to something approaching 84,000lb (38,102kg), when the Mk.IV Lancaster (the Lincoln described on page 137) would probably reach the limit of its development at 75,000lb. The Windsor was 10mph to 20mph (16km/h to 32km/h) faster than the Lancaster IV and, with a maximum 12,000lb (5,443kg) load, had a 490 mile (789km) range excess. To meet the long-range requirements of the Pacific War, in spring 1944 Vickers submitted a proposal to extend the Windsor's still air range with 4,000lb (1,814kg) of bombs to 4,000 miles (6,437km), which involved sacrificing most of the armour protection and some of the self-sealing material from the fuel tanks; the company stated that this version could be delivered from the start of Windsor production.

In April 1944 it was expected that Windsor production should begin in mid-1945 and during 1946 work up to a peak of forty per month. It was hoped that by mid-1947 thirty squadrons would be equipped with the type, mostly for operations in the Japanese theatre, but VCAS doubted, with its present armament, that the bomber would be suitable for that arena. Eventually the defensive armament problem, together with several other delays, meant that by the end of the war the Windsor was not offering a sufficient advance for production to proceed. In November 1944 the order for 300 machines was cut to 100, and later to just 40. Then on 17 November 1945, at a Ministry production meeting, the surviving B.Mk.Is were cancelled. On 23 November Vickers was told that 'the manufacture of Windsor aircraft should cease immediately.' At this point NN670 was almost complete and NN673 well advanced and both were eventually reduced to produce.

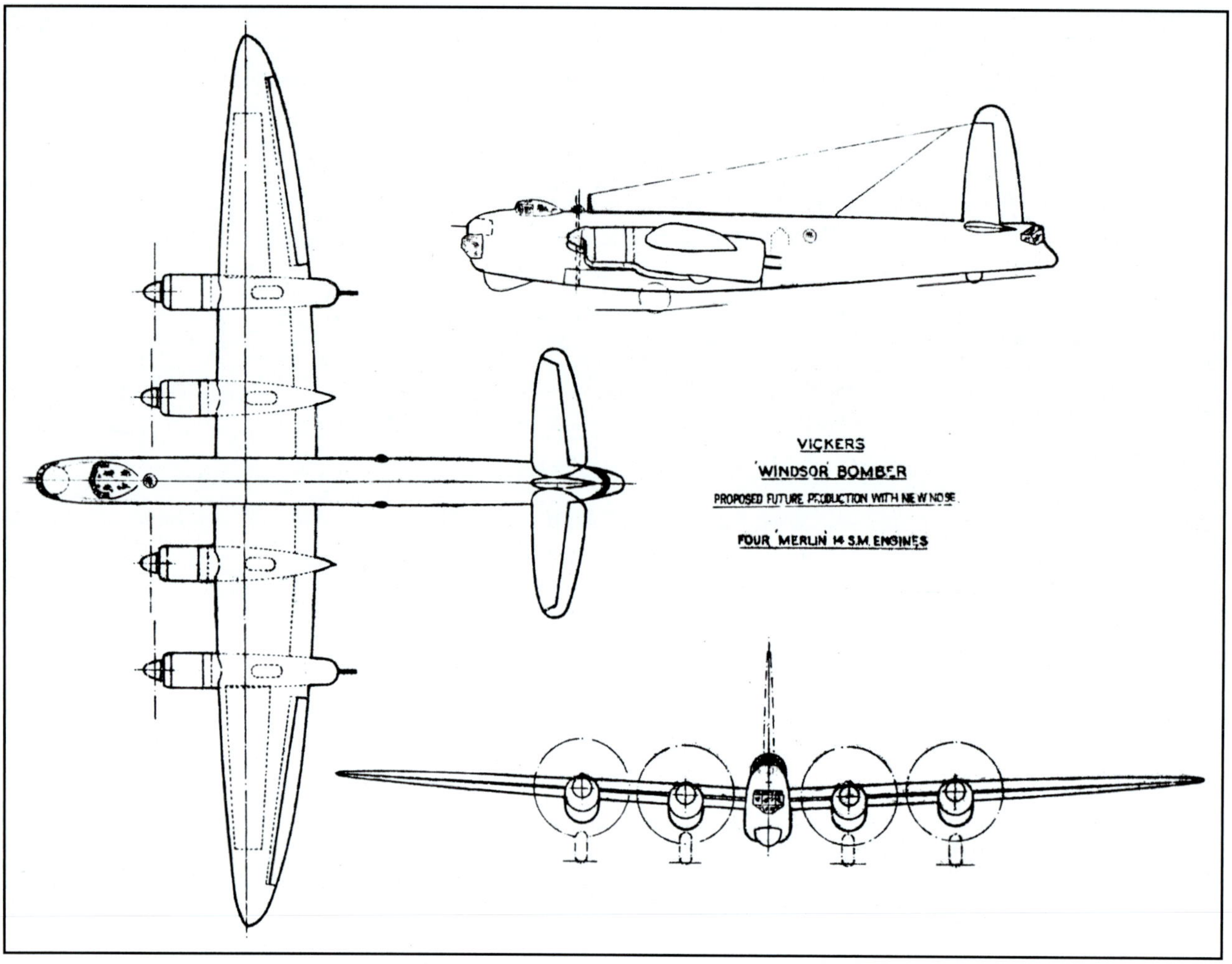

ABOVE The 'production' Windsor, complete with alternative nose (16.8.44). *Eric Morgan*

The Windsor was originally designed as a replacement for the obsolescent Wellington and was to be an aircraft that could take its place in the first line alongside the Lancaster and Halifax; its development life would also extend well beyond either of these types. As originally conceived the Windsor was a fast, lightly-armed and comparatively heavily armoured night bomber which was to carry a moderate load of 4,000lb (1,814kg) at a maximum cruise speed of 330mph (531km/h) but, when it became clear that it would be needed for the Pacific, the debate centred on just how suitable it might be. In its initial stages the type was found to be not sufficiently in advance of the Lancaster IV in range or general performance to justify the Ministry's plans to employ it actively in the war against Japan; it was also thought undesirable to introduce a new type in this theatre until it had been fully tried out in the UK.

BELOW Wind tunnel model of the 'production' Windsor.

Vickers 447 Windsor (3rd Prototype)	
Span	117ft 2in (35.71m)
Length	76ft 10in (23.42m)
Wing Area	1,248sq.ft (115.94sq.m)
All-Up-Weight	72,000lb (32,659kg)
Powerplant	4 × 1,750hp (1,305kW) Merlin 85
Max Speed/Height	c360mph (579km/h) at 21,000ft (6,401m)
Armament	12,000lb (5,443kg) bombs (B.Mk.I), 4 × 20mm cannon

Interest in the Windsor had gradually waned, Vickers became increasingly involved in the commercial aviation field and it was to be the Lincoln which entered production to serve the post-war RAF. The RAF also evaluated two American bombers, the Boeing B-29 Superfortress and the Consolidated B-32 Dominator, and at one point it was keen to have the B-29. In fact there were proposals to build the B-29 in Britain but this never happened. The RAF had to settle with the Lincoln as its main post-war heavy bomber until examples of the B-50 Washington, an upgrade of the B-29, were acquired in 1951.

Vickers Windsor Developments

A Rolls-Royce Griffon-powered Windsor had been considered by Rex Pierson and his team for some time but numerous difficulties, especially concerning weight, had shown such a project to be inferior to the Merlin-powered aircraft. Finally, in December 1944 Pierson produced a brochure for a Griffon Windsor fitted with four-blade 13ft 0in (3.96m) diameter propellers. The dimensions are unknown but presumed to be similar to the Merlin-powered machine. Internal fuel totalled 2,954gal (13,429lit) but this could be increased to 3,380gal (15,365lit) with 'reinforcing fuel' carried in the bomb compartment, and the range with 8,000lb (3,629kg) bombs on board was 2,500 miles (4,023km) when flying at at 230mph (370km/h). Rate of climb at 79,000lb (35,834kg) weight was 1,380ft/min (421m/min) at sea level and service ceiling 30,000ft (9,144m). On 2 November 1944, as the brochure was being prepared, Pierson wrote to N. E. Rowe, DTD, stating 'You will note that the maximum cruising speed is 322mph [518km/h], compared with 300mph [483km/h] for the Merlin with an increase in power plane weight of 2,000lb [907kg] and a corresponding increase in all-up weight, but retaining the same load factor. The ranges with the different engines was within 0.5%. It is anticipated the Griffons will be available to install in the fifth prototype machine in the middle of 1945 and this will mean that the fourth prototype and first batch of production machines will have the Merlin 100 engines.' An alternative Bristol Centaurus installation took the weight to 81,400lb (36,922kg) but reduced the ceiling to 27,000ft (8,230m).

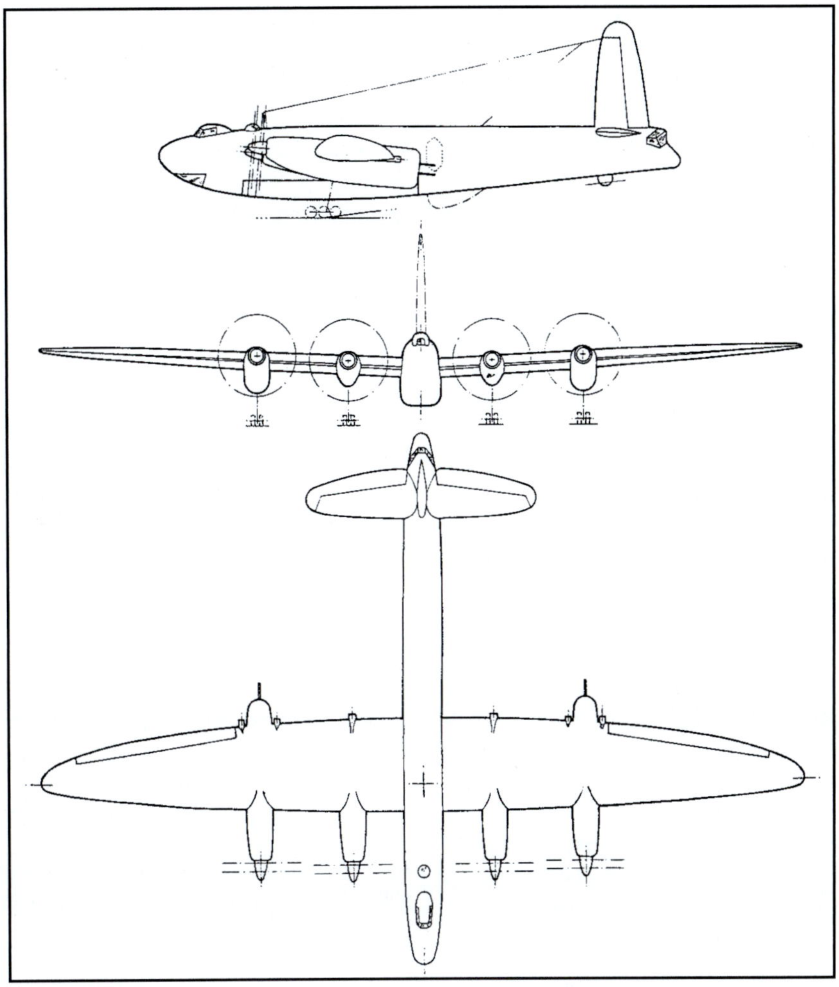

ABOVE Vickers drawing showing the Windsor fitted with four Rolls-Royce Clyde turboprop engines (11.44).

Vickers Windsor with Griffon engines (12.44)	
Maximum Loaded Weight	79,000lb (35,834kg)
Powerplant	4 × 2,070hp (1,544kW) Griffon RG.26SM
Max Speed/Height	382mph (615km/h) at 23,000ft (7,010m) at 65,500lb (29,710kg) weight
Armament	Maximum 12,000lb (5,443kg) bombs, 4 × 20mm guns in engine nacelle barbettes

In January 1945 Rex Pierson completed another brochure for a Windsor development, this time powered by four Rolls-Royce Clyde RCl.1.AC turboprop engines and fitted with four main undercarriage legs of a six-wheel bogie type then in the course of development. Visibly the airframe was unchanged, with a Windsor prototype nose, and only the engine nacelles had been altered; the rear nacelle guns were also retained. Cruise speed was estimated to be 390mph (628km/h) at 20,000ft (6,096m), sea level rate of climb 3,050ft/min (930m/min), time to 30,000ft (9,144m) 17.0 minutes and service ceiling 37,000ft (11,278m). A maximum 3,580gal (16,275lit) of internal fuel would have been carried and the range was 2,415 miles (3,887km). The Clyde turboprop, an example of a new concept of a jet engine and a propeller joined together, offered a combined

3,020bhp (2,252kW) and 1,225lb (5.4kN) of thrust at sea level and 3,310bhp (2,468kW) and 738lb (3.3kN) for maximum speed and climb. Contra-rotating propellers would have been fitted if they were available.

The extra power from the Clyde would have been very beneficial to the bomber, which was designated Type 601 Windsor B.Mk.II. In view of the attractive performance offered by the engine MAP informed Vickers on 27 February 1945 that it had been decided to fit NN673 with the new powerplant and asked that design work should proceed as soon as possible. Two more production Windsors were to be similarly converted (the same letter also stated that the idea of fitting the Griffon had been abandoned). Pierson replied that NN673 should be flying with Merlins by January 1946, but added that Rolls-Royce had reported that Clyde units would not be available until April 1946. By June 1945 this version had been given the revised 'ideal' nose with the twin 0.5in (12.7mm) turret, but the conversion and the whole project was cancelled on 16 January 1946.

Vickers 601 Windsor B.Mk.II (1.45)	
Span	117ft 2in (35.71m)
Length	77ft 8in (23.67m)
Wing Area	1,248sq.ft (115.94sq.m)
All-Up-Weight	79,800lb (36,197kg)
Powerplant	4 × 3,020hp (2,252kW) and 1,225lb (5.4kN) thrust Clyde RCl.1.AC
Max Speed/Height	409mph (658km/h) at 30,000ft (9,144m)
Armament	12,000lb (5,443kg) bombs, 4 × 20mm cannon

Giant Bombers

In 1937 Vickers produced a scheme for an aircraft of 180,000lb (81,647kg) all-up-weight and fitted with wings 7ft (2.13m) deep which carried all of its load in the wings. It was primarily intended to be a passenger carrier operating at 'normal' altitudes but a bomber variant was also shown. By July 1940 the scheme had become a high-altitude aircraft which had wings of normal depth with the bomb load transferred to the fuselage, and in November the proposals were submitted to Lord Beaverbrook. The first descriptive brochure was completed in January 1941 and forwarded to MAP and other officials.

Vickers Long-Range High-Altitude Bomber

Intended to undertake stratospheric bombing, this aircraft was expected to carry just one heavy bomb weighing 10 tons (22,400lb/10,160kg). Barnes Wallis at Vickers had realised that a single very heavy bomb could prove devastatingly destructive when dropped accurately but, as has been well documented, it took a great deal of effort to bring his ideas to fruition (in the form of the 6 ton [6,096kg] 'Tallboy' and 10 ton 'Grand Slam' bombs). In the event the Lancaster was adapted to carry these weapons but in the concept's early days it was thought that no current type would be capable of lifting them high and far enough to be effective. Consequently Wallis and Vickers had conceived this huge aeroplane to deliver the weapon; some accounts state that Wallis called it his 'Victory Bomber'.

It was intended to climb to its cruising height in the vicinity of its home base where the existing defence facilities and guns would be available; consequently the bomber's own defence was limited to a four-gun rear turret remotely controlled from the pressure cabin. Five crew were housed in this cabin, which formed the front portion of the fuselage, and the air pressure was maintained at a value corresponding to 10,000ft (3,048m) altitude by a blower driven by one of the engines (six Merlin RM.6.SM), which was triplicated for safety. At a take-off weight of 104,000lb (47,174kg), including the single bomb plus 4,020gal (18,275lit) of fuel, the aircraft would cruise at 40,000ft (12,192m) at a mean speed of 306mph (492km/h) on the outward trip and

BELOW A version of the Vickers High-Altitude Bomber was drawn with six Hercules VIII power units and no defensive guns (3.41). *Eric Morgan*

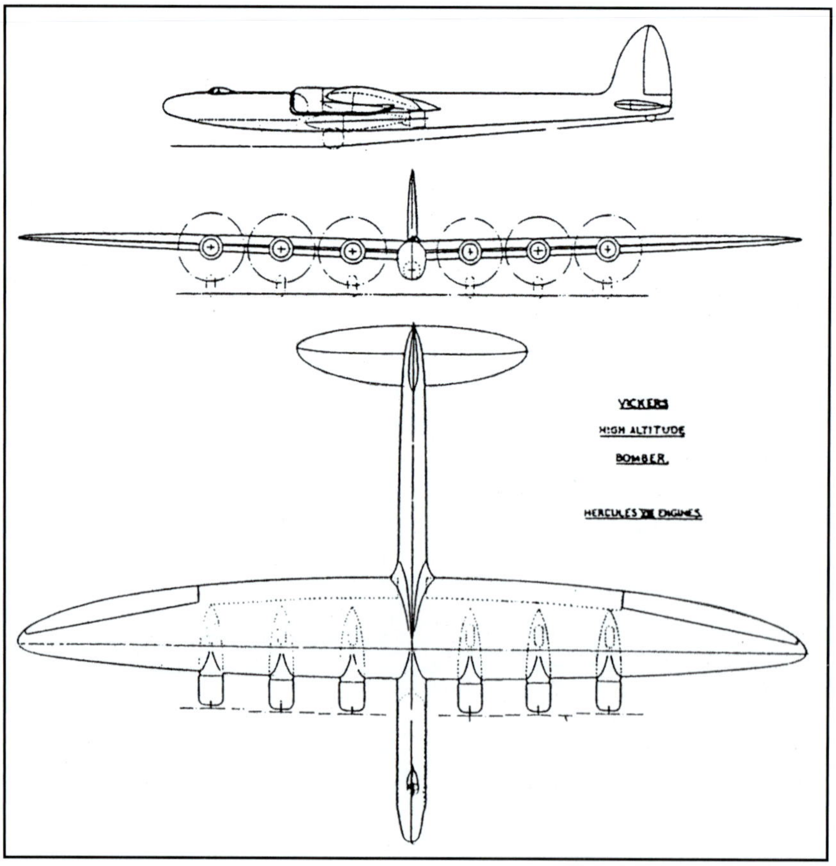

350mph (563km/h) on the return. At this weight the maximum rate of climb was 1,200ft/min (366m/min) at 10,750ft (3,277m), time to 35,000ft (10,668m) 37 minutes and radius of action 1,800 miles (2,897km) (that is, a range of 3,600 miles [5,794km]).

On 9 January 1941 Beaverbrook wrote to Vickers to suggest that, subject to certain high-altitude work taking preference, the company should continue its research into a 50 ton (50,802kg) six-engine bomber. On the 30th Sir Henry Tizard visited Weybridge to discuss Vickers' design programme and on 4 February W. S. Farren, DTD, met Wallis and Pierson to see an outline of their scheme. On the 9th Tizard and DGRD agreed that Vickers should be given an order and in March Farren proposed the allocation of a contract to allow the building of prototypes on a special step-by-step basis. Two machines were planned with the work probably to be undertaken in stages – 1) project design, 2) commencement of detailing in the Main Drawing Office and 3) release of drawings to the Experimental Shop for manufacture and assembly, but Vickers would not be permitted to go on to the next stage without authorisation from the Ministry. Farren added that it must not interfere with work of higher priority and, although in favour of the project, he was doubtful about the big bomb. Evidence then being collected on the damage to towns and factories from bombing raids did not support the concept beyond a size of 4,000lb (1,814kg).

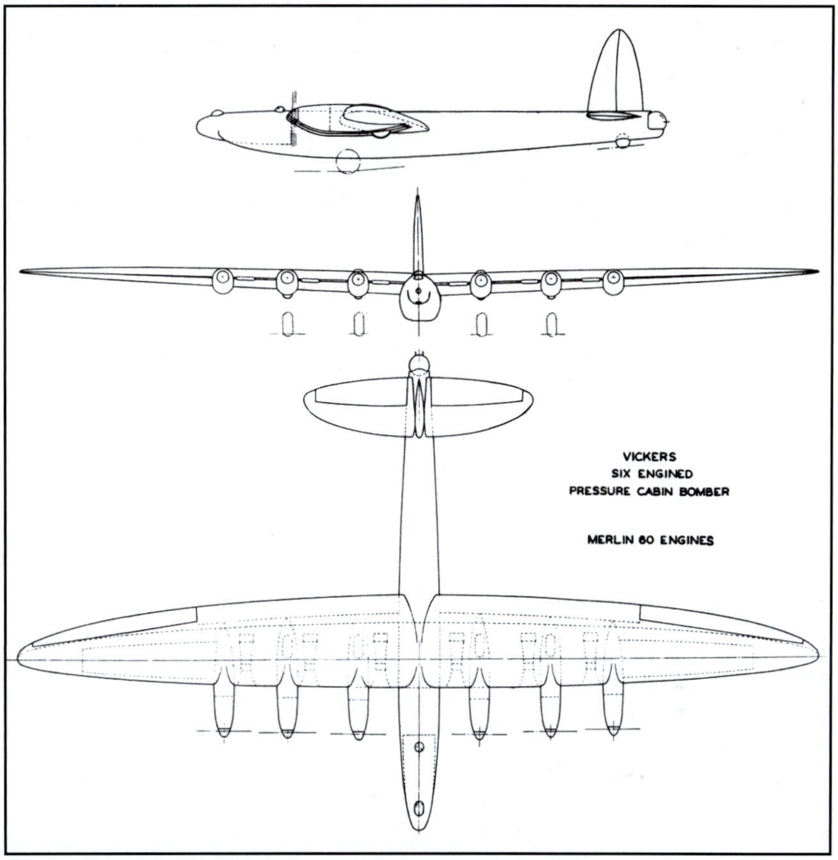

ABOVE Vickers High-Altitude Bomber at 1.42. *Eric Morgan*

Wallis pushed hard for his bomb and bomber. His objective was to produce a high velocity bomb of special streamlined shape and fineness ratio which could hit its target with great accuracy. In addition, because it was dropped from a great height, the substantial kinetic energy that would be generated at impact should produce a deep penetration. Wallis had calculated that a 16,000lb (7,257kg) HV bomb with a 9,000lb (4,082kg) explosive charge, when released from an altitude of 40,000ft (12,192m), would reach at impact the supersonic velocity of 1,400ft/sec (427m/sec), and give a penetration in sandy soil of approximately 100ft (30.48m).

BELOW Wind tunnel model of the Vickers High-Altitude Bomber.

On 20 May 1941, in a letter to Tizard, Wallis had assumed that the opposition to the 50 ton bomber was based on 'the reluctance of the Air Staff to order anything in the nature of a special purpose machine,' along with the feeling that its development period would be prohibitively long. Wallis felt that while the Air Staff's preference for all-purpose bombers up to the present time was unquestionably right, it was this policy which made the production time for a large bomber so great. This was due to the detail design and manufacture of the multifarious installations taking longer than that for the design and construction of the airframe itself, but Wallis thought that confining the design to one bomb with a single electrical circuit should reduce the development period by many months. As laid down the aircraft would involve as little new design as possible. The engine installation was six Wellington V units (with provision for alternatives such as four Centaurus); the undercarriages were the same as the Warwick but four would be used instead of two; the pressure cabin could be adapted from the Warwick or Wellington V; and the wing followed almost exactly that of the high-altitude Warwick III – there was little 'novelty' except in the tail unit.

Next day Tizard replied saying that 'the Air Staff has no interest in a specialised big bomber solely designed to carry one big bomb and your view that the single purpose bomber offers a high probability of winning the war is not accepted .... but I may say that I entirely agree with it. I would be far more interested in the development of the big bomber if there was real elasticity in its use and [if] you told me .... that you hoped to design it so that it could provide either for taking one large single bomb or for taking a very heavy total weight of smaller bombs. Please confirm this – it makes a great deal of difference to my interest in your proposals.'

Wallis had also put together a large report called 'A Note on a Method for Attacking the Axis Powers' which examined every aspect of bombs and bombing very closely, and his theories for large bombs. On 23 September 1941 Dr David Pye, DSR, informed Wallis that the document had been carefully reviewed by MAP in consultation with the Air Staff and it had been decided that no development work should be undertaken at the present time. On the same day DTD told Vickers that at present no development was to be undertaken on the large bomb and it was not proposed to proceed with the large bomber; the Minister had declared that in the current circumstances it was not justified.

However, Vickers kept the research ticking over and in January 1942 completed a brochure which recorded all of the latest work on performance and weight estimation. The aircraft was now designed to carry 32,000lb (14,515kg) of bombs over 2,000 miles (3,218km) or 16,000lb (7,257kg) over 4,000 miles (6,437km), and the ceilings over the target would be 43,500ft (13,259m) and 45,300ft (13,807m) respectively; Tizard's wish for alternative loads had also been addressed. Cruise speeds out were 272mph (438km/h) and 291mph (468km/h) respectively and 338mph (544km/h) and 334mph (538km/h) on the return journey while the ceiling on return would be 50,750ft (15,469m). Six Merlin 60s were still used and the rated height using the 'S' blower had increased from 30,000ft (9,144m) to 37,000ft (11,278m). It was thought that the only enemy aircraft likely to be encountered were fighters with forward-firing guns and so any attack would be expected from the rear hemisphere, thus the defence was still just a tail turret but this now had two 0.5in (12.7mm) machine guns and its own pressurised cell for the gunner.

Directly after the completion of this revision Vickers received notification from MAP, in the form of an official letter dated 9 January 1942, that it should stop all work on the six-engine heavy bomber project. Wallis' 'Victory Bomber' was finished but he persisted with his big bombs, which were eventually realised with 'Tallboy' and 'Grand Slam' and also the famous 'bouncing bomb' used by the Dambusters in May 1943.

Vickers Long-Range High-Altitude Bomber (1.41)

Span	172ft 0in (52.43m)
Length	96ft 0in (29.26m)
Wing Area	2,675sq.ft (248.52sq.m)
All-Up-Weight	104,000lb (47,174kg)
Powerplant	6 × Merlin RM.6.SM
Max Speed/Height	352mph (566km/h) at 32,000ft (9,754m)
Armament	1 × 10 ton (10,160kg) bomb, 4 × defensive guns

Vickers Long-Range High-Altitude Bomber (1.42)

Span	172ft 1in (52.45m)
Length	100ft 8in (30.68m)
Wing Area	2,676sq.ft (248.861sq.m)
All-Up-Weight	113,500lb (51,483kg)
Powerplant	6 × Merlin 60
Max Speed/Height	360mph (579km/h) at 40,000ft (12,192m)
Armament	32,000lb (14,515kg) bombs, 2 × 0.5in (12.7mm) machine guns

Despite these events, the idea of a very large bomber would not pass. Later in the year some new requirements appeared, but this time with a rather more modest cruise ceiling. As expected they generated much interest from Vickers which put together a complete set of designs, but other companies were also now involved.

In August 1942 the Air Staff passed draft operational requirements (for a bomber three or four times larger than existing machines) to MAP and, as a result, Linnell, CRD, held a meeting on 25 September with the Air Staff and leading designers from the industry. The requirements included an operational range of 2,500 miles (4,023km) with at least a 15 ton (15,241kg) bomb load and preferably 20 tons (20,321kg), cruise would be about 300mph (483km/h) at a normal operating height of 20,000ft (6,096m), but with the ability to cruise at 30,000ft (9,144m) if necessary, and a defensive armament of six 20mm cannon was to be carried covering all angles. The general opinion of the industry was that these requirements were too ambitious and would result in an aircraft of 250,000lb (113,398kg) to 320,000lb (145,150kg) all-up-weight, which was regarded as too big a step up from current four-engine types.

Nevertheless, the concept became known as the '75 Ton Bomber' (or in some documents '70 Ton Bomber') and on 17 October 1942 Avro's R. H. Dalna wrote to Linnell saying 'I, along with [Roy] Chadwick [Avro's chief designer], have been thinking quite a lot about this big bomber problem and matters are getting sort of crystallised in our minds, but one cannot get away from the fact that it is quite a big lot and a long job. Nevertheless, it is one which we are very anxious to do and I believe we could do it successfully and have a first class aeroplane. It might be a bit revolutionary, even though we are using and thinking around an entirely standard form of aircraft without anything fancy in it, and even without buried engines. The only semblance of anything fancy is the counter-rotating props, which we must have.'

By the end of December 1942 the 75 Ton Bomber was being considered as an undertaking of great importance; it was expected eventually to replace the Lancaster and all of the RAF's heavy bombers, and possibly also to form the basis of the UK's post-war civil aircraft. It was proposed that certain companies experienced in the design and manufacture of large aeroplanes should be asked for their rough views on the layout of such a type and in January 1943 five companies submitted a total of fifteen preliminary scheme designs.

Avro

Both of Avro's projects were conventional layouts based on the Lancaster, the smallest of 75 tons (76,204kg) and the larger 100 tons (101,605kg) and with a fuselage which the Ministry described as 'unnecessarily large'. The first had eight unnamed 2,000hp (1,491kW) conventional tractor engines, the second, ten, all in individual nacelles. Their monocoque fuselages would have used stringers, heavy frames and longerons and the undercarriages had front and midships wheels of equal diameter, although the brochure gave no details. Range for both was 2,500 miles (4,023km) and the maximum fuel loads were 57,300lb (25,991kg) and 78,800lb (35,743kg) respectively.

Avro 'Small' Design (18.1.43)	
Span	182ft 6in (55.63m)
Length	130ft 0in (39.62m)
Wing Area	3,030sq.ft (281.50sq.m)
All-Up-Weight	176,000lb (79,832kg)
Powerplant	8 × Unnamed engines giving 2,000hp (1,491kW)
Max Speed/Height	300mph (483km/h) maximum cruise at 20,000ft (6,096m)
Armament	19,595lb (8,888kg) bombs, defensive guns unknown

Avro 'Large' Design (18.1.43)	
Span	221ft 0in (67.36m)
Length	152ft 0in (46.33m)
Wing Area	4,880sq.ft (453.37sq.m)
All-Up-Weight	220,000lb (99,792kg)
Powerplant	10 x Unnamed engines giving 2,000hp (1,491kW)
Max Speed/Height	300mph (483km/h) maximum cruise at 20,000ft (6,096m)
Armament	15,000lb (6,804kg) bombs, defensive guns unknown

Bristol

Bristol completed an initial '100 Ton Bomber' drawing on 15 November 1942. It featured eight Centaurus pusher engines coupled in pairs and driving contra-rotating propellers, a massive fin and three defensive gun turrets each with four guns – a forward dorsal, rearward ventral and a tail turret. The undercarriage had four main wheels under the fuselage, another under each wing and a smaller tailwheel, and the bombs were housed in the fuselage; span was 225ft 0in (68.58m) and length 136ft 6in (41.61m). When submitted in January 1943 this project had been refined with a sleeker fuselage, apparently no defensive guns, a tricycle undercarriage with twin tyres on both main and nose legs and a V tail of 77ft 0in (23.47m) span had replaced the fin and rudder. The monocoque wings had no spars but were reinforced by thick skins and the bombs were still housed in the fuselage; maximum fuel load was 48,800lb (22,135kg). Rather less detail was supplied for Bristol's alternative '75 Ton Bomber' which had the same general layout but eight pusher Griffon 61s and four sets of propellers.

Bristol 'Small' Design (1.43)	
Span	180ft 0in (54.86m)
Length	126ft 0in (38.40m)
Wing Area	3,700sq.ft (343.74sq.m)
All-Up-Weight	170,000lb (77,111kg)
Powerplant	8 × Griffon 61
Max Speed/Height	?
Armament	?

Bristol 'Large' Design (1.43)	
Span	220ft 0in (67.06m)
Length	141ft 0in (42.98m)
Wing Area	4,900sq.ft (455.22sq.m)
All-Up-Weight	220,000lb (99,790kg)
Powerplant	8 × Centaurus CE.12.SM
Max Speed/Height	315mph (507km/h) maximum cruise at 25,000ft (7,620m)
Armament	64,000lb (29,030kg) bombs, no defensive guns (?)

BELOW Internal detail of the Bristol '100 Ton Bomber'.

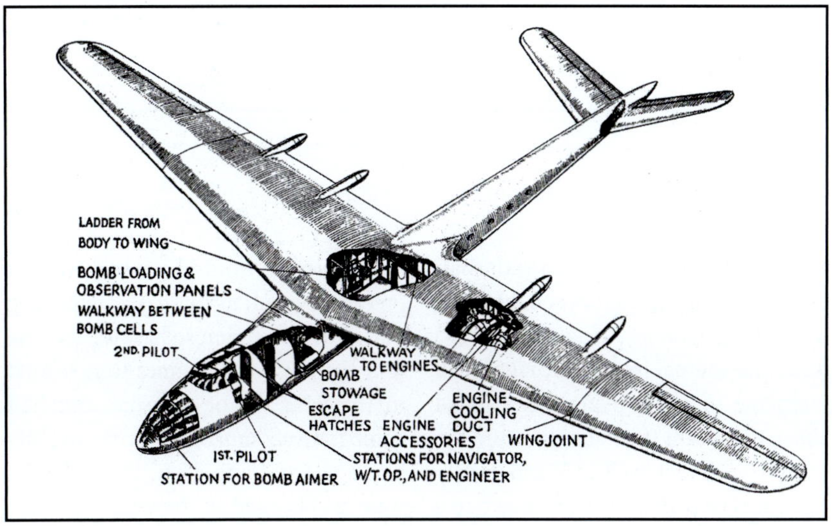

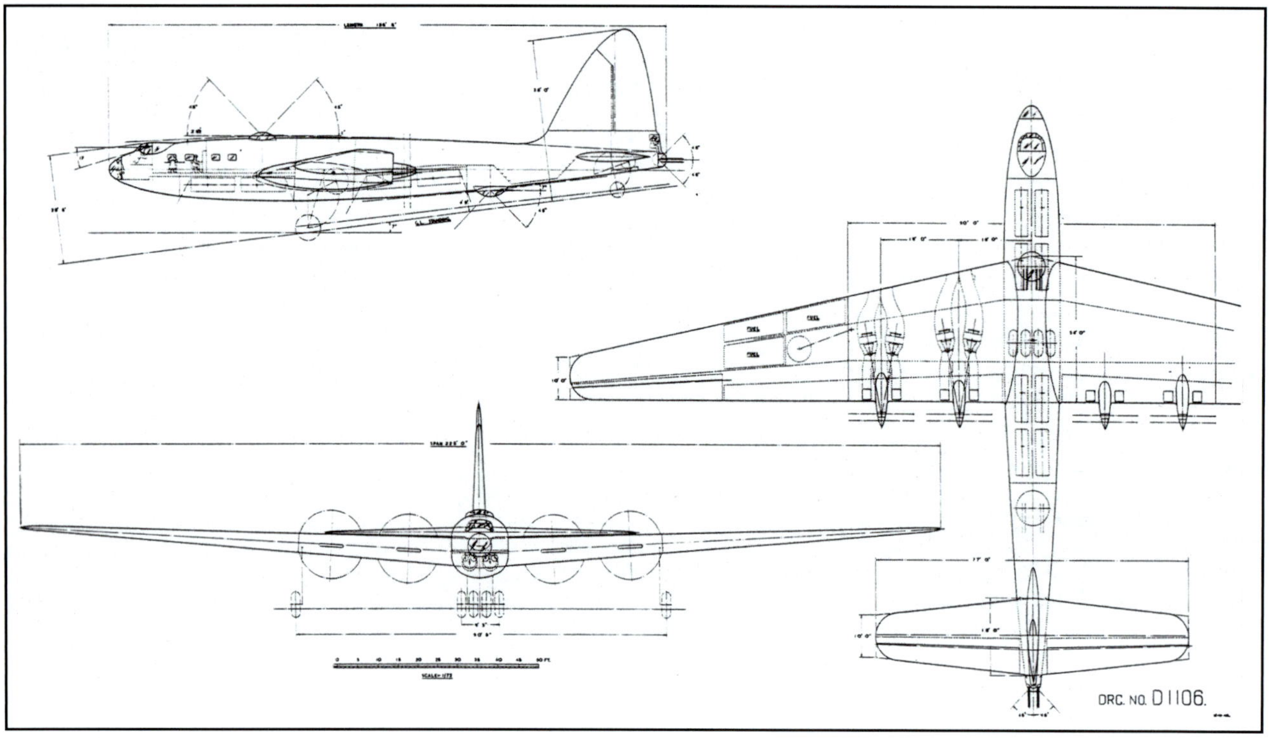

ABOVE Bristol '100 Ton Bomber' at 15.11.42. *Jim Oughton*

BELOW Bristol '100 Ton Bomber' at 30.12.42. Note the coupled engine arrangement. *Duncan Greenman, Bristol AiRchive*

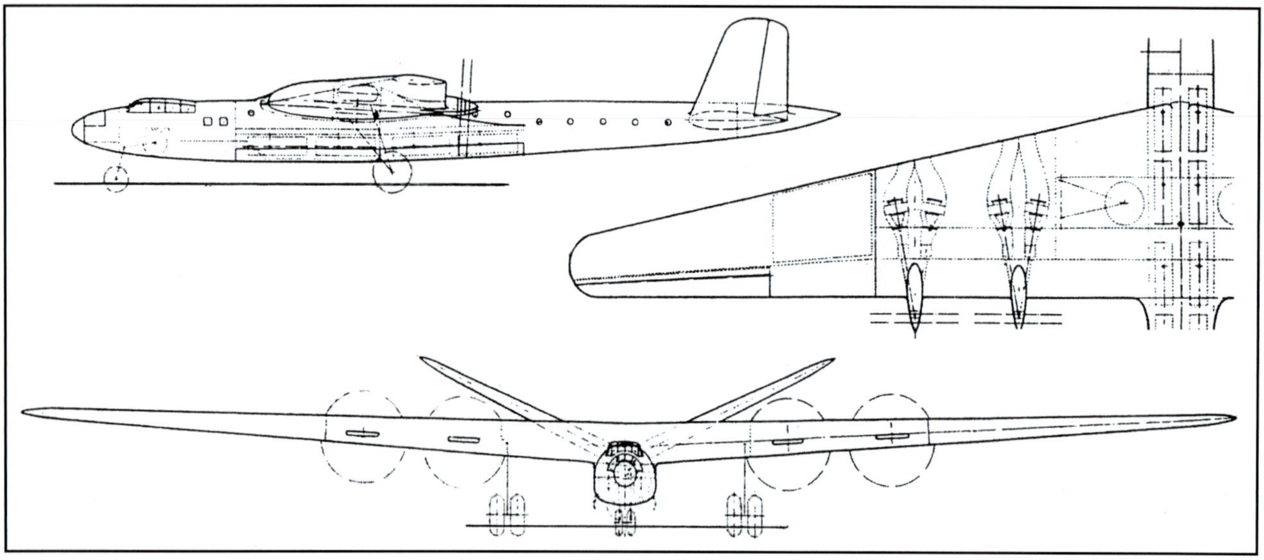

Handley Page

The two alternatives were described in Frederick Handley Page's covering letter as tailless developments, one with shaft drive Sabre piston engines and the other with Metropolitan-Vickers jets. To minimise mutual interference the small foreplane or 'rider-plane' was carried above the line of the mainplane and the wings were swept back 22.5° and heavily tapered. The Sabre version's wings had a D-nose and integral tanks, again holding 7,000gal (31,822lit) of fuel, and a tricycle undercarriage would have twin wheels on each leg with its main gear retracting outwards and the nose backwards. The four liquid-cooled engines were buried in the wing aft of the spar and had comparatively short shaft drives to four-blade pusher propellers; the radiators were also housed in the wing aft of the spar. All crew were located in a high level flight deck as per the orthodox layout and twin 20mm turrets were located in top rear, bottom front and tail fuselage positions, again with remote operation. Maximum load was 48,000lb (21,772kg) (6 × 8,000lb/3,629kg) or 40,000lb (18,144kg) (10 × 4,000lb/1,814kg) of bombs all carried in a bay immediately aft of the main spar.

The jet variant had a smaller wing, carried 5,000gal (22,730lit) of fuel and, because of the engine's lack of power, would have required an 'assisted take-off'. The assessors described this as the smallest, fastest and structurally the most efficient of any of these large bomber schemes, though it must be remembered that the quoted data was only an estimate. Powerplant was eight Metro-Vick unaugmented F.2 units.

Handley Page 'Conventional' Design (14.1.43)

Span	169ft 0in (51.51m)
Length	108ft 0in (32.92m)
Wing Area	2,600sq.ft (241.55sq.m)
Tailplane Area	520sq.ft (48.31sq.m)
All-Up-Weight	c157,000lb (71,214kg)
Powerplant	4 × 3,150hp (2,349kW) Napier 'Developed Sabre'
Max Speed/Height	400mph (644km/h) at 30,000ft (9,144m)
Max Cruising Speed/ Height	332mph (534km/h) at 30,000ft (9,144m)
Armament	Up to 48,000lb (21,772kg) of bombs, 6 × 20mm cannon

Handley Page 'All-Wing' Piston Design (14.1.43)

Span	155ft 0in (47.24m)
Length	67ft 0in (20.42m)
Wing Area	2,190sq.ft (203.45sq.m)
Rider-Plane Area	153sq.ft (14.21sq.m)
All-Up-Weight	c157,000lb (71,214kg)
Powerplant	4 × 3,150hp (2,349kW) Napier 'Developed Sabre'
Max Speed/Height	429mph (690km/h) at 30,000ft (9,144m)
Max Cruising Speed/ Height	354mph (570km/h) at 30,000ft (9,144m)
Armament	Up to 48,000lb (21,772kg) of bombs, 6 × 20mm cannon

Handley Page 'All-Wing' Jet Design (14.1.43)

Span	129ft 6in (39.47m)
Length	67ft 0in (20.42m)
Wing Area	2,190sq.ft (203.45sq.m)
Rider-Plane Area	285sq.ft (26.48sq.m)
All-Up-Weight	c157,000lb (71,214kg)
Powerplant	8 × 2,320lb (10.32kN) thrust Metro-Vick F.2
Max Speed/Height	500mph (805km/h) at 40,000ft (12,192m)
Max Cruising Speed/ Height	500mph (805km/h) at 40,000ft (12,192m)
Armament	Up to 48,000lb (21,772kg) of bombs, 6 × 20mm cannon

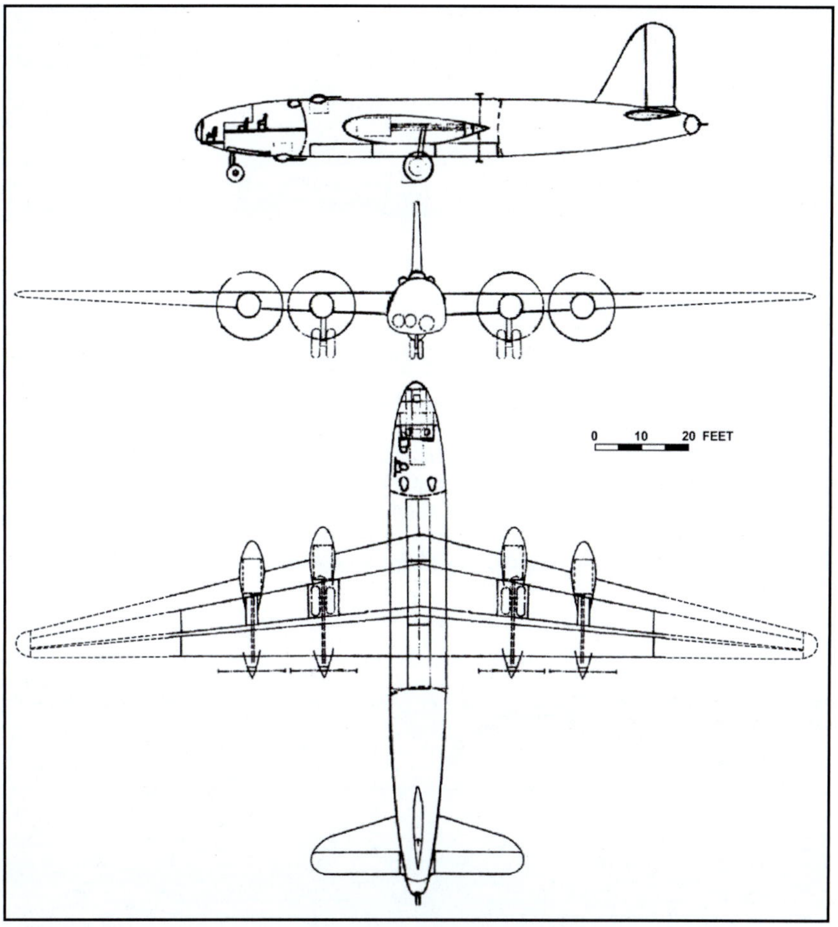

ABOVE The 'conventional' Handley Page '70 Ton Bomber' design (14.1.43).

BELOW The piston-powered Handley Page '70 Ton Bomber' design fitted with a canard or rider-plane (14.1.43).

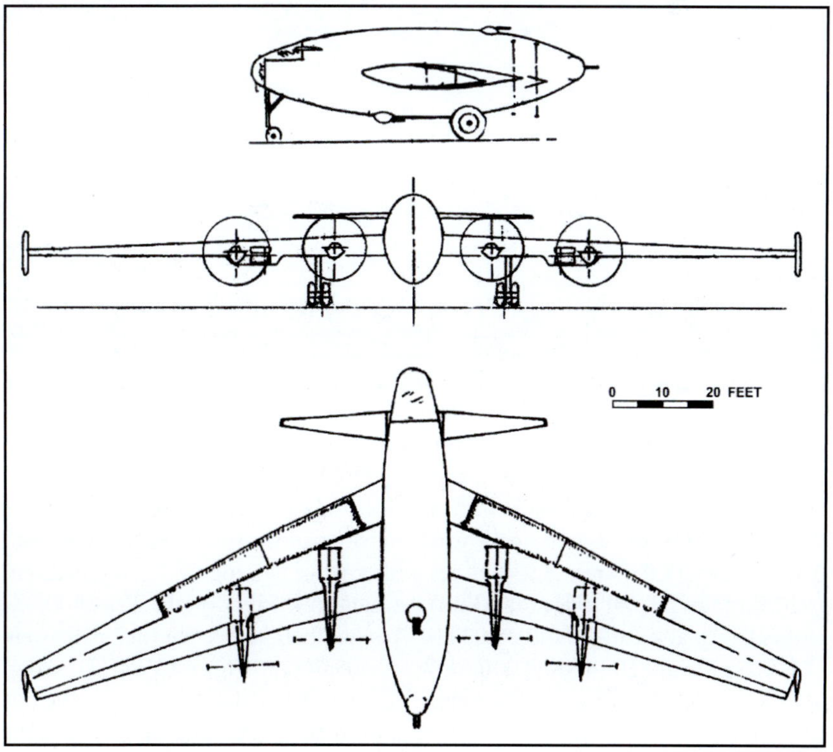

ABOVE AND RIGHT Had either of Handley Page's swept wing '70 Ton Bombers' been built then the HP.75 Manx research aircraft, with a rider-plane' attached to its nose, would have provided supporting data. This little aeroplane made its maiden flight on 25 June 1943. It had a span of 39ft 10in (12.14m) and length 18ft 3in (5.56m) and was powered by two 140hp (104kW) de Havilland Gipsy Major II engines.

ABOVE The Manx pictured in October 1945 with a Halifax bomber standing behind.

The wing thickness/chord ratio at the root on all three designs was 18%, and the estimated range for each with a 20,000lb (9,072kg) bomb load was 3,130 miles (5,037km), 3,930 miles (6,325km) and 3,730 miles (6,003km) respectively, and for the full 48,000lb (21,772kg) load 830 miles (1,336km), 1,460 miles (2,350km) and 2,000 miles (3,219km).

Shorts

This submission was essentially three versions of the same design fitted with alternative engine installations, Centaurus, Sabre or the Bristol Orion piston; their respective fuel loads were 41,400lb (18,779kg), 69,550lb (31,547kg) and 69,380lb (31,470kg). In general this was an orthodox scaled-up version of the Stirling powered by six engines housed in separate nacelles and driving tractor propellers. There was a remotely-controlled rear turret and a normal undercarriage with a tailwheel although, compared with other designs, the main wheels had a quite narrow track and did not retract fully into the inboard nacelles.

Shorts 'Design 1' (1.43)	
Span	168ft 0in (51.21m)
Length	157ft 6in (48.01m)
Wing Area	3,340sq.ft (310.30sq.m)
All-Up-Weight	170,000lb (77,111kg)
Powerplant	6 × Centaurus CE.12.SM
Max Speed/Height	302mph (486km/h) maximum cruise at 25,000ft (7,620m)
Armament	25,730lb (11,671kg) bombs, defensive guns unknown

Shorts 'Design 2' (1.43)	
Span	168ft 0in (51.21m)
Length	157ft 6in (48.01m)
Wing Area	3,340sq.ft (310.30sq.m)
All-Up-Weight	175,000lb (79,379kg)
Powerplant	6 × Sabre NS.46.SM
Max Speed/Height	317mph (510km/h) maximum cruise at 25,000ft (7,620m)
Armament	25,730lb (11,671kg) bombs, defensive guns unknown

Shorts 'Design 3' (1.43)	
Span	168ft 0in (51.21m)
Length	157ft 6in (48.01m)
Wing Area	3,340sq.ft (310.30sq.m)
All-Up-Weight	180,000lb (81,647kg)
Powerplant	6 × Bristol Orion
Max Speed/Height	329mph (529km/h) maximum cruise at 25,000ft (7,620m)
Armament	26,250lb (11,907kg) bombs, defensive guns unknown

Vickers

One of Vickers' first studies for this giant bomber 'programme' appears to have been a drawing dated 9 November 1942 which showed an elliptical wing, six Centaurus tractor engines with turbo-blowers and a very tall fin. By December this had been refined with a longer fuselage and broader fin to become Scheme 'A', one of five alternative layouts ('A' to 'E') included in a slim brochure completed on 14 January 1943. The permanent fuel tankage on each was 5,200gal (23,639lit) and the data was quoted for a range of 2,500 miles (4,023km); all were to be powered by the Centaurus. A great variety of bomb loads was available and in all cases the maximum load was 56,000lb (25,401kg). On 'A' to 'D' this comprised two 12,000lb (5,443kg) and four 8,000lb (3,629kg), but other combinations of six heavy bombs were possible including a load of four 12,000lb. The smallest quoted bomb size was 2,000lb (907kg) and sixteen of these could be taken on board. Scheme 'E' however, could make up 56,000lb with four 12,000lb and two 4,000lb (1,814kg), and could also take twenty 2,000lb.

On the subject of rear defence, CofG considerations meant that it was only possible to install four or five 20mm cannon when the Air Ministry specification requested six. The tractor propellers in 'A' (and 'C') permitted the four rear-facing 20mm guns to be split into two well-separated pairs mounted in the tails of two of the engine nacelles and remotely controlled by a single stern gunner ('C' had an extra 20mm in the rear fuselage). Vickers stated that the degree of decentralisation that the rear nacelle guns achieved rendered the tail defence much less likely to be completely crippled by enemy fire than a single stern turret and suggested that this very important advantage was worth far more than its weight penalty of 4,000lb (1,814kg). It was noted that in England the design of a remote control and sighting system was well advanced while in America it was understood to have already reached a satisfactory practical conclusion.

The pusher Types 'B', 'D' and 'E' had, by necessity, their four 20mm grouped in a single stern turret, which Vickers felt could be put out of action by a single burst of enemy fire. It was also remarked that, to Vickers' knowledge, no turret housing four 20mm was yet in existence. The beam and forward defence, common to each layout, comprised respectively a single 20mm gun turret and gunner per side and a twin 0.5in (12.7mm) bow turret remotely controlled by the bomb-aimer.

Types 'A' and 'B' both had a conventional tailplane and were designed to have a take-off weight of 168,000lb (76,204kg). To make a comparison to a neutral or downloaded tailplane, on 'C' and 'D' the wing was helped by the lifting foreplane, the difference being estimated as approximately 6% which added 10,000lb (4,536kg) to the disposable load and gave a take-off weight of 178,000lb (80,740kg) for the same effective wing loading as the conventional layouts; it would also reduce the landing speed. For the tailless Type 'E', the effect of the necessary washout of incidence progressively towards the tips was such that it limited the take-off weight to 174,000lb (78,925kg), in spite of the larger wing area which had been selected as the minimum required to enclose the engines.

Scheme 'A' had a tailplane, tractor engines in partly underslung nacelles and a tailwheel undercarriage with six wheels on each of four main gears; its wing was proportioned from the B.3/42 Windsor wing which was now under construction. Sea level rate of climb at full load would be 1,310ft/min (399m/min) and service ceiling 35,000ft (10,668m). Vickers felt this design offered a number of disadvantages, in particular difficulty in designing the controls in the tail owing to the presence of the slipstream; it would also be difficult to convert to jet propulsion because of changes in the CofG. 'B' was described as semi-conventional with a tailplane, pusher engines in nacelles mounted flush with the wing upper surface, six-wheel main gears and a tailwheel, but no fundamental departure from current design practice was expected. Here the full load sea level rate of climb would be 1,330ft/min (405m/min) and service ceiling 35,200ft (10,729m). Due to the absence of turbulent flow over the wing the pusher propellers were expected to result in a saving of drag over 'A'. Again a jet conversion could be difficult but here the CofG movement would be less.

Scheme 'C' was classed as experimental and had a foreplane, tip fins on the main wings, tractor engines and a tricycle undercarriage with six main legs, one per nacelle. When the brochure was submitted this layout was being subjected to some wind tunnel tests which appeared likely to lead to a

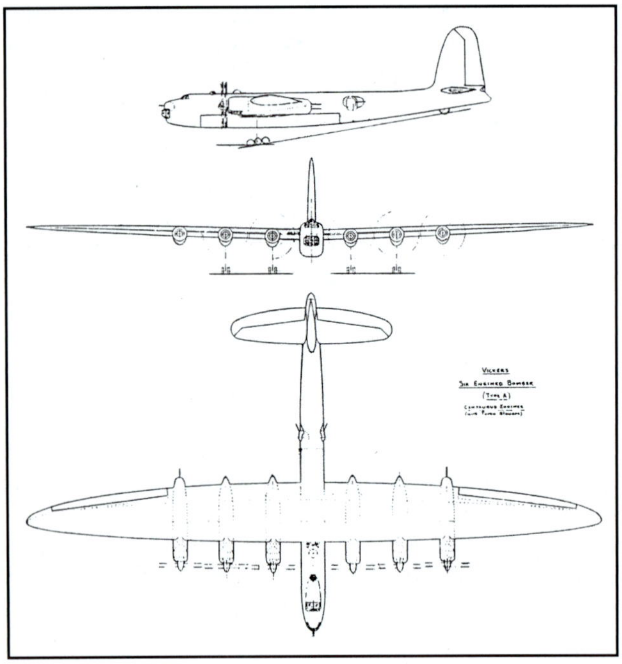

ABOVE **Vickers Scheme 'A' Six-Engine Bomber (14.1.43).** *Eric Morgan*

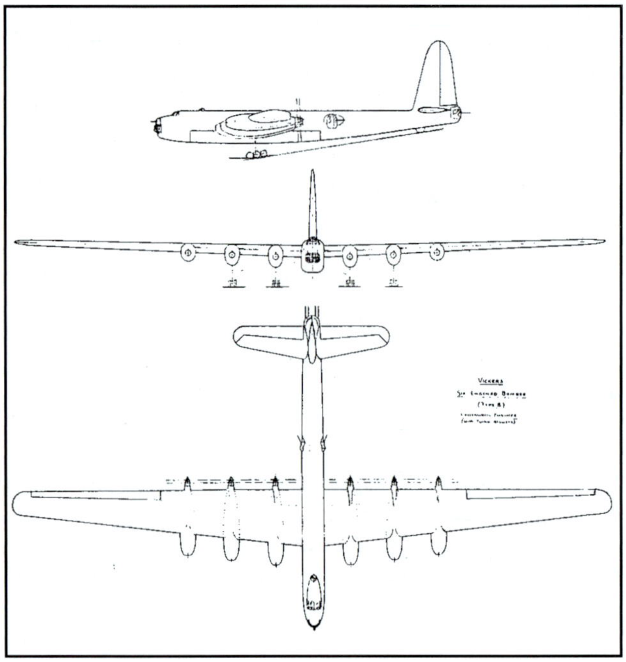

ABOVE **Vickers Scheme 'B' Six-Engine Bomber (14.1.43).** *Eric Morgan*

BELOW **Vickers Scheme 'C' Six-Engine Bomber with Centaurus engines and turbo blowers (drawing dated 12.42).** *Eric Morgan*

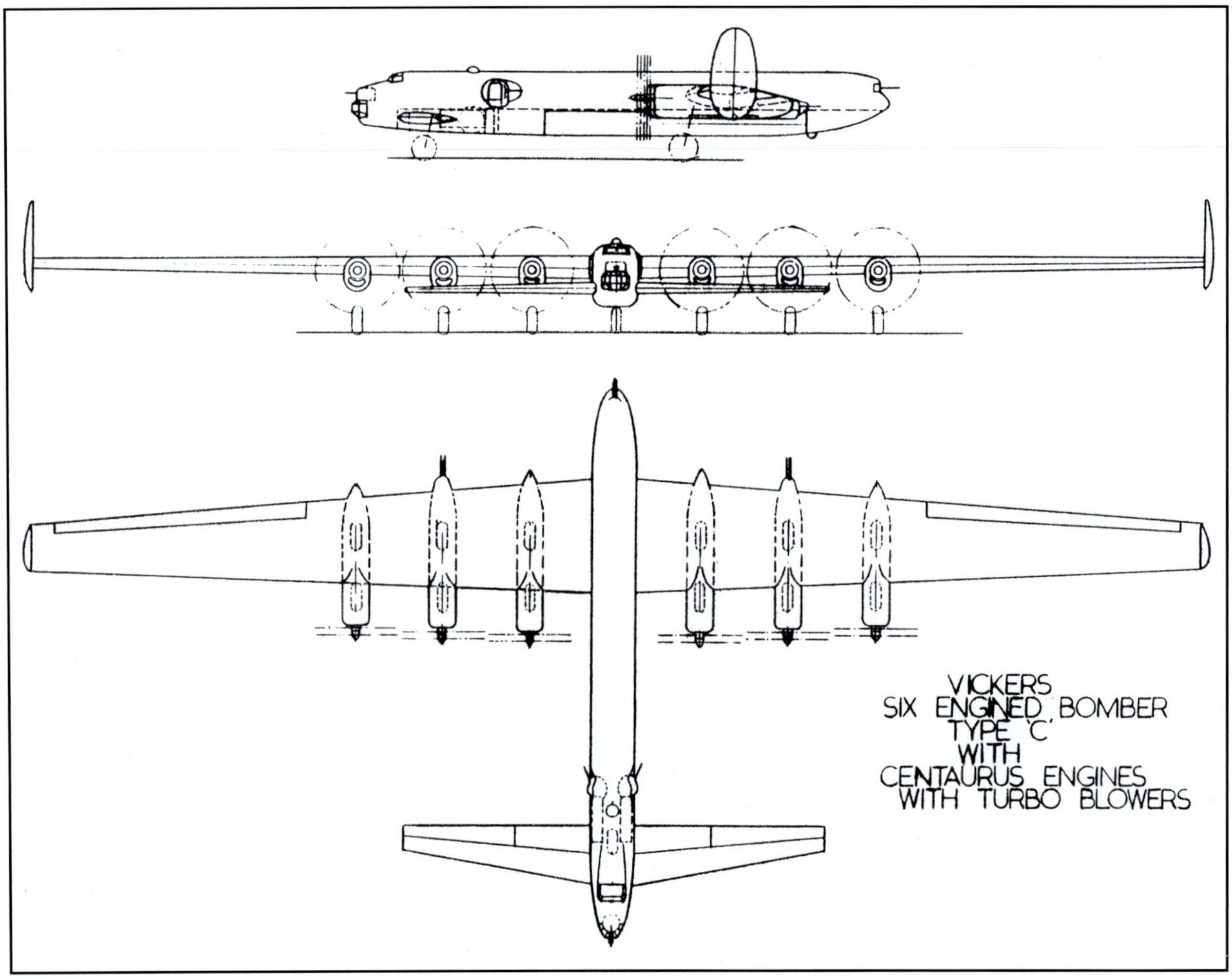

satisfactory solution to the problems of longitudinal and directional stability and control, though some wing sweepback might have to be introduced. To help the CofG, 25% of the fuel was carried in the foreplane and front fuselage. Sea level rate of climb was quoted as 1,280ft/min (390m/min) and service ceiling 34,800ft (10,607m). With such a novel design, it was considered essential to make use of a roughly ¼-scale flying model to confirm the aerodynamic behaviour. This would proceed in parallel with the design of the full prototype and would only need two engines and use the simplest and quickest wood or metal construction possible (manufactured by 'experts such as de Havillands.')

The absence of a tailplane meant that the engines were roughly in line with the fore and aft CofG positions, which made the layout eminently suitable for installing jets (in April 1943 Vickers drew a similar foreplane bomber which had six de Havilland jets in the wings). Flaps on the foreplane also helped to reduce the landing speed but one disadvantage, due to the large spanwise distribution of thrust necessitated by six separate piston engines, was a possible tendency to yaw should some of the engines be crippled.

Scheme 'D' was 'experimental' with a foreplane, pusher engines and a tricycle undercarriage. In order to reduce the maximum lateral displacement of the remaining thrust when two engines were dead, advantage had been taken with the pusher propeller arrangement to combine two engines in one nacelle. The drawing showed co-axial propellers with opposite rotation, each being driven separately by one engine through independent gearing, but Bristol had this matter under consideration and it was possible that they might advise combining the two engines to drive a pair of contra-rotating propellers through one set of gearing. Each outer nacelle housed a single engine driving a straight, direct shaft with a contra-rotating gearbox at the rear end.

ABOVE **Wind tunnel model of Vickers Scheme 'C'.**

BELOW **Vickers Scheme 'E' Six-Engine Bomber (drawing dated 20.12.42).** *Eric Morgan*

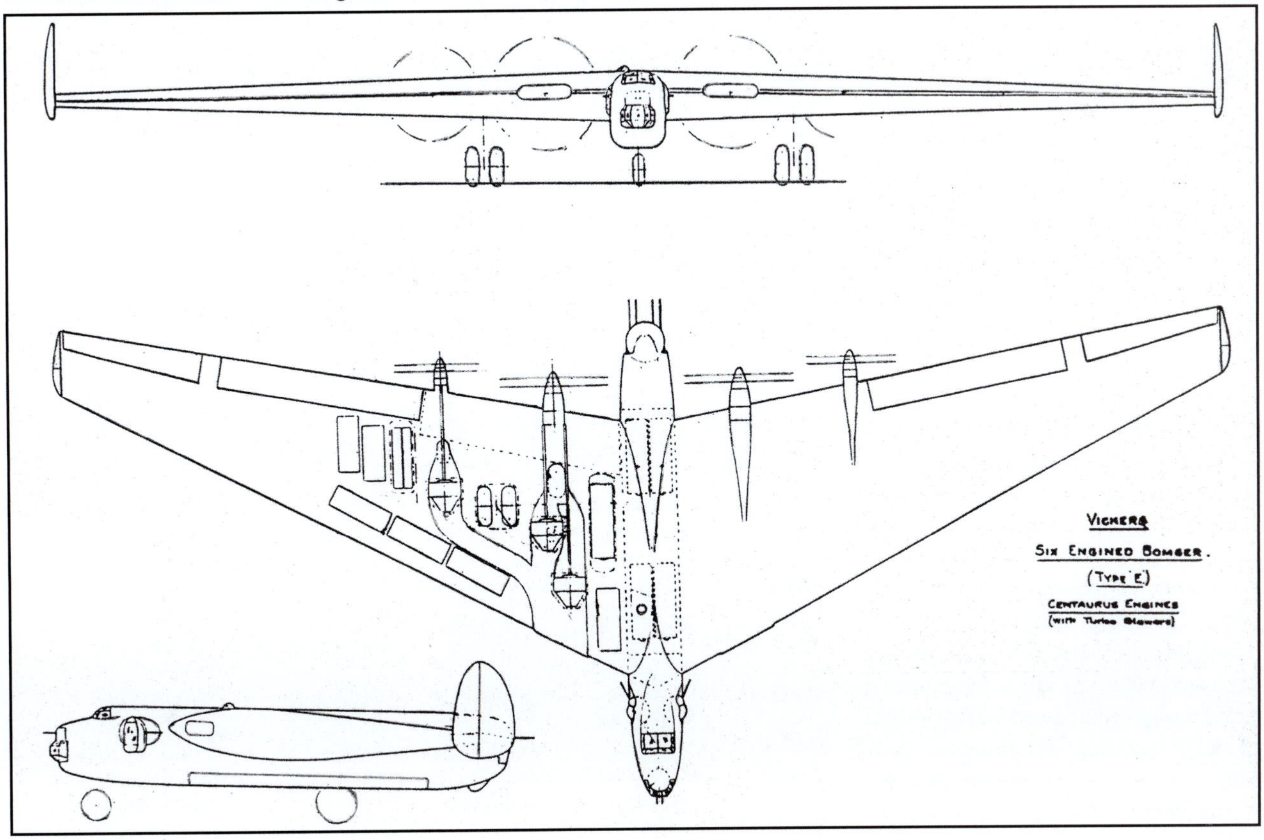

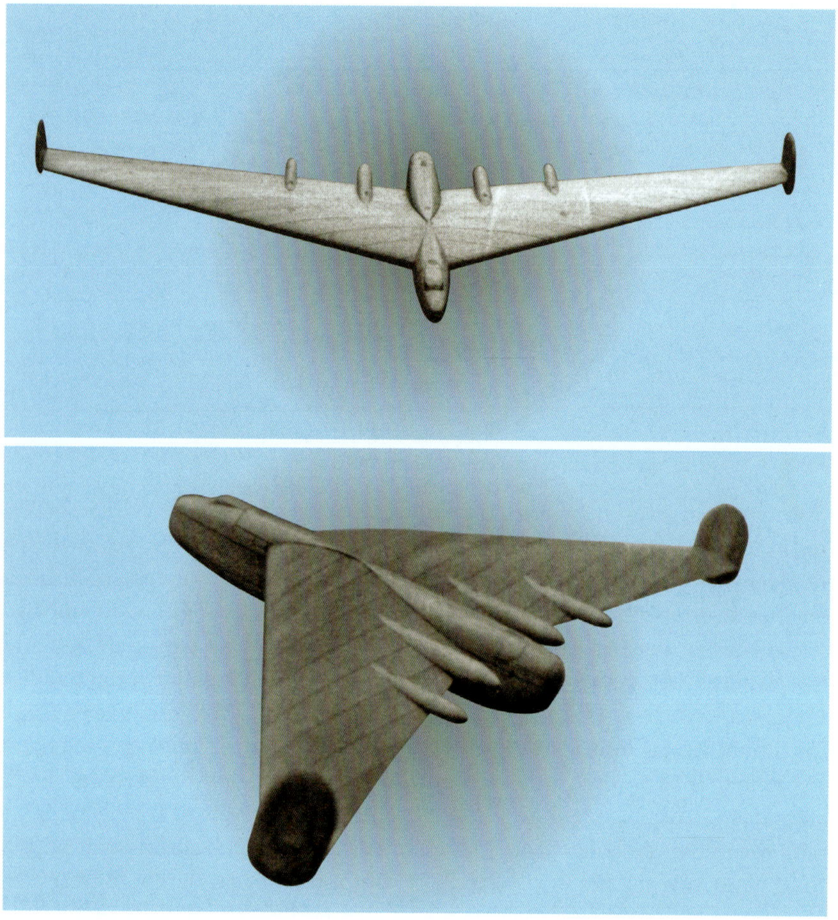

ABOVE Wind tunnel model of Vickers Scheme 'E'.

This design offered the take-off weight and landing speed advantages of 'C' and the drag reduction of 'B', but it would again suffer yawing if some engines were out; it also had the weaker rear defence. Its full load sea level rate of climb would be 1,280ft/min (390m/min) and service ceiling 34,800ft (10,607m).

Scheme 'E' was an experimental tailless design with pusher engines and a tricycle undercarriage with just two main gears. Its wings were swept back 15° and, to achieve longitudinal stability, they had been given appreciable washout towards to the tips. The wing depth was sufficient to enclose all six engines and there were ten fuel tanks, also all in the wings. Sea level rate of climb was 1,150ft/min (351m/min) and service ceiling 32,000ft (9,754m). Again such a novel design would need a flying model of about ¼-scale, built along the same lines as 'C', and it was thought that, due to the absence of a tail or foreplane, the design would suffer from a lack of damping in pitch which would be accentuated by an abnormally small longitudinal moment of inertia compared with the mean chord length. In addition, according to recently published reports, the permissible waviness for laminar flow was so small on such a large chord, as seen on most of this wing, as to be almost impossible to achieve in practice. The engine's cooling ducts were also very long and would present a considerable problem in air tightness; however, the absence of a tailplane was favourable for fitting jets but enclosing the power units in the wings might create problems in installing the intakes and jet pipes.

Vickers Design 'A' (14.1.43)	
Span	190ft 0in (57.91m)
Length	110ft 0in (33.53m)
Wing Area	2,900sq.ft (269.42sq.m)
All-Up-Weight	168,000lb (76,204kg)
Powerplant	6 × Centaurus with turbo blowers
Max Speed/Height	383mph (616km/h) at 25,000ft (7,620m)
Max Cruise Speed	318mph (512km/h) at 20,000ft (6,096m)
Armament	56,000lb (25,401kg) bombs, 6 × 20mm + 2 × 0.5in (12.7mm) guns

Vickers Design 'B' (14.1.43)	
Span	210ft 0in (64.01m)
Length	112ft 6in (34.29m)
Wing Area	2,900sq.ft (269.42sq.m)
All-Up-Weight	168,000lb (76,204kg)
Powerplant	6 × Centaurus with turbo blowers
Max Speed/Height	381mph (613km/h) at 25,000ft (7,620m)
Max Cruise Speed	316mph (509km/h) at 20,000ft (6,096m)
Armament	56,000lb (25,401kg) bombs, 6 × 20mm + 2 × 0.5in (12.7mm) guns

Vickers Design 'C' (14.1.43)	
Span	210ft 0in (64.01m)
Length	95ft 0in (28.96m)
Wing Area	2,900sq.ft (269.42sq.m)
All-Up-Weight	178,000lb (80,740kg)
Powerplant	6 × Centaurus with turbo blowers
Max Speed/Height	382mph (615km/h) at 25,000ft (7,620m)
Max Cruise Speed	317mph (510km/h) at 20,000ft (6,096m)
Armament	56,000lb (25,401kg) bombs, 6 × 20mm + 2 × 0.5in (12.7mm) guns

Vickers Design 'D' (14.1.43)	
Span	210ft 0in (64.01m)
Length	90ft 0in (27.43m)
Wing Area	2,900sq.ft (269.52sq.m)
All-Up-Weight	178,000lb (80,740kg)
Powerplant	6 × Centaurus with turbo blowers
Max Speed/Height	386mph (621km/h) at 25,000ft (7,620m)
Max Cruise Speed	318mph (512km/h) at 20,000ft (6,096m)
Armament	56,000lb (25,401kg) bombs, 6 × 20mm + 2 × 0.5in (12.7mm) guns

Vickers Design 'E' (14.1.43)	
Span	174ft 0in (53.04m)
Length	72ft 2in (22.00m)
Wing Area	4,000sq.ft (371.61sq.m)
All-Up-Weight	174,000lb (78,925kg)
Powerplant	6 × Centaurus with turbo blowers
Max Speed/Height	402mph (647km/h) at 25,000ft (7,620m)
Max Cruise Speed	330mph (531km/h) at 20,000ft (6,096m)
Armament	56,000lb (25,401kg) bombs, 6 × 20mm + 2 × 0.5in (12.7mm) guns

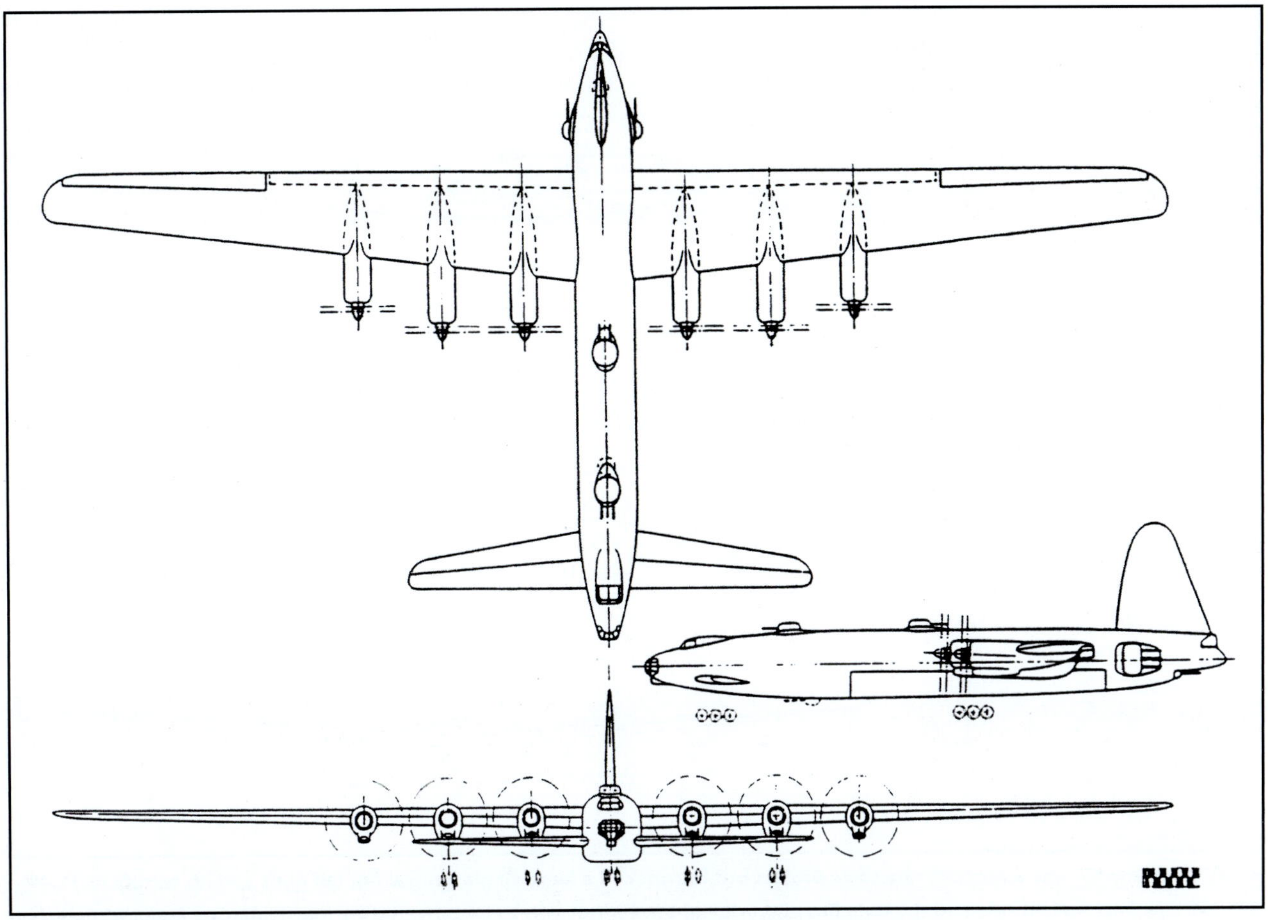

ABOVE **Revised Vickers Scheme 'C' with single fin and twelve 20mm guns (1943).** *Eric Morgan*

BELOW **Vickers High-Altitude Heavy Bomber Scheme 'C' with Clyde engines (5.11.44). (Relevant text on page 134.)**

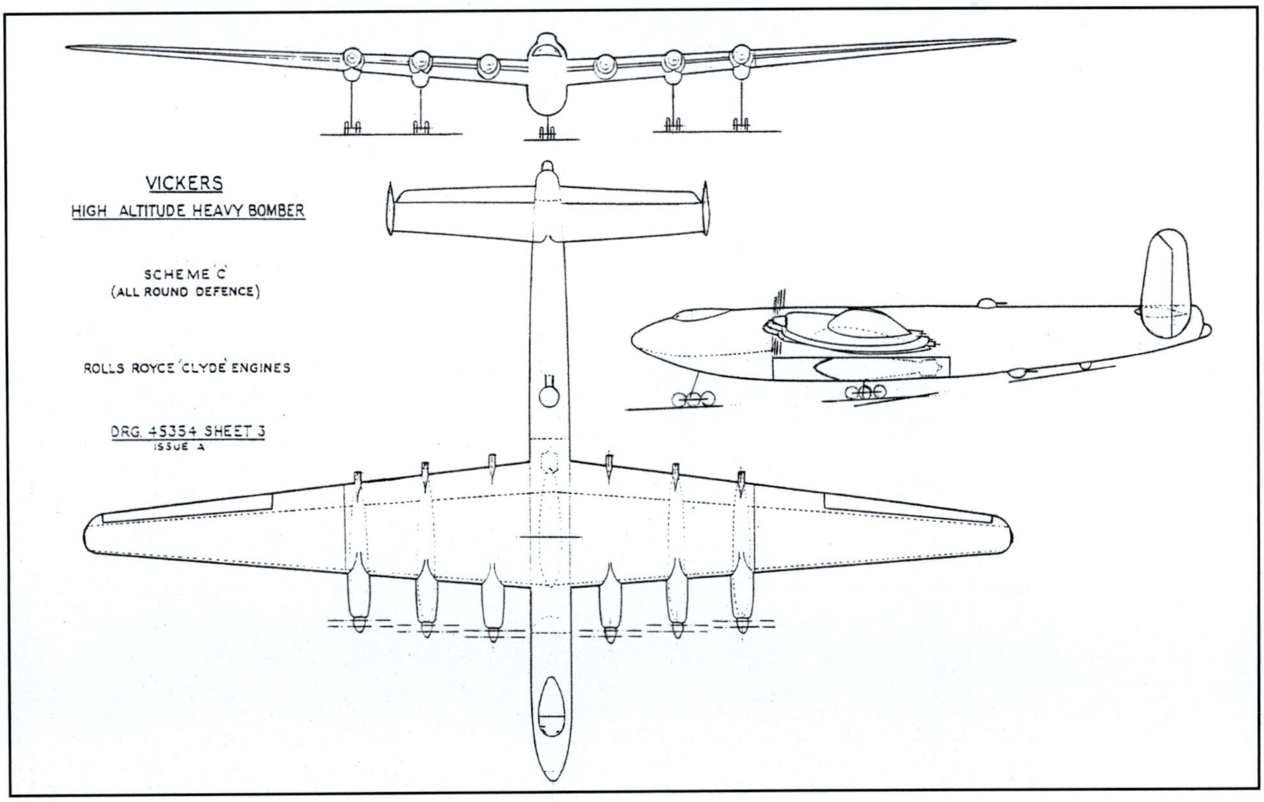

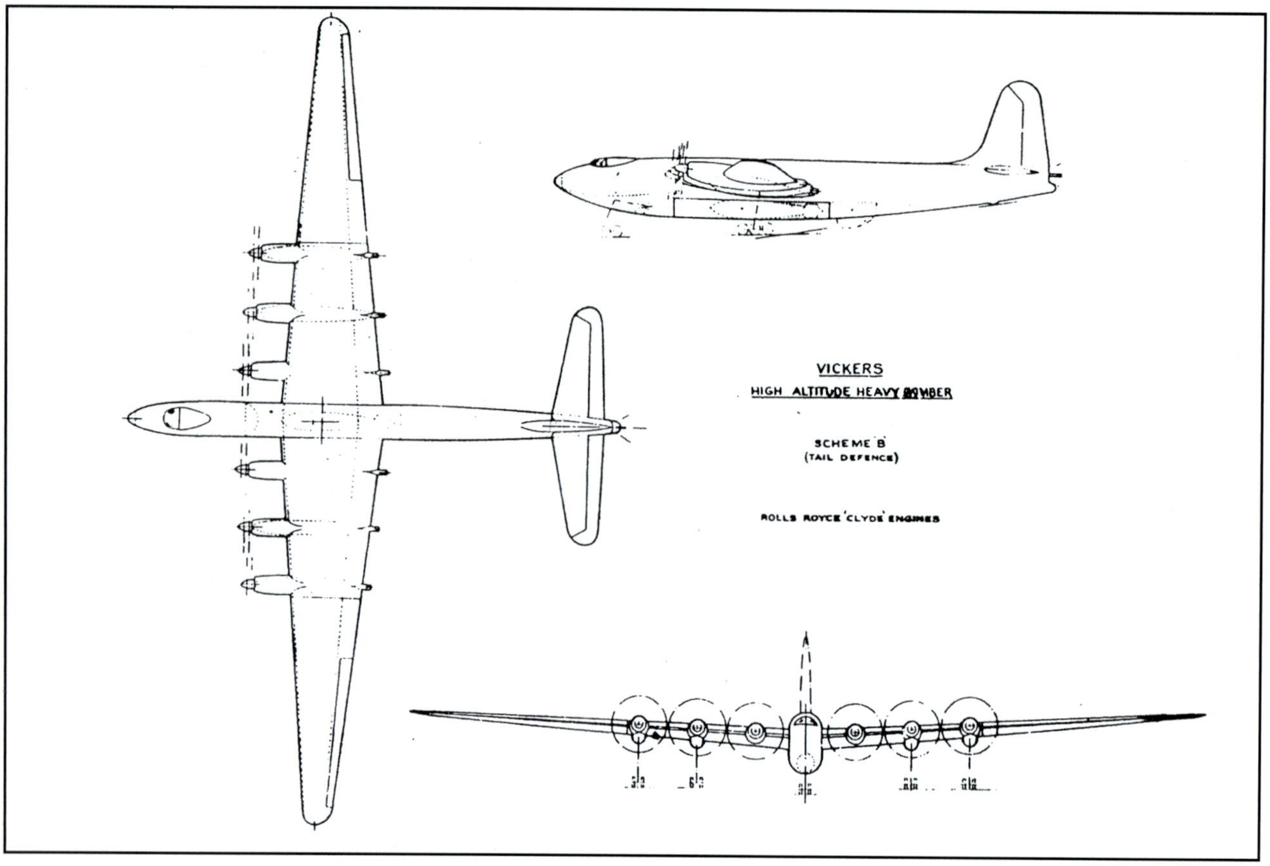

ABOVE Scheme 'B' was essentially the same project but introduced a large single central fin, tail guns and no turrets (8.11.44).

BELOW This final variant retained the twin fins and original turrets but was to be powered by four 'enlarged engines' based on the Clyde (9.11.44). In this drawing the bomb bay houses a Vickers Tallboy bomb. (Text for both on page 134.)

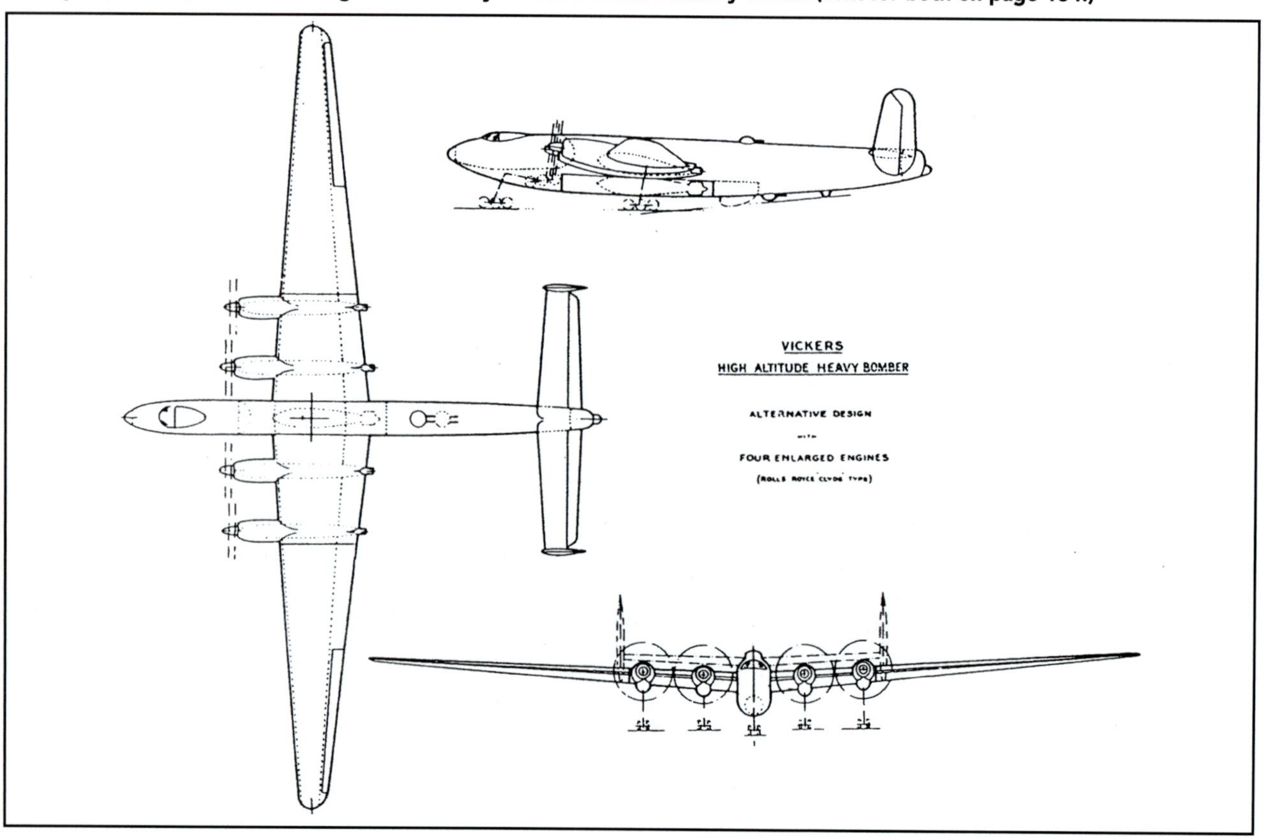

In his covering letter for the brochure Rex Pierson declared that, in his opinion, the most attractive design was 'C', and he did not favour the tailless 'E'.

None of these designs met the requirements entirely but, in their present form, N. E. Rowe, DTD, favoured Bristol's heavier layout. However it did present certain special problems, such as the installation and maintenance of buried engines, while the V-tail was also expected to give inadequate lateral stability which prompted suggestions for a return to a conventional tail. Rowe had deduced that the designs could not approach the requirements within a limiting weight of 75 tons (168,000lb/76,204kg), or with six engines which made a switch to eight essential (as suggested in the Bristol study). On 11 February 1943 Rowe stated that 'Bristol have made a thoughtful contribution showing buried engines and a particularly neat method for coupling pairs of engines. The fundamental features of their design spring from the decision to bury the Centaurus engines in the wing. This forced them to a comparatively low wing loading which is basically uneconomical. Nevertheless, theirs is the most promising approach to the problem and probably is near the optimum within the choice of engines available.'

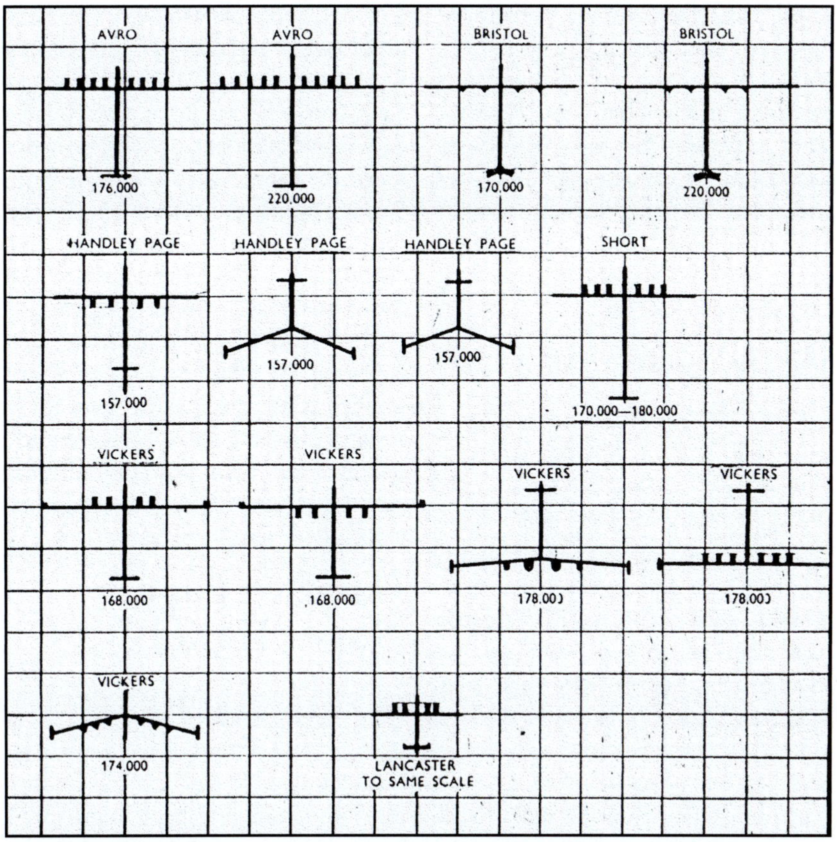

ABOVE **No drawings are known to exist for some of the '75 Ton' and '100 Ton' Bomber designs produced in January 1943, but this sketch illustrates their configurations.**

Rowe continued 'it was generally agreed that the all-wing layout is still experimental. We could not back ourselves in the present state of knowledge to develop it successfully in a reasonable time. The tail-first aircraft, according to RAE analysis, offers little or no advantage since the fuselage is not suppressed, hence that source of drag is not saved. Thus we are compelled to retain a conventional or near conventional aerodynamic form.' None of the tailless designs was actually a pure flying-wing and, consequently, they all fell well short of what might be possible. All of the Vickers projects had geodetic structures which gave percentage structure weights of around 26%, which was below anything built previously and, if achieved, would put these designs well ahead of any other; in addition their multi-wheel multi-leg undercarriages were intended to keep down the wheel size. The buried engines with common duct on the Vickers Scheme 'E', however, was not thought to be a satisfactory arrangement.

The Bristol design was indeed considered attractive and by February 1943 had become involved with Lord Brabazon's Committee on post-war civil aviation. After discussions to decide whether it should be designed primarily as a bomber or primarily as a transport, it was set on one side to make way for a civil version which became the Brabazon airliner, complete with a conventional and very large single fin. This was flown in September 1949 but remained a prototype, although Bristol later worked on another military variant. Both of the Vickers foreplane designs, 'C' and 'D', appeared to be unstable both longitudinally and laterally; sweepback would help but that would bring a major change to the layout. Type 'C' as submitted was felt to have a quite inadequate defensive armament and even its bomb load and range characteristics were disappointing. This design was later revised with a single fin and rearranged turrets that housed a total of twelve 20mm guns, six of which could be fired astern, and it was re-assessed by Rowe.

Initially, the objective of these requirements had been to find an aircraft to replace the present heavy bombers and which could be in production in the minimum of time, but as the assessments and study continued it became clear that an aircraft of such size could not enter production in less than five years. It would also be difficult for the type to achieve the proper balance between range, bomb load and defensive armament; long range was an essential feature but adequate defensive armament and an economic bomb load could only be obtained at the expense of range. Again the ever growing success of the Lancaster eventually removed the need for such large bombers. Although none of these projects was ever built as a bomber, they represent quite probably the most ambitious collection of design studies ever attempted by the British aircraft industry up to that date; the number of design man-hours spent on them must have been prodigious.

Vickers High-Altitude Heavy Bomber

After the end of 'official' research, Vickers continued studies into four, six and eight-engine bombers well into the autumn of 1944, and these culminated in a set of high-altitude bomber projects powered by Rolls-Royce RB.39 Clyde turboprops which were described in a small brochure dated November 1944. Scheme 'C' dated 5 November, shows a project with twin fins, six wheels on the nose gear and on each of the four main gears, and 20mm dorsal and ventral turrets for 'all round defence.' Its span was 185 ft 0in (56.39m), length 113ft 3in (34.52m) and gross wing area 2,860sq.ft (265.70sq.m) and the fuselage bomb bay would house a single 'Tallboy' or 'Grand Slam' bomb. No weight or performance data is available but the design had a pressure cabin. A second version, Scheme 'B' dated 8 November, showed the same project but had a large single central fin, tail guns and no turrets. Here the span was 182ft 0in (55.47m), length 112ft 9in (34.37m) and wing area 2,750sq.ft (255.48sq.m). Scheme 'A' was smaller at 175ft (53.34m) span while another variant, dated 9 November, retained the twin fins and original turrets but used four 'enlarged engines' based on the Clyde.

Handley Page 'Super Halifax'

Handley Page HP.65

In June 1943 proposals were made by Handley Page to develop the Halifax into a much more capable high-speed heavy bomber called the HP.65 'Super Halifax'. The brochure made no reference to any specification but the project makes an interesting companion and comparison to the Avro Lincoln (described shortly) and it was expected to show a greater bomb load and capacity, increased range and cruise speed and a greater operational height over any existing type. The aircraft had a new low-drag high aspect ratio wing with an extended span of 113ft (34.44m), new Hercules 38 turbo-supercharged engines and a new undercarriage, all fitted to a standard Halifax III fuselage and tail unit but with the bomb bay rearranged to take a maximum size of 12,000lb (5,443kg) with the doors closed. Further development would see the fuselage replaced by a pressurised alternative of circular cross-section, developed from the fuselage of the company's new transport project, but retaining the Halifax's fuselage in the first instance would help get the prototype airborne many months earlier.

It was of the utmost importance that the Halifax's altitude performance should be improved. The type's existing two-spar

BELOW None of the giant bombers described here was ever close to being built but the work at Bristol did help in the design of another giant aeroplane, the Brabazon transatlantic airliner first flown on 4 September 1949. The Brabazon is seen here at Filton in December 1948 with Lancaster RE131 alongside. The latter served as the development aircraft for the airliner's controls. *Bristol Aircraft photo*

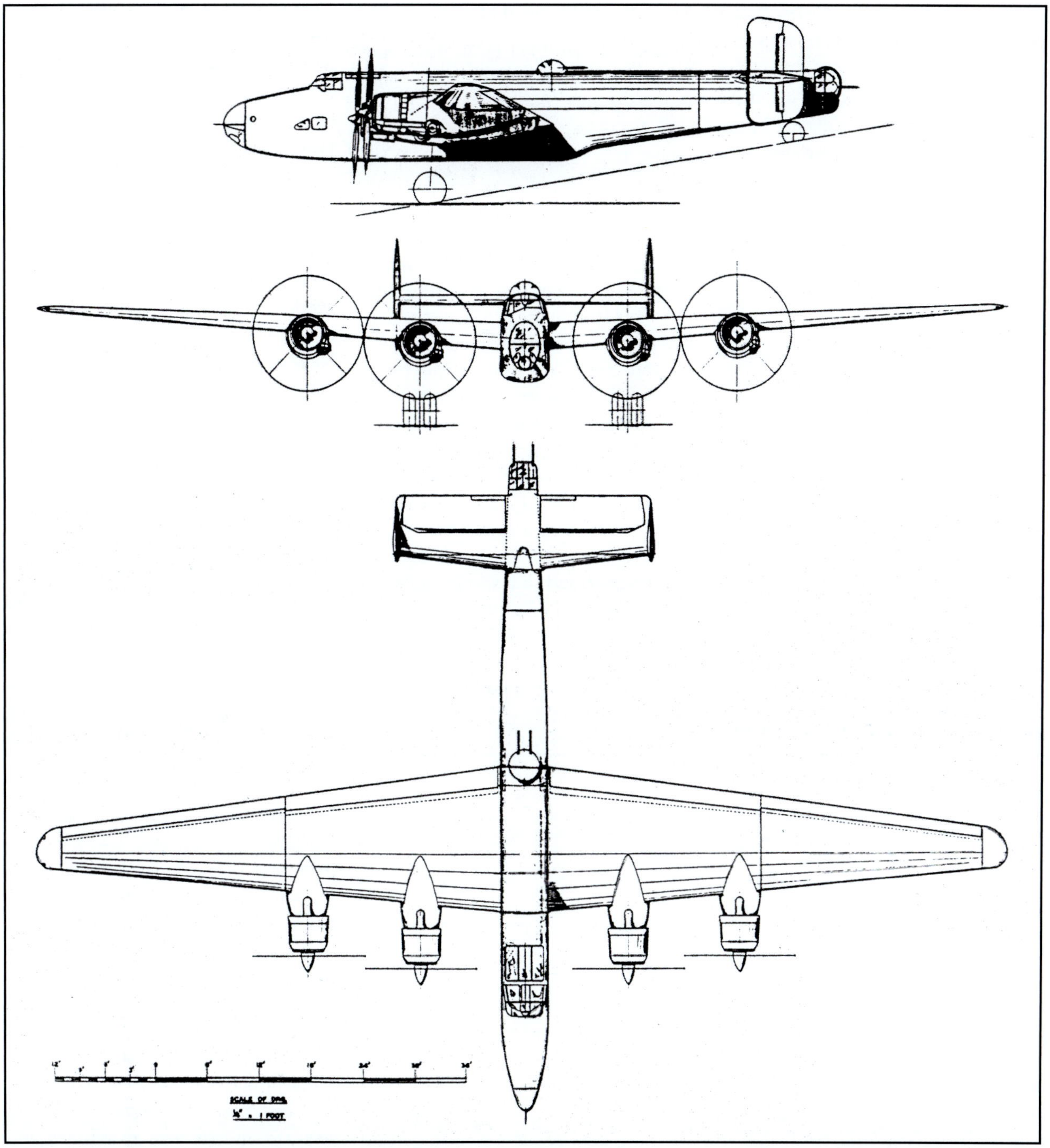

ABOVE Handley Page HP.65 (6.43). Note the twin-wheel main undercarriage.

wing gave spanwise seams that generated drag so the HP.65 was proposed to have the smoothest possible external form and lowest structural weight. The main stress-carrying portion of the wing section would be made of heavy-gauge skin to give a very smooth surface free from any appreciable waviness and the skin stiffeners were arranged so that, as far as possible, all the riveted seams would lie in a chordwise direction. The new single main spar was placed at 40% of the chord back from the leading edge and the entire skin contributed to the torsional strength of the wing. All of the internal fuel (2,500gal [11,365lit]) was carried in integral tanks built into the main wing and all external projections on the engine nacelles were suppressed – the duct entrances were in the leading edge while

Handley Page HP.65 (6.43)	
Span	113ft 0in (34.44m)
Length	76ft 0in (23.16m) overall
Wing Area	1,162sq.ft (107.95sq.m)
All-Up-Weight	70,000lb (31,752kg)
Powerplant	4 × Hercules 38 with turbo blowers
Max Speed/Height	350mph (563km/h) at 27,200ft (8,291m)
Armament	12,000lb (5,443kg) bombs, 4 × 0.5in (12.7mm) plus 1 × 0.303in (7.7mm) guns

the oil cooler, carburettor, air cleaner and intercooler were all housed within the nacelle fairing or the wing. There were two twin 0.5in (12.7mm) defensive turrets plus the Halifax's standard nose gun. A maximum operational altitude of 30,500ft (9,296m) was quoted at 66,500lb (30,164kg) weight while the cruise speed would be 285mph (459km/h) and range 3,710 miles (5,971km).

The Ministry compared the HP.65 to the Lancaster Mk.IV (later the Lincoln) but felt that the company's estimates for drag and weight were optimistic. On 1 October 1943 J. E. Serby noted that the new wing would create a vast amount of design work and so it was difficult to see the spring 1945 production date being met. The top speed quoted by Handley Page, 350mph (563km/h) at 27,000ft (8,230m), was revised by RDT to 326mph (525km/h) at 26,000ft (7,925m), with the maximum operational height 27,000ft (8,230m).

BELOW Handley Page HP.66 (15.11.43).

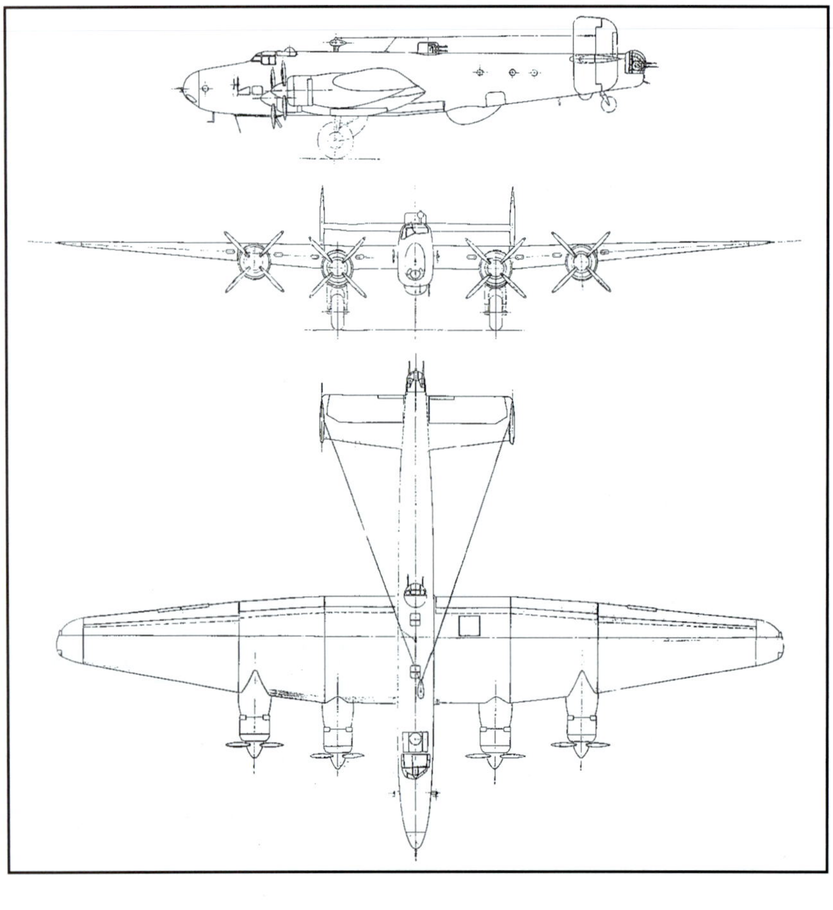

Handley Page HP.66

In late October 1943 N. E. Rowe met Handley Page representatives and suggested that the HP.65 should be abandoned for a simpler redesign which retained the Halifax's two-spar wing but with a new section attached. In mid-November the project was presented as the HP.66 and showed the old wing extended to 113ft (34.44m), which would save about 50% in design time over the HP.65 at the expense of a small loss in speed. This increase in span, the existing centre and outer planes being fitted with a new intermediate section and additional strengthening, took the wing to its limit in terms of retaining the greater part of the existing jigs and parts. Meanwhile the HP.65's 1,162sq.ft (107.95sq.m) wing area had been found to be inadequate for good take-off performance and so it was proposed to increase this to 1,408sq.ft (130.81sq.m).

On 2 December 1943 a contract was allocated to proceed with this aircraft and in February 1944 specification B.27/43 was raised to cover the project. Fitted with Hercules 100 engines it was proposed to call the type the Hastings B.Mk.I, while a version with turbo-blower exhausts would become the HP.69 Hastings Mk.II. Three prototypes were also ordered during February, SR650, SR654 and SR657, (two Hastings Mk.I and one Mk.II) and a fourth (SX553) was added in early April. A back-up arrangement was available to fit Merlin 65s in cylindrical nacelles and these interchangeable units with four-blade airscrews were tested on DG296, a Halifax Mk.II, and LV795, a Mk.III; these were standard power units already adopted for the Avro Lincoln and Vickers Windsor. Twin 0.5in (12.7mm) machine guns would be housed in upper, tail and nose turrets and remotely-controlled 20mm cannon would be fitted in the outer engine nacelles.

The all-up-weight was 70,000lb (31,752kg), a maximum load of 14,000lb (6,350kg) of bombs could be carried and the top speed was 321mph (517km/h) at 27,050ft (8,245m); the cruising ceiling was 31,750ft (9,677m) and the maximum internal fuel 1,802gal (8,192lit). It was hoped that the prototypes would be followed by two hundred production machines to be manufactured at Radlett from May 1945, after the completion of the Halifax run. However, the turbo-blower HP.69 was shelved in April 1944 when priority had to be given to two hundred Halifax A.Mk.IX transports needed for the European invasion; it was also clear that Bristol would be unable to take on the engine installation work. The HP.66 prototypes were retained but after VJ-Day these too were no longer required and so were abandoned and replaced by the HP.67 transport, which was also given the name Hastings.

On 26 October 1943 Rowe, when reporting his meeting with Handley Page to discuss the new proposal, had written 'we treat it not as a new starting off place for the Halifax, but rather as a final development in which we would use conventional armament, as used in the Lancaster IV'. He added that 'I had hoped that [Frederick] Handley Page might be prepared to open up on a tailless design, possibly in preference to sinking more design effort into the Halifax; I sounded him out on this but he is clearly not ready to take a major step of this sort.' Three days later Serby, CRD, added 'since we commenced to discuss the developed Halifax, Handley Page's ideas seem to have tended more and more to what would amount to a complete redesign. Although improvement in the Halifax as a bomber is desirable, it is fairly evident that by the time it can be ready the main requirements for bombers will be met by the Lancaster.'

Avro Lincoln

Avro 694

The development of the Lancaster was also taken to a stage at which the structural redesign was radical enough for the aircraft to deserve a new name, in this case Lincoln. In 1942 it was acknowledged that an improved Lancaster was needed and on 17 October Avro's R. H. Dalna wrote to Air Marshal Linnell, CRD, to suggest some ideas. He believed that 'we could have a replacement Lancaster, spliced into our production line, in a year's time. In this I am thinking about the Lancaster with either Sabres or Griffons with its speed pushed up by some 30 odd miles per hour (48km/h) from what it is at present, [while] maintaining the same bomb load and the same range. The great advantage of this would be, and I stress it as an interim measure, the retaining of a very large proportion of our detail tooling and even main assembly jigs.'

In fact the initial estimates showed a project with four Merlin RM.14.SMs and they indicated an all-up-weight of 70,000lb (31,752kg), top speed 346mph (557km/h) at 20,000ft (6,096m) and service ceiling 34,000ft (10,363m). The bomb load totalled 12,000lb (5,443kg) and the defensive armament comprised twin 0.5in (12.7mm) machine guns in nose and tail turrets and two 20mm cannon in a dorsal upper turret. This was initially known as the Lancaster B.Mk.IV and B.Mk.V and structural alterations were made to the wing, fuselage and undercarriage to increase the type's offensive performance. Its

ABOVE One of the prototypes of the Avro Lancaster Mk.IV (i.e. the Lincoln B.Mk.I) photographed on 27 July 1944 while undergoing testing by A&AEE Boscombe Down. **BELOW** Lincoln B.Mk.1 in flight.

ABOVE Lincoln RF352 pictured whilst serving with the Empire Central Flying School (ECFS) at Hullavington in about 1946.
Peter Arnold Collection

introduction, along with the Vickers Windsor, was thoroughly considered by the Air Staff's Defence Committee which decided at the end of the year that these two types 'were the best that could be brought into service in time to affect the future course of the war.' They would supplement and eventually replace Bomber Command's Lancasters.

A prototype contract was placed in July 1943 and the first order for 162 production aeroplanes followed a month later. Production specifications for two versions were issued under B.14/43 to cover 'The Design and Construction of Lancaster B.Mk.IV and Mk.V Bombers by the Parent Firm.' The operational requirements were essentially the same as the Lancaster B.Mk.III's but with improved defensive armament and protection and Merlin 85 or 68 engines for the respective marks. However, one objective was to make the new type suitable for operations in the Pacific theatre as a contribution towards helping America defeat Japan, but this needed a much greater range and ceiling.

The new type resembled the Lancaster but there were many differences and it was realised that a new name would be more suitable; an old name meant an old aircraft and Avro wanted a new one, but Bomber Command preferred to retain Lancaster. In June 1944 Avro suggested Lincoln which J. D. Breakey, ACAS(TR), noted was 'very appropriate as it falls within the bomber category (i.e. a city) and is moreover the name of a city within the area in which Bomber Command operates their aircraft.' The company also offered Sandringham and Stafford but Lincoln was the most favoured and was officially adopted in August. The Avro 694 Lancaster IV and V became the Lincoln B.Mk.I and B.Mk.II respectively.

Bomber Command had been critical of the Lancaster bomb-aimer's prone position and so during July and August 1943 a modified nose was fitted to Lancaster ED371 which provided a seat, flat-glass panelling and a new turret with twin 0.5in (12.7mm) guns. Flight testing began in September 1943 and proved a success; visibility was much improved while the aircraft's top speed rose by 6mph (10km/h) and, consequently, a similar nose was adopted for the Lincoln. The Lincoln was rather bigger than the Lancaster both in span and length and there were changes to the bomb bay and defensive armament. It was intended that the larger wing would considerably extend the high altitude and cruise performance but it also meant that many hangars could not cope with the extra span, so side-tracking skates fitted around the undercarriage had to be used to 'slide' the machines into their hangars.

The Lincoln prototype PW925 first flew on 9 June 1944 but the urgency to get the type into service was diluted by events. In 1944 the well-established Lancaster seemed quite adequate for 1945 and it left no spare manufacturing

ABOVE **RF570 was a Lincoln B.Mk.II which in about 1960 flew with the Bomber Command Bombing School based at Lindholme.**

capacity. As the situation in both Europe and the Pacific improved, the need for the new bomber receded and the priority for its production was reduced. When the war ended the need for so many bombers went with it and large numbers of Lincolns were cancelled. Nevertheless well over 500 were eventually built for the RAF, some operating throughout the 1950s, and other examples served in Argentina and Australia. There were also post-war proposals for a re-engined Lincoln II with Merlin 626s which it was hoped would get the bomber farther into Russia. In fact this variant offered an increase in ceiling and performance but not range and so the project was dropped in February 1949.

This and the previous chapter have shown that the British aircraft industry undertook a massive amount of heavy bomber design during the period 1935 to 1945, which accurately reflected the desire for the RAF to possess a powerful striking force. By the close of the Second World War this force was fully operational and very effective.

Avro 694 Lincoln B.Mk.I (flown)	
Span	120ft 0in (36.58m)
Length	78ft 3.5in (23.86m)
Wing Area	1,421sq.ft (132.01sq.m)
All-Up-Weight	82,000lb (37,195kg)
Powerplant	4 × 1,635hp (1,219kW) Merlin 85
Max Speed/Height	310mph (499km/h) at 18,300ft (5,578m) and 69,500lb (31,525kg) weight
Armament	22,000lb (9,979kg) bombs, 2 × 20mm + 4 × 0.5in guns

Chapter Six
Maritime Patrol

ABOVE Superb photo of war-weary Sunderland Mk.I L2163.

Until the 1950s the flying boat offered great benefits both to air forces and civil airlines. In particular, since it could take off with a higher all-up-weight it made possible longer range operations over the sea, although this was compromised a little by the poorer aerodynamics of the 'boat hull' which increased drag. In the short term it could also make use of any suitable landing area, thus maintaining an air presence when no land strip was available, but long-term operations would need extensive back-up facilities. The history of the RAF's wartime flying boats, used for maritime patrol and reconnaissance, is dominated by the Shorts Sunderland and the American Consolidated Catalina (over 650 Catalinas were supplied). In fact the Sunderland proved so successful that several attempts to find a replacement failed and the type stayed with the RAF until 1959.

Specification R.1/36 Blackburn B.20 and Saunders-Roe Lerwick

Prior to the outbreak of war there were plans for a smaller flying boat to undertake patrol duties. Specification R.1/36, dated 2 March 1936 and a refinement of an earlier document R.12/35, requested a cruising speed of at least 230mph (370km/h) and an all-up-weight not exceeding 25,000lb (11,340kg). Provision was to be made for 2,000lb (907kg) of bombs and the defensive armament was to comprise nose and midships twin-gun turrets and a four-gun rear turret. Saunders-Roe, Shorts and Supermarine only were invited to tender.

Blackburn B.20

Blackburn had already been given an order for a prototype of its experimental B.20 design as a 'development' item to Specification R.12/35, but this was subsequently modified to meet R.1/36. The B.20 had a horizontally-spilt body with the lower portion forming a retractable planing bottom, which was designed to cut the drag associated with deep hulls needed by monoplanes to keep their propellers above the water spray. On the water this was extended to form, in effect, a single 'float' which pushed the upper fuselage and the wings well above the water and also allowed the wing to give the precise angle of incidence required for take-off and low

Blackburn B.20 (flown)	
Span	(floats retracted) 82ft 2in (25.04m), (floats extended) 76ft 0in (23.16m)
Length	69ft 7.5in (21.22m)
Wing Area	(including floats) 1,066sq.ft (99.14sq.m)
Normal Loaded Weight	35,000lb (15,876kg)
Powerplant	2 x 1,720hp (1,283kW) Rolls-Royce Vulture
Max Speed/Height	(Estimated) 306mph (492km/h) at 15,000ft (4,572m)
Armament	(production aircraft): 8 x 250lb (113kg) bombs, 8 x 0.303in (7.7mm) machine guns

ABOVE **The Blackburn B.20 prototype V8914 afloat with its retractable planing bottom deployed.** *Phil Butler*

BELOW **This picture appears to show the Blackburn B.20 prototype itself but has all background removed. This would have been the aircraft's 'in-flight' configuration.**

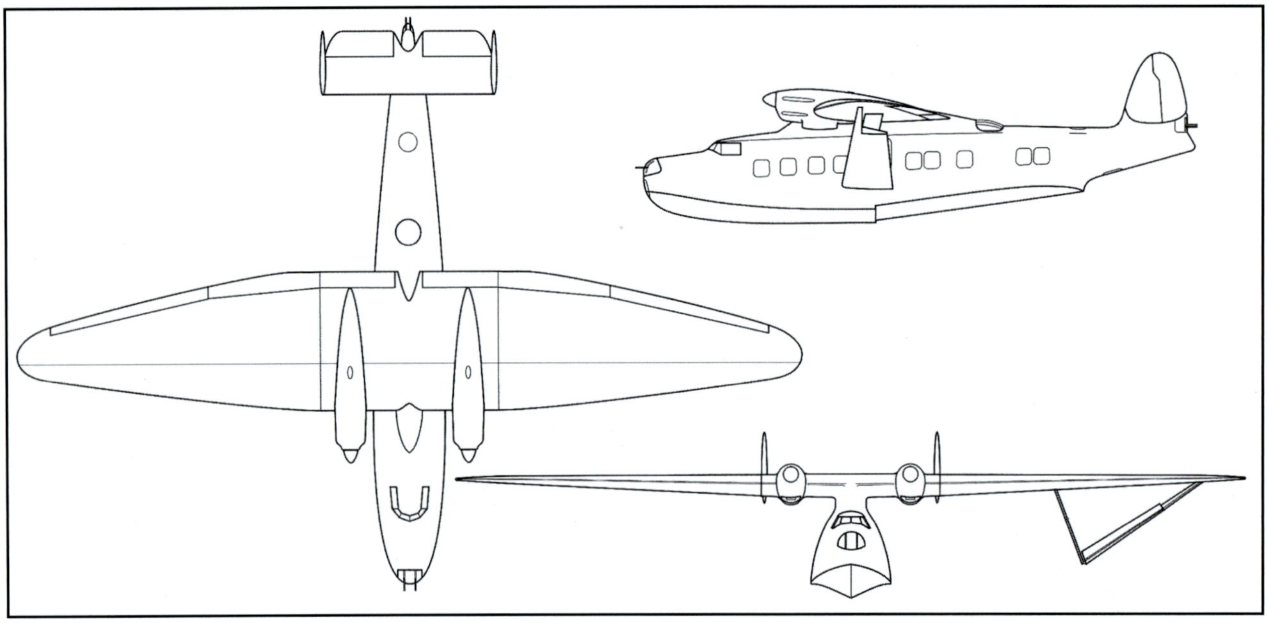

ABOVE Supermarine Type 314 (26.5.36). *Ralph Pegram*

cruise drag; in flight the retracted float formed a smaller solid fuselage and the wingtip floats would swing out sideways to form the wingtips. The B.20 was a proof of concept aeroplane and the sole prototype first flew on 27 March 1940, but then crashed into the sea on 7 April 1940 after experiencing aileron flutter.

Saunders-Roe S.36 (P.970)

The initial Saro submission to R.1/36 had a gull wing layout but was subsequently altered to the design which became the Lerwick. As first proposed here it had an estimated service ceiling of 31,600ft (9,632m).

Saro S.36 (c5.36)	
Span	75ft 0in (22.86m)
Length	64ft 6in (19.66m)
Wing Area	700sq.ft (65.10sq.m)
Normal Weight	23,000lb (10,433kg); overload 26,500lb (12,020kg)
Powerplant	2 x Bristol Hercules
Max Speed/Height	271mph (436km/h)
Armament	2,000lb (907kg) bombs, 8 x 0.303in (7.7mm) machine guns

Short R.1/36

No drawing is available for the Short Brothers project but this was to have been a monoplane with its wing supported on struts. Estimated service ceiling 27,500ft (8,382m).

Shorts R.1/36 (c5.36)	
Span	76ft 6in (23.32m)
Length	65ft 4in (19.91m)
Wing Area	750sq.ft (69.75sq.m)
Normal Weight	25,580lb (11,603kg)
Powerplant	2 x 1,700hp (1,268kW) Rolls-Royce Vulture
Max Speed/Height	258mph (415km/h)
Armament	2,000lb (907kg) bombs, 8 x 0.303in (7.7mm) machine guns

Supermarine 314

Supermarine had investigated two, three and four-engine flying boat concepts before settling on a development of its Type 308 twin-Vulture boat, which earlier had been the first formalised Supermarine design to feature bomb stowage in its wings. This cantilever wing proposal proved to be the last flying boat project developed by the team under R. J. Mitchell's leadership. Its service ceiling was expected to be 28,000ft (8,534m).

Saro Lerwick

At the Tender Design Conference held on 22 June 1936 the Supermarine 314 was considered to be the clear favourite, with at that point little to choose between Saro and Shorts. It was proposed to order the 314 into production 'off the drawing board', but Supermarine's workload with the Spitfire meant that the manufacturer

Supermarine 314 (26.5.36)	
Span	91ft 0in (27.74m)
Length	63ft 5in (19.33m)
Wing Area	1,055sq.ft (98.115sq.m)
Normal Weight	28,000lb (12,701kg), overload 33,000lb (14,969kg)
Powerplant	2 x 1,700hp (1,268kW) Rolls-Royce Vulture
Max Speed/Height	265mph (426km/h)
Armament	8 x 500lb (227kg) plus 4 x 250lb (113kg) bombs, 8 x 0.303in (7.7mm) machine guns

could not start work until 1939. By 13 November 1936 Saro had proposed a revised design where the gull-shape layout had been replaced by a cantilever design with a deeper hull so as to provide the necessary airscrew clearance above water. The bombs were also now carried in the wings instead of the hull and the service ceiling was given as

Saro S.36 (11.36)	
Span	81ft 0in (24.69m)
Length	65ft 0in (19.81m)
Wing Area	825sq.ft (76.725sq.m)
Normal Weight	24,000lb (10,886kg); overload 27,000lb (12,247kg)
Powerplant	2 x Bristol Hercules
Max Speed/Height	247mph (441km/h)
Armament	2,000lb (907kg) bombs, 8 x 0.303in (7.7mm) machine guns

ABOVE **The Saro A.36 Lerwick prototype L7248 pictured whilst in the hands of the Marine Aircraft Experimental Establishment (MAEE) at Felixstowe in October 1938. With the outbreak of war the MAEE moved to a safer location at Helensburgh in Scotland.** *Phil Butler*

BELOW **L7257 was one of a very small number of Saro Lerwicks to be built.**

25,600ft (7,803m). The Air Ministry assessment indicated that, in some respects, Saro's design, as it was now, was better than the Supermarine 314 and it was suggested that sufficient aircraft should be ordered to equip two squadrons. The performance of the revised project was, however, lower than the original S.36, so it was also proposed that the planned two prototype order for the faster Supermarine 314 should be retained (this was never confirmed).

As a result a replacement R.1/36 'off the board' contract went to Saro. The first S.36 was flown in early November 1938 and the type was named Lerwick, but only 21 were ever built. There were misgivings about the design itself and orders were cancelled and reinstated, and then the aircraft was found to have a disappointing performance with an even lower top speed. Its flight characteristics and water performance were also poor but the type did fulfil a limited service career before being withdrawn in 1942.

Saro S.36 Lerwick (flown)

Data	Saro S.36 Lerwick (flown)
Span	80ft 10in (24.64m)
Length	63ft 8in (19.41m)
Wing Area	845sq.ft (78.585sq.m)
All-Up-Weight	28,400lb (12,882kg)
Powerplant	2 x 1,375hp (1,025kW) Hercules HE.1.SM
Max Speed/Height	214mph (344km/h)
Armament	4 x 500lb (227kg) or 8 x 250lb (113kg) bombs or 4 depth charges, 7 x 0.303in (7.7mm) machine guns

Specification R.2/33

Saunders-Roe A.33 and Short Sunderland

Specification R.2/33 of 23 November 1933 requested a four-engine general purpose boat seaplane to replace the Shorts Singapore III. The projects selected for flight test were the Saunders-Roe A.33 and Shorts S.25 and in 1934 a single prototype of each was ordered, with serials K4773 and K4774 allocated respectively. Saro's A.33 had a fabric-covered parasol wing-mounted on struts well clear of the fuselage, the high position providing sufficient water clearance for the engines while also permitting the use of a relatively small low-drag hull. It had four Bristol Perseus XII engines, a streamlined all-metal hull and, instead of wing floats, huge hull-mounted sponsons to provide stability, an unusual feature in British design.

K4773 first flew on 14 October 1938, a full year after the S.25, but its water performance was poor. Porpoising (nose pitching both up and down) was experienced together with excessive wave pressure build up on the sponsons. On 25 October, during a take-off run, it hit the wake of a passing ferry which made it bounce and stall and resulted in a wing failure inboard of the starboard engines; one of the propellers also pierced the hull and it was clear that repairs were not worthwhile. The A.33's all-up-weight was 41,500lb (18,824kg), although all flight testing was performed at a take-off weight of 31,500lb (14,288kg), and it had a maximum speed of 200mph (322km/h). Initial production contracts for the A.33 and S.25 were placed in March 1936 before their prototypes were completed, but the order for eleven A.33s was now cancelled along with all further development.

Eleven Shorts S.25s were ordered and the type was named Sunderland. The Air Ministry and RAF voiced a few criticisms and one brought a change to the defensive armament (a large 37mm Vickers nose gun was replaced by a single machine gun while the rear turret was equipped with four Browning machine guns). This had an appreciable effect on the boat's layout in that just over 4° of sweep had to be introduced to the main wing spar. Originally the leading edge had been straight but sweepback was now required to compensate for the change in CofG caused by the heavy tail turret pushing back the centre of pressure. In turn this forced a redesign of the lower hull to accommodate a change in the hydrodynamics.

These alterations, however, evolved after the construction of K4774 had begun and it was decided to proceed with the straight wing on that aircraft. K4774 was launched into the River Medway on 14 October 1937 and its maiden flight followed two days later. Three more flights were completed before K4774 was returned to the factory to receive its swept wing, a repositioned main step on the planing bottom and the correct engines – Pegasus XXIIs (Pegasus Xs had been fitted as a temporary measure). The planing bottom, that part of the underside of a hull or float which is designed to develop hydrodynamic lift,

BELOW Saunders-Roe A.33 prototype K4773.

was tapered at its rear end to a vertical knife edge. In timing, the Sunderland came behind pre-war Shorts 'C' Class civil flying boats which allowed the military type to benefit from the former's development programme and a particular example was this improved knife-edge arrangement that replaced the transverse step of the civilian machine. The Sunderland prototype only was to receive a main step equipped with a retractable fairing, operated by a member of the crew inside the bomb loading compartment.

Sunderland hull shapes were tested on a Shorts S.22 Scion Senior seaplane, a four engine twin float machine about half of the size of a Sunderland. Since it appeared to make an ideal test model an example was bought by the Air Ministry in 1939 for hull experiments. The twin floats were removed and a central float fitted under the fuselage to act as a half-scale model of its big brother's planing bottom. Wingtip floats on long struts were added and the Scion Senior 'flying-boat', now serialled L9786, made a first flight in this form on 18 October 1939. It was sent to MAEE at Helensburgh to measure hull resistance during high-speed taxying (MAEE was based at Felixstowe before the outbreak of war) and the data collected helped in the design of a faired main step introduced on the Sunderland Mk.III. The Scion Senior was used until 1944 and its correlation with the behaviour of the full-size Sunderland proved far more accurate than small water tank models. By comparison Saunders-Roe's tank testing failed to indicate that its A.33 and Lerwick boats would both perform badly on the water.

ABOVE The first production Shorts Sunderland was L2158 seen here in 1939. *Crown Copyright*

BELOW Serial ML876, a Sunderland Mk.III, sits in the water at Belfast.

Shorts Sunderland Mk.I (flown)	
Span	112ft 9in (34.37m)
Length	85ft 7in (26.09m)
Wing Area	1,488sq.ft (138.24sq.m)
All-Up-Weight	56,000lb (25,401kg)
Powerplant	4 × 1,010hp (753kW) Pegasus XXII
Max Speed/Height	209mph (336km/h) at 5,000ft (1,524m)
Armament	2,000lb (907kg) bombs or depth charges, 7 × 0.303in (7.7mm) machine guns

The first Sunderland Mk.Is entered service in June 1938 and further updated versions followed with improved armament and engines. The final Mk.V was powered by the 1,200bhp (895kW) Pratt & Whitney R1830 Twin Wasp and a total of 749 aircraft was built. Sunderland production began before the war started and closed after the end of hostilities.

Shorts S.45 Seaford

A more powerful Bristol engine was the Hercules which Shorts used on its Stirling bomber (Chapter Four) and it was realised that this unit could improve the Sunderland's speed. Work began in late 1941 and the result was the Mk.IV, covered by Specification R.8/42 of November 1942, which received 1,700hp (1,268kW) Hercules XIXs. Orders followed for two prototypes, MZ269 and MZ271, and forty production aircraft. The changes to the airframe were minimal but they included an additional 3ft 3in (99cm) of hull length, 1ft (30.5cm) more maximum beam, a carefully redesigned planing bottom with a 3in (7.6cm) deeper main step and almost 5° of dihedral on the tailplane to keep it clear of spray. The wing was unaltered but a powerful defensive armament was fitted.

The Mk.IV was intended to serve against Japan and MZ269 first flew on 30 August 1944. It had been discovered that the normal Sunderland vertical tail had insufficient fin and rudder area for yaw control with both engines out on one side, so a bigger fin (2ft 9in [84cm] taller) plus a 20% larger tail were fitted which worked well but needed an additional dorsal fin to eliminate a new problem of rudder-locking. This upgrade was renamed the S.45 Seaford GR.Mk.I but the increase in maximum weight to 75,000lb (34,019kg) restricted the expected improvements in performance and, once the Pacific war was over, there was little point in putting it into service; the gain in speed over the Mk.III Sunderland was only about 32mph (51km/h). On 24 August 1946 Shorts was told that there would be no more orders for the Seaford, or any additional Sunderland Vs, after the eight Seafords then on order. These were completed but most were then converted for civilian use; the other production airframes were finished as Solent airliners or cancelled while the two Seaford prototypes were scrapped in 1947.

Shorts Seaford Mk.I (flown)	
Span	112ft 9.5in (34.38m)
Length	88ft 7in (27.00m)
Wing Area	1,488sq.ft (138.24sq.m)
All-Up-Weight	75,000lb (34,019kg)
Powerplant	4 × 1,700hp (1,268kW) Hercules XIX
Max Speed/Height	242mph (389km/h)
Armament	2,000lb (907kg) bombs or depth charges, 2 × 20mm cannon, 2 × 0.303in (7.7mm) plus 6 × 0.5in (12.7mm) machine guns

BELOW Shorts Seaford NJ205 in July 1946.

Specification R.5/39

In July 1938 draft proposals were prepared for Specification R.3/38 which was intended to produce a flying boat that was faster, and preferably smaller, than the Sunderland. The service load, 5,000lb (2,268kg), was broadly the same as Shorts' boat and investigations by RDT showed that there were good prospects of meeting the Air Staff's main requirement – speed – with four 1,000bhp (746kW) engines, either the Exe or the Taurus. Normal gross weight was estimated to be 45,000lb (20,412kg). While the details of R.3/38 were being discussed the Air Staff's policy on defensive armament was altered and a revised specification, issued as R.5/39 in April 1939, appeared with a four-cannon turret. A normal range of 1,500 miles (2,414km) was required with a minimum cruise speed of 235mph (378km/h). Four companies tendered designs, each using light alloy construction with fabric-covered control surfaces and each layout had a high position wing.

Blackburn B.32

Blackburn's brochure stated that this design met all of the military, operational and navigational requirements without any sacrifice in water or aerodynamic performance. The tailplane had pronounced dihedral which increased the clearance between the outer surface of the tailplane and the wave formation trailing from the main step, so the hull depth was kept to a minimum. Tip floats, retractable or fixed, were used which, when retracted, formed the wingtips and Handley Page type slotted flaps were fitted. The chosen engine was the Hercules, with the Griffon as an alternative (each tender used these), and the units were fitted well forward of the leading edge so that the full slipstream effect on lift was available for take-off. There were three bomb cells in each centre plane and two more bombs could be carried on swinging carriers at each side of the hull.

A four cannon turret was mounted between the two main wing spars close to the CofG and a large 12ft (3.66m) diameter cupola, shaped to form part of a sphere, rotated with the turret. The wing sections and thicknesses were adjusted so that the cupola was faired into the wing top surface. A single pillar-mounted cannon was placed in the tail turret with a two-piece transparent fairing which slid backwards on circular tracks to provide an opening for the gun to fire. The overload internal fuel totalled 3,190gal (14,502lit) and the normal load around 1,600gal (7,274lit). Maximum rate of climb for the Hercules version was 1,830ft/min (558m/min) at 2,000ft (610m), time to 5,000ft (1,524m) 3 minutes, cruise speed 262mph (422km/h) at 2,000ft (610m), maximum range 4,080 miles (6,566km)

Blackburn B.32 (19.6.39)	
Span	102ft 0in (31.09m) floats up, 95ft 6in (29.11m) floats down
Length	85ft 7in (26.09m)
Wing Area	1,650sq.ft (153.29sq.m)
All-Up-Weight	for 1,500 miles (2,414km) range Hercules 52,500lb (23,814kg) normal, 65,428lb (29,678kg) overload; Griffon 53,550lb (24,290kg) normal, 66,778lb (30,290kg) overload
Powerplant	4 × 1,580hp (1,178kW) Hercules HE.7.SM or 4 × 1,600hp (1,193kW) Griffon
Max Speed/Height	Hercules 299mph (481km/h) at 15,000ft (4,572m), Griffon 304mph (489km/h) at 15,000ft (4,572m)
Armament	6 bombs, 5 × 20mm cannon

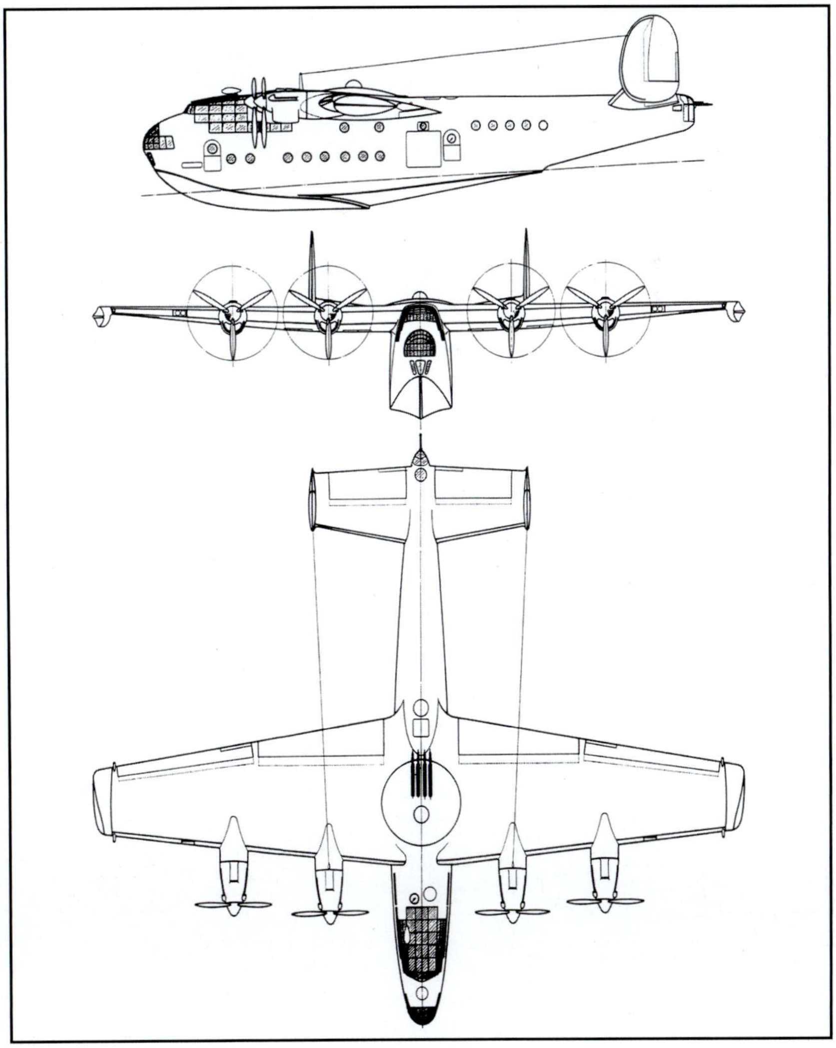

RIGHT Blackburn B.32 (19.6.39). *BAE Brough Heritage Centre*

and service ceiling 30,700ft (9,357m); for the Griffon the figures were 1,980ft/min (604m/min) at 6,800ft (2,073m), 2.6 minutes, 275mph (443km/h) at 6,400ft (1,951m), 4,000 miles (6,437km) and 28,500ft (8,687m). The prototype would take 24 months to produce.

Saunders-Roe S.38

This was a development of some early work done to R.3/38, which had begun with an aircraft powered by four Taurus engines. This new project's total fuel capacity was 3,830gal (17,411lit) with the normal load 2,030gal (9,228lit). The aircraft had a high wing with a single spar, inward retracting floats, four bomb cells in each wing, twin rudders, a four-gun amidships turret and a single gun tail turret. The Hercules gave a time to 5,000ft (1,524m) of 3.2 minutes and a maximum range of 4,130 miles (6,647km) while the cruise speed was 258mph (415km/h) (Griffon 265mph [426km/h]) at 15,000ft [4,572m]). The quote for producing the prototype was also 24 months.

Saunders-Roe S.38 (mid-1939)	
Span	110ft 0in (33.53m)
Length	97ft 0in (29.57m)
Wing Area	1,640sq.ft (152.36sq.m)
All-Up-Weight	Hercules 54,935lb (24,918kg) normal, 68,885lb (31,246kg) overload, Griffon 55,467lb (25,159kg) normal
Powerplant	4 × Hercules HE.1.SM or Griffon
Max Speed/Height	Hercules 284mph (457km/h) at 15,000ft (4,572m), Griffon 291mph (468km/h) at 15,000ft (4,572m)
Armament	bombs (up to 4,000lb [1,818kg]?), 5 × 20mm cannon

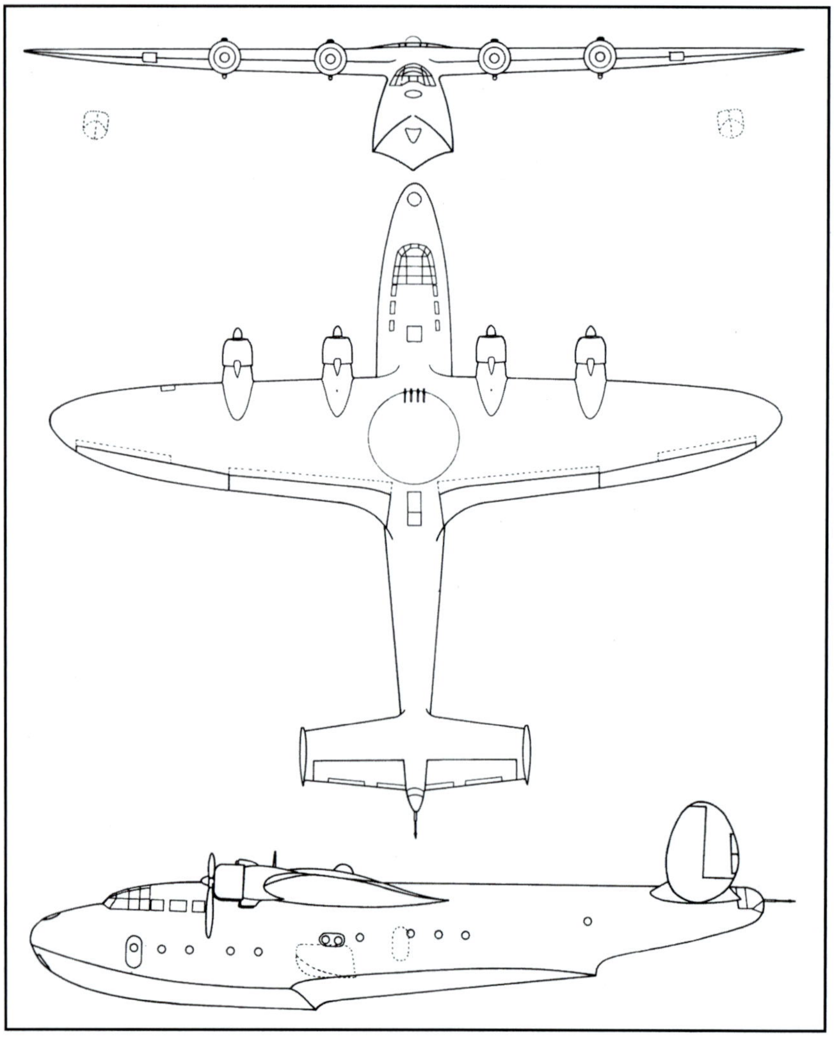

To support its R.5/39 studies and assess the aerodynamic and water properties, Saro built a flying scale model of this design called the S.37 Shrimp. Despite R.5/39 being abandoned in October 1939, Saro continued its flying boat studies as a private venture and the Shrimp itself was flown for the first time in early October.

Shorts R.5/39

This project used a two-spar wing system similar to the Stirling bomber and had fixed wing floats, a high wing and a single fin and rudder, eight bomb cells in each outer wing and the four cannon turret placed between the spar frames. Total fuel capacity was 3,360gal (15,274lit), cruise speed (Hercules) 236mph (380km/h) and (Griffon) 219mph (352km/h) at 5,000ft (1,524m), sea level rate of climb (Hercules) 1,470ft/min (448m/min) and range (Griffon) 3,645 miles (5,866km). Shorts expected to produce a prototype in 21 months.

Shorts R.5/39 (mid-1939)	
Span	115ft 6in (35.20m)
Length	94ft 0in (28.65m)
Wing Area	1,788sq.ft (166.11sq.m)
All-Up-Weight	for 1,500 miles (2,414km) range Hercules 60,700lb (27,533kg) normal, 71,800lb (32,568kg) overload, Griffon 61,850lb (28,055kg) normal, 73,290lb (33,244kg) overload
Powerplant	4 × Hercules HE.7.SM or Griffon
Max Speed/Height	Hercules 279mph (449km/h) at 15,000ft (4,572m), Griffon 273mph (439km/h) at 8,600ft (2,621m)
Armament	bombs (up to 4,000lb [1,818kg]?), 20mm cannon

Supermarine 328

The Type 328 flying boat was the culmination of Supermarine's pre-war thinking on large aircraft design. The brochure declared that this design offered

LEFT Saunders-Roe S.38 (mid-1939). *Saro via Michael J. F. Bowyer*

exceptional performance, a high degree of seaworthiness and an efficient bomb installation and the result was 'a very long range flying boat capable of operating away from its base for extended periods .... and a very serviceable bomber with a performance that contemporary bombers will be unlikely to equal.' Its wing construction and bomb layout closely followed those adopted on Supermarine's B.12/36 (Chapter Four) which was now under construction. The wing size and overall dimensions had been kept to a minimum and the single-spar construction allowed the interior of the wing to be put to the fullest use. Thus, with the torsion nose containing fuel ahead of the spar and all of the bombs and the retracting float placed aft of the spar, the wing was almost completely filled and could not be made any smaller; slotted flaps were employed.

It had also been found possible to design a hull of 'excellent form' to provide aerodynamic cleanliness but without sacrificing water performance. A simple scheme had been worked out for the retraction of the main step in flight and a hydrofoil type of float had been developed that was housed completely within the wing, features which saved a large amount of fuel weight. The float retracted into the wing using a method which was similar in principle to the Spitfire's undercarriage. Each wing had eight bomb cells, level with and between the two engine nacelles, and could take 250lb (113kg) bombs; the four inner cells were also large enough to take 500lb (227kg) bombs and the four cannon turret was housed in the rear centre section with a single cannon at the rear. Respective cruise speeds for Hercules or Griffon were 268mph and 250mph (431km/h and 402km/h) at 5,000ft (1,524m), time to 5,000ft 3.6 and 3.0 minutes and service ceilings 22,000ft (6,706m) and 25,500ft (7,772m). The normal fuel load was 1,830gal (8,319lit) and overload 3,810gal (17,320lit), maximum range 5,000 miles (8,047km) and 24 months was the time quoted to produce the first machine.

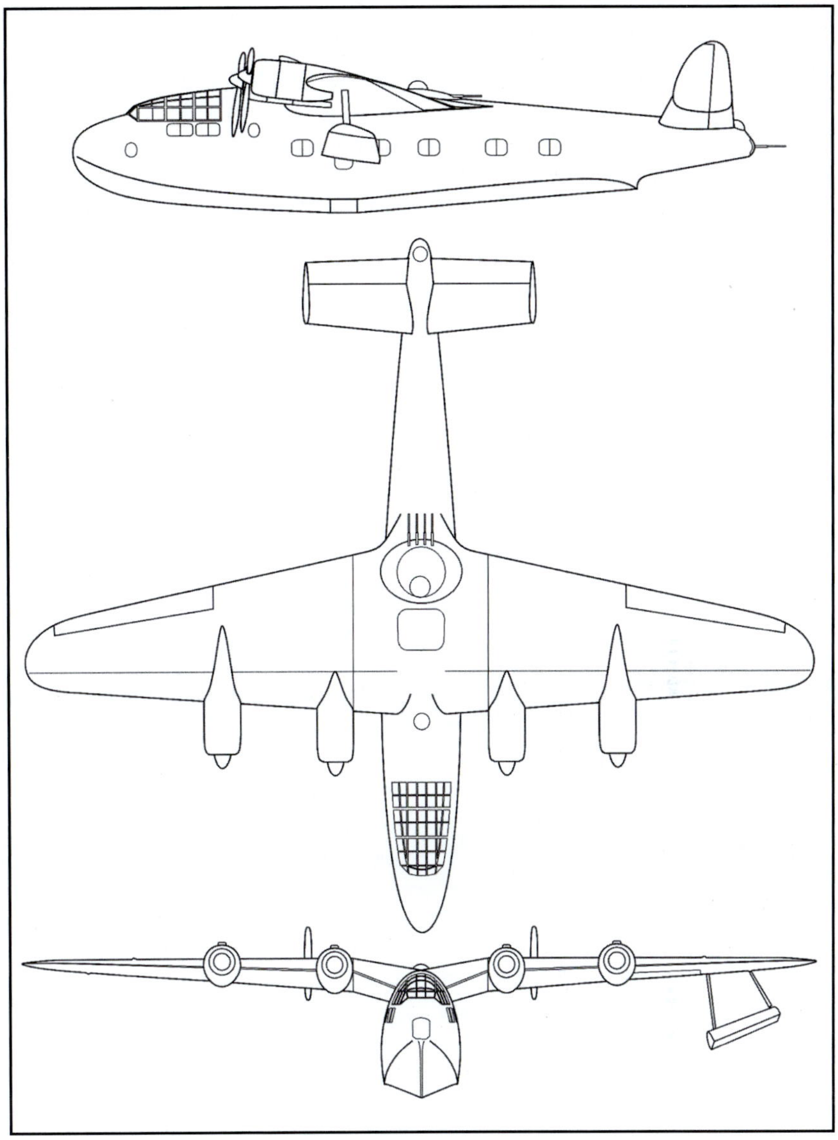

ABOVE Supermarine 328 (6.39). *Ralph Pegram*

BELOW Photo of a manufacturer's model of the Supermarine 328 which would have been included in the project brochure. *Ralph Pegram*

Supermarine 328 (6.39)	
Span	97ft 0in (29.57m)
Length	82ft 9in (25.22m)
Wing Area	1,360sq.ft (126.35sq.m)
All-Up-Weight	for 1,500 miles (2,414km) range Hercules 49,890lb (22,630kg) normal, 63,690lb (28,889kg) overload, Griffon 49,710lb (22,548kg) normal, 65,610lb (29,760kg) overload
Powerplant	4 × Hercules HE.7.SM or Griffon
Max Speed/Height	Hercules 323mph (520km/h) at 17,500ft (5,334m), Griffon 326mph (525km/h) at 17,500ft (5,334m)
Armament	4,000lb (1,814kg) bombs, 4 × 20mm cannon

On 18 July 1939 RAE Farnborough reported on these designs and noted that Shorts' single rudder restricted the rear field of fire while Blackburn had poor bomb stowage. It placed Supermarine as the best general layout and Saro second; Shorts and Blackburn were 'inferior'. The Tender Design Conference, held on 28 July, generally agreed. Saro's retractable float was described as 'an excellent feature' but Shorts' experience in constructing large flying boats gave extra confidence because, while that company's design had very conservative general features, if the R.5/39 type was required at an early date it was the only one that could be ordered with a guarantee of delivery; this design would also have to have twin rudders.

The Conference considered that the Supermarine 328 was the best compromise but, if it was adopted, it was recommended that the design's wing area should be slightly increased and Saro's retractable wingtip float should be included together with larger airscrews; the latter would be made possible by moving the inboard engines some 10in (25.4cm) further outwards. The question of Supermarine agreeing to provide a half-scale model would also need investigation. The second string was carefully discussed and Saro's project was felt to be 'very enterprising', while the company was also developing a half-scale model. The spars and integral tanks would need some redesign but it was agreed that, with these changes, the design should be recommended. Blackburn's B.32 was placed last on all counts and contained so many disadvantages that it was not worth pursuing.

In August 1939 a decision was taken to go ahead with the Supermarine 328. However, at a meeting held on 4 October to discuss the future experimental aircraft programme, it was stated that the Air Staff would not call for a replacement for the Sunderland for some time and so R.5/39 as a requirement could be abandoned. By 4 December the Air Staff had proposed some modifications to produce a Mk.II Sunderland with an extra 500gal (2,273lit) of internal fuel, changes to the hull forebody, redesigned bomb gear, folding wingtip floats (which increased the cruise speed by 4mph [6.4km/h] and added a little range) and twin fins in place of the existing single fin (to reduce a slight tendency to swing on take-off). However, some strong voices complained that a replacement aircraft should have been put in hand over twenty months ago and that the R.5/39 prototype should by now have been well on the way to completion. R.5/39 had suffered delays but its requirements came very close to the American Consolidated Coronado boat now in production. In contrast, others felt that R.5/39 had grown from 'a smaller and faster Sunderland' to almost a 'boat version of the B.1/39' (Chapter Four).

On 13 January 1940 CinC Coastal Command, in a letter to the Air Staff, expressed his concern regarding the decision to abandon R.5/39 and he urged the continuance of flying boat development in general, perhaps at an all-up-weight of 84,000lb (38,102kg). R5/39's requirements were now reconsidered in relation to the newly proposed 'smaller flying boat' (later called R.13/40 and described below) and to the improved Sunderland (the latter was continued and a great deal of work completed, which made it possible for the type to take-off at 56,000lb [25,401kg] weight). A meeting convened on 24 April recommended that an order should be placed with Shorts and Saro for a flying boat to R.5/.39, but with Centaurus or Sabre engines instead of the original Hercules which would increase the all-up-weight from 65,000lb (29,484kg) to roughly 100,000lb (45,359kg).

Saunders-Roe S.38A & S.39

In the meantime Saro's private venture work had continued and the S.38A was drawn in April 1940 with Centaurus engines, the same guns as the S.38, all-up-weight 62,000lb (28,123kg), 4,000lb (1,814kg) bombs and maximum speed 285mph (459km/h) at 15,000ft (4,572m). Saro also produced the alternative S.39 design which offered a range of 5,000 miles (8,047km) and had four turrets with machine guns. It was powered by four Centaurus but the Napier Sabre was an alternative engine. (Blackburn had also replaced its B.32 project with the twin Centaurus B.39, again prepared to R.5/39).

Saunders-Roe S.38A & S.39 (4.40)	
Span	137ft 0in (41.76m)
Length	105ft 0in (32.00m)
Wing Area	2,200sq.ft (204.39sq.m)
All-Up-Weight	80,000lb (36,287kg) normal, 96,000lb (43,545kg) overload
Powerplant	4 × Centaurus
Max Speed/Height	300mph (483km/h) at 15,000ft (4,572m)
Armament	bombs, 4 guns

The momentum for a new flying boat grew and on 25 May 1940 instructions were given for development orders to be placed with Shorts and Saunders-Roe. In July a new specification, R.14/40, replaced R.5/39 which detailed a maximum load approaching 100,000lb (45,359kg) and 20,000lb (9,072kg) of bombs.

Saunders-Roe S.41

Saro revised its S.39 project to R.14/40 and it now had a span of 137ft 6in (41.91m) and length 101ft 6in (30.94m) with the same wing area; it also returned to the four-cannon turret. There was also the S.39A with four Hercules, a four cannon turret and a

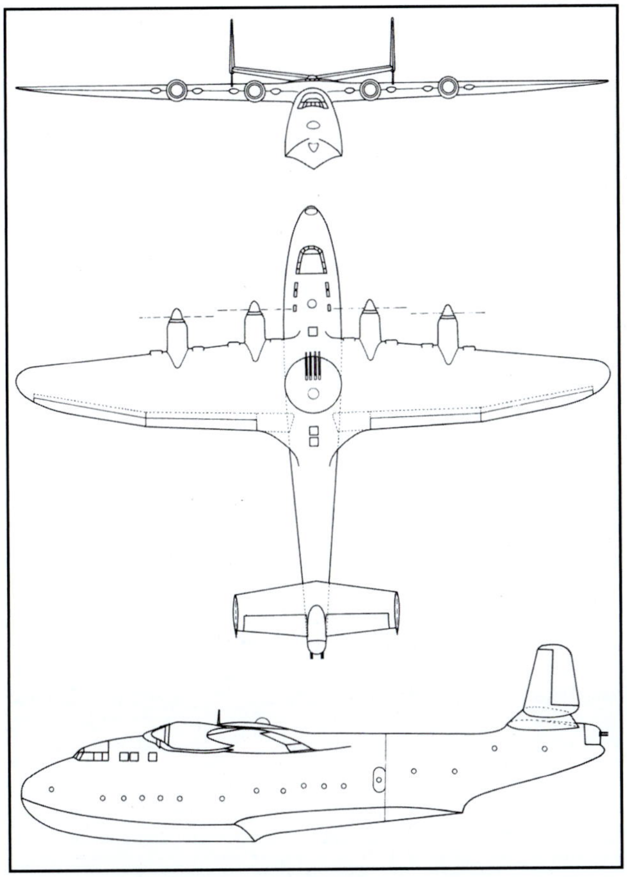

ABOVE Saunders-Roe S.39 (4.40). *Saro via Michael J. F. Bowyer*

ABOVE Saunders-Roe S.41 (1.41 onwards). *Saro via Michael J. F. Bowyer*

retractable planing bottom along the lines of Blackburn's B.20 (this project was not tendered). In January 1941 the company began the S.41 which had a powerful defensive armament of four cannon in a rear turret and twelve machine guns, four in each of two dorsal turrets and in a nose turret. This had four Centaurus, an all-up-weight of 110,000lb (49,895kg) and a range of 3,800 miles (6,116km), and was also offered to R.14/40. (Drawings and more information for the Saro S.38, S.39 and S.41 projects, and the P.162 below, can be found in the books *Aircraft for the Royal Air Force, From Sea to Air* and *Saunders and Saro Aircraft since 1917*).

Shorts S.35 Shetland

Shorts too had continued its work although details of the company's efforts to R.14/40 have not been found. In the event the two rivals were asked to submit a combined project, otherwise no order would be forthcoming, which resulted in the Shetland. This was primarily a Shorts design but Saro and Shorts agreed to co-operate on the aircraft's manufacture, the former having the responsibility for the 150ft (45.72m) wing and, thanks to the work achieved with the Shrimp, some of the hull's hydrodynamic design, while Shorts did the hull and tail unit and undertook final assembly. The first prototype, DX166, made its maiden

Shorts Shetland Mk.I (flown)	
Span	150ft 4in (45.82m)
Length	110ft 9in (33.76m)
Wing Area	2,636sq.ft (244.89sq.m)
All-Up-Weight	125,000lb (56,699kg)
Powerplant	4 × 2,525hp (1,883kW) Centaurus VII
Max Speed/Height	at 120,000lb (54,431kg) weight 268mph (431km/h) at 2,000ft (610m)
Armament	Maximum 12 × 2,000lb (907kg) bombs, 2 × 20mm cannon, 10 × 0.5in (12.7mm) machine guns

BELOW The scale-model Saro S.37 Shrimp research aircraft.

ABOVE Shorts Shetland prototype DX166 in 1944. When completed this was the biggest British aircraft built to date.

LEFT One of the Shetlands caught on camera flying just above the water.

flight on 14 December 1944 and performed well both in the air and in the water, but the end of the war meant that its time had passed. This aircraft was accidentally burnt at its moorings on 28 January 1946. As early as mid-1943 the RAF was looking at converting the Shetland for transport duties and an order for six such aeroplanes was seriously considered in mid-1945. The second prototype, DX171, was converted for civil use but this took some time to complete and it did not fly until 17 September 1947; it was too late and the aircraft was scrapped in 1951.

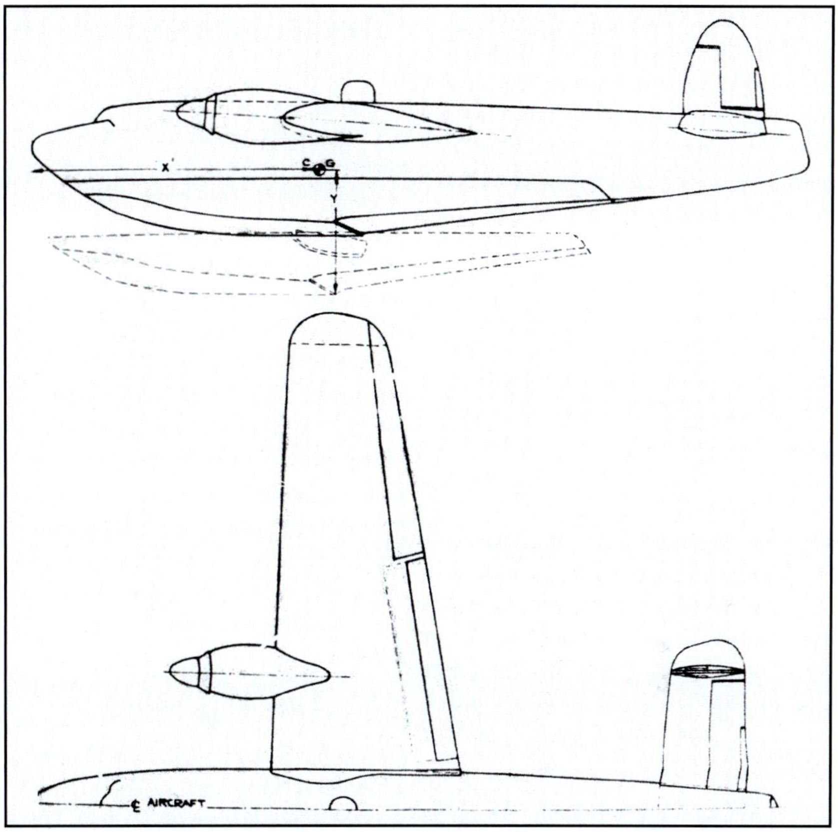

ABOVE Rough drawing showing how the Blackburn B.40 would have looked.

Blackburn B.40

This was a proposed improvement of Blackburn's B.20. At a meeting held on 24 April 1940 the development of the B.40 was recommended to meet a requirement for a small flying boat of high performance and long range. It was thought that, with two Sabres or Centaurus and based on the Lerwick specification, an aircraft of about 38,000lb to 40,000lb (17,237kg to 18,144kg) would meet the speed requirements but might be too small to reach some of the range limits. The B.40 was initiated as a DTD experiment to acquire information on the retracting hull method of improving the performance of small flying boats and Specification R.13/40 was subsequently allotted to the design.

By January 1941 the B.40 had become a 'replacement' for the Sunderland 'to do better and more economically what the Sunderland already does well,' but not for duties beyond the Sunderland's powers (which were some of the objectives of R.14/40). On 28 January W. S. Farren reviewed the B.40 which, in comparison with the Sunderland, had a better top speed (by 35mph [56km/h] to 40mph [64km/h]), a better cruise speed (25mph [40km/h] to 30mph [48km/h]), at least equal range and a heavier armament. Farren described the B.40 as a single central float plane in which the 'float' or 'pontoon' could be drawn up to the fuselage and faired with it; the wingtip floats were also retractable. Due to the need to keep the airscrews and tail clear of the sea, the hull depth for a boat the size of the Sunderland was several feet more than was needed to accommodate the crew and equipment, consequently the hull's air drag was high. With a retractable single pontoon both fuselage and pontoon could be made the correct size and their combined air drag was about 75% of that from the corresponding boat hull. All of the fuel would go in the pontoon.

Farren added that the case for development depended on whether there was a continuing need for a seaplane of this general size, whether the Sunderland was good enough, or could be developed to be good enough, and whether the technical promise of the R.13/40 was backed by sound evidence. He felt that the loss of the smaller B.20 experimental prototype was irrelevant – the cause was known (aileron flutter and nothing to do with the retracting pontoon) and the retracting gear was simple and had given no trouble. The Sunderland could 'scarcely be taken much further' and it could not carry engines that would give it the speed of the R.13/40; this older type was being developed as far as possible but it remained a Sunderland – well tried, reliable, slow and over-roomy. The B.40 had two Centaurus which, at their present power, was equivalent to the Sunderland's four Pegasus and there was good reason to believe that the newer engine would eventually give 20% more power.

The B.40 would cruise at 165mph (265km/h) and potentially offered a range of 2,300 miles (3,701km), dependent on the engine manufacturer's figures for fuel consumption. Its defensive armament was one 20mm cannon in a power mounting, two turrets each with two 0.5in (12.7mm) machine guns and four hand-held 0.303in (7.7mm) machine guns. Farren concluded that, providing the appropriate duties for a Sunderland size of seaplane remain to be carried out, duties for which an R.14/40 was extravagant and for which a landplane was unsuited, the technical case for building the B.40 was good. It offered advances in air and water performance and a number of operational advantages.

However, on 3 March 1941 DD/RDT stated that the required range, now 3,500 miles (5,632km), could not be met by the B.40 and ACAS(T) observed that the aircraft therefore ceased to be of operational interest. Nevertheless work continued and on 19 September two prototypes, ES966 and ES979, were ordered. On 20 December N. E. Rowe, DTD, declared that the 'range now available, viz. 3,050 miles [4,909km] without a bomb, is not acceptable to the Air Staff. Moreover the single-engined performance of the aeroplane is quite unacceptable.' The single-engine case had grown steadily worse since the design had been first put forward, when the emphasis was on high performance rather than very long range and a weight of around 52,000lb (23,587kg) was in mind.

The Air Staff saw no requirement for a small high-performance boat of the R.13/40 class and pointed out that, compared to the Sunderland Mk.III, it showed very little advance in range – which was now the major requirement. In addition it had been found that landplanes were acceptable for ranges of 2,500 miles to 3,000 miles (4,023km to 4,828km) and were now being used. Rowe added that at the present weight and size, made necessary to approach Air Staff requirements, the retracting hull showed practically no advantage and so the value of the experiment would be lost. Since the Air Staff had no operational use for the boat it was now necessary to cancel it, and this had been agreed.

Blackburn B.40 (1940)	
Span	98ft 1in (29.89m)
Length	?
Wing Area	1,400sq.ft (130.06sq.m)
All-Up-Weight	52,500lb (23,814kg)
Powerplant	2 × 2,080hp (1,551kW) Bristol Centaurus
Max Speed/Height	245mph (394km/h) at 5,000ft (1,524m)
Armament	bombs, 1 × 20mm cannon, 4 × 0.5in (12.7mm) and 4 × 0.303in (7.7mm) machine guns

Specification R.2/48

This 1948 requirement almost falls outside the period covered by this book but it belongs here because it represents, for the RAF at least, pretty well the last throw of the dice for the military flying boat. R.2/48, dated 12 November 1948, was the last British specification to be issued for a maritime reconnaissance and anti-submarine flying boat and asked for a 4,000lb (1,814kg) bomb load (or 8,000lb [3,629kg] with reduced fuel), a maximum speed of 350 knots (403mph/648km/h) and a design that was suitable for the economic production of eighty aeroplanes. Some published sources have stated that the Blackburn B.78 was designed to R.2/48 but official documents make no reference to it.

Saunders-Roe P.104

During the period 1948 to 1953 fourteen schemes of flying boat were prepared by Saro to the requirements of R.2/48. These all had four engines (Centaurus, Griffon or Nomad); used either single or twin fins and rudders or a V-tail; had a retractable ASV radar scanner mounted in the underside either in the nose or behind the wing; and spans varying between 134ft (40.84m) and 168ft (51.21m). The layout proposed to R.2/48 in early 1949 was a high-wing cantilever monoplane having four individual engines and to be fitted with either a twin-finned or a 'V-type' tail unit. The stabilising floats would retract upwards and outwards to the extreme tips of the wing. P.104's hull had been designed with a larger deadrise angle and a greater length-to-beam ratio than had hitherto been chosen for British flying-boats in order to improve its performance in rough-water (the merits of this type of hull had been substantiated by tests in the Saunders-Roe tank and wind tunnel). The airframe would be constructed of high grade Duralumin and Alclad.

The various bombs and other weapons were carried on slides on the inside of two large doors, one on each side of the flying-boat, which were hinged along their upper edges to the hull. Provision would be made to carry a 6ft (1.83m) radar scanner below the hull aft of the main step, in such a position that the entire lower hemisphere could be scanned. When not in use, this scanner would retract to a position inside the hull above the water-line. Armament would consist of a twin 20mm turret mounted in the top of the hull between the wing and tail unit, and eight forward-firing 3in (76.2mm) rocket projectiles, the latter carried inside the hull on the lower deck and fired from retractable slides.

The powerplant was four compounded Rolls-Royce Griffons fitted with 14ft (4.27m) diameter single disc propellers though, if necessary, standard Griffon 57 engines could be used as an interim measure, the performance remaining unaltered except for a reduction in range. The power cell was also interchangeable with that used on the Avro Shackleton (described shortly), and the Bristol Centaurus or Napier Nomad were also available as alternatives. A crew of nine would be carried; the wing's thickness/chord

Saunders-Roe P.104 (3.49)	
Span	134ft 0in (40.84m)
Length	105ft 0in (32.00m)
Wing Area	(excluding floats) 1,664sq.ft (154.59sq.m)
All-Up-Weight	(with 4,000lb/1,814kg bombs) 89,900lb (40,778kg),
Powerplant	4 × 2,500hp (1,864kW) Compounded Griffon RGT.30.SM
Max Speed/Height	290mph (467km/h) at 10,000ft (3,048m)
Armament	Maximum 8,000lb (3,629kg) bombs, Pentane, mines, 8 × 3in (76.2mm) rockets, 2 ×20mm cannon
Saunders-Roe P.104 Modified (6.49)	
Span	134ft 0in (40.84m)
Length	109ft 6in (33.38m)
Wing Area	1,736sq.ft (161.28sq.m)
All-Up-Weight	(4,000lb/1,814kg bombs) 94,250lb (42,751kg)
Powerplant	4 × 2,850hp (2,125kW) Turbo Griffon
Max Speed/Height	310mph (498km/h) at 10,000ft (3,048m)
Armament	As previously(?)

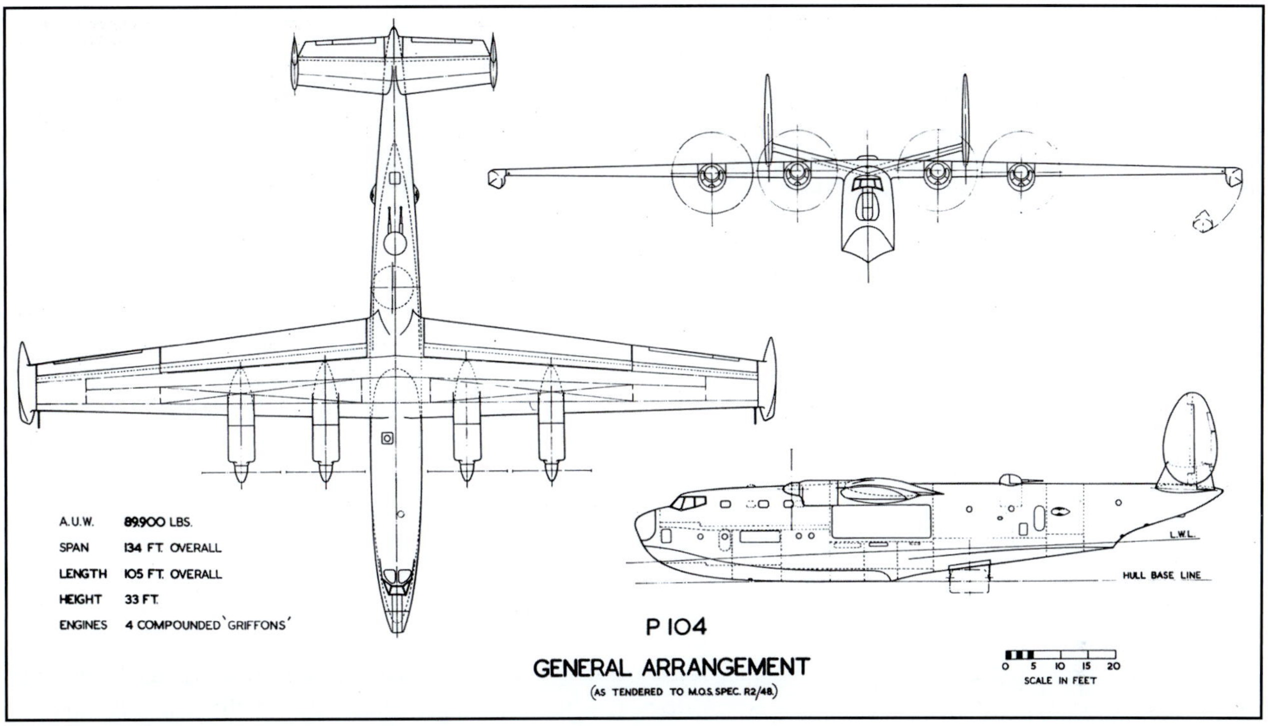

ABOVE Saunders-Roe P.104 in March 1949. *National Aerospace Library*

BELOW Saunders-Roe P.104 in June 1949. *National Aerospace Library*

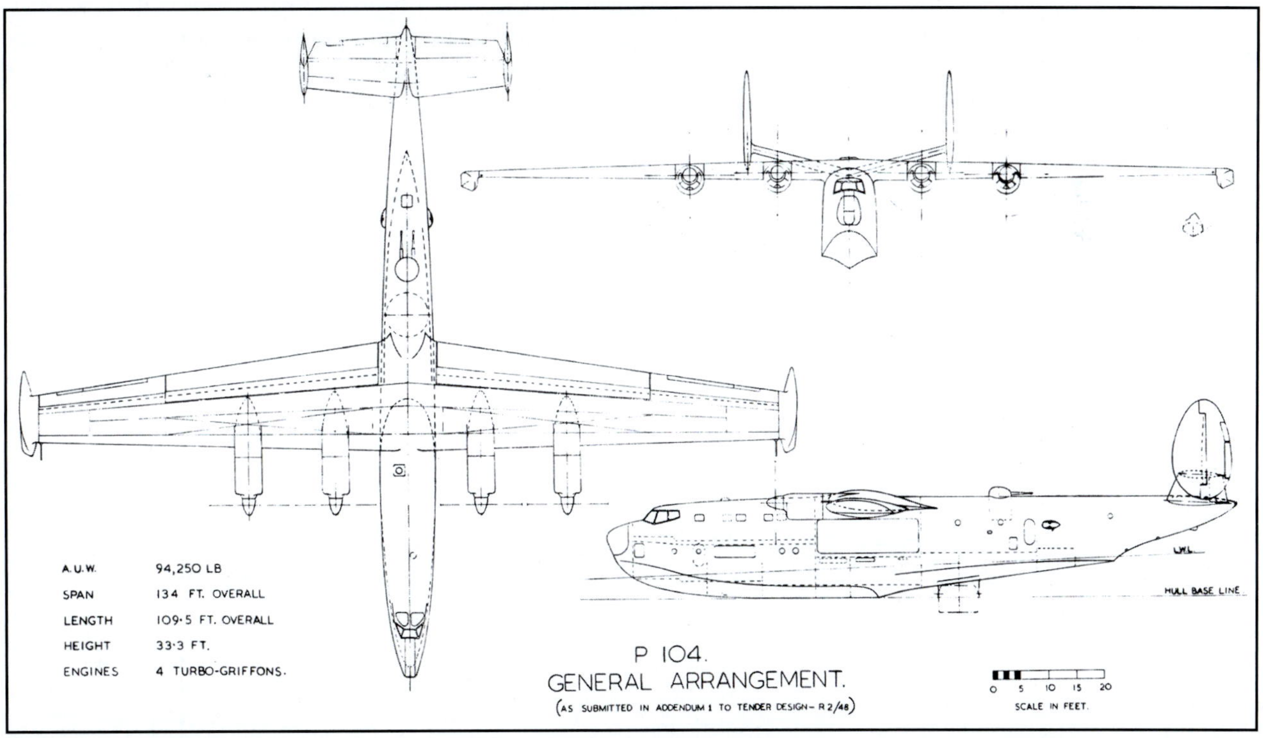

ratio was 18% at the root and 12% at the tip; and at the gross (all-up) weight the maximum rate of climb at sea level was 1,210ft/min (369m/min) and service ceiling 21,000ft (6,401m). This data relates to the twin-fin design, but the version with a V tail would have the same dimensions and weight. A first flight would be made 152 weeks from ITP.

An addendum, dated June 1949, showed a slightly stretched fuselage to accommodate recent developments in Sonobouys, ASV radar and radio equipment. This development was powered by four more powerful Turbo Griffons engines, which at the gross (all-up) weight gave a maximum rate of climb at sea level of 1,390ft/min (424m/min) and a service ceiling of 23,500ft (7,163m).

Shorts P.D.2

Three projects were offered by Shorts, one a new design called the P.D.2, the second a development of the R.14/40 Shetland set at 128,500lb (58,287kg) all-up-weight and giving a maximum speed of 281mph (452km/h) at 10,000ft (3,048m), and the third a Seaford fitted with new engines. The modified Shetland had a ceiling of 24,500ft (7,468m) and an endurance of 15.7 hours, the Nomad-powered P.D.2 32,000ft (9,754m) and 14.6 hours and the Centaurus P.D.2 27,600ft (8,412m) and 13.7 hours. For a maiden flight the Shetland variant would only need 12 months from ITP but the P.D.2 would take 35 months to reach completion.

Shorts P.D.2 (early 1949)	
Span	155ft 0in (47.24m)
Length	97ft 10.5in (29.83m)
Wing Area	2,132sq.ft (198.07sq.m)
All-Up-Weight	Nomad 105,000lb (47,627kg), Centaurus 107,000lb (48,534kg)
Powerplant	4 × Napier Nomad or Centaurus 661
Max Speed/Height	Nomad 326mph (525km/h) at 10,000ft (3,048m), Centaurus 299mph (481km/h) at 10,000ft (3,048m)
Armament	Pentane, bombs, mines and RPs, 2 × 20mm cannon in a twin dorsal turret

Supermarine 524

Supermarine's investigations had shown that it was quite feasible to design a flying boat to take any of three alternative engines and still meet the requirements. The Napier Nomad compound engine resulted in the lightest boat, with a fuel requirement of 2,620gal (11,910lit), but this engine was untried and Supermarine felt it was unwise to rely on it at the exclusion of other types. The Centaurus piston needed 3,700gal (16,820lit) of fuel but by the time the boat was in production this engine could be obsolescent. However, there appeared to be no conventional British alternative and for this reason the Centaurus could remain in service for many years. The Bristol Proteus turboprop called for a slightly larger boat and the fuel requirement was 5,000gal (22,730lit); in each case all of the fuel was housed in the wings. The maximum continuous cruising speeds were Centaurus 326mph (525km/h), Proteus 389mph (626km/h) and Nomad 381mph (613km/h), sea level rates of climb 1,410ft/min (430m/min), 2,060ft/min (628m/min) and 1,420ft/min (433m/min) and service ceilings 32,000ft (9,754m), 35,200ft (10,729m) and 34,600ft (10,546m); each version offered a twelve hour endurance.

Apart from what Supermarine called 'the powerplant adaptability', its proposals were conventional. A single-spar light alloy wing was used and a retractable twin 20mm turret was fitted in the hull roof just forward of the wing. The ASV scanner was mounted in the bottom of the hull in a retractable drum set level with the wing trailing edge. During operations this projected beneath the hull so that the field of search embraced the whole lower hemisphere and then for landing it retracted into a watertight compartment, the aperture in the hull bottom being closed by electrically-operated doors. The bombs and Pentanes (anti-submarine missiles) were carried in compartments let into the sides of the hull beneath the wings, which for release were run out on carriers along the inner wing. Aft of the entrance door a compartment was provided on each side to take four rockets with 25lb (11.3kg) or 60lb (27.2kg) heads and these were carried on frames and rollers so that they could be run out for firing. The first flight would take 160 weeks from ITP.

An RAE assessment dated 17 June 1949 noted that the Shetland variant

BELOW Supermarine 524 with Proteus engines (early 1949).

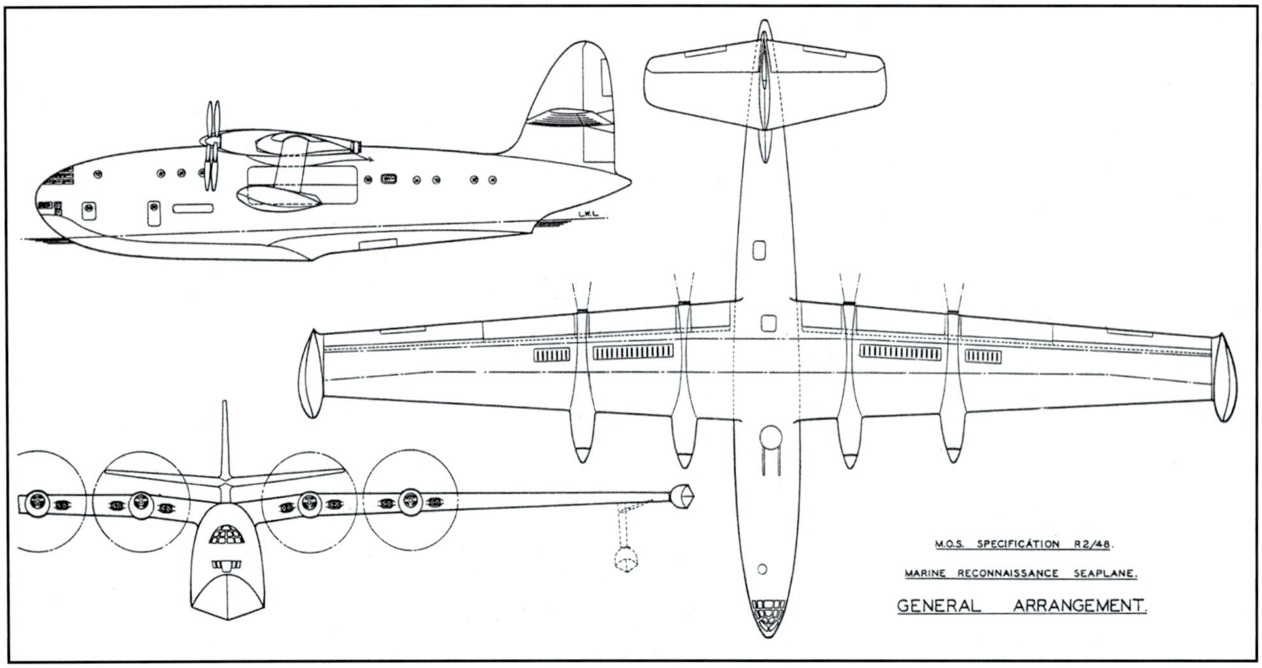

was considered to be too experimental, so it was decided to recommend that a contract should be placed with Fairey for two or three prototypes while Hawker and Westland should be informed of the drawbacks to their designs and be invited to submit revised proposals, with a view to one of them being ordered as a prototype.

Their revisions were assessed at a further conference held on 16 May 1938. DTD said that both were good and Westland was free to undertake the design effort but Hawker was about to begin work on a single-seat fighter to replace the Hurricane. No decision was taken but on 30 July the Admiralty declared that both projects used experimental features which were important to the FAA and so it wanted two prototypes ordered from each company. On 5 August Liptrot recommended that two prototypes should come from Hawker 'as a spur to Fairey,' but ten days later the Air Ministry recommended placing an order with Fairey for four prototypes while both the Hawker and Westland designs should be reconsidered in January 1939.

Then, on 22 September 1938 it was learnt that Fairey had gone right ahead with its design while Hawker was very much behind, so there would be a delay of perhaps five or six months in getting a comparative prototype. It was also thought that it would be difficult to get Hawker really interested. By the end of the month Westland was out of the picture because it now had too much work in hand (the Lysander army co-operation aircraft and a fighter) whereas Hawker had not made much progress when Fairey had made a great deal. On 30 November 1938 the Admiralty commended to the Air Ministry that no further progress should be made with the Hawker and Westland proposals.

Fairey Barracuda

The prototype contract for the Fairey project was placed on 30 January 1939 and in February a production order for 300 examples was agreed. A Ministry document noted that the Exe had to be discarded but it was over two and a half months before it was finally decided to fit the Rolls-Royce Merlin. Replacing the Exe was a 1,250bhp (932kW) Merlin 30 which forced Marcel Lobelle, Fairey's chief designer, to redesign the aircraft. His answer was a low-wing type with the rest of the airframe not dissimilar to the final shape. Fairey also wished to use its own and far more powerful P.24 engine, but the Merlin stayed.

In due course, to ensure that the requirements were met in full and to satisfy the CofG, the wing was pushed up to the shoulder position. Fitted with the low wing, and loaded with all of its equipment, the aeroplane would have fallen outside its safe operating envelope, so if the low wing was to be retained its leading edge would have to be moved forward and this would affect part of the pilot's view. Also the wing had to be foldable with the undercarriage fully retractable (on the Swordfish and Albacore the latter was fixed). The Barracuda was also fitted with large Fairey-Youngman flaps which, apart from their usual function, could be set at a negative angle of 30° to serve as dive brakes. The first prototype became airborne on 7 December 1940 and the type was eventually named Barracuda. Despite numerous development problems 2,600 were built, the first entering service in 1943 and the last lasting into 1953.

Fairey Barracuda Mk.I (flown)	
Span	49ft 2in (14.99m)
Length	39ft 9in (12.12m)
Wing Area	414sq.ft (38.46sq.m)
All-Up-Weight	13,177lb (5,977kg) with torpedo
Powerplant	1 × 1,260hp (940kW) Merlin 30
Max Speed/Height	250mph (402km/h) clean
Armament	3 × 500lb (227kg), 6 × 250lb (113kg) bombs, 1 × torpedo or 3 × depth charges, 3 × 0.303in machine guns

BELOW Fairey Barracuda Mk.II P9791 takes off using rocket assistance.

ABOVE RK409 was a Barracuda Mk.III of Ship's Flight, HMS *Theseus*. It is pictured in late 1946. *Fred Motley*

BELOW Rare colour photo of a Fairey Barracuda, here serving with 767 Squadron Fleet Air Arm. What appears to be a mobile control tower stands behind.

Supermarine 322 'Dumbo'

Despite its dismissal for being 'too experimental', in 1939 an order was placed for two Type 322 prototypes, R1810 and R1815, to test the variable-incidence wing, the fitting of which precluded a retractable undercarriage. However, Supermarine's Spitfire commitments meant that the first example (built entirely of wood) did not fly until 6 February 1943 but it was found that, despite the fixed undercarriage, the second prototype (with Duralumin wings and the same 1,640bhp [1,223kW] Merlin 32) flew rather faster than the Barracuda Mk.II (240mph [386km/h] against 279mph [449km/h]). The 322 was nicknamed 'Dumbo'.

Supermarine 322 (flown)	
Span	50ft 0in (15.24m)
Length	40ft 0in (12.19m)
Wing Area	319.5sq.ft (29.68sq.m)
All-Up-Weight	12,000lb (5,443kg) design figure
Powerplant	1 × 1,300hp (969kW) Merlin 30
Max Speed/Height	279mph (449km/h) at 4,000ft (1,219m)
Armament	3 × 500lb (227kg), 6 × 250lb (113kg) bombs or 1 torpedo, 2 × 0.303in (7.7mm) machine gun

Bristol Beaufort/ Blackburn Botha

This story brings together three different specifications and resulted in two different aeroplanes, one quite successful

ABOVE Well known photo of the Supermarine Type 322 'Dumbo' prototype. *Phil Butler*

but the other less so. Specification M.15/35 requested a shore-based torpedo bomber while G.24/35 called for a general purpose land-based reconnaissance aircraft, both were approved by DTD in September 1935 and then issued to tender; later they were combined into 10/36. M.15/35 resulted in the following designs.

Avro 672

This was a much modified development of Avro's Anson reconnaissance and training aircraft first flown on 24 March 1935. It was powered by two Armstrong Siddeley Terrier engines and had a dorsal turret with two machine guns. Span was 59ft 8in (18.19m), length 45ft 2in (13.77m).

Blackburn M.15/35

An unnumbered high-wing design was submitted which used Armstrong Siddeley Terrier or Aquila engines.

Boulton Paul P.83

Fitted with either Bristol Pegasus X or Rolls-Royce Goshawks, this aircraft had an all-metal monocoque structure and carried four bombs or a single torpedo in a recess in the lower fuselage. A dorsal turret housed twin Lewis guns and one forward-facing 0.303in (7.7mm) Browning was mounted in the port fuselage side level with the pilot. The Goshawk variant required 413gal (1,877lit) of fuel while the Pegasus pushed this up to 457gal (2,078lit), but the two engines gave a near identical performance including a 2,000ft/min (610m/min) rate of climb at sea level and 28,000ft (8,534m) service ceiling.

Boulton Paul P.83 (12.35)	
Span	67ft 0in (20.42m)
Length	47ft 9in (14.55m)
Wing Area	575sq.ft (53.42sq.m)
All-Up-Weight	13,846lb (6,280kg) or 13,739lb (6,232kg)
Powerplant	2 × Bristol Pegasus X or RR Goshawk
Max Speed/Height	254mph (409km/h) at 10,000ft (3,048m)
Armament	4 × 500lb (227kg) or 250lb (113kg) bombs or 1 × torpedo, 3 × 0.303in (7.7mm) machine guns

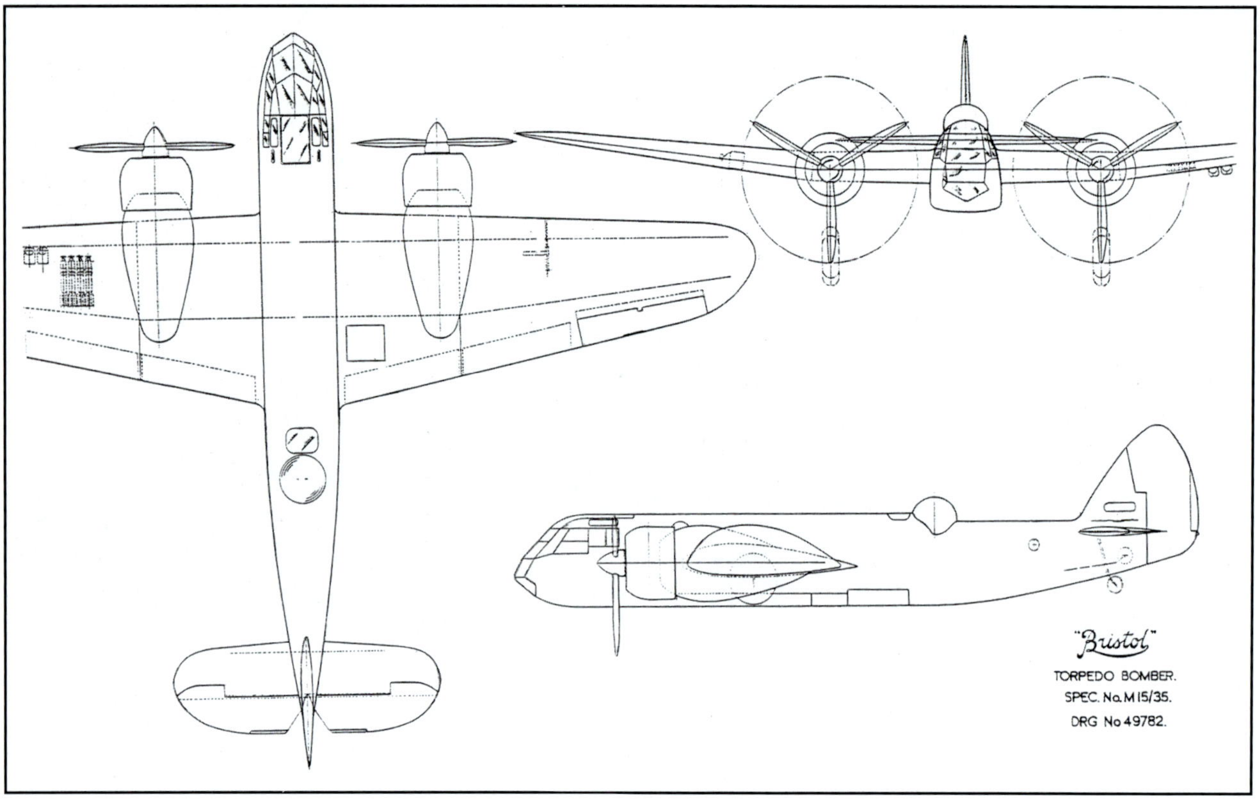

ABOVE Bristol 150 to M.15/35 (3.12.35).

Bristol 150

The Type 150 was similar in most respects to Bristol's Type 142M (Blenheim) medium bomber, and the company's G.24/35 project, with the only differences those necessitated by M.15/35's requirements for equipment or strength. For example the cabin was wider and longer to allow, respectively, more comfortable navigation and for the torpedo to be stowed internally; in fact an extra 4ft 6in (1.37m) of cabin had been added between the front spar and the pilot's seat. The rear turret was identical to the G.24/35 and the single fixed Browning gun in the starboard wing and the bomb cells were the same as the 142M. Maximum rate of climb was 2,070ft/min (631m/min) at 5,000ft (1,524m) and service ceiling 26,500ft (8,077m).

Bristol 150 (3.12.35)	
Span	58ft 0in (17.68m)
Length	44ft 3in (13.49m)
Wing Area	492sq.ft (45.71sq.m)
All-Up-Weight	12,022lb (5,453kg)
Powerplant	2 × 870hp (649kW) Bristol Perseus PER.3.M
Max Speed/Height	286mph (460km/h) at 5,000ft (1,524m)
Armament	4 × 500lb (227kg) or 250lb (113kg) or 1 × 2,000lb (907kg) bombs or 1 × torpedo, 3 × 0.303in (7.7mm) machine guns

Handley Page and Vickers

Both companies converted their B.9/32 medium bombers (the Hampden and the original Type 271 'Wellington' prototypes) to M.15/35.

A Tender Design Conference, held on 8 January 1936, described Blackburn's armament scheme as excellent, particularly the torpedo and bomb installation, and noted that a high wing specially suited the requirement. Bristol's Perseus was not very good and the Handley Page and Vickers conversions were both too big, but these did show that it was quite possible for a medium bomber to carry an alternative torpedo without an adverse effect on its design. The following G.24/35 designs were actually submitted ahead of the M.15/35 projects and their Tender Design Conference was held on 10 December 1935.

Avro 675

This was a further development of the Anson, again powered by Terriers (the Aquila was an alternative), but featuring a nose observer's position plus a long glazed cockpit roof. Span 50ft 6in (15.39m), length 42ft 6in (12.95m).

Blackburn G.25/35

No information survives on this Aquila-powered machine but the Tender Conference rated it as good.

Boulton Paul P.84

This was a near identical aeroplane to the P.83 and shared interchangeable wings, tail unit, undercarriage and (derated Goshawk) engines; the principal differences were small changes to the body layout, a slightly lower weight and reduced internal fuel. An alternative engine was the Aquila AE.3.M radial

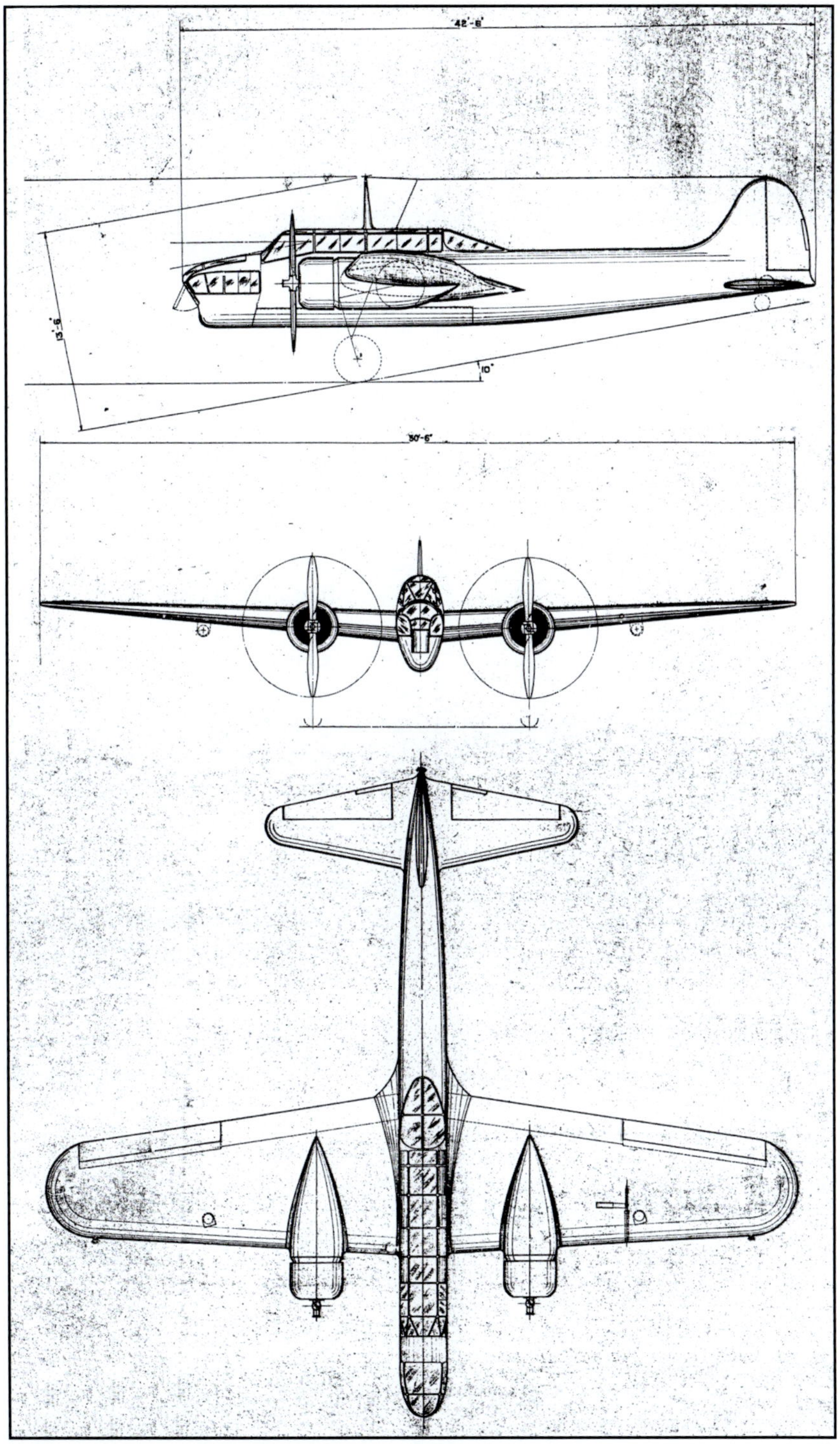

ABOVE Avro 675 (2.11.35). *Avro Heritage Centre*

which also required a smaller wing, had a slightly shorter tail (but the same body), carried less fuel (297gal [1,350lit] against 317gal [1,441lit]) and gave a sea level rate of climb of 1,750ft/min (533m/min) when the Goshawk offered 2,000ft/min (610m/min); service ceilings were 25,500ft (7,772m) and 26,500ft (8,077m) respectively. The gun and bomb carrying arrangements were unchanged from the P.83. G.24/35 specified a maximum all-up-weight of 9,500lb (4,309kg) but Boulton Paul had concluded that the range and performance could not be met within this limit.

Boulton Paul P.84 (12.11.35)	
Span	60ft 0in (18.29m) or 67ft 0in (20.42m)
Length	45ft 6in (13.87m) or 47ft 9in (14.55m)
Wing Area	495sq.ft (45.99sq.m) or 575sq.ft (53.42sq.m)
All-Up-Weight	11,430lb (5,185kg) or 12,915lb (5,858kg)
Powerplant	2 ×Aquila AE.3.M or Goshawk
Max Speed/Height	239mph (385km/h) or 245mph (394km/h) at 5,000ft (1,524m)
Armament	2 × 500lb (227kg) or 4 × 250lb (113kg) bombs, 3 × 0.303in (7.7mm) machine guns

Bristol G.24/35

This aircraft was another conversion of the 142M with a wider cabin and a larger rear turret but with the same bomb cells and fixed Browning gun. Sea level rate of climb was 1,613ft/min (492m/min) and service ceiling 26,200ft (7,986m).

Bristol G.24/35 (18.11.35)	
Span	56ft 0in (17.07m)
Length	39ft 9in (12.12m)
Wing Area	469sq.ft (43.57sq.m)
All-Up-Weight	10,920lb (4,953kg)
Powerplant	2 × 670hp (500kW) Aquila
Max Speed/Height	254mph (409km/h) at 5,000ft (1,524m)
Armament	2 × 500lb (227kg) or 4 × 250lb (113kg) bombs, 3 × 0.303in (7.7mm) machine guns

Gloster G.24/35

No details available.

Westland G.24/35

A project with two Perseus engines, recesses for four 500lb (227kg) bombs or two torpedoes on each side of the lower fuselage (described at the Design Conference as a 'novel feature') and a dorsal turret. Span was 57ft 0in (17.37m) and wing area 475sq.ft (44.13sq.m). The Conference declared that neither Gloster's or Westland's proposals were acceptable.

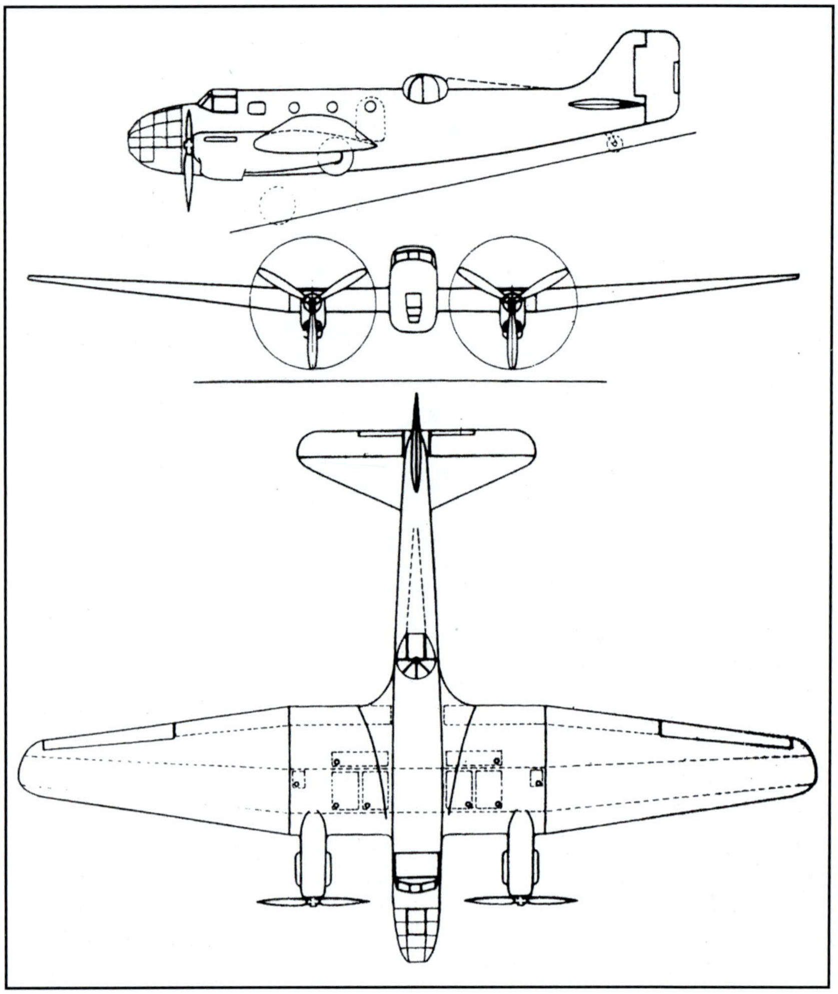

The Air Ministry had thought that the most that could be done with these specifications was to produce a single basic design that could be converted at some stage of production to either of the two different types. However, Bristol's Leslie Frise had always envisaged making a single aircraft type that would combine the functions of general reconnaissance and torpedo bombing and he pressed these ideas on the Air Ministry. The two Bristol designs described above were both Blenheim developments that were intended to use some of the same parts. Frise felt that Squadron Leader Oxland was a great stumbling block to this, declaring that he had no vision and was always thinking of details. Nevertheless, in December 1935 the Air Staff discussed the prospects of such a union and concluded that it would be possible for both of these roles to be combined in one class of aircraft.

On 14 January 1936 DTD recommended merging the two specifications and ordering duplicate prototypes from Avro, Blackburn and Boulton Paul. On 26 January CAS agreed that Avro, Blackburn, Boulton Paul and Bristol, who had all submitted good designs, should be asked to submit new projects that merged the two

ABOVE Boulton Paul P.84 with Goshawk power units (12.11.35). *Les Whitehouse*
BELOW Bristol design to G.24/35 (18.11.35).

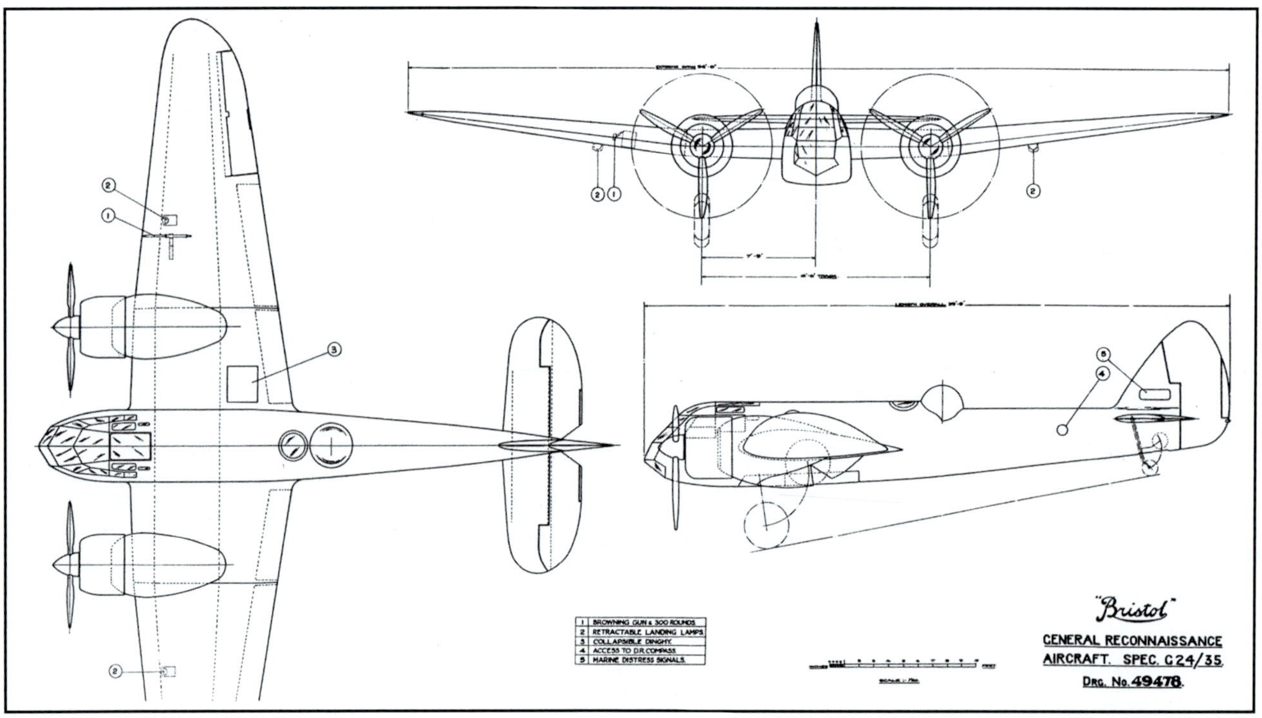

requirements and this was the direction that was taken. The resulting designs were discussed individually with their companies during January and February 1936 and in March CAS decided to amalgamate the two documents, at the same time giving approval for production orders 'off the drawing board' to both Blackburn and Bristol. The new specification, 10/36 approved in June, contained some revisions including a speed with a normal weapon load of 220mph (354km/h) at 15,000ft (4,572m) and a range with a 1,000lb (454kg) load of 1,250 miles (2,012km).

Avro 10/36

This appears to have been a revision of the Type 675.

Blackburn B.26

This was ordered as the Botha and the first production example, which doubled as a prototype, made its maiden flight on 28 December 1938. However, its Perseus engines gave insufficient power and in October 1940, after a brief career, it was decided not to use the type as an operational aircraft any longer. A total of 580 were built (over 670 were cancelled) and most were used for training.

Blackburn Botha Mk.I (flown)	
Span	59ft 0in (17.98m)
Length	51ft 1in (15.57m)
Wing Area	518sq.ft (48.12sq.m)
All-Up-Weight	17,628lb (7,996kg)
Powerplant	2 × 880hp (656kW) Perseus X
Max Speed/Height	253mph (407km/h) at 15,000ft (4,572m)
Armament	2 × 500lb (227kg), 4 × 250lb (113kg) or 1 × 2,000lb (907kg) bombs or 1 × torpedo, 3 × 0.303in (7.7mm) machine guns

Boulton Paul P.86

This aircraft was identical to the Aquila-powered P.84 except that it had a longer nose, extra observation windows, alternative torpedo accommodation and increased tankage to cope with the longer range limit; these additions added 120lb (54kg) to the weight and reduced

ABOVE Photos of Blackburn Botha W5065 taken in August 1941. *Blackburn*

BELOW Botha L6507 poses for publicity photos in 1940 or 1941.

ABOVE The 'prototype' Bristol Beaufort L4441 in October 1938. *Crown Copyright*

the maximum speed by about 2mph (3.2km/h). In the general reconnaissance role the service ceiling would be 32,000ft (9,754m), as a torpedo bomber 29,000ft (8,839m).

Bristol 152

On 21 February 1936 Bristol completed a brochure for a design which was much altered from its previous studies. The body length ahead of the wings was increased but the fixed forward-firing gun was still as per the 142M and a dorsal turret was still in place. There was permanent tankage in the wings for 415gal (1,887lit) of fuel and construction was to be all-metal, the wings being covered in Alclad. The general reconnaissance version could carry the required bomb loads – one 2,000lb (907kg), two 500lb (227kg) or four 250lb (113kg) – and the only change for the torpedo role concerned the body floor for loading the 1,900lb (862kg) torpedo, the weapon being slung with half of its diameter protruding. At a late stage of the airframe's construction the necessary modification would be made to suit either type. Alternative powerplants were the Perseus or Aquila which gave respective sea level rates of climb 2,000ft/min (610m/min) and 1,670ft/min (509m/min), and service ceilings 27,000ft (8,230m) and 26,500ft (8,077m). The initial production order was placed on 22 August 1936.

Bristol 152 (with Perseus - 2.36)	
Span	58ft 0in (17.68m)
Length	44ft 3in (13.49m)
Wing Area	492sq.ft (45.71sq.m)
All-Up-Weight	11,725lb (5,318kg)/12,230lb (5,547kg) torpedo/general bomber
Powerplant	2 × 870hp (649kW) Perseus
Max Speed/Height	288mph (463km/h) at 5,000ft (1,524m)
Armament	2 × 500lb (227kg), 4 × 250lb (113kg) or 1 × 2,000lb (907kg) bombs or 1 × torpedo, 0.303in (7.7mm) machine guns

Bristol 152 (with Aquila - 2.36)	
Span	56ft 0in (17.07m)
Length	44ft 3in (13.49m)
Wing Area	492sq.ft (45.71sq.m)
All-Up-Weight	10,895lb (4,942kg)/10,910lb (4,949kg) torpedo/general bomber
Powerplant	2 × 670hp (500kW) Aquila
Max Speed/Height	262mph (422km/h) at 5,000ft (1,524m)
Armament	2 × 500lb (227kg), 4 × 250lb (113kg) or 1 × 2,000lb (907kg) bombs or 1 × torpedo, 0.303in (7.7mm) machine guns

Bristol and Blackburn were the only companies to build aeroplanes to 10/36. Although originally intended to meet the one document and to use Perseus engines, the Botha's structural weight was 2,000lb (907kg) more than the Bristol design, which was later named Beaufort.

In early 1937 the Air Staff changed its requirements and decided that bombing should now be the type's primary role, which meant that the aircraft would now have to operate at 15,000ft (4,572m) altitude instead of 5,000ft (1,524m). Since the planned engine for the Beaufort was only moderately supercharged, a fully supercharged alternative was introduced to allow cruise at 15,000ft. At about the same time the engines themselves were changed because Bristol felt that the Perseus had no development potential, and in July 1937 permission was given to switch to the company's new engine, the Taurus. Blackburn stayed with the Perseus and the Botha suffered accordingly.

Construction of the first Beaufort production aircraft was accelerated so that it could act as a prototype while the airframes following were purposely retarded to allow all necessary alterations and modifications to be incorporated. However, progress was

ABOVE AW304 was a Beaufort Mk.II.

slow and compared unfavourably with the Botha, whose Mock-up Conference took place in January 1937. By the following April the Beaufort mock-up was only two-thirds complete and its Conference finally took place in September. The mock-up included a four-gun turret but Oxland told Bristol to take that out and replace it with a single Lewis gun, because it appeared that Browning production would be insufficient to satisfy every aircraft type that needed it. The first Beaufort, L4441, was much delayed and did not get airborne until 15 October 1938, but part of the problem was that Bristol was also preparing the Beaufighter to follow closely behind the Beaufort. The first true production Beaufort was delivered in October 1939 and eventually over 1,100 were built, later examples receiving American Pratt & Whitney Twin Wasp radial engines.

Bristol 152 Beaufort Mk.I (flown)	
Span	57ft 10in (17.63m)
Length	44ft 7in (13.59m)
Wing Area	?
All-Up-Weight	21,228lb (9,629kg)
Powerplant	2 × 1,130hp (843kW) Taurus
Max Speed/Height	265mph (426km/h) at 6,000ft (1,829m)
Armament	2,000lb (907kg) bombs, mines or 1 × torpedo, 4 × 0.303in (7.7mm) machine guns

BELOW T9540 was the first of a batch of Beaufort Mk.Vs.

ABOVE Bristol Beaufort in flight.

Specifications S.6/43 and S.11/43 Shorts Sturgeon

Fairey Shore-Based Torpedo Bomber

This unsolicited work does not appear to have been prepared against any specific requirement. A brochure was completed on 8 April 1942 for a machine powered by two Merlin 32s and armed with two 0.5in (12.7mm) Colt machine guns in an upper turret, one 0.5in lower rear gun, two 0.303in (7.7mm) Browning machine guns in the nose and one 21in (53.3cm) torpedo carried in a fuselage bay. It carried 450gal (2,046lit) of fuel, had a top speed of 210mph (338km/h) at sea level and would take 9 minutes to reach 10,000ft (3,048m) and 27.5 minutes to 20,000ft (6,096m); service ceiling was 21,750ft (6,629m) and range 840 miles (1,352km). An extra 300gal (1,364lit) could be carried to give an overload weight of 28,205lb (12,794kg) and a range of 1,500 miles (2,414km). A second brochure dated 12 July described a revised version with two 1,980bhp (1,476kW) Griffon 61s, all-up-weight 34,100lb (15,468kg), maximum speed 279mph (449km/h) at 5,000ft (1,524m), time to 5,000ft 4.5 minutes, normal range 1,500 miles and overload range 2,000 miles (3,219km).

Fairey Torpedo Bomber (8.4.42)	
Span	c70ft 3in (21.41m)
Length	c47ft 8in (14.53m)
Wing Area	660sq.ft (61.32sq.m)
All-Up-Weight	26,090lb (11,834kg)
Powerplant	2 × 1,650hp (1,230kW) Merlin 32
Max Speed/Height	249mph (401km/h) at 10,000ft (3,048m)
Armament	3,500lb (1,588kg) torpedoes, 5 × machine guns

During the first months of 1943 the Admiralty began putting together Specification S.6/43 for a torpedo bomber and reconnaissance aircraft, which included a maximum all-up-weight of 24,000lb (10,886kg) and an overall length of 46ft (14.02m). Design studies were requested from Armstrong Whitworth, Cunliffe-Owen, de Havilland (who were unable to comply), Fairey and Westland. Before the studies were received the CNR (Chief Naval Representative), in the light of advance information from the companies concerned, was able to forecast that, in general terms, a twin-engine aircraft to meet S.6/43 was unlikely to weigh less than 26,000lb (11,793kg), but a top speed of 300mph to 340mph (483km/h to 547km/h) might be possible. On the other hand a single-engine type would be lighter but, inevitably, would have a disappointing performance that would be little better than the Barracuda.

Therefore, at a Design Committee meeting held on 27 March 1943, it was accordingly decided to split the functions, and draft requirements were begun for i) a torpedo bomber and ii)

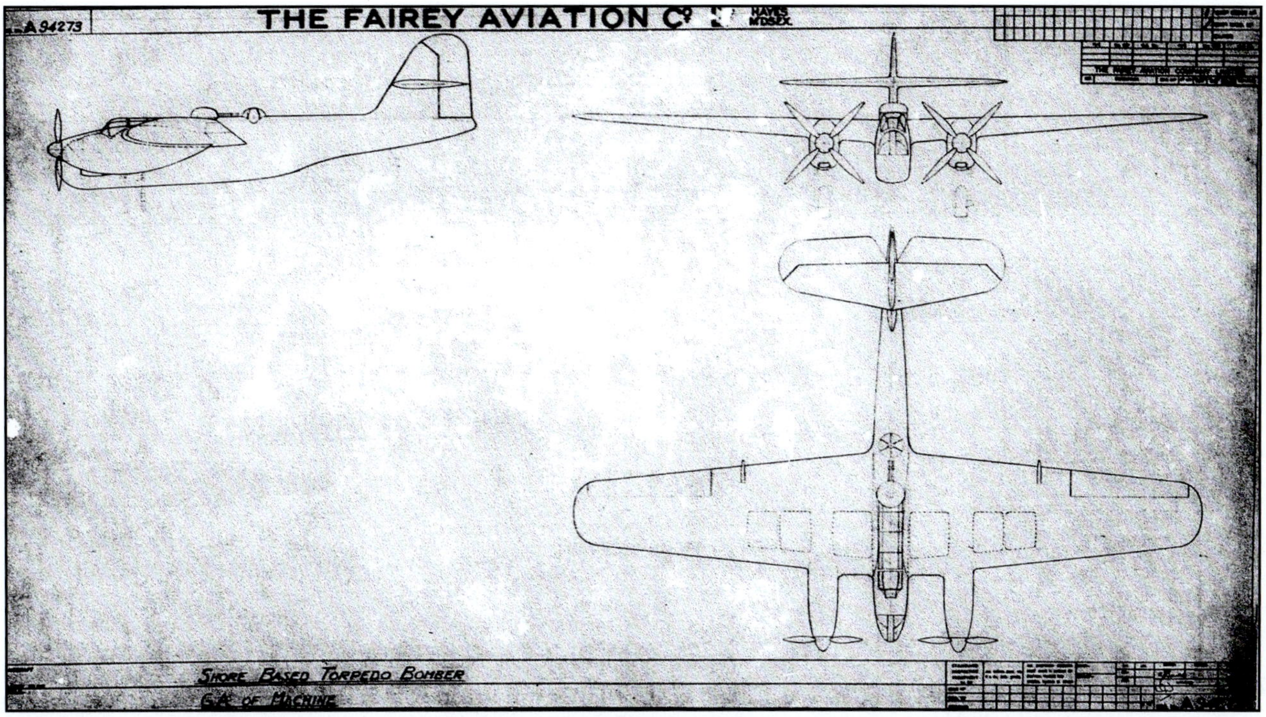

ABOVE **The only known drawing of the Fairey Shore-Based Torpedo Bomber, with twin Merlin 32s (9.4.42).**

BELOW **Poor quality but unique manufacturer's impression of the Fairey twin Merlin torpedo bomber.**

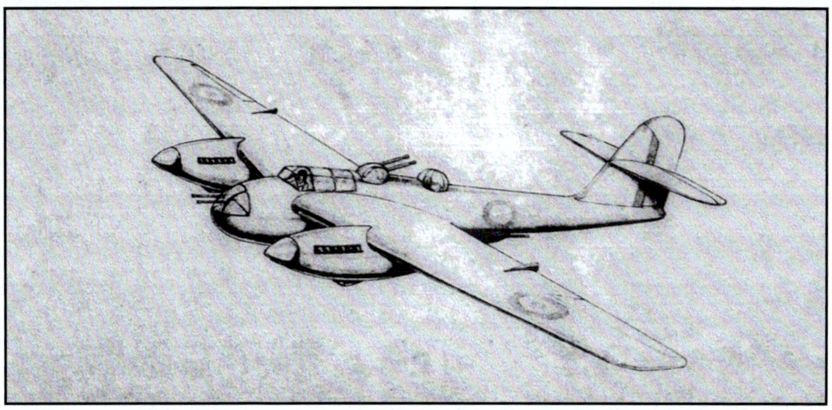

a reconnaissance bomber with reconnaissance as its primary function. The former became O.5/43 and was to lead to the Fairey Spearfish described later; the latter became S.11/43. The S.6/43 proposals, however, were not cancelled since it was felt that they should be examined with a view to confirming the decision. These were as follows:

Armstrong Whitworth AW.53

AWA declared that the weight and length limits could not be met. The latter would certainly not provide sufficient yawing movement to counteract the effect of losing one engine, particularly during take-off, and even with a large fin and rudder the length could not be kept below 48ft (14.63m). The defensive armament comprised twin 0.5in (12.7mm) machine guns in a mid-upper turret and the offensive load, carried in an internal bomb bay, could be a torpedo or up to six 500lb (227kg) bombs; four rocket projectiles could also be loaded under each wing. Sea level top speed was 288mph (463km/h) and rate of climb fully loaded 1,280ft/min (390m/min); less the torpedo and half fuel this became 1,820ft/min (555m/min).

For the approach, Fowler flaps were fitted which moved backwards for 15% of the wing chord, while both ailerons were drooped to give the effect of full-span flaps. When the ailerons were in this position, differential gearing automatically came into action which ensured that the control remained light in operation. To counteract the adverse yawing moments due to drooped ailerons, a spoiler was automatically coupled to the control system, but this was inoperative when the ailerons were in their normal position. A tricycle undercarriage was provided with an exceptionally long vertical travel that would absorb the kinetic energy of landing with a vertical velocity of 17ft/sec (5.18m/sec); AWA's experience with the Albemarle bomber's gear had been very beneficial here. A laminar flow wing had been rejected but, to ensure a smooth surface free from dimples, the light alloy wing covering was fairly thick. Orthodox construction with light alloy sheeting was used throughout, except for the three fabric-covered control surfaces. The outer wings folded backwards on an inclined hinge at the rear spar and the arrester gear comprised a hook attached to the fuselage underside.

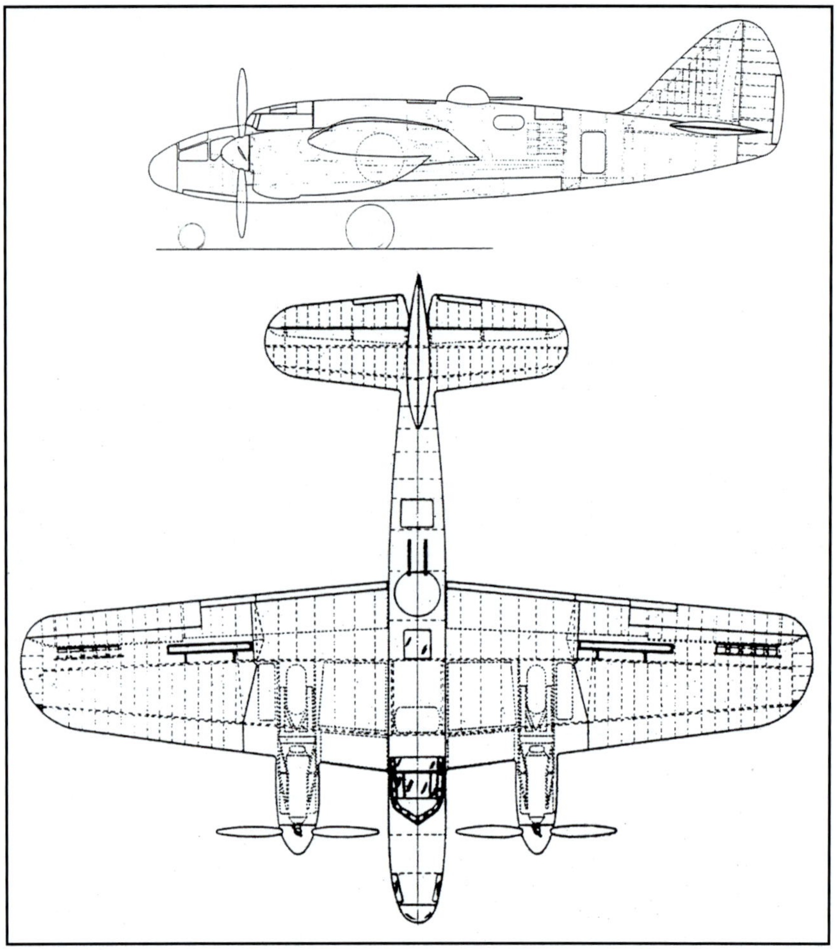

ABOVE Armstrong Whitworth AW.53 (4.43). *Ray Williams*

BELOW Model of the AW.53. *Ray Williams*

Cunliffe-Owen S.6/43

No details are available for the Cunliffe-Owen design save that this machine weighed about 25,000lb (11,340kg) and the Admiralty noted that it was 'over-span and made poor provision for the observer's view.'

AWA AW.53 (4.43)	
Span	60ft 0in (18.29m)
Length	48ft 0in (14.63m)
Wing Area	?
All-Up-Weight	24,930lb (11,308kg)
Powerplant	2 × 1,600hp (1,193kW) Merlin 26
Max Speed/Height	304mph (489km/h) at 9,500ft (2,896m)
Armament	6 × 500lb (227kg) bombs or 1 × torpedo, 8 × RP, 2 × 0.5in (12.7mm) machine guns

Fairey S.6/43

Fairey had explored both of the main alternatives to meet the requirements, either single or twin-engine tractor monoplanes, and had concluded that the single-engine type would virtually be a development of the Barracuda. Such a project was currently being undertaken within the present dimensional limits of the Barracuda specification, but this limited the range and weapon load and so Fairey had concentrated on a twin which offered a greatly improved view for the observer and pilot, a better power/weight ratio, the ability to carry a higher wing loading and the possibility of getting home on one engine. The engines examined included the Hercules 12.SM and Griffon 14.SM, but the Merlin RM.14.SM had been chosen which offered 1,960bhp (1,462kW) on MS power and 1,840bhp (1,372kW) on FS. The Griffon 61 offered a considerable increase in weight but a handsome dividend in performance; the Hercules weighed the same as the Griffon but gave an inferior performance.

The powerplant included the main cooling radiators installed in the wing leading edge for low drag, with oil and intercooler radiators, while the air intake was placed in the nose of the power egg; the variable pitch propellers were to be reversible for braking the aircraft during torpedo or bombing attacks and full-span flaps were to be fitted, based on the Youngman scheme. The outer wings were of all-metal two-spar stressed skin construction, the fuselage was light alloy monocoque throughout, eliminating the need for stringers, and the tail unit had a stressed skin all-metal structure with

Supermarine 524 (early 1949)	
Span	148ft 0in (45.11m) with floats extended
Length	98ft 0in (29.87m)
Wing Area	2,190sq.ft (203.46sq.m)
All-Up-Weight	Centaurus 106,400lb (48,262kg), Proteus 117,100lb (53,116kg), Nomad 103,200lb (46,811kg)
Powerplant	4 × 2,700hp (2,013kW) Centaurus 160, 4 × 3,400hp (2,535kW) Proteus 3, or 4 × Nomad giving 1,580hp (1,178kW) and 324lb (1.44kN) thrust at sea level
Max Speed/Height	Centaurus 326mph (525km/h), Proteus 389mph (626km/h), Nomad 381mph (613km/h)
Armament	4 × 2,000lb (907kg) Pentane, 8 × 1,000lb (454kg) or 16 × 500lb (227kg) bombs, 4 × 1,800lb (816kg) mines, 16 × 300lb (136kg) anti-submarine bombs, 8 × RPs, 2 × 20mm cannon

(essentially an attempt to resuscitate an old design) did not adequately meet the requirement while Shorts' new design had a very poor flight deck layout. The latter was in fact a disappointment and gave the impression that Shorts' project office had concentrated on performance to the exclusion of all other features; for example the brochure barely mentioned strength and stiffness. In addition the hull design was quite old and, in general, the tender showed 'little imagination.' Saro's design (the most comprehensive submitted) was 'a very good attempt' but the hull form left little room for future needs; it did, however, employ the latest ideas on hulls to improve the rough water characteristics. Supermarine's 524 was very attractive and looked good for long-term development but its hull form and method of bomb carriage were inferior to Saro. Supermarine's design was placed second to Saro's.

At the Tender Design Conference held on 25 July 1949 Shorts' modified Shetland was ruled out because of its high weight, but there was general agreement that Saro's P.104 was technically superior to the others. However, it would have to be re-engined with the Centaurus while the question of a further change to the Nomad would need to be considered later. Despite these opinions, in due course a decision was made to place a development contract with Shorts for an R.2/48 aircraft powered by four compound Nomad or Centaurus and the company was told in early 1950 that this project was likely to come to them. Consequently Shorts began reserving capacity, but the programme was then put in suspension pending a decision as to whether a future flying boat was needed.

In July 1951 the whole future of the military flying boat was in question. The venerable Sunderland was still in service but needed replacing and a decision was required as to what aircraft should fill its role. VCAS produced a long report examining the full subject of maritime reconnaissance worldwide and gave support to the R.2/48. The Ministry of Supply (which had replaced MAP) felt strongly that the contract should be placed with Shorts but the Air Staff felt that Saro's design was still the best. VCAS declared that he considered the R.2/48 should be developed and that the work should go to Saunders-Roe, and he invited the Air Council to agree that they should proceed and the Ministry of Supply to place the work with Saro.

Saunders-Roe P.162

In 1952 Saro refined its R.2/48 project into the P.162 long-range reconnaissance and anti-submarine flying boat. The compounded Griffons gave way to four Centaurus, then four Nomads or a mixture of four Centaurus with two more Avon jet engines. The highest weight of the various studies was 155,000lb (70,307kg), the maximum span 157ft (47.85m) and length 126ft 6in (38.56m). The ultimate P.162 had four Rolls-Royce RB.109 turboprops with bomb bays in the lower inboard nacelles, a span of 136ft (41.45m), length 114ft 7in (34.92m) and all-up-weight 148,000lb (67,132kg).

In the early 1950s R.2/48 was renumbered and updated to R.112D but, despite VCAS's thoughts, the flying boat era was all but over. By 1952 it was clear that a flying boat was not required for Atlantic operations because these were now well covered by land-based types like the Avro Shackleton. By the mid-1950s British interest in the military flying boat had ceased. (For a further account of the R.2/48 competition, and the demise of the flying boat in general as an RAF patrol aircraft, the reader is directed towards Chris Gibson's book *Nimrod's Genesis*.)

BELOW This artwork almost certainly shows the Saunders-Roe P.162 project of early 1952. The image was published in *Flight* magazine for 14 March of that year.

ABOVE **This model is thought to represent a later version of Saro's P.162.**

Avro Shackleton

The need to deal with German U-boats in the Battle of the Atlantic was a key driving force behind the introduction of wartime land-based patrol aircraft. Very long range was essential to try to close, as much as possible, the gap in the centre of the ocean which lacked maritime air cover and to assist naval surface ships in defending their merchant convoys. Versions of several bomber types were employed in this task and by the end of the war RAF Coastal Command had used Handley Page Halifaxes and American Boeing B-17 Fortresses and Consolidated B-24 Liberators in the very long-range role. The close of hostilities however, did not mean the end of the RAF's commitment to these duties because the creation of NATO ensured that long-range ocean patrol and air-sea rescue was just as vital as before. To replace the American types a maritime adaptation of the Lancaster was brought into service (which served until 1956) but there was a need for an all-new aircraft specially dedicated to this task.

Avro 696 Shackleton

The result was this development of Avro's Lincoln bomber (Chapter Five) and Tudor airliner and the first brochure was dated 29 January 1946. It described an aeroplane composed of the Tudor's outer wings and

BELOW **The second Avro Shackleton MR.Mk.1 prototype VW131 seen in January 1950.**

ABOVE Shackleton MR.Mk.2 WG531 pictured in transit to the industry show and display at Farnborough in September 1952.

undercarriage, a modified Lincoln wing centre section, a Lincoln tail unit, plus a new fuselage that was deeper and wider than before. One 12,000lb (5,443kg) or a mix of smaller bombs could be carried and power would be supplied by four Merlins to give a top speed of 300mph (483km/h) at 18,300ft (5,578m). The project was selected for RAF Coastal Command service (there is no evidence of any competing designs) and R.5/46 was written around it. As built the 696 had a tail and fin slightly modified from the Lincoln arrangement plus four Griffon 57s with contra-rotating propellers. The prototype flew on 9 March 1949 and the aircraft entered service in April 1951 as the Shackleton. A grand total of 191 Shackletons was built in three versions and the type served until the early 1990s.

Avro 696 Shackleton Mk.I (flown)	
Span	120ft 0in (36.58m)
Length	77ft 6in (23.62m)
Wing Area	1,421sq.ft (132.02sq.m)
All-Up-Weight	82,000lb (37,195kg)
Powerplant	2 × 2,450hp (1,827kW) Griffon 57 & 2 × 57A
Max Speed/Height	294mph (473km/h) at 12,000ft (3,658m)
Armament	Up to 4,000lb (1,814kg) bombs, 2 × 20mm cannon

Chapter Seven
RAF and Fleet Air Arm Torpedo Bombers

ABOVE Bristol Brigand RH747 was photographed for recognition purposes whilst flying from Boscombe Down. *Crown Copyright*

During the war the RAF operated shore-based torpedo bombers whilst the FAA employed both shore and carrier-based types. All of these have been grouped together in this chapter.

Fairey Swordfish

The Swordfish was easily the most famous of the Fleet Air Arm's wartime torpedo bombers and resulted from Specification S.15/33, which requested a general purpose spotter-reconnaissance and torpedo aircraft. Prototypes (all biplanes) were built by Blackburn (the Shark which also entered production), Gloster (the TSR.38) and Fairey. Fairey's prototype first flew on 17 April 1934 and the subsequent production order was covered by Specification 38/34. By the opening of the Second World War the Swordfish was considered rather out of date but it was to prove highly successful during the early years of the conflict and on several occasions covered itself with glory.

ABOVE Fleet Air Arm Fairey Swordfish fly over their parent carrier.

RIGHT Fairey Albacore Mk.I BF759. *Crown Copyright*

Fairey Albacore

The Albacore was a follow-on to the Swordfish and shared its biplane configuration, albeit with an enclosed cockpit, but it was never to acquire the fame of its predecessor. The initial design stemmed from Specification M.7/36 of 8 September 1936 which described a torpedo spotter reconnaissance aeroplane. This document was later cancelled but a replacement, 41/36, was produced in February 1937 to allow the project to be completed. It appears that no competition was forthcoming from any other company and the prototype, L7074, made its maiden flight on 12 December 1938. The first production aeroplanes entered service in 1940 and eventually 800 were built, but by the end of 1943 most of the squadrons using the type had moved on the more advanced aircraft like the Barracuda and the American Grumman Avenger.

Fairey Albacore (flown)	
Span	50ft 0in (15.24m)
Length	39ft 10in (12.14m)
Wing Area	?
All-Up-Weight	10,460lb (4,745kg)
Powerplant	1 × 1,065hp (794kW) Bristol Taurus
Max Speed/Height	161mph (259km/h) at 4,500ft (1,372m)
Armament	4 × 500lb (227kg), 6 × 250lb (113kg) bombs or 1 × 18in (45.7cm) torpedo, 3 × 0.303in (7.7mm) machine guns

Specification S.24/37, Fairey Barracuda and Supermarine 322

In July 1937 two private venture 'TSR Replacement' designs submitted to DTD by Blackburn and Fairey were discussed at the Ministry (details have not been traced but they were probably intended to replace the Swordfish). Fairey's layout had a low wing, Blackburn's a high wing and, since the Admiralty held strong views on high wings, Fairey's low wing could be ruled out. Blackburn's was thought to be 'on the right lines' but it was based on requirements produced about a year previously and, at this stage, a cruise speed of 200mph (322km/h) was considered 'scarcely adequate for an aircraft not likely to be flying until about 1939'. (It is worth noting that the Swordfish's top speed in 1940 was only around 140mph [225km/h], but few could have predicted how long that aircraft would last.) Fairey's rejected low-wing design used two of its own P.24 engines and had an all-metal monocoque structure and two crew; a big feature was a 'high-speed' wing fitted with an early version of the Fairey-Youngman flap. However, the Ministry did not like the idea of twin-engine aircraft operating from carriers and so new requirements were drawn up, which became Specification S.24/37 of 6 January 1938.

S.24/37 requested a carrier-based torpedo bomber, dive bomber and reconnaissance aircraft all in one. Maximum all-up-weight had to be 10,500lb (4,763kg), including one 1,500lb (680kg) torpedo or three 500lb (227kg) or six 250lb (113kg) bombs. An alternative float undercarriage for use in sheltered waters was to be provided in the design but was not required to be constructed (this was later dropped) and in February the document was sent to six companies. The following tenders were submitted.

Blackburn B.21, B.29 and B.36

The design actually tendered to S.24/37 was probably the B.29. The B.21 was drawn in 1937 but was dropped in favour of the B.29 high-wing monoplane project, for which Blackburn built a mock-up. The design was seen as a replacement for the Shark torpedo bomber; it had a high sided fuselage and a single fin and was to be powered by a Rolls-Royce Exe engine (which was originally called the Boreas). After

Blackburn B.29 (1938)	
Span	c50ft 0in (15.24m)
Length	c40ft 0in (12.19m)
Wing Area	?
All-Up-Weight	?
Powerplant	1 × Exe
Max Speed/Height	?
Armament	3 × 500lb (227kg), 6 × 250lb (113kg) bombs or 1 × torpedo, 1 × machine gun

Blackburn's S.24/37 proposals had been rejected a further scheme to S.24/37 called the B.36 was completed which was dated 16 June 1938.

ABOVE Model of the Bristol S.24/37. *Jim Oughton*

BELOW Bristol S.24/37 fitted with floats. *Jim Oughton*

Bristol S.24/37

This high-wing cantilever monoplane project was to be powered by a single Bristol Taurus and could carry the torpedo, or four of the bombs, under the fuselage; a single bomb could also be loaded under each wing. There were two 115gal (523lit) fuel tanks, one to each side of the fuselage, and the folded span was just 12ft 0in (3.66m), the wings folding backwards from the roots. Three crew were carried and for defensive purposes a single Vickers K gun was mounted in the rear cockpit.

Bristol S.24/37 (8.3.38)	
Span	50ft 0in (15.24m)
Length	40ft 0in (12.19m)
Wing Area	450sq.ft (41.81sq.m)
All-Up-Weight	?
Powerplant	1 × 1,035hp (772kW) Taurus TE.1.M
Max Speed/Height	229mph (369km/h) at 5,000ft (1,524m)
Armament	3 × 500lb (227kg), 6 × 250lb (113kg) bombs or 1 × torpedo, 1 × machine gun

Fairey Type 100

This had a shoulder wing arrangement and was powered by a 1,200bhp (895kW) Exe.

Hawker S.24/37

Another shoulder-wing Taurus-powered design, this carried its torpedo beneath the fuselage but all of the bombs went under the wings, three per side. Again the wings folded rearwards a little outside the

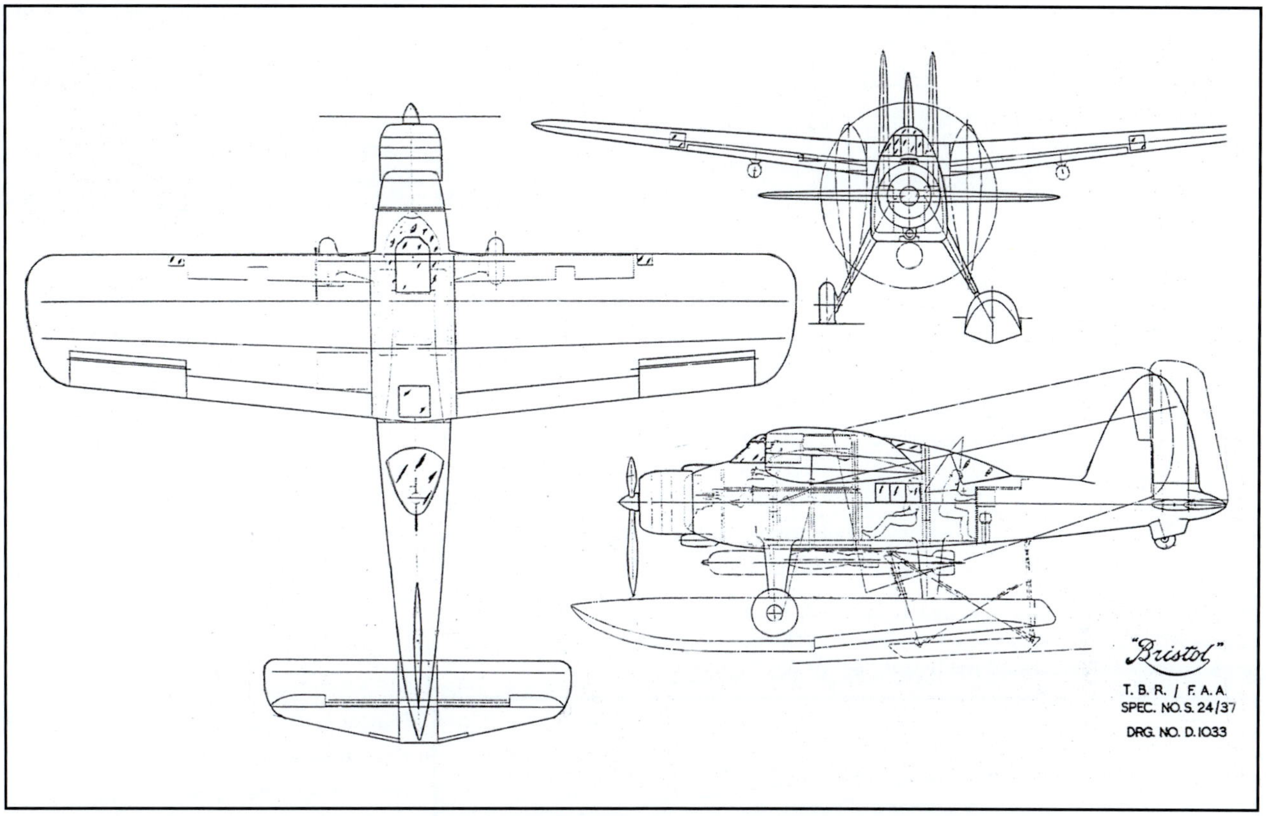

ABOVE **Bristol S.24/37 (8.3.38). This 'combined' drawing shows both ship and float versions.** *Jim Oughton*

BELOW **'Combined' drawing of ship and float versions of the Hawker S.24/37 (3.3.38).** *Chris Farara*

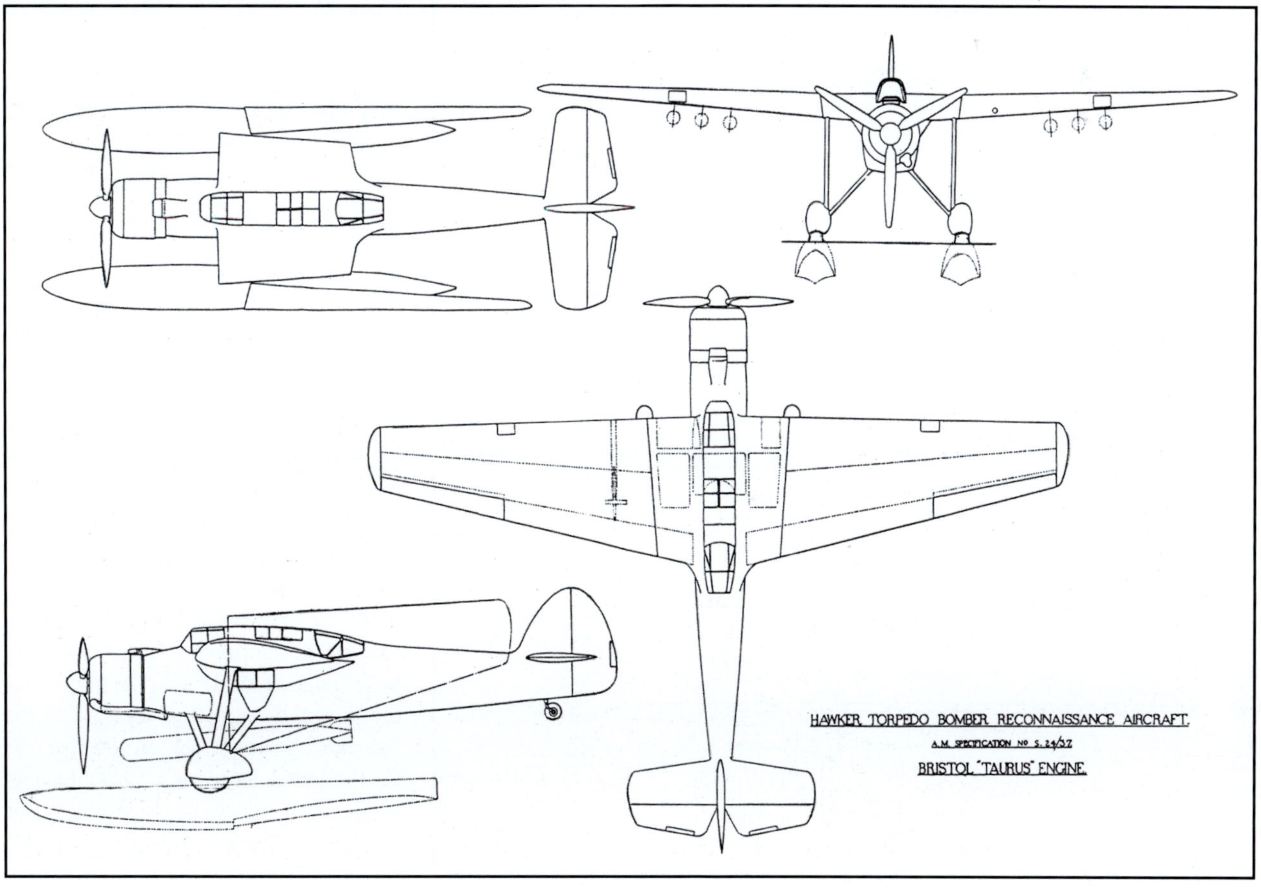

roots (folded width 13ft 6in [4.11m]) and approximately 200gal (909lit) of internal fuel were carried. A single 0.303in (7.7mm) Browning machine gun was housed in the port wing.

Hawker S.24/37 (3.3.38)	
Span	50ft 0in (15.24m)
Length	38ft 6in (11.73m)
Wing Area	?
All-Up-Weight	?
Powerplant	1 × Taurus
Max Speed/Height	?
Armament	3 × 500lb (227kg), 6 × 250lb (113kg) bombs or 1 × torpedo, 1 × machine gun

Supermarine 322

This high-wing design could use the Rolls-Royce Exe (as drawn) or the Bristol Taurus and had its bombs recessed under the underside of the fuselage; folded width was 13ft 6in (4.11m). In the reconnaissance role the all-up-weight would be 10,500lb (4,763kg) and the service ceiling with the Exe was 26,000ft (7,925m), and with the Taurus 27,400ft (8,352m). A novel feature was the variable-incidence wings which, because they offered desirable low-speed characteristics, were seen as a solution to the problem of increasing the angle of descent and reducing the landing run of a 'clean' carrier-based torpedo aircraft. None of the surviving general arrangement drawings shows a Taurus installation.

BELOW The Supermarine Type 322 as originally tendered with a Rolls-Royce Exe engine (7.3.38). The water-based version used the same fuselage but had two very large floats which increased the length to 44ft 0in (13.41m). *Ralph Pegram*

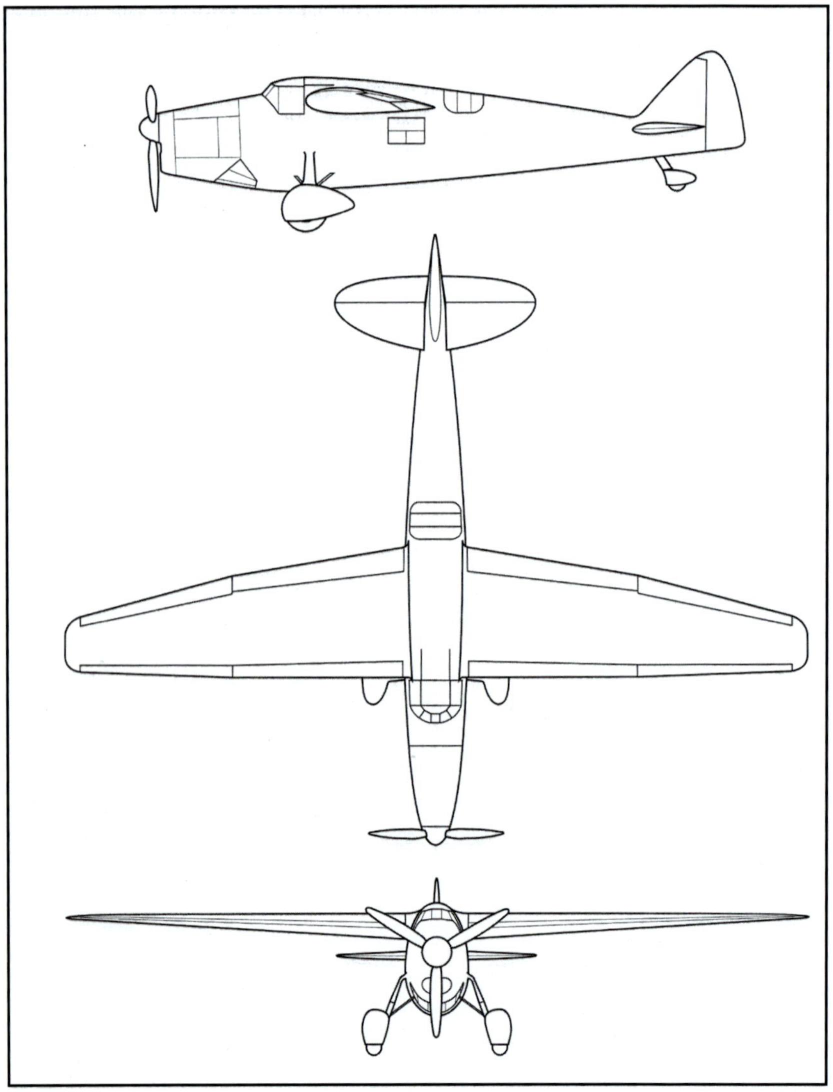

Supermarine 322 (7.3.38)	
Span	50ft 0in (15.24m)
Length	40ft 0in (12.19m)
Wing Area	?
All-Up-Weight	10,070lb (4,568kg) as bomb/TT carrier
Powerplant	1 × 1,100hp (820kW) Exe or 1 × 1,250hp (932kW) Taurus TE.3.SM
Max Speed/Height	(recce role) 255mph (410km/h) or 264mph (425km/h) at 5,000ft (1,524m)
Armament	3 × 500lb (227kg), 6 × 250lb (113kg) bombs or 1 × torpedo, 1 × machine gun

Westland P.10

Another to employ the Taurus, this layout had a braced high wing with a tailwheel landing gear.

Westland P.10 (3.38)	
Span	47ft 9in (14.55m)
Length	?
Wing Area	370sq.ft (34.37sq.m)
All-Up-Weight	10,500lb (4,763kg)
Powerplant	1 × Taurus
Max Speed/Height	213mph (343km/h)
Armament	3 × 500lb (227kg), 6 × 250lb (113kg) bombs or 1 × torpedo, 1 × machine gun

The Tender Design Conference was held on 31 March 1938. Fairey's design was considered the best while Blackburn's was 'inferior' and it was agreed to recommend Fairey, eliminate Blackburn and then reconsider the other four in order to choose an alternative to Fairey. The designs were powered either by the Bristol Taurus radial or the Rolls-Royce Exe air-cooled in-line unit and, at this point, the Taurus was a little ahead of the Exe in development, but both were expected to be available at the same time; the power ratings were similar but the Exe was heavier (work on the Exe was suspended in December 1939). Back at the conference Bristol's project was eventually deleted and Supermarine's

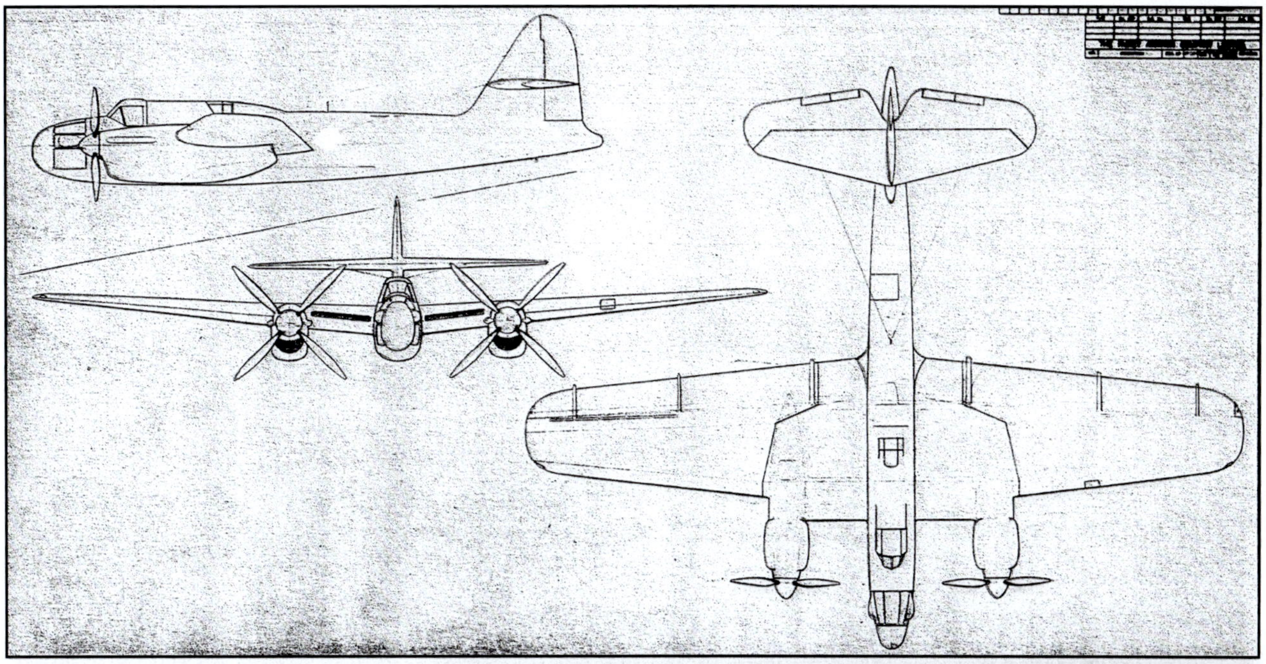

ABOVE Fairey S.6/43 (17.4.43).

an all-metal fin. All of the offensive stores were housed within the fuselage to give a minimum cross sectional area and a centimetric ASV scanner, covering an arc of 150° ahead, was installed in the extreme forward position of the observer's cockpit.

The rear defence comprised either two 0.5in (12.7mm) machine guns on a Rose type mounting or one 20mm cannon. At 25,670lb (11,644kg) weight, the maximum speed at sea level was 312mph (502km/h), time to 10,000ft (3,048m) 8.17 minutes and 20,000ft (6,096m) 17.33 minutes, service ceiling 29,400ft (8,961m) and normal range 900nm (1,667km). Internal fuel was 550gal (2,500lit) but this could be increased to 880gal (4,000lit) to give a range of 1,500nm (2,778km).

Fairey S.6/43 (4.43)	
Span	c56ft 8in (17.27m)
Length	c45ft 10in (13.97m)
Wing Area	?
All-Up-Weight	25,670lb (11,644kg)
Powerplant	2 × 1,960hp (1,462kW) Merlin RM.14.SM
Max Speed/Height	341mph (549km/h) at 17,000ft (5,182m)
Armament	bombs or torpedoes, 2 × 0.5in (12.7mm) machine guns or 1 × 20mm cannon

ABOVE Impression of the Fairey S.6/43.

BELOW Poor quality but unique manufacturer's illustrations showing the Fairey S.6/43 design being loaded with bombs or a torpedo.

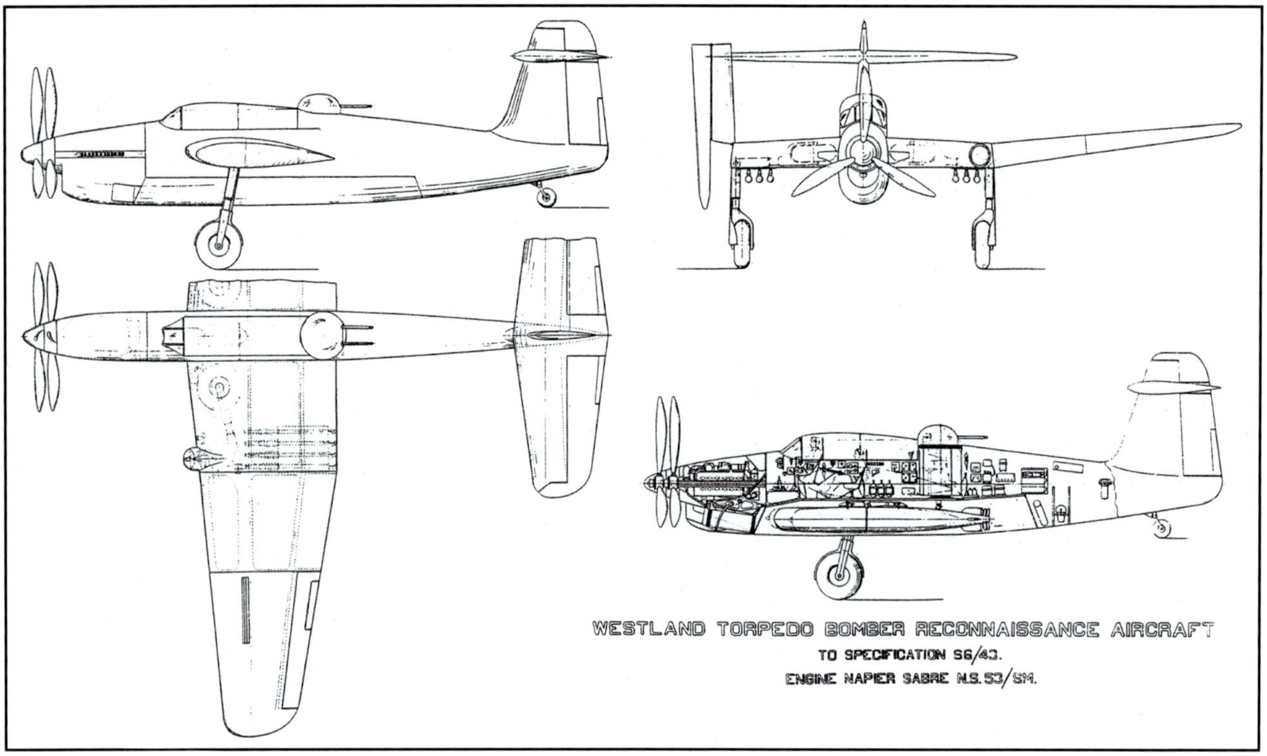

ABOVE Westland S.6/43 (drawing P.1005) (4.43). *Fred Ballam, Westland*

Westland S.6/43

Westland's design was powered by a single Napier Sabre NS.53.SM and could carry a single torpedo or its bomb load internally in a lower fuselage bay (each of these S.6/43 designs could take an 18in [45.7cm], 21in [53.3cm] or 22.4in [56.9cm] diameter torpedo). Four rocket projectiles could be carried under each wing and the wing folded in two positions from just outside the undercarriage position, which meant that the flaps came in two parts. A total of 400gal (1,818lit) of fuel were housed in each wing.

Westland S.6/43 (4.43)	
Span	60ft 0in (18.29m)
Length	45ft 6in (13.87m)
Wing Area	550sq.ft (51.10sq.m)
All-Up-Weight	24,000lb (10,886kg)
Powerplant	1 × 2,850hp (2,125kW) Sabre NS.53.SM
Max Speed/Height	265mph (426km/h) at 16,000ft (4,877m)
Armament	1 × 2,000lb (907kg), 2 × 1,000lb (454kg), 5 × 500lb (227kg) or 8 × 250lb (113kg) bombs, 1 × torpedo or 1 × mine, 8 x RP, 2 guns

The AW.53 was described as 'a fair conventional effort' while, to comply fully with S.6/43, Fairey's project worked out at 27,200lb (12,338kg) and made use of somewhat experimental high-lift devices and control arrangements, but was still 'generally a fine attempt to meet the specification.' Under close examination its top speed (340mph [547km/h] at 17,000ft [5,182m]) would probably have been reduced since the brochure employed two Merlins in their highest projected stage of development and there was little doubt that, by the time the aircraft entered service, it would be close to the Admiralty's 30,000lb (13,608kg) limit. If the full specification was to be met Westland's single-engine machine would need an all-up-weight of 25,800lb (11,703kg); this design was based on the Sabre V and, even allowing that this engine would materialise, it would clearly have been overloaded.

These design studies confirmed the wisdom of abandoning the torpedo bomber reconnaissance aeroplane, although the Design Committee recognised the implications of departing from this 'maid of all work' type which had proved so successful. However, with an increase in the number of aircraft carriers expected to be available in the future, an increase in the number of aircraft types could now be more readily accepted than in the past, the prime objective here being to secure machines of generally better performance.

Shorts S.6/43

The book *Shorts Aircraft since 1900* states that during the summer of 1943 this company proposed two designs to S.6/43, but official documents make no mention of them. One was to be powered by a single Centaurus, the second by two Merlins, and the latter was the 'preferred' choice. The second design was certainly in the picture during the next stage, the reconnaissance bomber to S.11/43. The Staff requirements were sent to several companies and the Admiralty had little doubt that a high-performance three-seater, with a top speed in the 300/350mph (483/563km/h) zone, could be provided. It seemed certain that the highest performance would be offered by a twin-engine type.

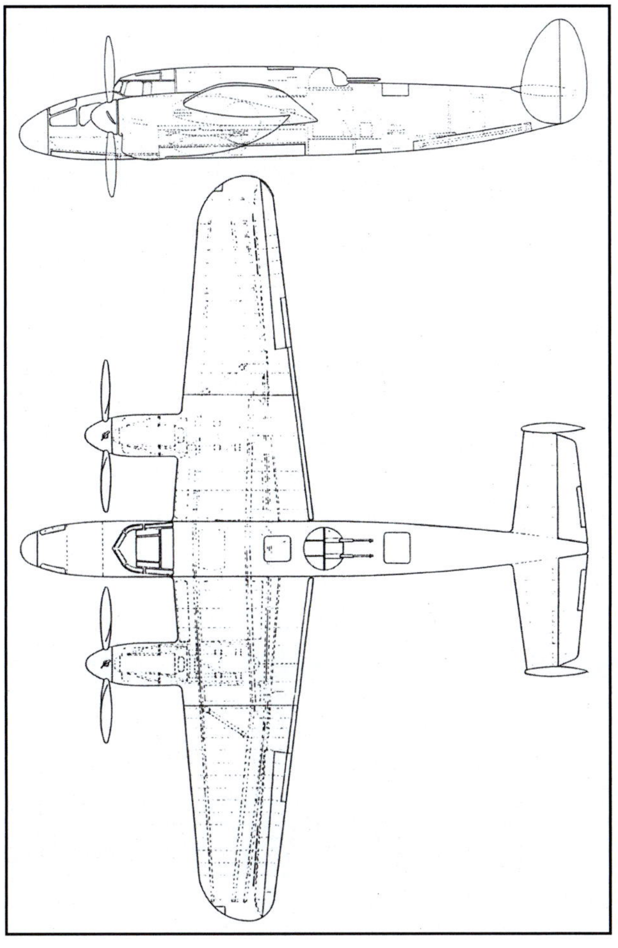

ABOVE Armstrong Whitworth AW.54 (6.43). *Ray Williams*

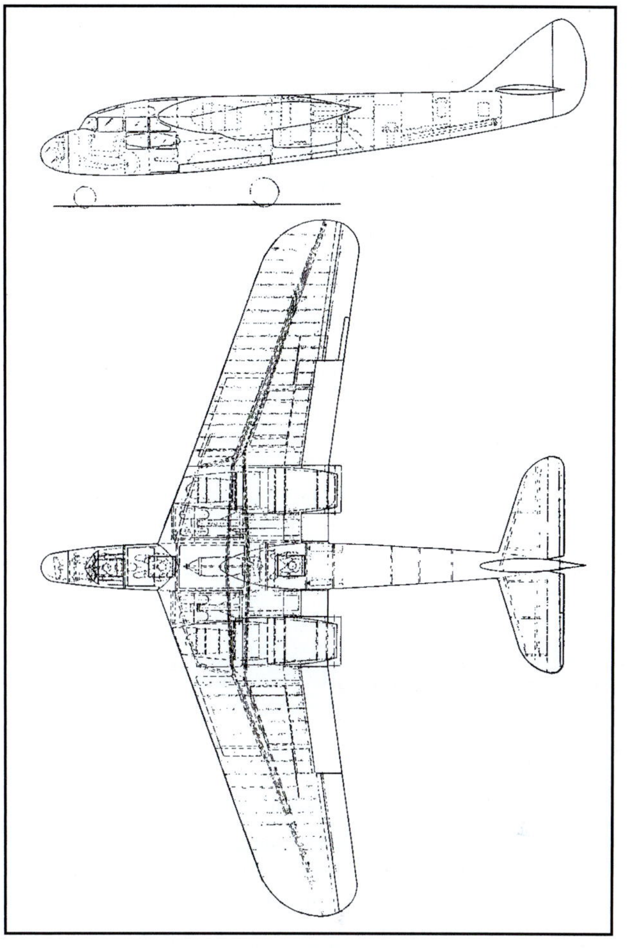

ABOVE Armstrong Whitworth AW.54A (1943). *Ray Williams*

Armstrong Whitworth AW.54

This aircraft's general layout was similar to the AW.53, except that it was slightly smaller and had twin fins. AWA believed that it could design the aircraft to a weight not exceeding 20,000lb (9,072kg) but it would need a folded span of 27ft (8.2m). Top speed was 310mph (499km/h) at sea level and rate of climb 2,020ft/min (616m/min) at full load. Many of the features of the AW.53, such as the undercarriage, wing, Fowler flap and aileron arrangement, dorsal turret and the equipment for carrier operation, were retained but twice the specified bomb load (1,000lb [454kg]) could be carried. However, the design was criticised for lack of performance and so AWA chief designer John Lloyd scrapped his piston proposals and switched to jet power.

AWA AW.54 (6.43)	
Span	59ft 0in (17.98m)
Length	45ft 0in (13.72m)
Wing Area	500sq.ft (46.45sq.m)
All-Up-Weight	19,780lb (8,972kg)
Powerplant	2 × 1,600hp (1,193kW) Merlin 26
Max Speed/Height	330mph (531km/h) at 9,500ft (2,896m)
Armament	2,000lb (907kg) bombs or depth charges, 2 × 0.5in (12.7mm) machine guns

Armstrong Whitworth AW.54A

This AWA design introduced a much higher performance, particularly in regard to speed. It had swept laminar flow wings with two Metropolitan-Vickers F.3 jet engines (with augmented thrust) mounted on the trailing half just outboard of the roots; the wings, together with a reduced fuselage cross section, were intended to help the performance. The long-travel main gears had twin tyres and a variable-incidence tailplane was fitted so that any large change of trim caused by the flaps could be easily corrected. The flap/aileron combination used by the AW.53 and AW.54 for the approach was retained, except that slotted flaps were now fitted, and the main wings folded backwards on an inclined hinge.

Thanks to its speed, defensive armament was thought to be unnecessary and had been taken out. Top speed and rate of climb at sea level were 440mph (708km/h) and 4,300ft/min (1,311m/min) and, despite the known problems of high fuel consumption associated with jets, the 900nm (1,669km) range could be met using only the internal capacity. However, despite its promise, the proposal was turned down – the possible effects of jet efflux on aircraft carrier decks were, at the time, still uncertain and contributed to this decision.

AWA AW.54A (1943)	
Span	53ft 0in (16.15m)
Length	43ft 6in (13.26m)
Wing Area	530sq.ft (49.24sq.m)
All-Up-Weight	18,840lb (8,546kg)
Powerplant	2 × Metro-Vick F.3
Max Speed/Height	450mph (724km/h) at 15,000ft (4,572m)
Armament	2,000lb (907kg) bombs or depth charges, 2 × 0.5in (12.7mm) machine guns

Blackburn S.11/43

A drawing of this unnumbered project shows a twin dorsal turret and what looks like two Merlin engines. No data available.

Blackburn S.11/43 (25.6.43)	
Span	c60ft 6in (18.44m)
Length	c43ft 6in (13.26m)
No other details	

Fairey S.11/43

The main Fairey S.11/43 submission was made on 19 June 1943. As a design it was very similar to the July 1943 study made for O.5/43 (described below) and used a dual powerplant comprising a Merlin 26 plus a 3,000lb (13.3kN) thrust jet engine.

Westland S.11/43

Westland's S.6/43 was modified into a propeller-cum-jet machine with a Pratt & Whitney R4360 radial in the nose and a Halford H.1 jet farther back, the jet being used for take-off and boosting the top speed. The wings were not dissimilar to the S.6/43 but the unusual butterfly tail was highly swept with twin rudders at the tips. Two cannon were mounted in each wing's leading edge and, surprisingly, a torpedo could be carried externally beneath the cockpit.

Westland S.11/43 (8.43)	
Span	55ft 0in (16.76m)
Length	?
Wing Area	470sq.ft (43.66sq.m)
All-Up-Weight	26,600lb (12,066kg)
Powerplant	1 × 3,000hp (2,237kW) P&W R4360 plus 1 × 3,000lb (13.3kN) thrust Halford jet
Max Speed/Height	370mph (595km/h) at 15,000ft (4,572m)
Armament	bombs?, 1 × torpedo, 4 × 20mm cannon

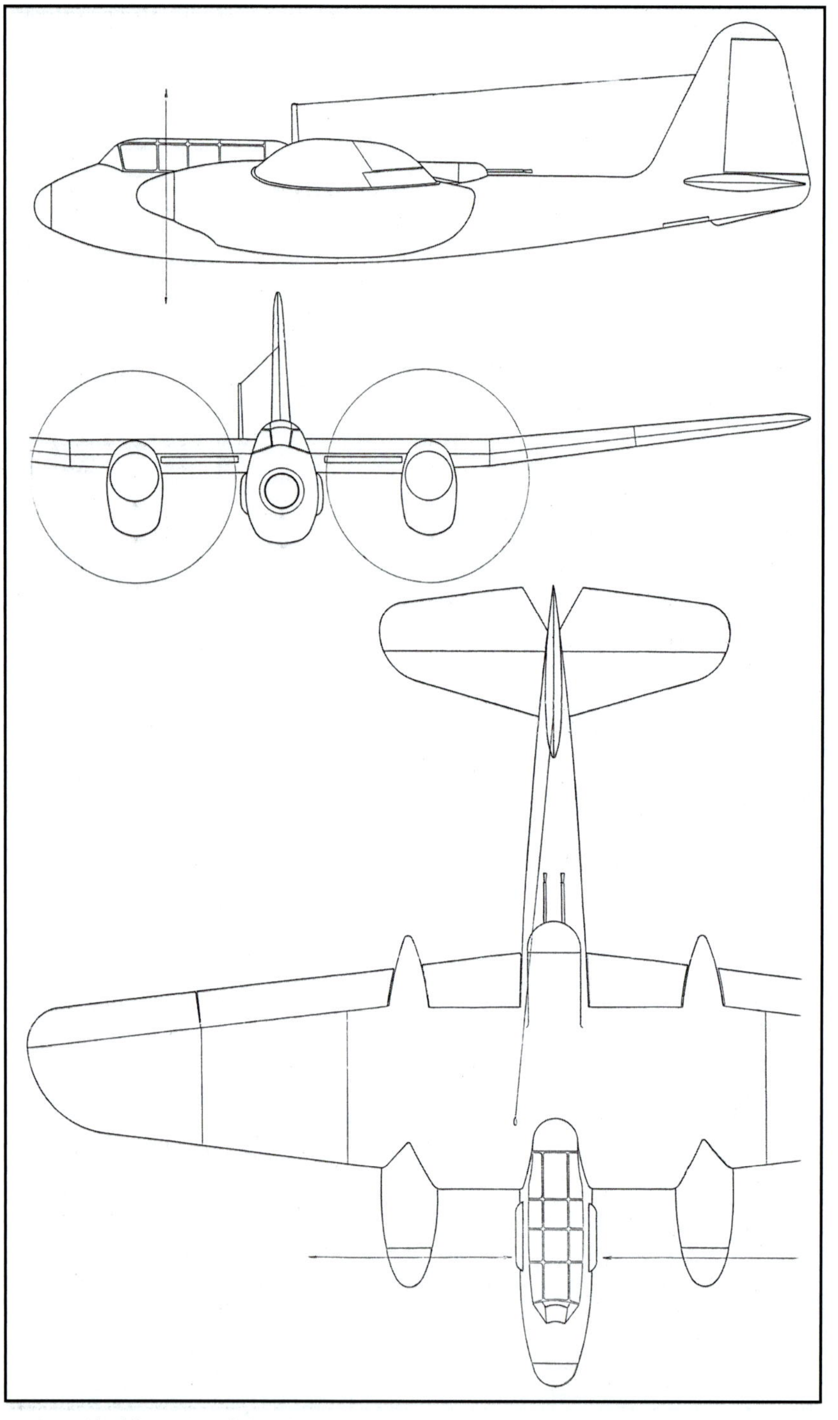

ABOVE Blackburn S.11/43 (25.6.43). *BAE Systems Brough Heritage Centre*

Shorts S.38 and Sturgeon

The above designs were eventually rejected and an ITP was given to Shorts in October 1943 for its twin-Merlin project, now numbered S.38, which was eventually called the S.A.1 Sturgeon. Details of the original proposals have not been traced but S.11/43 was rewritten around them and reissued to the company on 12 February 1944 to cover three S.Mk.I prototypes, RK787, RK791 and RK794 ordered on 19 October 1943. Provision for the subsequent installation

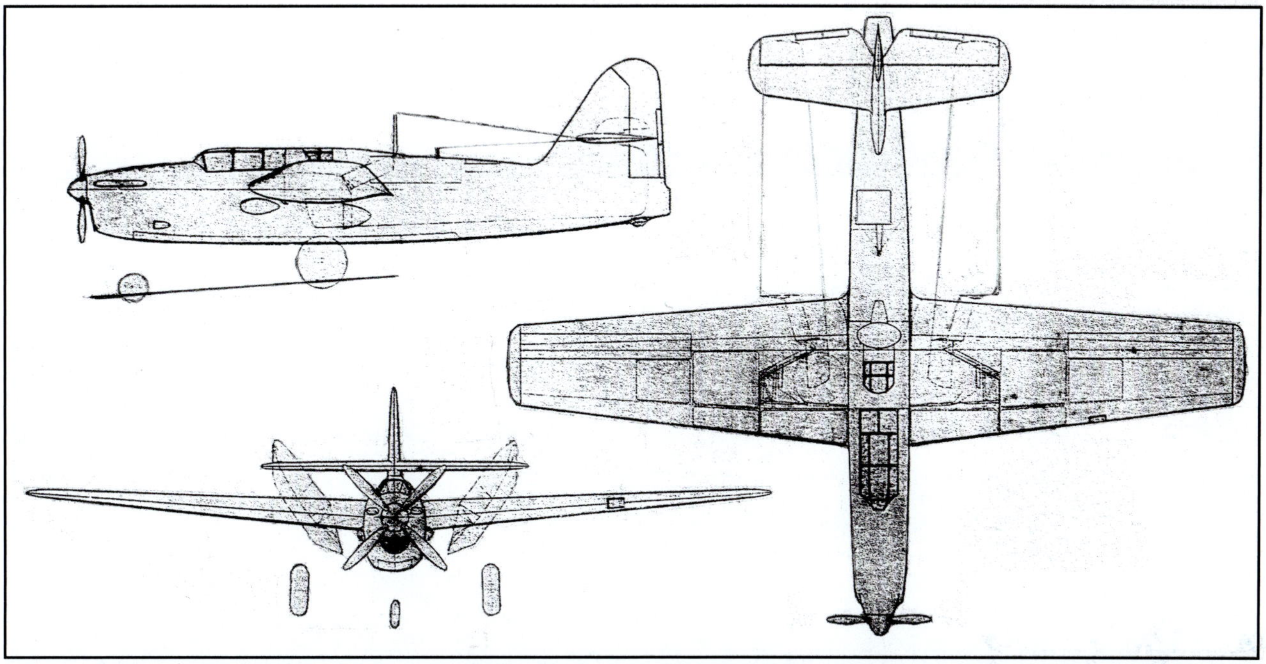

ABOVE **The Fairey S.11/43 combined powerplant design (24.5.43). The variant to O.5/43 (2.7.43) was nearly identical.**

BELOW **Rough sketch of the Westland S.11/43 (8.43).** *Fred Ballam, Westland*

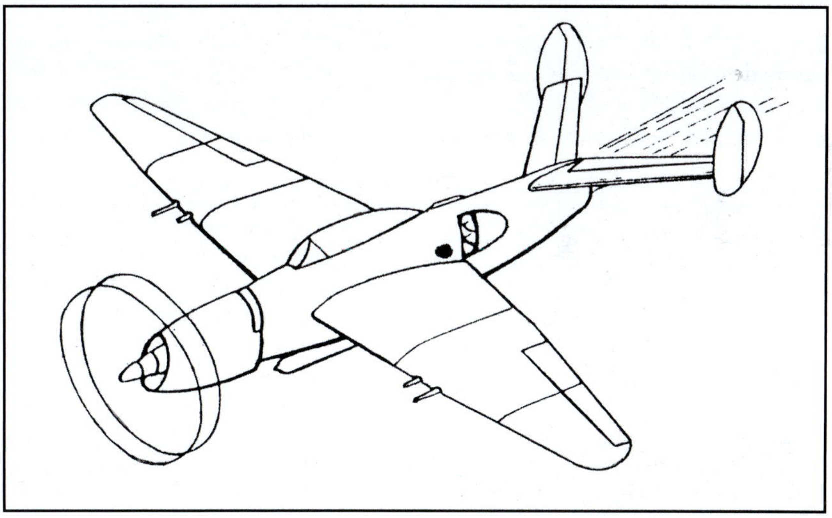

of Griffons was also requested. Designed by the team led by C. P. T. Lipscombe, RK787 made its maiden flight on 7 June 1946 and the type was the first twin-engine aircraft designed specifically for FAA service, although by the time RK787 flew two de Havilland creations, the Mosquito and Hornet, had found their way on to the deck of an aircraft carrier.

Both Hornet and Mosquito highlighted a major problem of twin-engine aircraft landing on aircraft carriers, the lack of asymmetric control with one engine out that was required during the high-power/low-speed approach. Due to this the conventional Mosquito could not be deck-landed on one engine and, in addition, its propellers rotated in the same direction which gave the added problem of swing on take-off. The naval Sea Hornet received handed engines and propellers which removed the swing problem, but the asymmetric difficulty remained. It was hoped that the Sturgeon might prove better suited for single-engine landings since the shorter blades of its contra-rotating propellers allowed the engines to be placed closer to the fuselage centreline, thus easing the asymmetry weakness. In the event however, single-engine deck landings still proved to be impractical.

The Sturgeon was essentially designed for operations in the Pacific as part of preparations for the final drive against Japan, but after that conflict ended the Navy was left with a new bomber and nowhere to use it. The type was intended to operate from Ark Royal Class and Hermes Class carriers but post-war economies were to cancel or suspend the construction of these ships (none was to commission before 1952) with the result that the only possible home for the Sturgeon could be the wartime Illustrious Class or the Colossus Class Light Fleet Carrier. Operation on the former would require a stronger arrester gear while the Sturgeon itself would have to remain above deck at all times. As a result the reconnaissance-bomber Sturgeon did not enter production, but before the end of the war it was adopted as a humble target-tug. Conversion to the TT.Mk.2 variant, which Shorts originally called the S.39 and then S.A.2, was undertaken to Specification Q.1/46 and the third S.A.1 prototype, RK794, was modified to act as the prototype. Reserialled VR363 it made its maiden flight on 18 May 1948 and 24 production aeroplanes were built.

ABOVE AND OPPOSITE **Views of Shorts Sturgeon prototype RK787. Production Shorts Sturgeons were built as target-tugs.**
Aeroplane & Short Bros.

RK787

Shorts S.38 Sturgeon Mk.I (flown)	
Span	59ft 11in (18.26m)
Length	44ft 0in (13.41m)
Wing Area	560sq.ft (52.05sq.m)
All-Up-Weight	21,700lb (9,843kg) normal load
Powerplant	2 × 2,080hp (1,551kW) Merlin 140
Max Speed/Height	401mph (645km/h) at 18,850ft (5,745m)
Armament	1 × 1,000lb (454kg) or 2 × 500lb (227kg) bombs or 4 × 250lb (113kg) depth charges in bomb bay, 8 × RP, 2 × 0.5in (12.7mm) machine guns in nose

Specification O.5/43 and O.21/44

Fairey Spearfish

After the decision to abandon the S.6/43 torpedo bomber/reconnaissance aircraft, staff requirements for a torpedo/dive bomber were considered at a Design Committee meeting held on 12 April 1943. It was agreed that the tactics of torpedo and dive bombing had much in common and it was far easier to combine these two tasks rather than the torpedo role with reconnaissance. The original requirement for a dive bomber had centred around the carriage of a 1,600lb (726kg) bomb and, although replacing it with a torpedo was not expected to be detrimental to the dive bomber's performance, it was decided to wait for the arrival of the dive bomber design studies and then, picking the best, to consider carrying a torpedo. Much discussion centred round whether the type should be single or two-seat. The specification was numbered O.5/43 and brought the following proposals.

Cunliffe-Owen O.5/43

A single-engine design for which no data has been found.

Blackburn B.47

A single-engine two-seat design with a rear defensive turret.

Blackburn B.47 (19.4.43)	
Span	c52ft 3in (15.93m)
Length	c37ft 2in (11.33m)
No other details	

Fairey O.5/43 Single-Engine

Since the O.5/43 was envisaged to be a heavy aeroplane, one of the available 'large' engines would be needed which Fairey placed in the order Griffon 61, Centaurus or Sabre. It was proposed to limit the diving speed near to the maximum level speed and, following conversations with Rotol and de Havilland, Fairey had formed the opinion that deceleration by airscrew drag had reached a stage of development where it could be a practical possibility in about a year's time. Retarding the aircraft by airscrew drag was so attractive, with no effect on the aircraft, that the designers suggested that reliance

Fairey O.5/43 single engine (17.4.43)	
Span	52ft 0in (15.85m)
Length	42ft 3in (12.88m)
Wing Area	415sq.ft (38.55sq.m)
All-Up-Weight	Griffon 17,250lb (7,824kg), Sabre 17,285lb (7,840kg), Centaurus 17,760lb (8,056kg)
Powerplant	1 × 2,100hp (1,566kW) Griffon 61, 2,310hp (1,723kW) Sabre III or 2,425hp (1,808kW) Centaurus 7.SM 2
Max Speed/Height	Griffon 321mph (517km/h) at 18,000ft (5,486m), Sabre 304mph (489km/h) at 16,000ft (4,877m), Griffon 305mph (491km/h) at 13,250ft (4,039m)
Armament	6 × 250lb (113kg) bombs or larger or 1 × torpedo, RPs, 1 × 0.5in (12.7mm) machine gun

BELOW Blackburn B.47 (19.4.43). *BAE Systems Brough Heritage Centre*

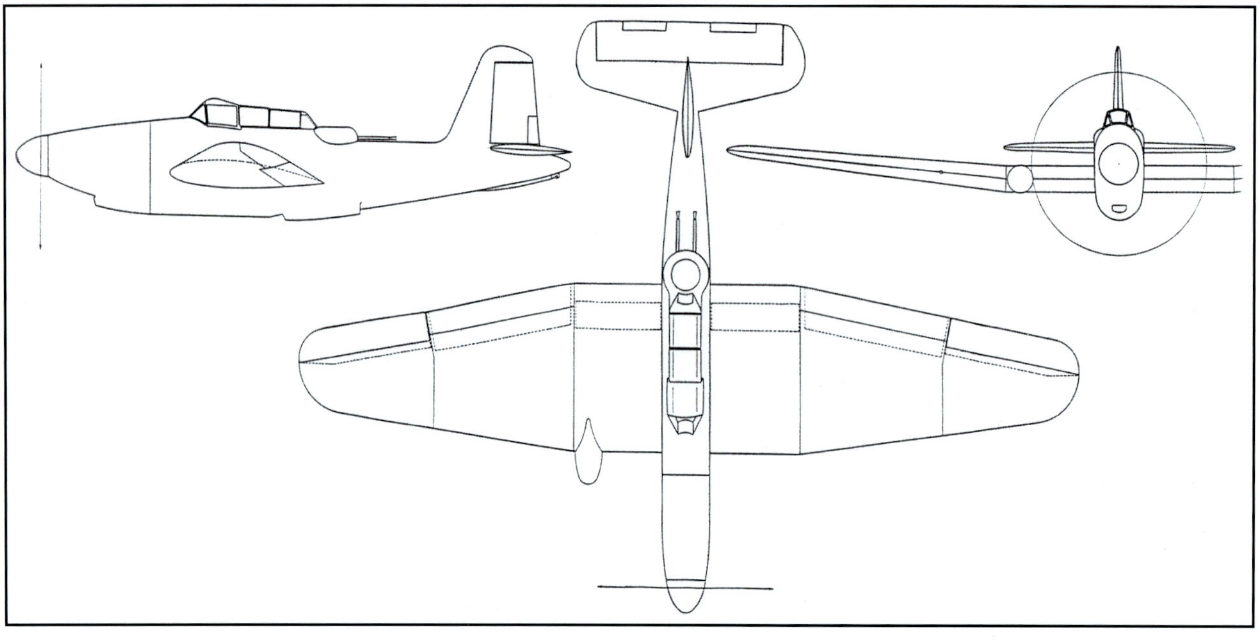

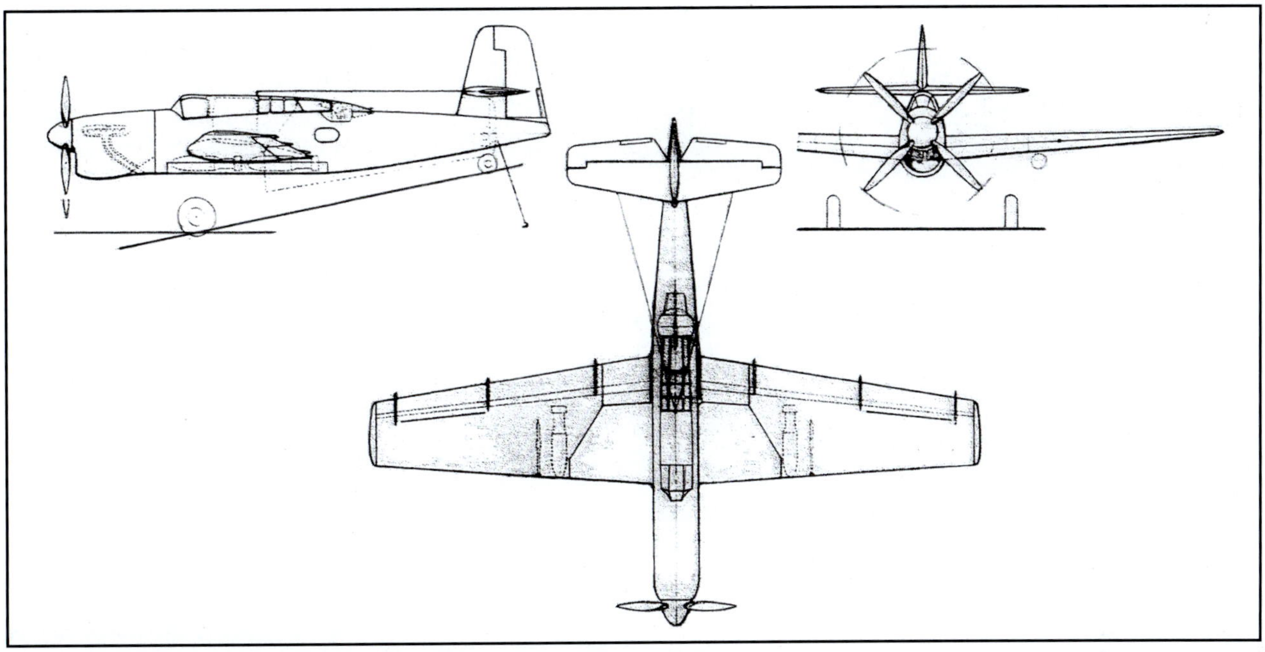

ABOVE **Fairey single-engine O.5/43 with Griffon 61 (17.4.43).**

BELOW **Fairey twin-engine O.5/43 (14.4.43).**

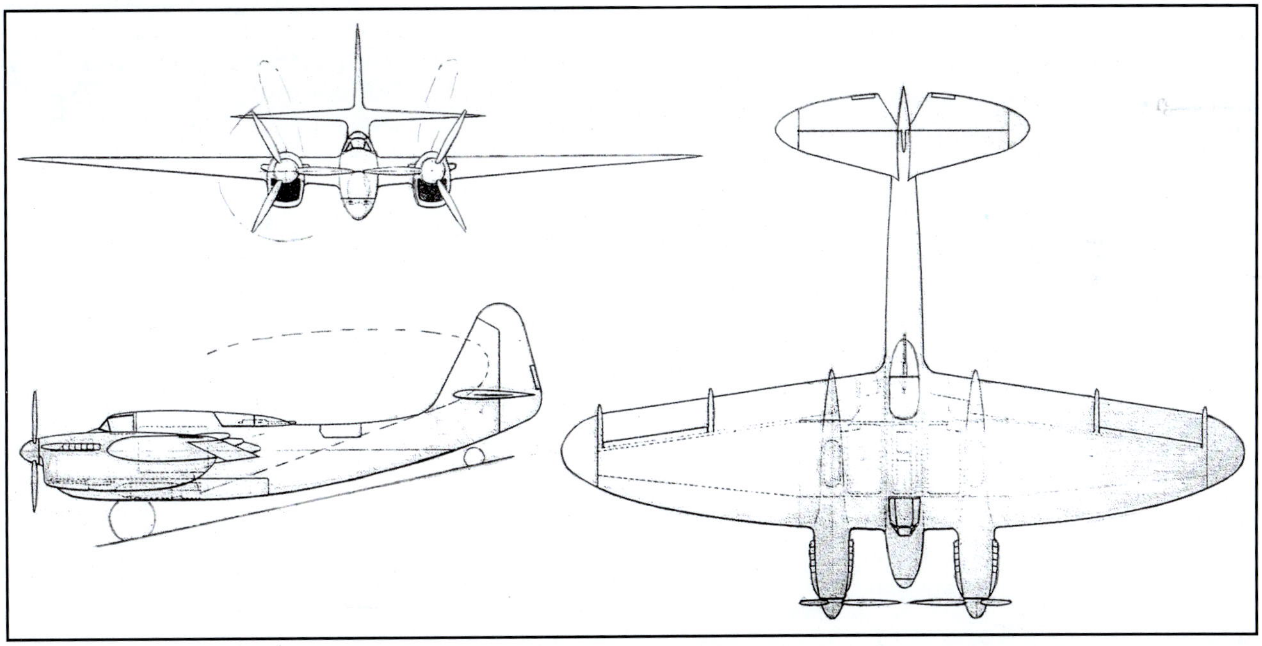

should be placed on it as a first string with development of the reversing airscrew to be accelerated. Although experimental, much progress had already been made on this concept.

Full-span flaps were fitted which offered the chance to increase the wing loading by 15% but a tricycle undercarriage was rejected. Stressed skin construction was used throughout and the Griffon 61 power egg had annular type air intakes as developed for the Halifax bomber. Except for two 250lb (113kg) bombs or some rockets under the outer wings, the bomb load was carried beneath the fuselage. A defensive turret had been ruled out because of its weight and drag but a single 0.5in (12.7mm) was available. With Griffon 61, Sabre III and Centaurus 7.SM respectively, time to 10,000ft (3,048m) was 8.67, 7.5 and 7.0 minutes, service ceiling 28,500ft (8,687m), 26,000ft (7,925m) and 25,300ft (7,711m), and each could achieve the 900nm (1,667km) range, or 1,500nm (2,778km) with extra fuel. In fact, to save weight, half of the specified endurance fuel had been termed 'overload' which reduced the stressing required and had produced a smaller aircraft – 'Scheme A'. An alternative 'Scheme B' carried all of the specified fuel but this was larger with a span of 56ft (17.07m) and length 45ft (13.72m) and it was not examined closely.

ABOVE Artist's impression of the rather ugly Fairey twin-Merlin O.5/43 project.

Fairey O.5/43 Twin-Engine

Fairey declared that the advantages of this alternative included a perfect view for the pilot at all times, the ability to get home on one engine and a greatly improved performance over the single-engine type. It was principally built of stressed skin construction and all of the bomb load was totally enclosed in a fuselage bay. For rear defence the second crewman had a hydraulically-operated 'Rose' type gun pillar with one 0.5in (12.7mm) Browning gun while, to combat a forward attack, two forward-firing fixed 0.5in were mounted in the nose of the bomb compartment. An alternative cannon armament of four 20mm or one 37mm could be carried instead of the bombs, or an auxiliary fuel tank could be housed in the bomb compartment to give the 1,500nm (2,778km) range. Full-span flaps were used and the wing fold rotated about two axes. Time to 10,000ft (3,048m) was 7.1 minutes and service ceiling 31,200ft (9,510m). Fairey stressed its preference for this design over the single-engine on the score of performance and view.

Fairey O.5/43 twin-engine (17.4.43)	
Span	56ft 0in (17.07m)
Length	43ft 0in (13.11m)
Wing Area	?
All-Up-Weight	24,125lb (10,943kg)
Powerplant	2 × 1,680hp (1,253kW) Merlin RM.14.SM
Max Speed/Height	356mph (573km/h) at 17,000ft (5,182m)
Armament	1 × 1,600lb (726kg) or 1,000lb (454kg), 3 × 500lb (227kg) or 250lb (113kg) bombs, or 3 depth charges, 3 × 0.5in (12.7mm) machine guns

Folland Fo.119

Folland's single-engine proposal 'arrived late' (the drawing is dated 1 June 1943) and was rejected by the Ministry on 11 September 1943. It had contra-rotating propellers and the drawing shows the slats and flaps extended for landing, but no other details are available.

After close analysis MAP concluded that the two Fairey projects, adapted to carry a torpedo, were worthy of serious consideration. Both depended on some experimental features in the form of full-span flaps which were to be power operated to give lateral control. Spoiler lateral control was to be brought into play under conditions when, due to the limited movement of the full-span flaps in the retracted position, lateral control by power operation of the flaps alone would not be wholly satisfactory. Similar expedients were under development in America by the Vought company and such features were desirable if the best was to be obtained from this type of aeroplane.

The real issue, however, was the relative merits of the two projects. With a 2,200lb (998kg) torpedo, it seemed that the twin-Merlin design could be built at around a 26,000lb (11,793kg) weight with a top speed of about 350mph (563km/h) at 19,000ft (5,791m). Apart from the obvious objections in regard to numbers that could be stowed aboard carriers, it was clear that the margin between 26,000lb (11,793kg) and the Admiralty's absolute limit of 30,000lb (13,608kg) was too small for an ultimate development using more powerful engines such as the Griffon. The single-engine design with Griffon, Centaurus or Sabre would work out at about 19,000lb+ (8,618kg), making it underpowered with any of these units. However, the adoption of the Centaurus appeared to permit the possibility of fitting the more powerful Rolls-Royce Exe 45 (a 45-litre air-cooled inline development of the original smaller Exe designed for the Barracuda) or the new American Pratt & Whitney R4360 later. The new Exe appeared to have the potential for 3,000bhp (2,237kW) but would begin with a take-off power and dry weight comparable to the Centaurus. The 4360 also promised 3,000bhp (2,237kW) but it was a larger and heavier engine.

It was thought that when carrying a 1,800lb (816kg) 18in (45.7cm) torpedo, the single-engine Fairey might start at 20,000lb (9,072kg) all-up-weight and give a maximum 310mph (499km/h) at 19,000ft (5,791m), but there was potential for another 30mph (48km/h) later. Therefore, apart from its greater ease of stowage in carriers, the type had a better potential improvement than the twin-Merlin whilst keeping well within the Admiralty's maximum weight limit. It was agreed that a closer examination of the single-engine Fairey should be pursued and a further design study followed based on the lines of the original.

Fairey O.5/43 Developments

At the request of CNR Fairey remodelled its O.5/43 single-engine layout by improving the power loading and extending the bomb bay to carry an 18in

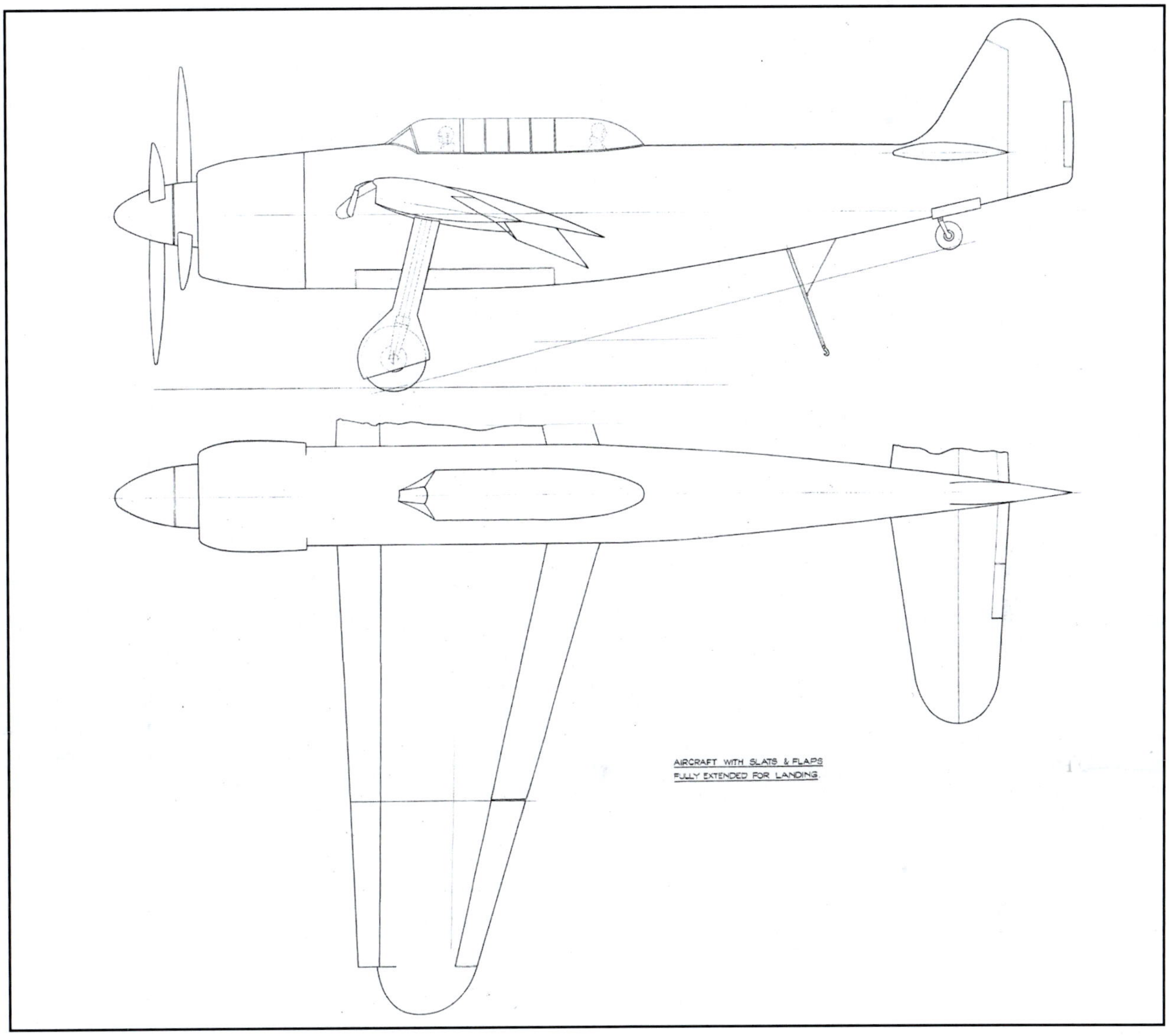

ABOVE Folland Fo.119 (1.6.43). *Solent Sky Museum*

BELOW Fairey O.5/43 dive/torpedo bomber with Exe 45 (2.6.43).

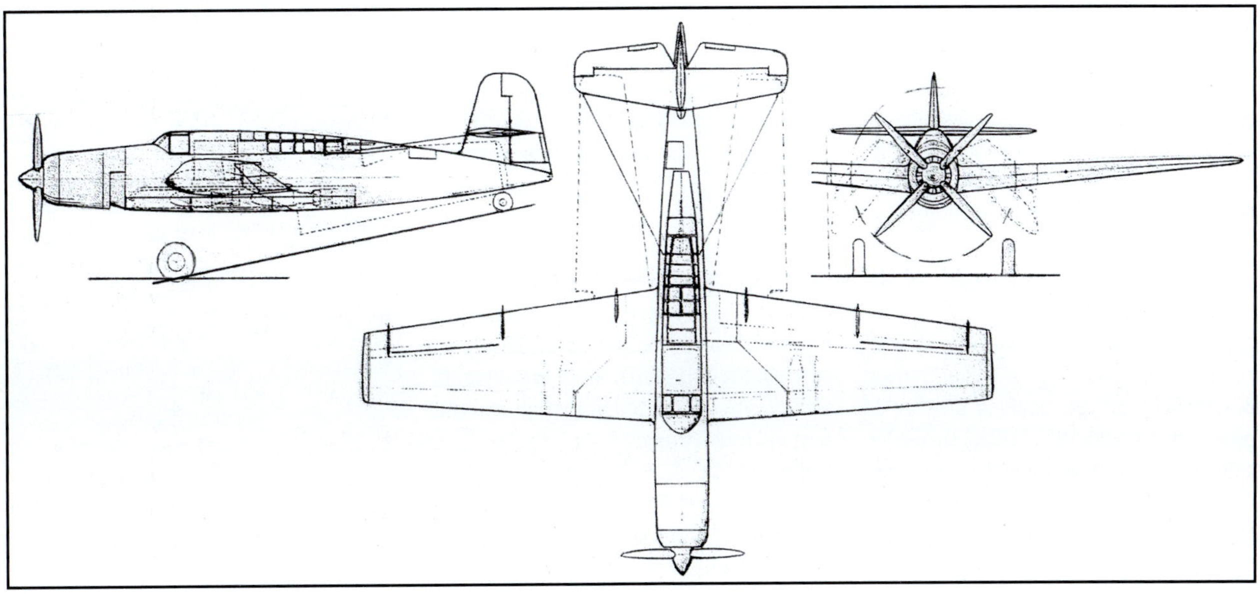

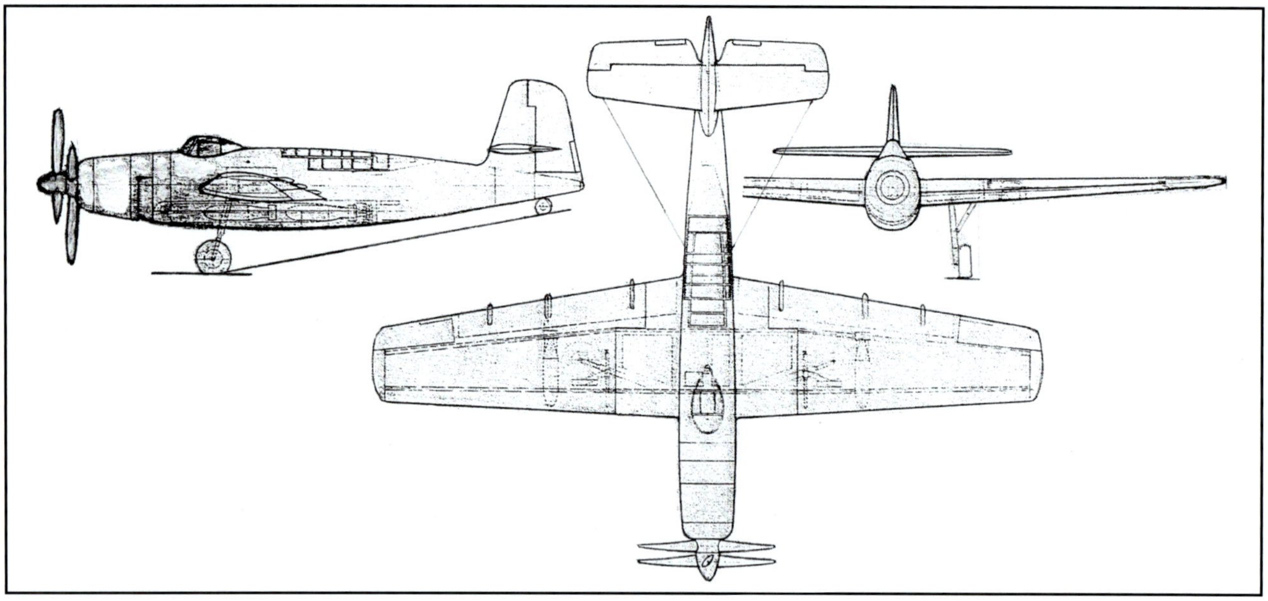

ABOVE Fairey O.5/43 with Exe powerplant at 2.8.43. Span 56ft 0in (17.07m), length 45ft 6in (13.87m).

(45.7cm) torpedo, stowed internally. This was completed on 7 June 1943 and the company felt that this type was now a logical follow-on from the Barracuda; the proposed engine was an Exe 45. The net result was an increase in the total weight of the aircraft by 1,070lb (485kg) with a consequent increase in size which, with the Exe 45's provisional rating, actually gave a reduction in performance compared to the original submission's Centaurus. This change had been made to accommodate the Exe 45 with its possible development to 3,000bhp (2,237kW) but Fairey suggested that, since the Centaurus was an available engine, a prototype should be built around this unit but with an eye to future adoption of the Exe 45 or one of the big American engines. To accommodate the torpedo it had been necessary to introduce a cranked centre section spar. The Centaurus would take the aircraft to 10,000ft (3,048m) in 6.45 minutes, the service ceiling was 24,000ft (7,315m) and this engine reduced the length of the fuselage by 2ft (61cm).

On 3 July Fairey followed this up with a brochure showing a combination powerplant design using a Merlin 26 piston and a 3,000lb (13.3kN) thrust jet. This investigation, which also embraced very similar work to S.11/43, was primarily intended to find if the co-axial arrangement of engines had any advantage over the large single engine. Fairey found that this design provided all of the advantages of a twin without any of the drawbacks associated with deck flying. The use of a relatively small piston engine for cruising, with a consequent small diameter propeller, reduced the length required for the bomb projector arms which meant that the whole arrangement could be mounted on a short tricycle undercarriage. The design had a ceiling of 36,000ft (10,973m), would take five minutes to get to 10,000ft (3,048m) and with the jet switched off had a top speed of 261mph (420km/h) at 9,500ft (2,896m).

However, a prototype order for the piston-only type was placed in mid-August 1943 and on the 23rd Fairey confirmed that a Centaurus 7 or 12.SM would be fitted in the first instance with the Exe 45 later. A drawing was enclosed showing how the aircraft would look with the Exe (including a contra-rotating propeller) but it differed quite markedly from what was eventually built; at 23,700lb (10,750kg) weight the top speed would be 360mph (579km/h) at 15,000ft (4,572m). This big aircraft was eventually named Spearfish and the first of four prototypes to fly became airborne on 5 July 1945. A fifth prototype never flew and two more, plus 150 production examples, were to be cancelled. On 18 April 1945 a Spearfish conversion was proposed to act as a test bed for the Rolls-Royce Clyde turboprop, which gave 1,850bhp (1,380kW) and 750lb (3.3kN) thrust; at 18,374lb (8,334kg) weight this was expected to give 335mph (539km/h) at 15,000ft (4,572m).

Fairey O.5/43 (7.6.43)	
Span	54ft 0in (16.46m)
Length	45ft 0in (13.72m)
Wing Area	?
All-Up-Weight	18,830lb (8,541kg)
Powerplant	Prototype 1 × 2,500hp (1,864kW) Centaurus, later 1 × 3,000hp (2,237kW) Exe
Max Speed/Height	Centaurus 300mph (483km/h) at 13,000ft (3,962m), Exe with 3,000hp rating 352mph (566km/h)
Armament	4 × bombs or 1 × torpedo in bay, 1 × bomb under each wing, 1 × 0.5in (12.7mm) machine gun

Fairey O.5/43 mixed powerplant (3.7.43)	
Span	56ft 0in (17.07m)
Length	46ft 0in (14.02m)
Wing Area	?
All-Up-Weight	21,850lb (9,911kg)
Powerplant	1 × 1,620hp (1,208kW) Merlin 26 plus 1 × 3,000lb (13.3kN) thrust jet engine
Max Speed/Height	373mph (600km/h) at 20,000ft (6,096m)
Armament	4 × bombs or 2 × torpedo, 1 gun in each wing, 1 rear facing machine gun

ABOVE The Fairey Spearfish prototype seen at Heston on 17 September 1945.

RIGHT Spearfish RN241 was photographed during a publicity flight on 27 September 1946.

Fairey Spearfish (flown)	
Span	60ft 3in (18.36m)
Length	44ft 7in (13.59m)
Wing Area	?
All-Up-Weight	normal 21,642lb (9,817kg), overload 22,083lb (10,017kg)
Powerplant	1 × 2,600bhp (1,939kW) Centaurus
Max Speed/Height	292mph (470km/h) at 14,000ft (4,267m)
Armament	1 × 2,000lb (907kg) or 1,000lb (454kg) or 4 × 500lb (227kg) bombs, 1 × torpedo or 4 depth charges, RPs, 4 × 0.5in (12.7mm) machine guns

Fairey O.21/44

Although a considerable demand was expected for the O.5/43 Spearfish the type had hardly got into its stride when the Naval Air Staff felt the need for a strike aircraft of higher performance. To meet this line of thought, in September 1944 Fairey put forward a brochure that modified the O.5/43 with a twin coupled-Merlin arrangement, this used the same airframe components and showed on estimate a considerable improvement in performance. Fairey felt that the O.5/43's value could be greatly improved if its speed could be increased from the present 300mph (483km/h) to at least 350mph

BELOW One of the first Spearfish prototypes. The number '244' does not relate to a serial, but rather shows that the type was number 244 in a series of experimental general arrangement drawings.

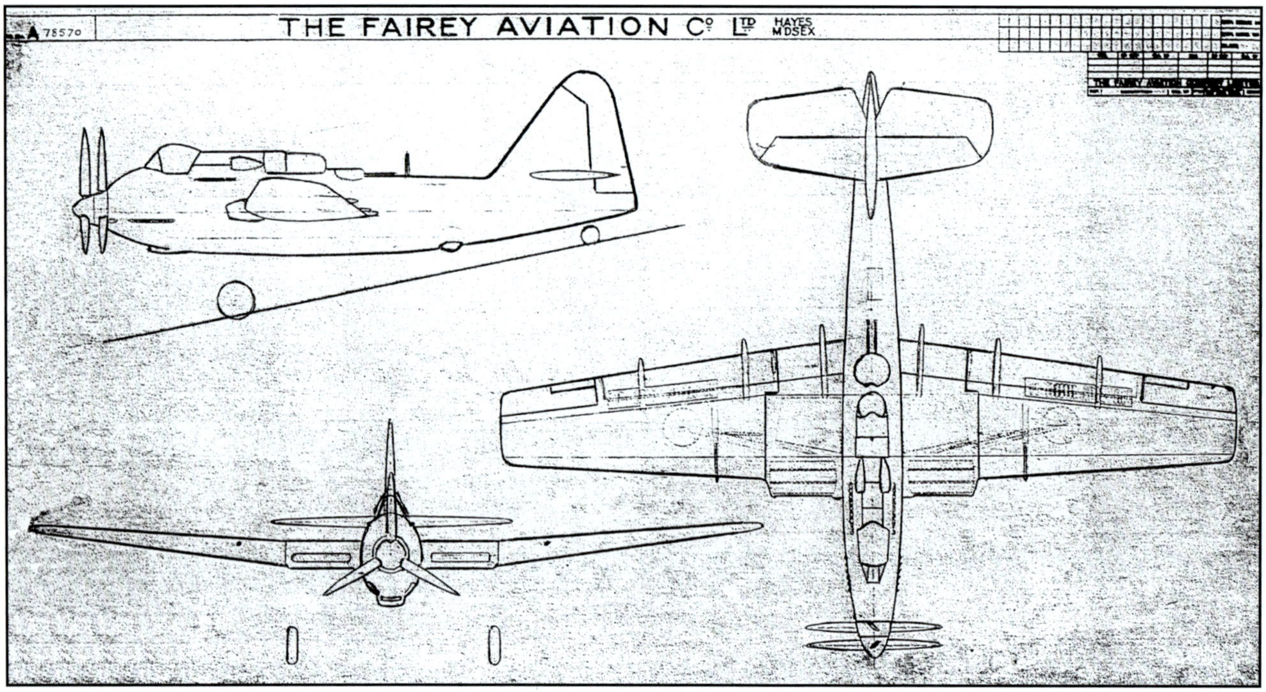

ABOVE Fairey O.21/44 (21.7.44). This design had a single 0.5in (12.7mm) machine gun in each wing and two more in a defensive turret.

(563km/h) and a small separate design team had been working on this problem for several months. As a result the use of large engines like the American R4360 was now rejected because the length became inconvenient while the pilot's view suffered.

During these investigations, which included contact with Rolls-Royce to discuss an extension shaft drive with a single engine which enabled the pilot to sit forward of the engine to obtain the best possible view, Fairey had conceived the idea of utilising two Merlins arranged in tandem within the fuselage. The forward engine incorporated and drove a special nose gearbox with a single pair of contra-rotating propellers, to which the rear engine was coupled by means of an extension shaft. The front engine drove the rear propeller and the rear engine the front propeller, the two drives being quite independent of each other so that the machine might be flown with one engine and one propeller only. By this route Fairey could see a way of installing 4,000bhp (2,983kW) in the aircraft with a minimum increase in drag and weight. Besides having twin-engine reliability without the danger of asymmetry with one engine out, and a high performance due to the low frontal area, this arrangement appeared more desirable than the piston-plus-jet because only one type of fuel was necessary while the thrust efficiency was much higher, giving a better take-off and landing performance. The jet's high fuel consumption was also taken out of the equation.

To investigate the twin piston in tandem system a long and comprehensive series of design studies was prepared, all of them around the O.5/43 specification except that the machine was considered as a single seater with no rear defence. The alternatives studied were a normally situated single tractor Rolls-Royce Pennine or Eagle engine, a conventionally arranged twin Merlin 14.SM, a tandem twin single-stage Griffon 23.SM or one Pennine plus a 3,000lb (13.3kN) Halford jet. The investigations showed that the tandem engine arrangements gave a performance which, at the time, was superior to any other powerplant and it was decided to submit to CNR and DTD three projects to illustrate the new principle and its advantages:

1. A normal two-seat aircraft to O.5/43 in standard production form, except for a new fuselage forward of the front wing spar which incorporated twin tandem Merlin 14.SMs. (The initial project was dated 21 July 1944 and became the core of the September brochure.)

2. A single-seat torpedo/dive bomber to the O.5/43 specification but without rear defence. This had twin 2,400bhp (1,790kW) Griffon 71s in tandem which gave an all-up-weight of 24,800lb (11,249kg), a top speed of 420mph (676km/h) and a maximum rate of climb of 1,770ft/min (539m/min) (dated 13 September 1944).

3. A single-seat conversion of the O.5/43 with one 2,520bhp (1,879kW) Rolls-Royce Pennine RX.2.SM piston and one 2,000lb (8.9kN) jet in tandem, which weighed 21,900lb (9,934kg) and gave a speed of 370mph (595km/h) (also dated 13 September 1944).

In due course a contract was placed for four twin-Merlin two-seaters to the general requirements of O.5/43, the actual specification for these machines, O.21/44, being written around the new design. The project would have an

ABOVE Manufacturer's model of the Fairey O.21/44.

RIGHT Artwork showing examples of the Fairey O.21/44 project.

internal fuel capacity of 470gal (2,137lit) and a range of 900nm (1,667km). Fairey was very enthusiastic about the idea and design work commenced at the beginning of 1945 in the hands of a special team at Fairey's Stockport works – it was intended that the detail design and construction of these four machines should be carried out at Stockport. During August 1944, whilst the three projects submitted to MAP were being discussed, Fairey was requested to investigate the possibilities of the tandem twin-engine scheme in a new project, a naval strike aircraft. The resulting Fairey Strike Fighter was submitted in October (and is described in the sister volume covering World War Two fighter designs).

Fairey O.21/44 (7.44)	
Span	60ft 0in (18.29m)
Length	45ft 5in (13.84m)
Wing Area	?
All-Up-Weight	23,700lb (10,750kg)
Powerplant	2 × 2,200hp (1,641kW) Merlin RM.14.SM
Max Speed/Height	360mph (579km/h) at 15,000ft (4,572m)
Armament	bombs, torpedoes, 1 × 0.5in (12.7mm) machine gun in each wing, 2 × 0.5in (12.7mm) machine gun in rear turret

However, developments in jet and propeller turbines were beginning to reveal their value and the general feeling was that all reciprocating types would rapidly become obsolete. Therefore, after a few months of effort in the Fairey drawing office, the O.21/44 contract was cancelled; this same reasoning also brought the demise of the O.5/43 contract.

Bristol Brigand

On 18 May 1942 Air Chief Marshal Sir Philip Joubert, AOC-in-C Coastal Command, informed Air Marshal F. J. Linnell, CRD, that the stage had been reached where, because its losses had become so severe, the American Lockheed Hudson was 'virtually useless' as an anti-shipping aircraft. Consequently experiments were under way to put torpedoes, bombs and rocket projectiles onto the Bristol Beaufighter. The Beaufighter eventually succeeded the Beaufort in the torpedo bomber role and proved such a success that suggestions for a more advanced aircraft gained momentum. The Beaufighter was essentially the first of a new class of 'strike' aircraft.

On 8 July 1942, at Bristol's wartime design headquarters and project office at Ivor House, some rough ideas for a future requirement were laid down by Sorley, Rowe and Boothman of the Ministry, Frise, Russell and Morgan from Bristol and the company's RTO, H. J. Webb. Bristol offered two alternatives:

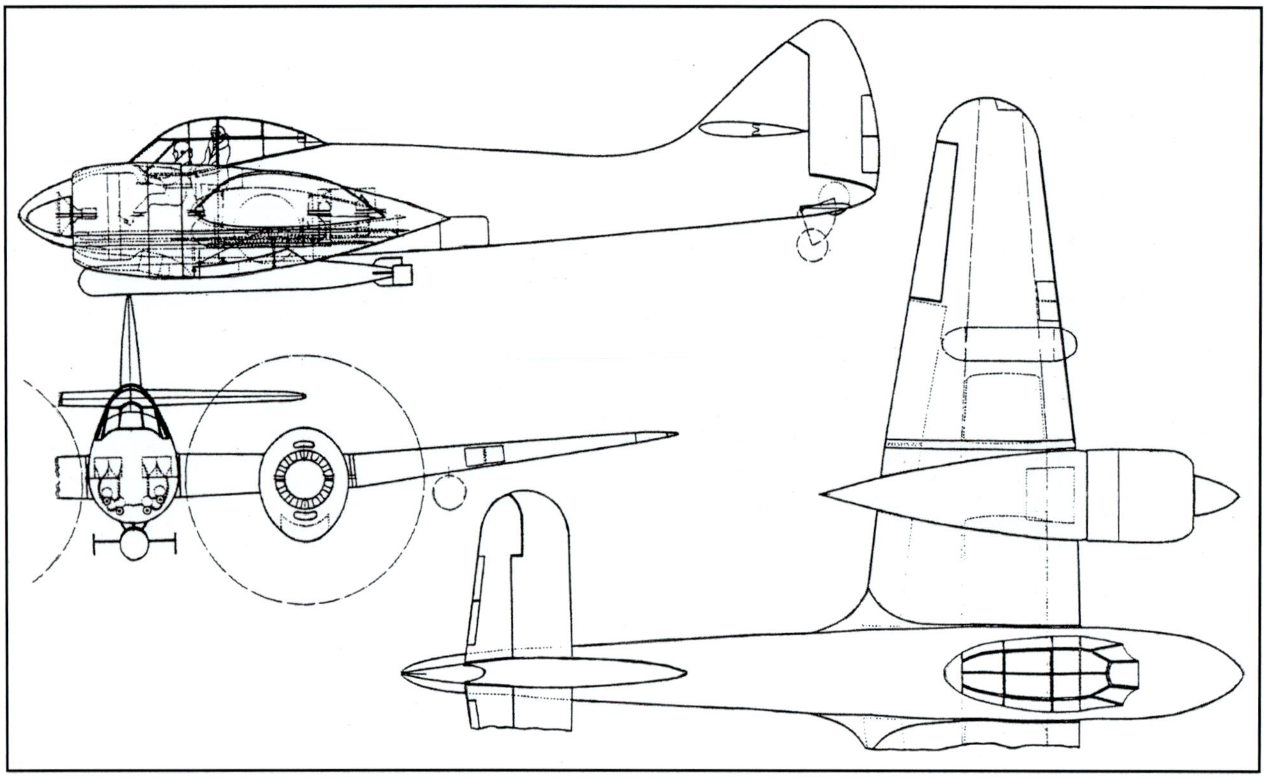

ABOVE The Bristol H.7/42, tentatively named Buccaneer, as at 3 November 1942. The four cannon were mounted in the lower nose. *Duncan Greenman, Bristol AiRchive*

1. An aircraft derived from the Beaufighter with one torpedo and four 20mm cannon, 24,900lb (11,294kg) take-off weight, a wing area of 503sq.ft (46.73sq.m) and a maximum speed at sea level of 327mph (526km/h), or

2. A Buckingham II derivative of 32,500lb (14,742kg) with two torpedoes, a 708sq.ft (65.78sq.m) wing and capable of 340mph (547km/h) at sea level.

A redesigned Beaufighter with a new body was eventually selected; drawings were issued for a fuselage mock-up and on 26 August Specification S.7/42 was raised to cover the project (this was renumbered H.7/42 on 15 September). Bristol suggested that the new aircraft might be called Buccaneer and hoped for a possible first flight in November 1943. The Beaufighter's navigator was moved to a position just behind the pilot which made the task of torpedo direction somewhat simpler.

As the work proceeded the design reached a stage where it no longer had much in common with the Beaufighter. The estimated all-up-weight rose to 27,000lb (12,247kg) and so the span had to be increased to keep down the wing loading, which meant that the new fuselage and tail unit now had a completely redesigned wing to go with them, and even the strengthened Beaufighter undercarriage would need further alteration should the weight go any higher. All of this reduced the top speed and left only a very small margin for development, a bad policy for a type not due to enter production for two years. Attempts were made to cut the drag, the most obvious way on the Beaufighter being the engine nacelles.

Frise and Russell were so concerned that they suggested fitting Centaurus engines instead of the Hercules or, in other words, combine the Buckingham wings and power units with the present H.7/42 fuselage of smaller cross-sectional area; the predicted all-up-weights for this machine with either Centaurus and Hercules were 34,086lb and 26,136lb (15,461kg and 11,855kg) respectively. This change was practicable since the spar centres were the same for the two types and Bristol considered that such an adaptation would not only produce a better aeroplane but save time both in design and flight testing. Brake flaps would need to be added to the Buckingham's wings but this would entail far less design work than needed for the current H.7/42 wing, and the Buckingham tail unit could also be adapted although, at this point, Bristol favoured a single fin and rudder.

The result would be a fast aircraft with a crew of three and a fuselage layout identical to that already mocked-up and agreed for the H.7/42, and this was accepted on 11 March 1943 as the Type 164. The Beaufighter-based project had become overloaded and its performance had forced this switch to a new aircraft, a decision that put much less strain on the Bristol design organisation. Specification H.7/42 had been issued 10 December 1942 and called for a high-speed torpedo attack aircraft and dive bomber with a maximum speed at sea level of not less than 345mph

ABOVE **Bristol Brigand MX991 photographed on 5 July 1945.** *Crown Copyright*
BELOW **Another Brigand, RH749, is seen armed with an underfuselage torpedo.**

(555km/h). In early February 1943 the new aeroplane was officially called the Brigand TF.Mk.I and the go-ahead to proceed was given in April. Four Brigand prototypes were ordered on 12 April, all powered by the Centaurus VII, and the first, MX988, made its maiden flight on 4 December 1944. On 14 August 1945 MX994 reached 390mph (628km/h) at 13,000ft (3,962m) in a dive.

With the end of Beaufort production, there would no longer be an aircraft available for the training requirements of the Beaufighter and Brigand OTUs so, in May, N. E. Rowe, DTD, made a dual-control version an urgent requirement. Consequently the Type 165 Brigand II was prepared but then, to simplify matters and not complicate the torpedo bomber's development, in August Bristol proposed a dual-control Buckingham which became the Type 166 Buckmaster to Specification T.13/43, the first example flying on 27 October 1944. Since many components, such as the undercarriage, were the same for all three types – Buckingham, Brigand and Buckmaster – it was planned to attach a flight of Buckmasters to each Brigand squadron for conversion training.

The Brigand was too late to see action in the Far East against Japan and most TF.Mk.Is were quickly returned to Filton for conversion into B.Mk.I light bombers with the rear gun removed. In fact during this period the need for an RAF anti-shipping aircraft was abandoned. At the end of the war the RAF had a wide-ranging anti-shipping role but this was rapidly cut down and by 1947 only one Mosquito strike wing remained, which was to be re-equipped with the Brigand. However, instead of waiting any longer, the RAF got out of the maritime strike business altogether and disbanded its last strike wing before the Brigand was ready. In September 1947 it was decided that the Brigand should operate only as a general purpose bomber and it was finally cleared for Service use on 6 March 1948. A total of 147 was built, some as T.Mk.IV trainers, and many served in the Far East before the type was retired in 1958.

BELOW Brigand RH754 pictured on 3 September 1947 prior to the SBAC Show at Radlett. It carries eight rocket projectiles and a torpedo. Note the aerofoil attached to the latter, to help the weapon maintain stability on its descent into the water.

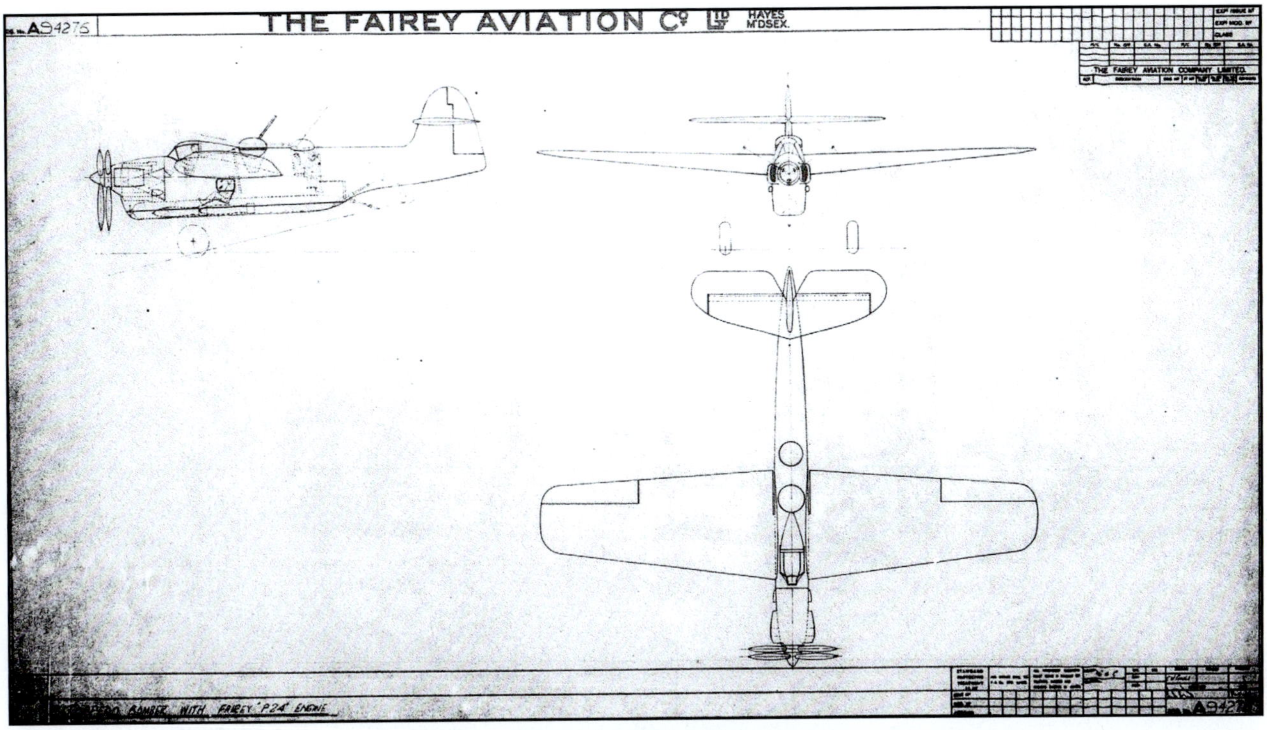

ABOVE While Fairey was conducting its studies into the requirements that brought forth the Spearfish and Sturgeon, it also produced this recently discovered torpedo bomber reconnaissance design. No data are available but it was to be powered by one of Fairey's own P24 piston engines driving a contra-rotating propeller. It has a crew of three; two bombs are loaded in tandem in the bomb bay; and there are two defensive turrets. The drawing is dated 9 March 1943.

Bristol H.7/42 'Buccaneer' (8.42 onwards)	
Span	c58ft 2in (17.73m)
Length	c45ft 1in (13.74m)
Wing Area	503sq.ft (46.73sq.m)
All-Up-Weight	24,900lb (11,294kg)
Powerplant	2 × Hercules
Max Speed/Height	327mph (526km/h) at sea level,
Armament	1 × torpedo, 4 × 20mm cannon

Bristol 164 Brigand TF.Mk.I (flown)	
Span	72ft 4in (22.05m)
Length	46ft 5in (14.15m)
Wing Area	718sq.ft (66.70sq.m)
All-Up-Weight	39,296lb (17,824kg)
Powerplant	2 × 2,500hp (1,864kW) Centaurus 57
Max Speed/Height	359mph (578km/h) at 16,100ft (4,907m)
Armament	1 × 2,000lb (907kg) or 2 × 1,000lb (454kg) or 600lb (272kg) bombs, 1 × torpedo or 1 × 1,000lb (454kg) mine, 4 × 20mm cannon, 1 × 0.5in (12.7mm) machine gun

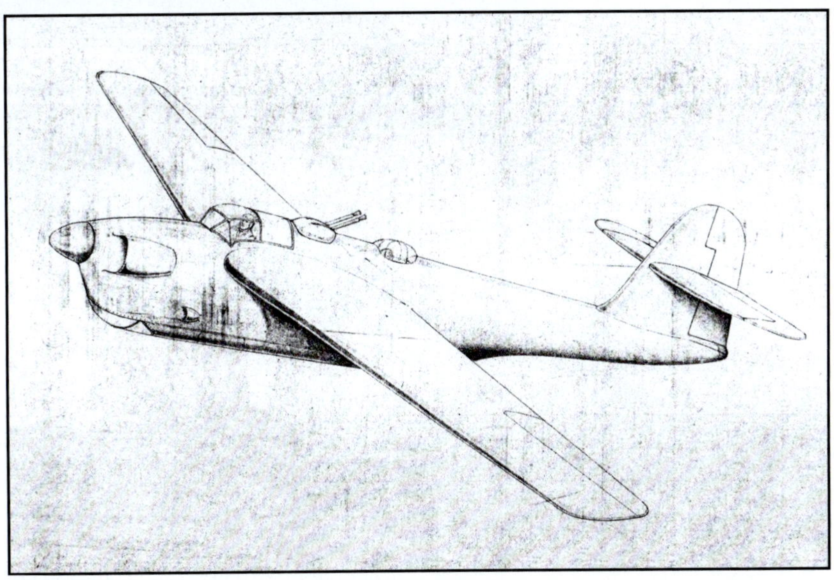

ABOVE Original artwork for the Fairey P24-powered torpedo bomber. Note the twin machine guns in the dorsal turret. *Chris Stainer*

Chapter Eight
Jet Bombers

ABOVE Model of the first version of the Gloster Jet Bomber with engines mounted in individual nacelles.
Joe Cherrie

The early stages of the development of the jet engine were characterised by the new power unit's high fuel consumption and consequent lack of range, with the result that fighter and interceptor type aircraft seemed to be the obvious place for this exciting invention. However, as early as January 1942, a memorandum from RAE Farnborough stated that 'contrary to popular belief, the jet-propulsion engine in its present state of development will make a substantially faster and more effective day bomber than is possible with the conventional reciprocating engine-airscrew combination. The attainment of this superior performance imposes a possible operational limitation on the jet propelled aeroplane, in that for longish ranges it must be cruised at a high altitude – in the neighbourhood of 40,000ft [12,192m] – and meteorological conditions may not always favour this procedure. This limitation does not debar the bomber from descending to ground level at the target where its enormous speed and high rate of climb render it relatively immune from ground and air attack.

The great majority of early British jet aircraft design work was indeed devoted to fighters, but it was not long before proposals followed for bombers powered by jet engines. A Ministry review of 'Future Gas Turbine Aircraft Projects' held on 8 June 1942 in fact listed four bomber designs:

1. A Gloster proposal with four 1,700lb (7.6kN) thrust W.2B engines, 31,000lb (14,061kg) all-up-weight, 4,000lb (1,814kg) bomb load, 440mph (708km/h) top speed at 40,000ft (12,192m) and 1,500 miles (2,414km) range.
2. The same aircraft with 4,500lb (2,041kg) bombs giving a 35,000lb (15,876kg) all-up-weight and 1,350 miles (2,172km) range.
3. A de Havilland proposal with two 3,000lb (13.3kN) thrust de Havilland H.1 engines, 22,000lb (9,979kg) all-up-weight, 2,000lb (907kg) bombs, 445mph (716km/h) maximum at 40,000ft and 1,500 miles range.
4. An RAE Farnborough tail-first proposal with two 4,000lb (17.8kN) Metropolitan-Vickers F.3 engines, 30,000lb (13,608kg) all-up-weight, 4,000lb of bombs, 435mph (700km/h) top speed at 40,000ft and 2,100 miles (3,380km/h) range.

It was agreed that, at the present time, the obvious engine choices for bomber types were the F.3 and H.1 (the Metro-Vick F.3 was to be the first British turbofan engine to be designed and built and to undergo testing).

In terms of bomber schemes the Review concluded that:

1. Although engines were not yet sufficiently developed, they were within striking distance and it was now time to start a bomber design to come to fruition with the engines in two years' time.
2. Although a conventional type of gas turbine bomber could be built, the CofG position would be sensitive to changes in load distribution and any rear armament would probably upset the balance.
3. Therefore an attempt should be made on 'the optimum design which appears to be the unconventional tail-first type.'

The conventional unarmed bomber would be at the mercy of jet fighters but it could be built if the Air Staff wanted a jet-powered bomber quickly.

Gloster Jet Bomber

Probably the first ever British design for a jet bomber was a brochure completed by Gloster on 12 August 1941 which showed a machine powered by four 2,000lb (8.9kN) thrust Whittle (Power Jets) W.2B engines, with each unit in its own individual wing-mounted nacelle sufficiently outboard of the wing centre section to avoid interference. George Carter explained that the proposal took the development of the jet beyond his company's fighter studies but this was

Gloster Jet Bomber (12.8.41)	
Span	84ft 0in (25.60m)
Length	62ft 6in (19.05m)
Wing Area	900sq.ft (83.61sq.m)
All-Up-Weight	31,500lg (14,288kg)
Powerplant	4 × 2,000lb (8.9kN) Power Jets W.2B
Max Speed/Height	454mph (731km/h) at 36,000ft (10,973m)
Armament	4,000lb (1,814kg) bombs normal load, 8,000lb (3,629kg) overload

BELOW The first Gloster Jet Bomber in model form.

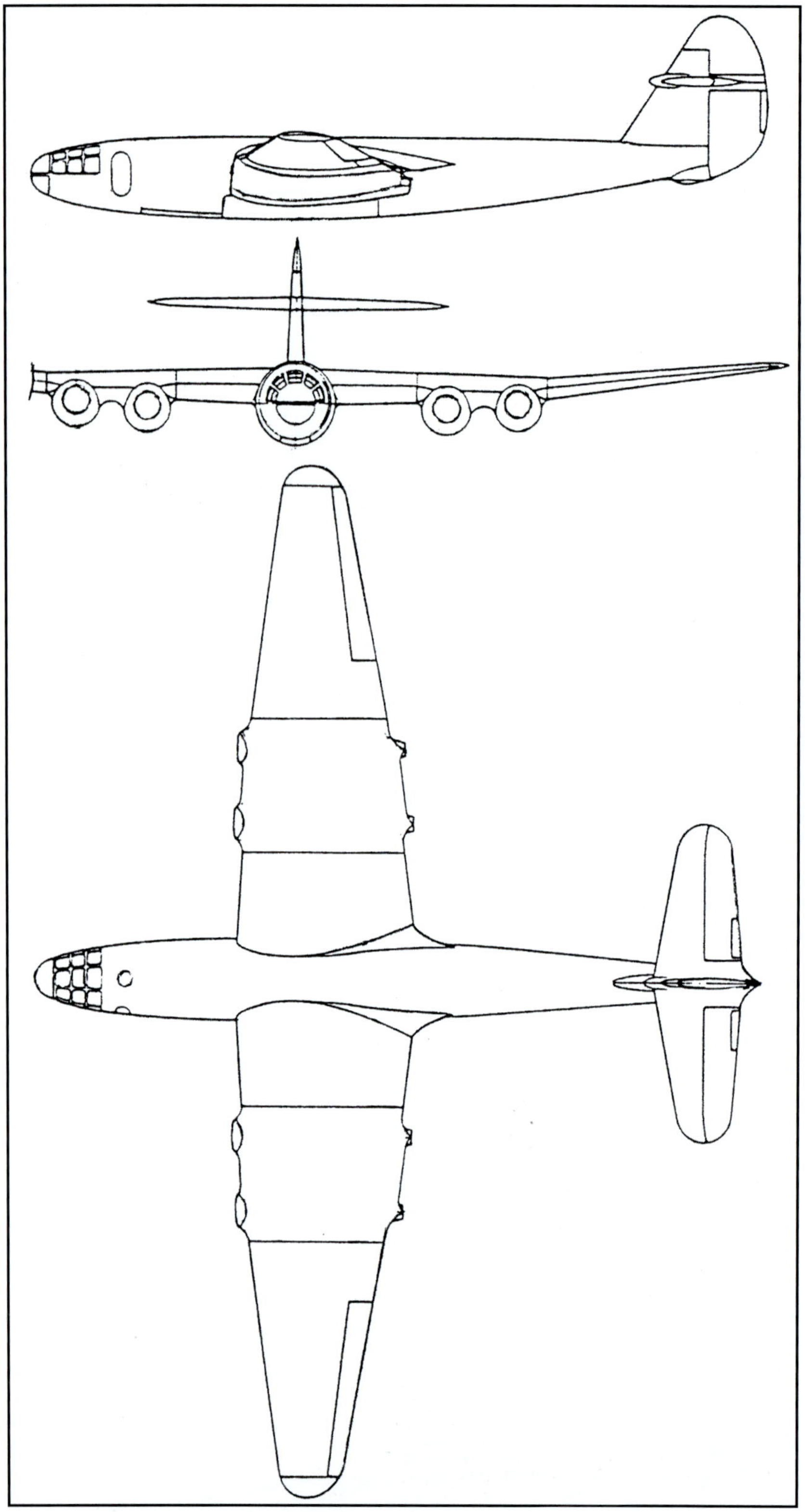

LEFT Gloster Jet Bomber (12.8.41). *Jet Age Museum*

not a finalised scheme. Two crew were carried; there was no provision for defensive armament; and the nosewheel of the tricycle undercarriage was a problem to the design of the front fuselage. The project was regarded as a rational development of the F.9/40 (Meteor) fighter with the same basic layout; its range was 1,500 miles (2,414km) plus twenty minutes over the target, ceiling 55,300ft (16,855m) and internal fuel 1,225gals (5,569lit).

Gloster P.109

In December 1941 Carter completed a revised study (drawing P.109 dated 24 November) with the same powerplant but with the power units now closely coupled in a common nacelle; this also provided a suitable housing for the fore and aft retracting undercarriage. The units were mounted ahead of a single-spar structural member and the exhaust pipes passed through elongated apertures at the rear of the nacelle. This arrangement, with a common entry and exit, was regarded as the most efficient installation for a pair of jet engines. Carter felt the design was perhaps the best that could presently be done with four W.2Bs (the possibility of six engines was being considered with the all-up-weight increased to 41,000lb [18,597kg]).

The main design conditions were substantially the same as the earlier project but the normal bomb load was now 4,500lb (2,041kg) to give a range of 1,750 miles (2,816km) and the maximum was 6,000lb (2,722kg) for a range of 1,500 miles (2,414km); the bomb load could comprise six 1,000lb (454kg) or nine 500lb (227kg). The cruise speed on the outward journey would be 395mph (636km/h) at 40,000ft (12,192m) and over the target 405mph (652km/h), and the time needed to get to 40,000ft was 40 minutes. Carter concluded that the main purpose of the proposal was to outline the general suitability of jet propulsion units for a bomber type, and more particularly to indicate the practicability of a scheme using four standard W.2B engines.

Gloster P.109 (24.11.41)	
Span	100ft 0in (30.48m)
Length	72ft 0in (21.95m)
Wing Area	1,120sq.ft (104.05sq.m)
All-Up-Weight	34,500lb (15,649kg) normal load, 36,000lb (16,329kg) overload
Powerplant	4 × 2,000lb (8.9kN) Power Jets W.2B
Max Speed/Height	?
Armament	4,500lb (2,041kg) bombs normal load, 6,000lb (2,772kg) overload

On 6 February 1942 Capt Liptrot completed his appraisal of this work for N. E. Rowe and declared that Gloster had underestimated the service load by some 700lb (318kg) and the structure by 300lb (136kg) – he expected the total weight to be 35,500lb (16,103kg), the cruise speeds to be about 25mph (40km/h) lower and maximum range 1,350 miles (2,172km). In addition the mean thrust needed to be increased by some 2,500lb (11.1kN) during a take-off to cut down the take-off distance and his main objection was the use of Whittle power units. The new Halford (de Havilland) jet engine would be far more appropriate to this type, not only by virtue of its better static thrust which would tend to satisfy the take-off situation, but also by its better cruising conditions. Liptrot added that the analysis showed that it was perfectly feasible, even now, to undertake the design of a pressure cabin unarmed bomber comparable, so far as bomb load and range were concerned, with the Hawker P.1005 (Chapter Three).

The same day Rowe wrote to CRD noting that 'these proposals were not sent by Carter with any idea that we would adopt them. You can take this scheme as an idea of a 'practical design' – an explanation of how the W2B could be used in a bomber. The conclusion from this work is that the power/weight ratio and fuel consumption of the unit are not good enough for the maximum range we require from bombers nowadays. If the Halford engine comes up to promise, there is little doubt that we shall be able to put it into a bomber type with upwards of 2,000 miles (3,219km) range.' CRD replied three weeks later 'Once we've got a 3,000lb (13.3kN) thrust engine, the bomber projects begin to get attractive.' He also stated that the 'day of the jet bomber may not be yet but I do not want such projects pushed into the background.' On 10 April 1942 however, Rowe stated that he felt the promise of suitable jet engines for powering medium-range bombers of 1,600 miles (2,575km) was still not strong enough and the best course now was to go forward with the jet fighter.

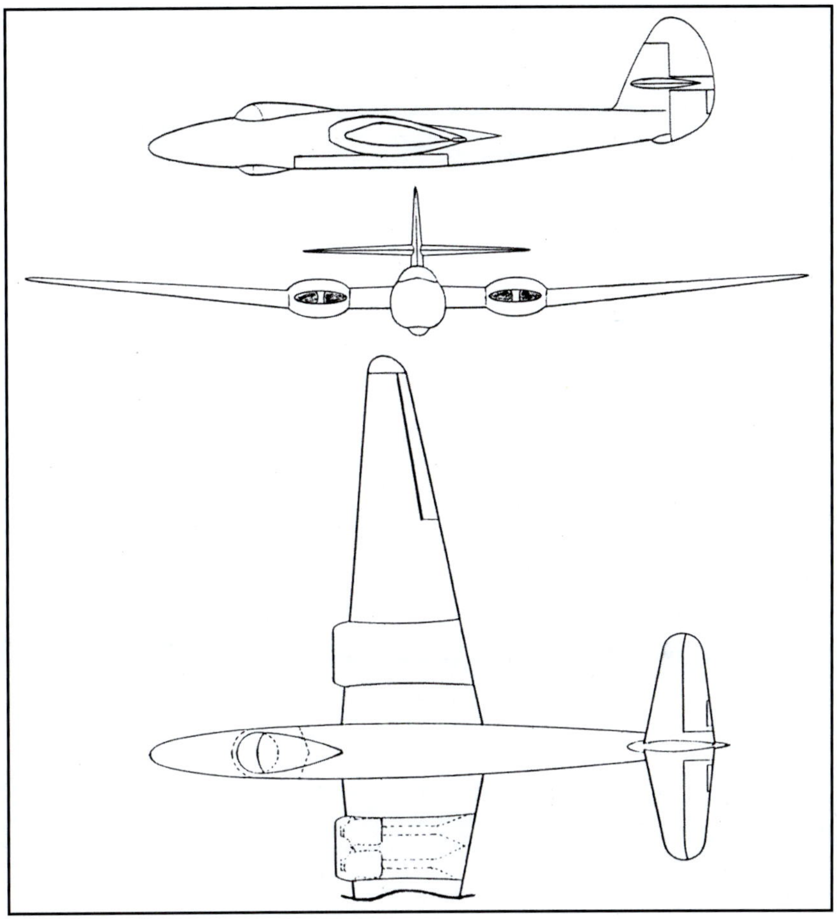

ABOVE Gloster P.109 four-jet bomber (24.11.41). *Jet Age Museum*

de Havilland Jet Bomber

It is unknown just how much work de Havilland put into the design of a jet bomber but in February 1942 the company was asked to examine the question of designing a twin-jet bomber instead of the single-jet fighter on which it was engaged (the DH.100, which became the Vampire). de Havilland's C. C. Walker told Rowe on 13 February that the case for proceeding with the fighter was as strong as it was before. He added that 'so far as the design of a jet-propelled bomber is concerned, this most interesting proposal depends on everything coming out exactly according to plan, and while there is no reason to doubt that the expected figures will eventually be obtained, we should have to wait until the altitude power and other features had been substantiated before starting it.'

There was also the domestic side of the question. de Havilland had had the greatest difficulty in getting enough design capacity to do the new DH.102 bomber (Chapter Three), to look after Mosquito development and production, and to do the new jet fighter. By making special arrangements with the Airspeed company it had been able to do this but if de Havilland was to try to substitute a twin-jet bomber for the fighter in its design programme, it (being a much bigger job) would put the programme definitely out of the company's reach. Walker hoped that, for all these reasons, de Havilland could go straight ahead with the fighter.

It due course it did, although Walker added a postscript on 23 February – 'We do fully realise the importance of producing a bomber with twin H.1 units when they have shown that they can deliver the anticipated thrust/consumption. So far as our capacity to produce is concerned, if we were engaged on the fighter, the Sabre bomber and Mosquito development, we could do no more. There is,

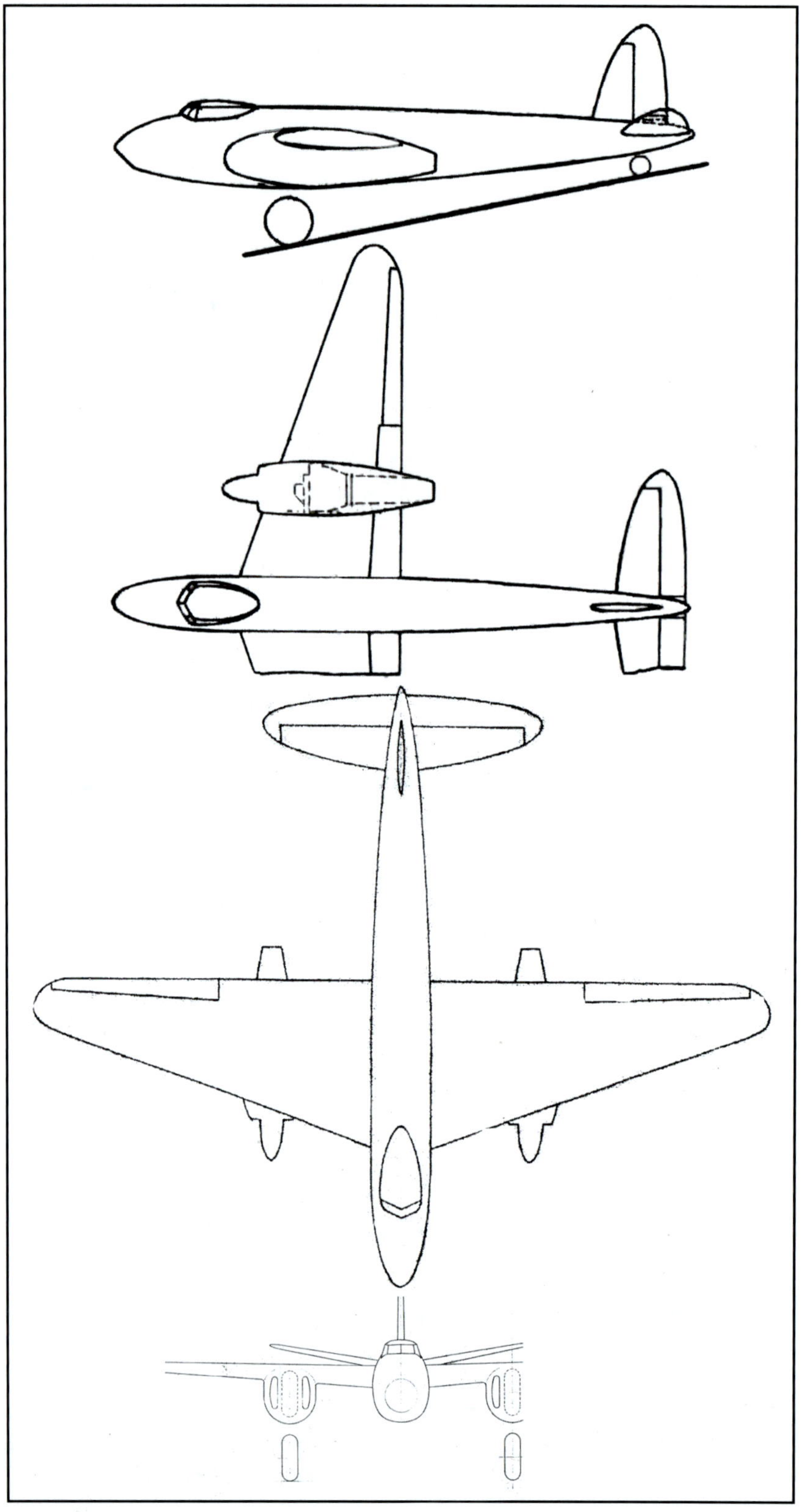

ABOVE The de Havilland 'Jet Mosquito' was to be powered by two Halford H.1 jet engines. *Bill Taylor*

however, this further possibility. If the H.1 soon shows that it can do what is expected, we could do the H.1 bomber instead of the Sabre bomber. It would do the same job with a higher performance and would only be subject to the duration-at-low-altitude limitations we have indicated. Much of

de Havilland Jet Mosquito (at mid-1942)	
Span	57ft 0in (17.37m)
Length	46ft 8.5in (14.24m)
Wing Area	483sq.ft (44.87sq.m)
All-Up-Weight	(2,000lb/907kg bombs) 22,150lb (10,047kg)
Overload weight	(4,000lb/1,814kg bombs) 24,150lb (10,954kg)
Powerplant	2 × 3,000lb (13.3kN) H.1 jets
Max Speed/Height	451mph (726km/h) at sea level, 483mph (777km/h) at 35,000ft (10,668m)
Armament	Internal provision for 4,000lb (1,814kg) bombs

the work we have done on the Sabre version would be of use in such a design, and two could be produced for the same production effort as one Sabre machine. The problem of getting a Sabre machine into production with its counter-rotating propellers – new installation and equipment problems with the skilled labour position as it is, is one which makes us look rather hungrily at the much simpler H.1 version. Substituting the H.1 bomber for the Sabre bomber is one of the possible alterations to be considered.'

Just how long the de Havilland jet bomber design lasted as a project is unknown. An undated de Havilland report, comparing the Jet Bomber with a version of the firm's twin-Napier Sabre bomber (Chapter Three), gave the data in the adjacent table. This report also declared that the jet propelled aircraft could be made considerably smaller and lighter than the conventionally engined aircraft, though some weight and drag would be incurred in accommodating the fuel (7,030lb/3,189kg in total) and locating the CofG correctly. The report also listed an initial rate of climb of 3,270ft/min (997m/min), operational ceiling 40,300ft (12,283m), dive speed 550mph (885km/h) IAS and still air range 1,550 miles (2,494km). No DH-number was allocated to the 'Jet Mosquito' project, but in summary it was stated that the aircraft 'possesses an overwhelming superiority in performance at all altitudes over the conventional bomber with the same range and bomb load.'

ABOVE Model of the 'Jet Mosquito' made by Joe Cherrie. *Joe Cherrie*

ABOVE AND LEFT An idea by Petter of Westland for a jet-powered fighter bomber (c1944). The models indicate three versions, all with a nose intake and a tricycle undercarriage. Two had engines possibly stacked one above the other, an outlet in the upper fuselage which required either a V tail or a conventional tail with tip fins, and possibly another outlet in the lower fuselage. A third version had side-by-side engines, side intakes and jetpipes in the fuselage sides just to the rear of the wing. The date is unknown but they would have been quite large aeroplanes. Unfortunately these images are of poor quality. *Westland Archive*

Westland P.1056

In early 1944 Westland's technical director W. E. W. Petter, after discussions between his company and two members of MAP, Sir Wilfred Freeman (now a civilian and its Chief Executive) and N. E. Rowe, completed a design study for a high-speed twin jet-powered fighter bomber called the P.1056. Petter sent off his first drawings on 1 February and suggested a substantial mix of weapons – two, four or six 20mm cannon (mounted beneath the nose intake), two six pounder guns, nine 500lb (227kg), three 1,000lb (454kg) or two 2,000lb (907kg) bombs in a lower fuselage internal bomb bay, or 90lb (41kg) rocket projectiles. Various mixes of guns and bombs were listed together with their effect on the aircraft's range – six 20mm alone gave a range of 1,375 miles (2,213km) but a large bomb load plus alternative gun arrangements reduced this to 790 miles (1,271km).

Initially the P.1056 had the tailwheel arrangement used by most piston aircraft but later a tricycle undercarriage with a nosewheel was introduced and this version was called P.1061. Power was supplied by a pair of Metro-Vick F.2/4 Beryl axial jets mounted side-by-side in the centre fuselage and fed by a large nose intake. To avoid the tailwheel the exhaust was ejected through holes in the side of the fuselage ahead of the tailplane, but introducing the tricycle gear meant a more effective single pipe at the very end of the fuselage could be

Westland P.1056 (3.44 onwards)	
Span	56ft 4in (17.17m)
Length	45ft 5in (13.84m)
Wing Area	550sq.ft (51.09sq.m)
All-Up-Weight	32,000lb (14,515kg)
Powerplant	2 × 3,500lb (15.6kN) Metro-Vick F.2/4 Beryl
Max Speed/Height	520mph (837km/h) at 25,000ft (7,620m)
Armament	See text

fitted to serve both engines. The two crew sat side by side. (The P.1056 and P.1061 are described more fully, and shown in drawing and model form, in the author's *British Secret Projects: Jet Bombers since 1949*, published by Crécy in 2018.)

On 20 February 1944 J. D. Breakey wrote 'we have found it difficult to associate this project with the fighter/bomber role as we understand it. Petter has obviously intended this aircraft to be a ground attack close-support weapon as he calculates his range on a basis of 250 miles [402km] at ground level and provides for protection from forward and ground fire. For the fighter/bomber we require a highly manoeuvrable aircraft which will not be required to operate above 10,000ft [3,048m] and I find it difficult to believe that the jet reaction type of power unit is the most suitable for such an aircraft. With any of Petter's proposals we get an aircraft which has to go over 20,000ft [6,096m] to obtain reasonably economic cruising conditions for the range requirement and has a poor take-off of 1,500 yards [1,372m] to [clear] 50ft [15m], which is very undesirable in an aircraft which might be expected to operate from improvised airfields. I also find it difficult to reconcile the size of the twin Metro-Vick F.2 Mk.4 aircraft with the manoeuvrability required in the fighter/bomber role.'

However, Breakey had recently discussed the project with Petter and found that the design lent itself to a very much more flexible bomber arrangement than was suggested in the brochure, with a maximum capacity of 4,500lb (2,041kg) bombs, and he could foresee a better future for something of this sort as a high-speed bomber. He suggested that the whole project should be re-examined on these lines and in this idea he was correct because the concept was eventually to become the post-war Canberra flown in 1949, although built by English Electric (which Petter had joined) and not Westland. In May 1944 Breakey wrote 'the scheme offered in the twin Metro-Vick form is attractive and I should like to see it put in hand.' A mock-up of the nose and central fuselage was constructed while Petter displayed a scale model on his desk complete with bombs, engines and internal fittings, but this particular design was never built.

Handley Page Research

Before the war ended there were several other proposals for jet-powered combat aircraft including the 'giant' jet bomber from Handley Page listed in Chapter Five; several jet conversions of piston types like the Mosquito; and a 'Jet Sturgeon' fighter version of the naval bomber covered in Chapter Seven, but details for most are very sketchy. By late December 1942 agreement had been reached to put in hand an 'experimental design' of jet bomber of 40,000lb to 50,000lb (18,144kg to 22,680kg) all-up-weight and Handley Page had been selected to do this project, which was essentially expected to take the form of a tailless aircraft. At the time Handley Page was the only company with a current active interest in tailless aeroplanes (although Armstrong Whitworth had made a paper study of the problems of tailless bombers with jet propulsion) and it had a small twin-engine model ready for flight (the Manx which actually did not fly until 25 June 1943 – Chapter Five). The Ministry felt that the company should be ready to get down to design work by about April 1943 although this depended on its Halifax workload, but the project appears never to have got going.

Bristol 'Jet Buckingham'

Some references have been found in official documents for a 'Jet Buckingham'. The first suggestions for fitting jets in combination with normal piston engines, which would turn the Buckingham into a very high-speed bomber, were made in September 1941. The jets would be fitted in the rear half of the nacelles behind the piston units and give, for short periods only, an increment of speed at full throttle at moderately low altitudes. It was indicated that at 15,000ft (4,572m), from the piston only maximum of 340mph (547km/h), this increase could perhaps reach 430mph (692km/h) with Rolls-Royce engines and 407mph (655km/h) with Whittle units; at 20,000ft (6,096m) the new maximum speeds from the piston-powered 368mph (592km/h) would be 450mph (724km/h) and 430mph (692km/h) respectively. However, on 17 January 1942 N. E. Rowe noted that they 'do not propose to add this to Bristol's burden at the moment but would like details worked out as soon as the way is clear.' The 'Jet Buckingham' was another idea that never came to fruition.

Appendix One British 'Wartime' Aircraft Project Summary

ABOVE **An Armstrong Whitworth Whitley displays its characteristic nose-down attitude when in flight.**

During their years of independence many of Britain's aircraft firms became wedded to certain types of aeroplane or areas of manufacture. Hawker, for example, was always a fighter specialist while Avro, Handley Page and Vickers usually built or designed heavy bombers and larger types. Blackburn and Fairey were regular suppliers of aircraft to the Fleet Air Arm and this often influenced their lines of development.

The following lists all known bomber designs and projects produced by the companies between 1935 and the mid to late 1940s. Selected earlier types that were still in production are also included together with research types that were developed essentially to advance the designer's art. In theory, all projects are 'official,' despite some schemes having such a brief life that they really have no right to be here but sneak in, as one cannot always determine which they are; in fact some of the designs that are here can really only be considered as draft or provisional layouts. Information for some Second World War bomber projects does not appear to have survived and has probably been lost forever. In fact, with so many firms and specifications (to which many projects were prepared without project numbers) it is impossible to say how complete this list is. Finally, some wartime jet bomber projects are listed here only briefly because they were covered in more depth by the jet bomber volume in this series, where they essentially formed part of the post-war story.

AIRSPEED (taken over by de Havilland in 1940)

AS.15 Speculative four-engine heavy bomber design by Hessel Tiltman, 5.35. Span 166ft (50.60m) and powerful armament but far too large for its time.

AS.29 Bomber to Specification B.1/35, 2.36.

AS.47 High-speed all wood twin-boom bomber project with two Napier Sabre engines, 1939/40.

AS.52 Bomb-carrying glider based on Horsa to Specification X.3/41, 1941. Serials given to two prototypes under Ministry contract but not proceeded with.

ARMSTRONG WHITWORTH

AW.38 Heavy bomber developed to B.3/34 and first flown 17.3.36. Entered service as Whitley.

AW.39 Whitley bomber development to B.1/35, 7.35.

AW.41 Albemarle bomber, first flown 5.40.

AW.42 Four-engine bomber to B.12/36, 9.36.

AW.44 Development of Albemarle with four RR Merlins, 10.39. Span 84ft 6in (25.76m), length 59ft 11in (18.26m).

AW.45 Twin-Merlin aircraft, probably for bomber or reconnaissance role, 23.10.39.

AW.46 Four-engine scaled-up version of AW.45 near identical in shape and layout to earlier form, drawing traced 16.1.40. AWA long-travel tricycle undercarriage fitted with main wheels retracting into inboard engine nacelles, all metal monocoque structure, three crew, no defensive armament, ten bombs in wings, two in fuselage. Span 70ft 2in (21.39m), length 47ft 1in (14.35m).

AW.47 Bomber project believed prepared to B.3/40, 9.40.

AW.48 Heavy bomber to B.1/39, 17.4.39.

Light High-Speed Day Bomber Unnumbered project to B.7/40, 11.9.40.

Four-engine Whitley Unnumbered scheme prepared in 1941 to meet RAF need for high-performance heavy bomber. To ensure use of existing Whitley jigs and tools, as much original Whitley structure as possible retained and four Bristol Centaurus III or Wright Cyclone engines fitted, two replacing the Merlins, two more mounted on new wing sections placed between existing centre and outer wing sections. Tailplane and elevators enlarged, four standard Whitley fins and rudders fitted and structure strengthened; bomb load increased to 24,000lb (10,886kg). Span 135ft (41.15m), length 72ft 6in (22.10m), all-up-weight 90,000lb (40,823kg), top speed 295mph (475km/h). Little Ministry interest (Whitley by now considered obsolete).

AW.49 Ground attack aircraft, 9.42.

AW.50 Flying wing jet bomber; design study tendered to MAP mid-12.42 but soon abandoned.

AW.51 One-third scale wood glider to test aerodynamics of highly experimental AW.50, 1943.

AW.52 Experimental tailless aircraft to E.9/44 to test flying wing concept for large aircraft. AW.52G scale model glider flown 2.3.45. First of two AW.52s flown 13.11.47.

AW.53 Twin-engine torpedo bomber to S.6/43, 4.43.

AW.54 Redesign of AW.53 to S.11/43, 6.43.

AW.54A Reconnaissance bomber with two Metro-Vick F.3 turbojet engines, 1943.

AVRO

672 Torpedo bomber/reconnaissance aircraft to Specification M.15/35, 10.35. Based on Anson reconnaissance and training aircraft.

675 Torpedo bomber general reconnaissance aircraft to G.24/35, late 1935.

679 Bomber project to P.13/36. Became Manchester, first flown 25.7.39. Several proposals with alternative engines plus, c1939, development with cannon turrets.

680 Heavy bomber to B.1/39, 4.39. No detail drawings completed.

681 Heavy bomber project, c1939.

682 Heavy bomber project, c1939.

Close-Support Bomber Unnumbered project possibly prepared for B.20/40, 11.40.

683 Heavy bomber development of Manchester with four Merlins. Became Lancaster, first flown 9.1.41.

684 Stratosphere bomber development of Lancaster, 16.8.41.

High-speed Lancaster Version with streamlined nose, 1942.

'75 Ton Bomber' Two designs, 18.1.43.

694 B.Mk.IV and B.Mk.V Lancaster developments to B.14/43. Renamed Lincoln and first flown 9.6.44.

696 Anti-submarine aircraft to R.5/46. Became Shackleton, first flown 9.3.49.

BELOW Manufacturer's impression of the 'Four-Engine Whitley' of 1941.

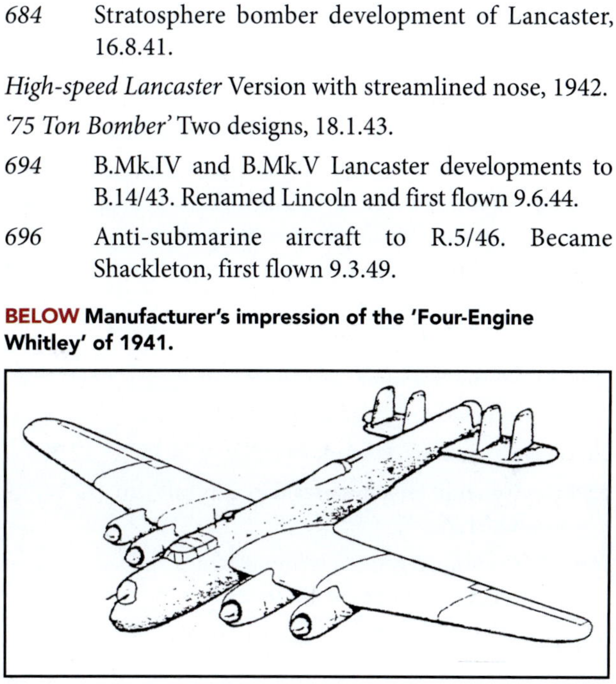

BLACKBURN

B.20 Flying boat to R.1/36 first flown late March/early April 1940.

B.21 Torpedo bomber reconnaissance monoplane to S.24/37, 1937.

B.22 Torpedo bomber reconnaissance aircraft to S.30/37, 5.37. Two Bristol Aquila A.E.3 or Napier Rapier VI engines.

B.23 Botha Mk.II private venture project, 1938. Abandoned for B.27.

B.26 Unnumbered projects proposed to M.15/35 and G.24/35 (both late 1935). Combined into B.26 for Specification 10/36 (1.36) and, as Botha Mk.I, first flown 28.12.38.

B.27 Botha Mk.II private venture project with two 1,400hp (1,044kW) Bristol Hercules engines, late 1930s.

B.28 Private venture high-speed light bomber and reconnaissance development based on Botha to B.3/40, 1939.

B.29 Torpedo bomber reconnaissance monoplane to S.24/37 with RR Exe engine, 1938. Was replacement for Blackburn Shark but cancelled in favour of B.36.

B.30 Heavy bomber to B.1/39, 4.39.

B.32 Four-engine flying boat to R.5/39, 19.6.39. Replaced by B.39.

B.36 Torpedo reconnaissance aircraft to S.24/37, 16.6.38.

B.39 Flying boat to R.5/39 with two Bristol Centaurus engines, 1940.

B.40 Proposed improvement of B.20 with Centaurus, 1940. Covered by R.13/40.

B.47 Dive and torpedo bomber project to O.5/43, 19.4.43.

Reconnaissance Bomber Project to S.11/43, 25.6.43.

B.50 Jet-powered FAA strike aircraft with one RR Nene engine submitted to Air Ministry 17.2.45. Two variants with single and twin booms.

B.78 Maritime flying boat to R.2/48(?), 1949.

BOULTON PAUL

P.79 Heavy bomber originally proposed to B.3/34; updated to B.1/35 in 6.35.

P.83 Shore-based torpedo bomber to M.15/35, 12.35.

P.84 General reconnaissance aircraft to G.24/35, 12.11.35.

P.86 Combined general reconnaissance and shore-based torpedo bomber to 10/36, 2.36.

P.87 Heavy bomber with two modified Merlin engines, 1936.

P.90 Heavy bomber to B.12/36 with four RR Kestrel KV.26, 1.10.36.

P.91 Medium bomber to P.13/36 with two RR Vultures, 6.1.37.

P.95 Single-engine two-seat bomber to B.20/40 with Bristol Hercules VI, c11.40.

P.99 Low-level single-seat pusher ground attack fighter with twin booms, 6.10.42. One RR Griffon and contra-rotating propellers.

P.100 Low-level single-seat tail-first pusher ground fighter, 6.10.42. One Griffon and contra-rotating propellers.

P.101 Low-level biplane ground attack fighter with one Bristol Centaurus CE.12.SM, 6.10.42.

Jet Barracuda Project to add one Power Jets W2B/37 engine in Fairey Barracuda torpedo bomber (Boulton Paul then undertaking production), c1942. Aimed at boosting aircraft's attacking performance in anti-shipping mode by putting jet in tail to 'augment' piston unit. No project number issued.

BRISTOL

Heavy Bomber Project to B.1/35, 3.7.35.

142M Medium bomber development of Type 142 airliner to 28/35. Became Blenheim first flown 25.6.36. Developments tendered to M.15/35 (3.12.35) and G.24/35 (18.11.35).

143 Initial military development of Type 142 and flown 20.1.36 as testbed for Bristol Aquila engine.

144 Heavy bomber tendered to B.3/34, mid-1934.

'Standard Bomber' Four-engine development of Blenheim, 12.35. Potential of Blenheim examined in terms of land-based bomber and torpedo bombers and this variant proposed using B.1/35 specification and extrapolating Type 142 performance data. Attached drawing, believed to be this project, had same front fuselage as Blenheim I, a large all-new wing and large fin, four Bristol Mercury IX or Bristol Taurus engines, four crew. Span 96ft (29.26m), length 68ft (20.73m), top speed 275mph (443km/h) (Mercury IX) or 300mph (483km/h) (Taurus), all-up-weight 37,500lb (17,010kg) (Mercury) or 38,500lb (17,463kg) (Taurus), range 225 miles (362km). As result, company invited to tender to B.12/36 and P.13/36. Little is known about the 'Standard Bomber', but for the Bristol design team it formed a link between the original Blenheim and the new four-engine types.

149 Bolingbroke Mk.I and Blenheim Mks.II and IV.

150 Torpedo bomber to M.15/35, 3.12.35.

152 Beaufort to 10/36, first flown 15.10.38.

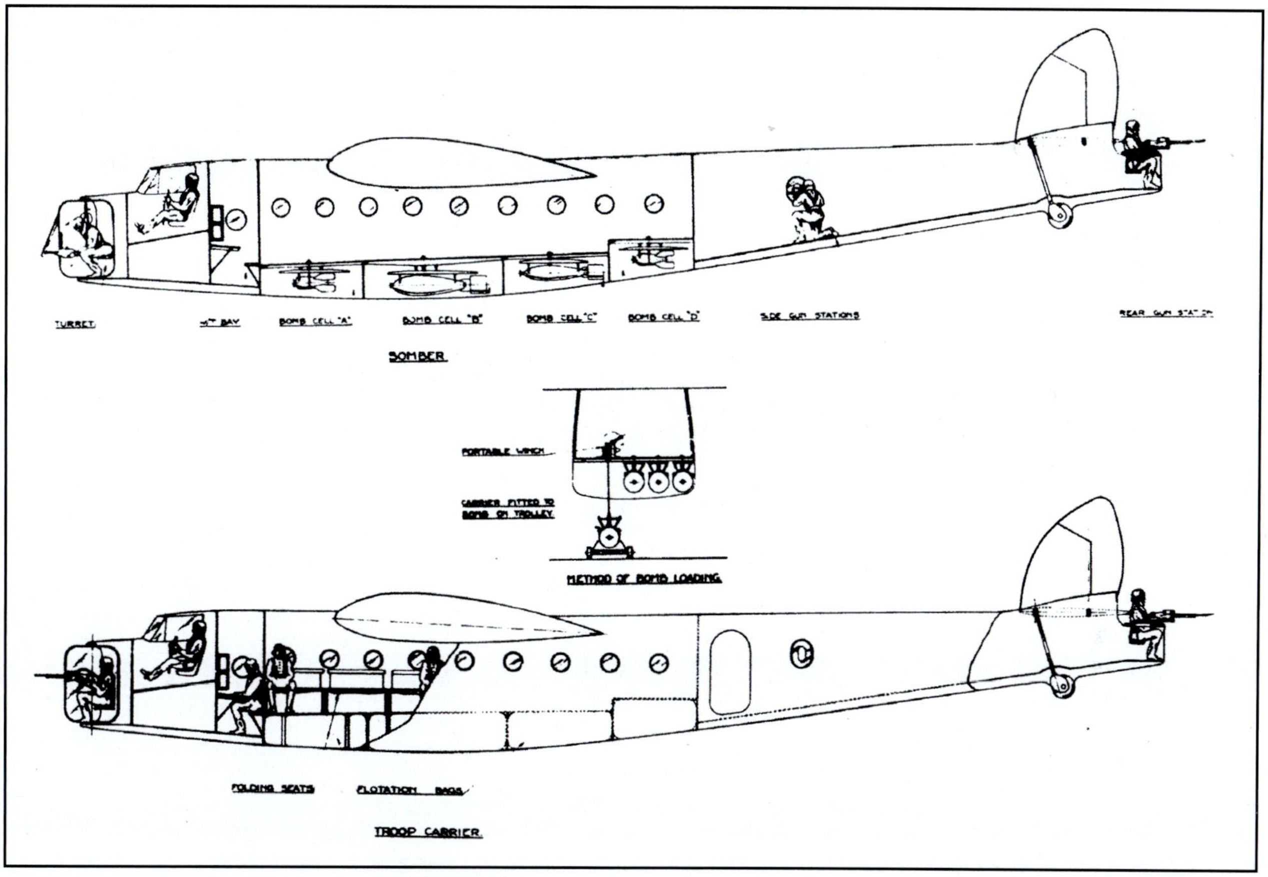

ABOVE **Side view cut-away drawings of the Type 144, Bristol's competing design to what became the Whitley (mid-1934).** *Duncan Greenman, Bristol AiRchive*

BELOW **An early mark of Bristol Blenheim in flight.**

ABOVE Later marks of Blenheim had a longer nose. This view shows a Mk.IV, possibly Z9815.

BELOW The Type 160 Blenheim Mk.V was originally called the Bristol Bisley Mk.I. This view was taken in July 1941.

Medium Bomber Unnumbered project to P.13/36, 6.1.37.

Heavy Bomber Unnumbered project to B.12/36, 15.4.37.

Torpedo Bomber Unnumbered project to S.24/37, 8.3.38.

155 Twin-engine wood and steel composite bomber to B.17/38, 1938.

159 Heavy bomber to B.1/39, 4.39.

160 Bisley Mk.I to B.6/40 first flown 24.2.41. Later entered service as Blenheim Mk.V.

161 Medium bomber, mid-1940.

162 Medium bomber ('Beaumont'), 2.10.40.

163 Revision of Type 162 Beaumont to B.2/41 which became Buckingham medium bomber first flown 4.2.43. Jet-powered Buckingham suggested 9.41.

164 'Buccaneer' torpedo bomber prepared to H.7/42, 8.42 onwards. Further developed as Type 164 Brigand, first flown 4.12.44.

'75 Ton Bomber' First proposals 15.11.42; two designs submitted 1.43.

CUNLIFFE-OWEN

Ground Attack Aircraft Design studies in response to Air Staff enquiries, 8 and 10.42.

Torpedo Bomber Reconnaissance Aircraft Study to S.6/43, 4.43.

Dive/Torpedo Bomber Project to O.5/43, 4.43.

DE HAVILLAND

DH.98 Unarmed bomber proposal of 9.39 onwards which became Mosquito. First flown 25.11.40 and built in many versions.

DH.99 High-speed bomber development of Mosquito to B.11/41, first considered early 1941. Soon renumbered DH.101. DH.99 reallocated to jet fighter and then to civil design.

DH.101 High-speed bomber to B.11/41. Abandoned 4.42.

High-Speed Unarmed Night Bomber Believed to be Mosquito development with four Merlins put forward as 'fast' heavy bomber, 1941. Span given as 80ft (24.38m), gross wing area 825sq.ft (76.64sq.m), operational weight 41,955lb (19,031kg), fuel 1,150 gallons (5,232lit). Possible alternative two Sabre NS.8.SM engines, bomb load 12 × 500lb (227kg), 6 × 1,000lb (454kg) plus 2 × 500lb (227kg), 4 × 1,900lb (862kg), or 2 × two 4,000lb (1,814kg). Maximum speed 385mph (620km/h) at 25,000ft (7,620m), range 2,150 miles (3,460km), service ceiling 31,000ft (9,449m).

'Jet Mosquito' Unnumbered development of Mosquito with two H.1 jet engines, first half 1942.

DH.102 'Mosquito II' high-performance bomber to B.4/42, 5.42. Cancelled 12.42.

FAIREY

Fairey did not make full use of project numbers and, consequently, this list only contains projects known to have existed. There almost certainly will have been more, particularly for the late 1930s, but details are lacking.

Battle Light bomber first designed to P.27/32 and first flown 10.3.36.

Swordfish Torpedo spotter reconnaissance (TSR) aircraft produced under Specification 38/34. Prototype first flown 17.4.34.

P.4/34 Light bomber prototype based on Battle and first flown 13.1.37. Used as a flying mock-up for Fulmar fighter.

Heavy Bomber Project to B.1/35, 6.35.

Albacore Torpedo bomber designed originally to M.7/36. First flown 12.12.38.

Medium Bomber Project to P.13/36, late 1936.

Reconnaissance Torpedo Bomber Project believed proposed to S.30/37, 1938.

Heavy Bomber Design to B.1/39, 4.39.

Dive Bomber Dive bomber conversion of Fulmar naval fighter, 31.5.40. Two bombs under each wing.

Barracuda Torpedo bomber to S.24/37 first flown 7.12.40.

Close-Support Bomber High-wing monoplane project to B.20/40, late 1940.

Note: During 1940 Fairey also worked on a twin Wright Cyclone-engine bomber, a twin-Merlin bomber [possibly to B.7/40] and a twin-engine dive bomber/fighter. In late 1942 single-engine Barracuda 'replacements' were being considered with either a Napier Sabre, RR Griffon or Fairey P24.

Barracuda Development Installation of RR Griffon or Bristol Hercules studied second half of 1941. Brochure for Barracuda with 1,560bhp (1,163kW) Hercules X 31.1.42, all-up-weight 12,025lb (5,454kg), maximum 259mph (417km/h) at 4,000ft (1,219m), 3.6 minutes to 5,000ft (1,524m).

Torpedo/Reconnaissance Aircraft Twin-Merlin project with special hinged engine mountings interconnected with wing fold gear. When wings folded, propeller spinners swung towards each other enabling aircraft to fold within 18ft (5.49m) width, despite engine centres 14ft 8in (4.47m) apart and prop diameter 12ft (3.66m).

Torpedo Bomber Twin Merlin project, 8.4.42. Revised with Griffons 12.7.42.

Torpedo Bomber Reconnaissance Aircraft Study to S.6/43, 4.43.

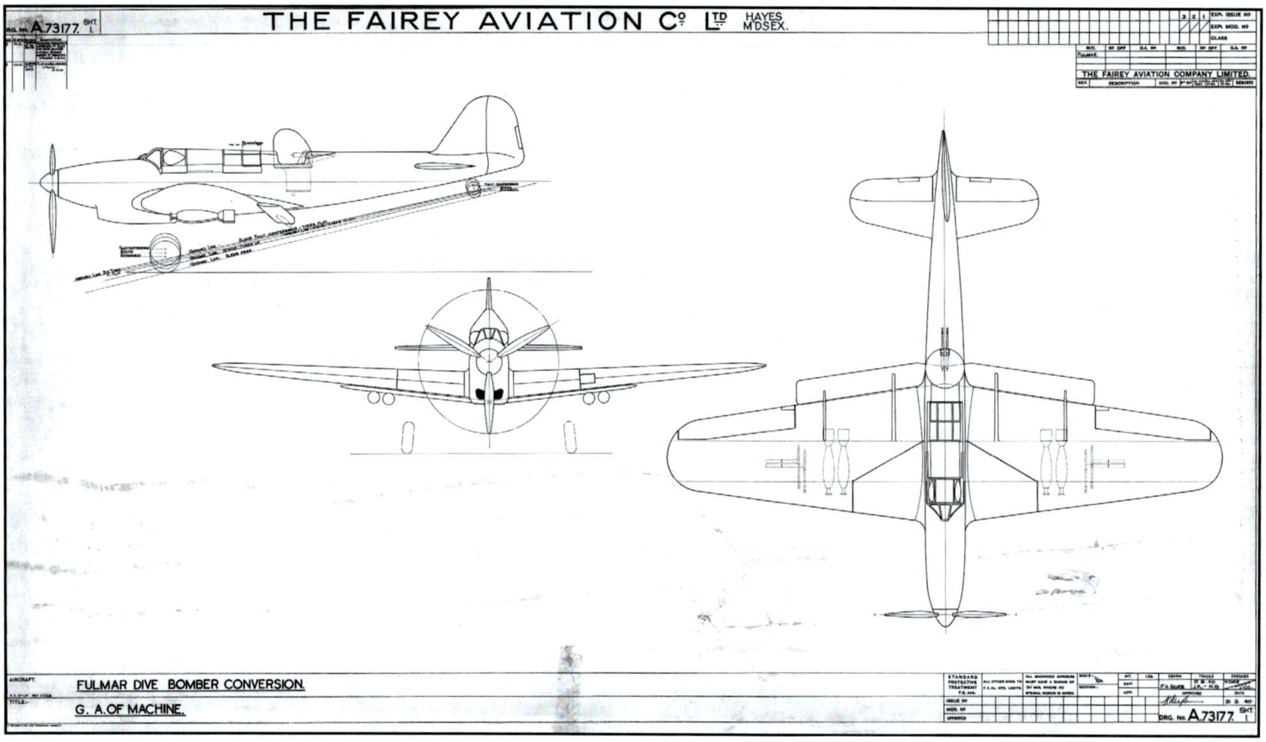

ABOVE Fairey dive bomber based on Fulmar fighter (31.5.40). *Chris Stainer*

Dive/Torpedo Bombers Series of designs to O.5/43, 4.43 onwards. Resulted in Spearfish first flown 5.7.45. Proposed RR Clyde testbed conversion 18.4.45.

Torpedo Bomber Reconnaissance Aircraft Design powered by Fairey P24 engine, 9.3.43.

Naval Bomber Combined piston/jet project to S.11/43, mid-1943.

Strike Aircraft Spearfish developments to O.21/44 with different engine arrangements, 7.44 onwards. Various development proposals with different engines.

Gannet Various studies for anti-submarine aircraft to GR.17/45. First brochure 14.12.45. As Type Q became Gannet, first flown 19.9.49.

FLIGHT REFUELLING

FR.5 Medium bomber with in-flight refuelling capability, 10.38.

FR.7 High-speed unarmed bomber, 1.39.

FOLLAND

Fo.100 Believed to be a bomber powered by a single RR Vulture, 4.37.

Fo.100A Bomber with one Vulture, 8.37.

Fo.104 Torpedo spotter reconnaissance (TSR) type with two Bristol Aquila engines, 7.37.

Fo.108 Testbed aircraft to 43/37 (Folland 'Frightful') first flown 1940. Used to test different versions of Bristol Hercules and Centaurus, Napier Sabre and RR Griffon, plus various propellers.

Fo.111 Single-engine bomber, 22.11.39. To form upper component of composite project – lower component never established. Single-engine high speed bomber design described in 8.39 issue of *Aeronautics* may be associated but was different aircraft.

Fo.111A Bomber with single Pratt & Whitney Twin Wasp radial, 1.40.

Fo.112 Unarmed bomber, single Wasp or Sabre, 1.40.

Fo.112A Single Napier Sabre-powered unarmed bomber, 9.40.

Fo.113 Twin-engine two-seat bomber to B.1/40, 1940/41.

Fo.114 As Fo.113 but powered by two Griffons, 1940/41.

Fo.115 Sabre-powered 'torpedo reconnaissance' aircraft to E.28/40, 1940/41.

Fo.116 As Fo.115 but variable-incidence wing and 2,400hp (1,790kW) Bristol Centaurus III, 19.1.41. E.28/40 called for research aircraft to examine problem of increasing weight during carrier deck landings and prototypes DX160 and DX165 ordered 8.41 with Centaurus replacing Sabre. Variable incidence (range between –1° and +14° with wing moving on spar pivots) would allow pilot to keep fuselage horizontal throughout landing; wing also had leading-edge slots and Fowler trailing-edge flaps for maximum lift. Normal construction used in fuselage, twin-0.50in (12.7mm) dorsal turret mounted behind pilot's cockpit and fixed 'spatted' undercarriage. Span 51ft 2in (15.60m), folded span 18ft 0in (5.49m), length 44ft 2in (13.46m), wing area 380sq.ft (35.30sq.m), estimated top speed 288mph (463km/h) at 20,000ft (6,096m) and sea level rate of climb 1,420ft/min (433m/min). All-up-weight for stressing 19,000lb (8,618kg) which, without the special wing, would have given minimum speed too high to achieve carrier landing. Cruising range 800 miles (1,287km) for which 360gal (1,637lit) fuel provided. Mock-up built and by 1943 DX160 well advanced, but by then many of problems to be examined had been solved and project cancelled. DX165 never started.

Fo.116A Revised development of Fo.116 with same basic layout but different wing and retractable undercarriage, 28.2.42. Span 56ft 0in (17.07m), length 45ft 0in (13.72m), wing area 450sq.ft (41.81sq.m), maximum all-up-weight for stressing 17,600lb (7,983kg), maximum overload weight 20,000lb (9,072kg).

Fo.119 Single-engine dive bomber to O.5/43, 1.6.43.

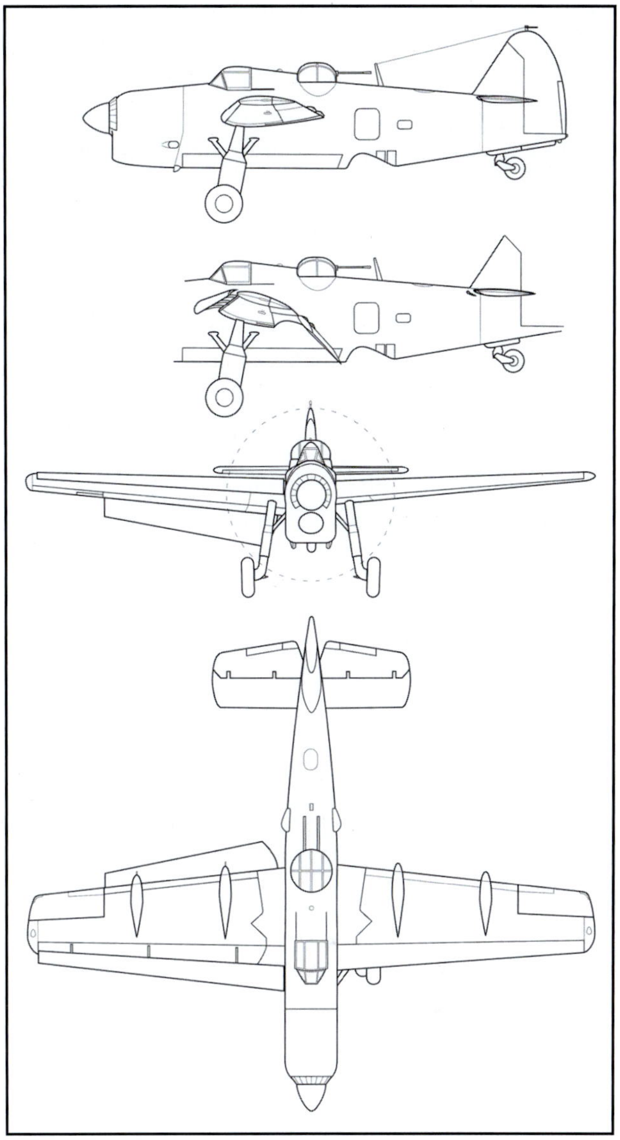

RIGHT The original version of the Folland Fo.116 project (19.1.41). *Ralph Pegram*

BELOW The Folland 'Frightful' engine testbed was flown with various different units installed, including the Napier Sabre and Bristol Hercules.

ABOVE Model of the Folland Fo.116.

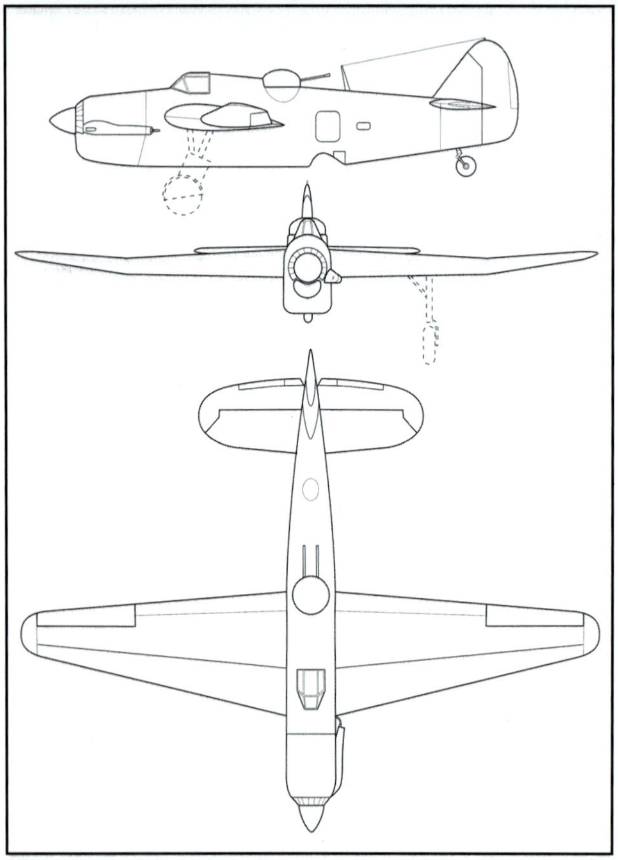

ABOVE A much later version of Folland's naval research aircraft introduced a retractable undercarriage and a different wing. It was labelled Fo.116A (28.2.42). *Ralph Pegram*

GENERAL

GAL.39 Covered two projects, GAL.39A and B, latter with variable area wing (more accurately a monoplane-to-biplane arrangement), 2.3.38 and 30.4.38 respectively. To Specification S.30/37 of 1.38 for general-purpose two-motor three-crew carrierborne aircraft to perform reconnaissance and spotting, level and dive bombing and torpedo attacks. Requested warload one 1,500lb (680kg) torpedo or three 500lb (227kg) or six 250lb (113kg) bombs, one forward-firing Browning machine gun and one Vickers K gun for air gunner. GAL.39B featured double upper surface on outer wing panels – to increase wing area for slow flying, the upper surface could be raised so that aircraft virtually became a biplane. Both powered by two 1,000hp (746kW) Bristol Aquila engines, and both 40ft 0in (12.19m) long. GAL.39A span 50ft 0in (15.24m) and folded 18ft 4in (5.59m). GAL.39B 44ft 9in (13.64m) and folded 18ft 0in (5.49m).

GAL.43 Covered two engine testbed projects, GAL.43A and GAL.43B, to 43/37, mid-1938.

GLOSTER

The P number here refers to a drawing, not a project.

Heavy Bomber Project to B.1/35, 6.35.

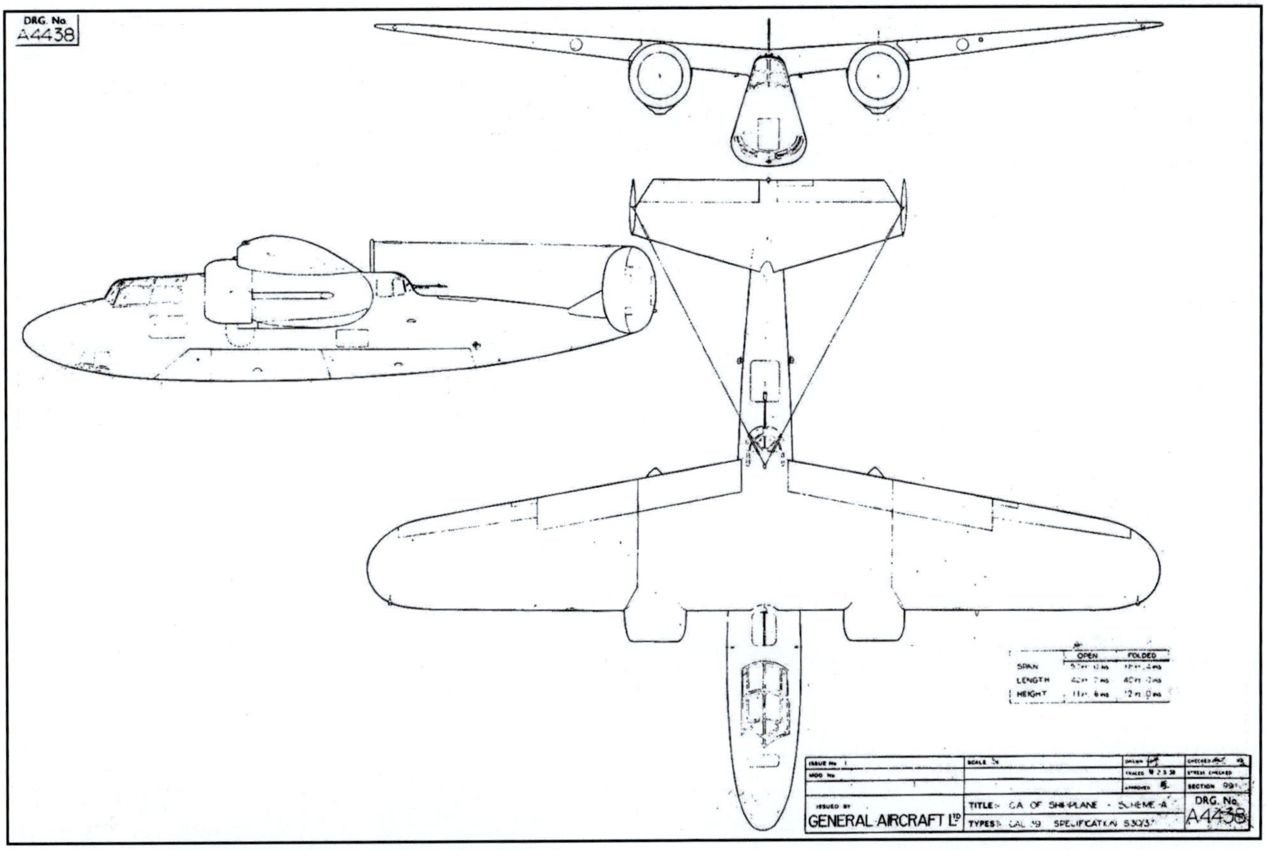

ABOVE **General Aircraft GAL.39A (2.3.38).** *Ralph Pegram*

BELOW **General Aircraft GAL.39B (30.4.38).** *Ralph Pegram*

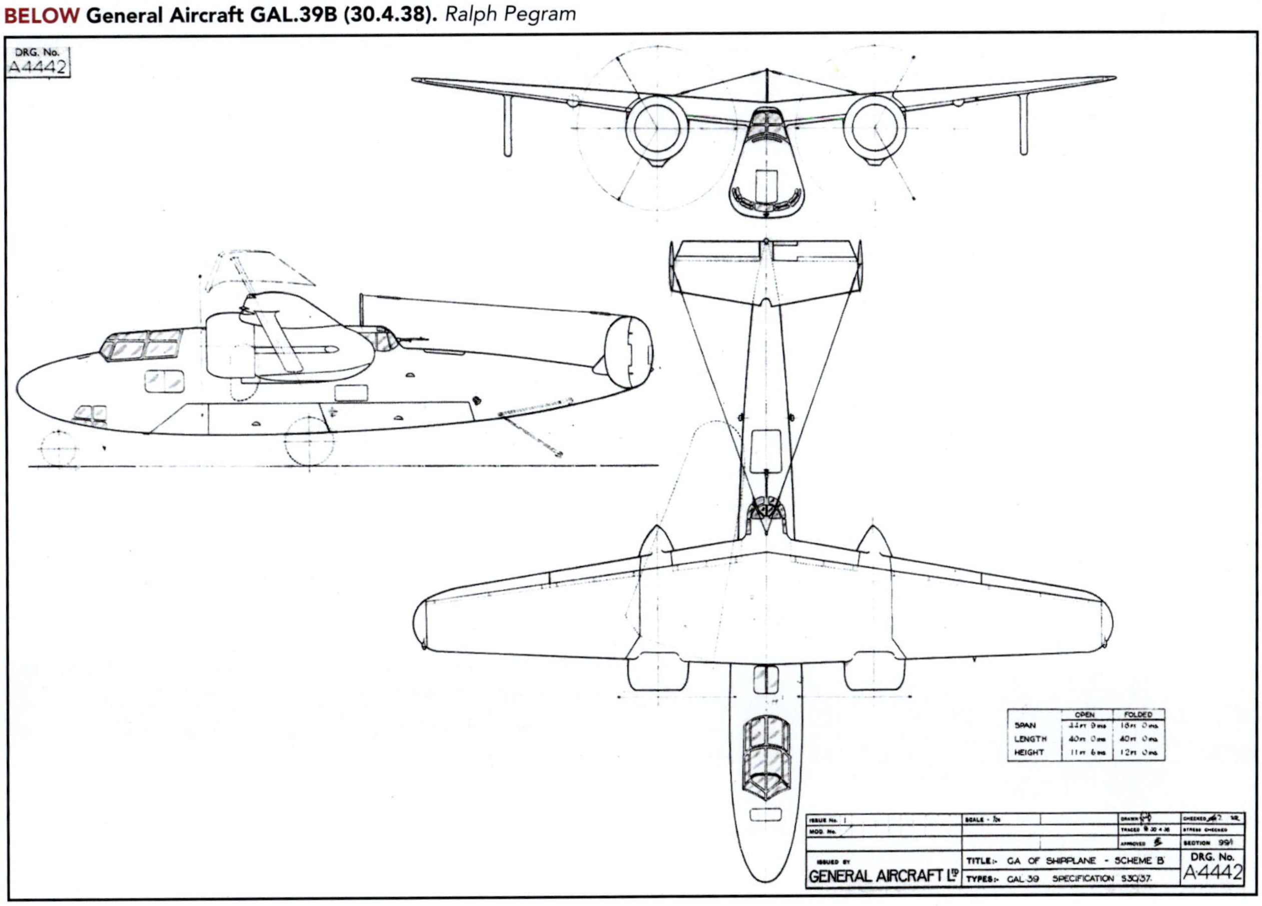

ABOVE Original General Aircraft model of its GAL.39B reconnaissance torpedo bomber project which shows the type's large weapons bay. The underwing 'struts' confirm this is the 'B' version.

BELOW Original manufacturer's artwork for the GAL.39 with fictitious serial K7559 (a serial in fact given to a Fairey Battle light bomber).

Reconnaissance Bomber Project to G.24/35, late 1935.

'Mayo Composite' Long-range high-speed bomber forming upper component of composite arrangement, 12.6.36. Lower component unknown but would have been larger.

Heavy Bomber Project to B.1/39, 4.39.

P.109 First 'Gloster Jet Bomber' proposal with four Whittle W.2B jets in individual pods 12.8.41 (drawing number unknown). Modified P.109 produced 24.11.41 with engines podded in pairs.

HANDLEY PAGE

A company that, from a warplane point of view, concentrated entirely on bombers.

HP.52 Hampden bomber to B.9/32 (Bristol Pegasus engines) first flown 21.6.36.

HP.53 Hereford development of Hampden to 44/36 with Napier Dagger engines first flown 6.10.38.

HP.54 Harrow bomber transport first flown 10.10.36.

HP.55 Heavy bomber to B.1/35 with two Hercules or Merlin, 6.35.

Torpedo Bomber Conversion of HP.52 to M.15/35, late 1935.

HP.56 Medium bomber to P.13/36 with twin RR Vultures, 1.1.37.

High-Speed Bomber Unnumbered project for unarmed high-speed bomber, 5.37. Further versions or designs appear to have followed with one dated 2.38.

HP.57 Heavy bomber with four Merlin X, 8.37. Became Halifax Mk.I first flown 25.10.39.

HP.58 Heavy bomber project intended to be (first) Halifax Mk.II, 1939. Had dorsal and ventral turrets mounting 20mm cannon and four Merlin X. L7244 earmarked for conversion as a prototype but work suspended autumn 1940. Project never left drawing board through problems developing turrets but mock-up inspected 12.39.

ABOVE Handley Page Hereford L6067.

TOP Handley Page Hampden Mk.I.

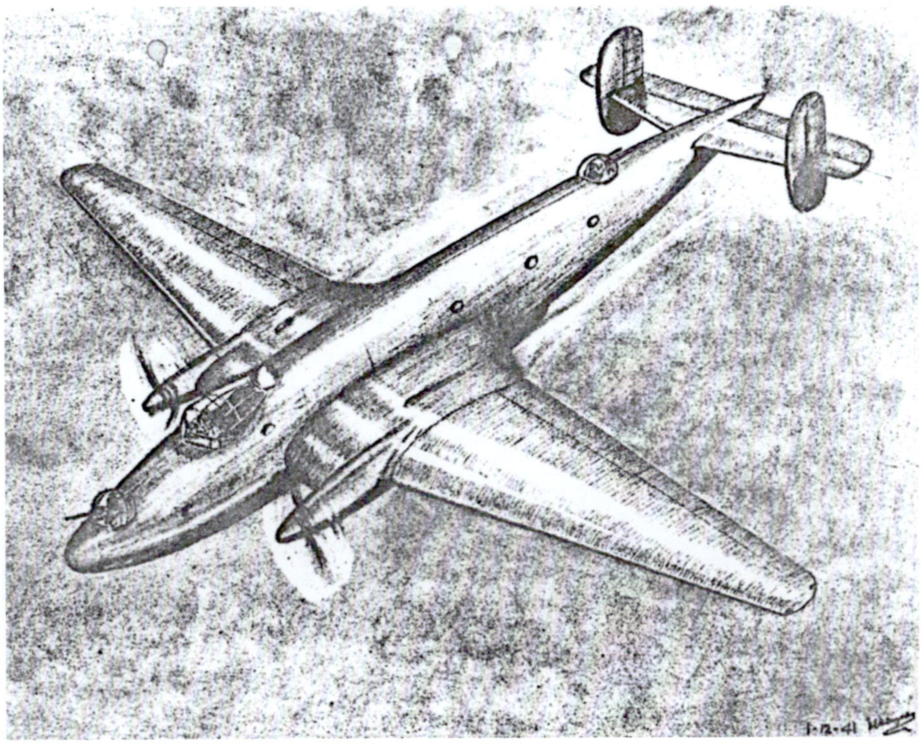

RIGHT Manufacturer's artwork for the Handley Page High Altitude Bomber.

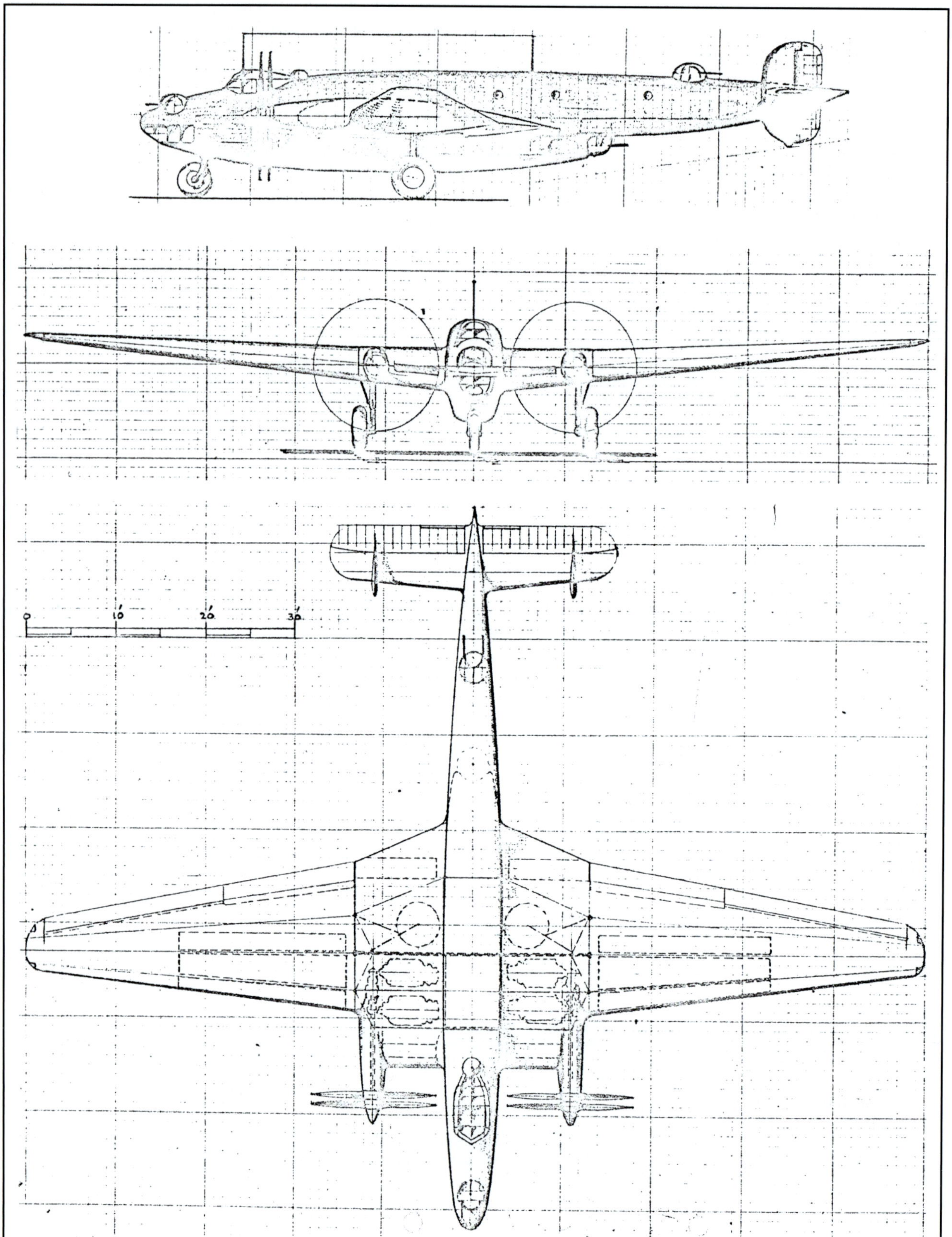

ABOVE Handley Page High Altitude Bomber (1.12.41).

HP.59 Halifax Mk.II as built.

HP.59A Half-scale B.1/39 project with four Pobjoy Airmotors Niagara V engines, 1940.

HP.60 Heavy bomber to B.1/39, 4.39.

HP.60A Halifax IV with Merlin 60 engines, c1940.

HP.61 Halifax III with Hercules VIs first flown 10.42. Also covered Halifax VI and VII.

HP.62 Hampden II medium bomber project with twin Wright Cyclone G.102 engines, 1941.

High-Altitude Bomber Little-known unnumbered project dated 1.12.41. Four RR Merlin 60s buried sideways in pairs in wing roots and driving contra-rotating propellers. Wing roots thus very thick and deep behind powerplants and also used to stow main wheels of tricycle undercarriage. Large central body, relatively small twin fins, nose, dorsal and ventral turrets. Elevators and rudders appeared to be fabric-covered but rest of airframe had metal skinning. Span 100ft (30.48m), length 74ft 5in (22.70m).

'70 Ton Bomber' Study embracing three designs, one conventional, two with canards including one powered by jets, 14.1.43.

HP.63 Halifax Mk.V with Merlin 22 engines, 1943.

HP.65 Development of Halifax IV ('Super Halifax') with Hercules 38s to B.14/43, 6.43.

HP.66 'Stretched' Halifax with Hercules 100 turbo-blower engines to B.27/43, 15.11.43. Proposed as alternative to HP.65. To be called Hastings B.Mk.I and prototypes ordered, but cancelled 4.44 and name transferred to HP.67 transport.

HP.69 Hastings B.Mk.II bomber project with four Hercules HE.15.MT engines, 11.43.

HP.75 Experimental Manx tailless aircraft with two de Havilland Gipsy Major II engines and built by Dart Aircraft at Dunstable in 1939. First flown 25.6.43. No project number until 1945.

HAWKER

One of the most famous of fighter firms, Hawker rarely forayed into bomber development. The P.1000-series of project numbers was introduced in 1940 but, at the time of writing, drawings for most of the projects listed up to P.1050 have not been traced and may no longer exist. Even into the war, not every project received a number.

Henley Light day bomber to P.4/34 first flown 10.4.37.

Medium Bomber Project with two Vultures to P.13/36, 1.1.37.

Torpedo Bomber Project to S.24/37, 3.3.38.

P.1001 Close-support bomber based on Henley to B.7/40, 1940.

P.1005 Twin-engined high-speed bomber with Sabre engines to B.11/41, 12.40.

P.1006 Henley-based close-support bomber to B.20/40, late 1940.

P.1041 Design investigation into Mosquito replacement, 1944/45.

MARTIN-BAKER

Tankbuster Unnumbered twin-boom design for ground attack, 24.3.43.

MILES (Phillips & Powis up to October 1943)

M.34 Project design for twin-Merlin aircraft to undertake both ground attack and target tug duties, 1941. Latter task eventually fulfilled by Miles M.33 Monitor. Heavily tapered wing had large root fillets and narrow fuselage. One or two crew dependent on role, proposed four 40mm cannon armament heaviest for any aircraft so far. Design never completed due to company's workload.

M.35 Libellula aerodynamic research aircraft fitted with de Havilland Gipsy Major I pusher engine. Flown 1.5.42 with B Conditions number U0235.

M.39 Libellula high-speed high-altitude three-seat medium bomber to B.11/41, 7.42. M.39B scale model flown 22.7.43 but full size M.39 never completed. M.39C with twin Merlin 68s drawn 8.10.43. Plans to fit three Power Jets units never fulfilled.

Heavy Bomber Unnumbered project with Libellula wing arrangement, c5.42. Miles stated Libellula concept, with forward ('canard') wing contributing to lift, would give bomber with same overall dimensions as existing types but much greater bomb load. Six Centaurus CE.3.SM engines (two mounted on smaller forward wing, four on rear main wing), tip and central fins, nose, dorsal, ventral and rear turrets. Total wing area c2,700sq.ft (250.84sq.m), all-up-weight c150,000lb (68,039kg), normal bomb load 51,000lb (23,133kg).

M.42 Ground attack fighter proposal to Air Staff requirement, 8.42. Shipborne torpedo bomber variant also considered by 1.43.

M.43 Ground attack fighter proposal to Air Staff requirement, 8.42. Shipborne fighter variant also considered by 1.43.

M.44 Ground attack fighter proposal to Air Staff requirement, 9.42.

ABOVE **The Miles M.34 project was never completed but its target tug role was taken on by the specially produced Miles Monitor. This nose view shows the Monitor's thick wing.** *David O'Neill*

BELOW **Miles 'Libellula' heavy bomber (c5.42).** *Peter Amos*

BELOW **Close-up view of a Miles Monitor taken in July 1946.**

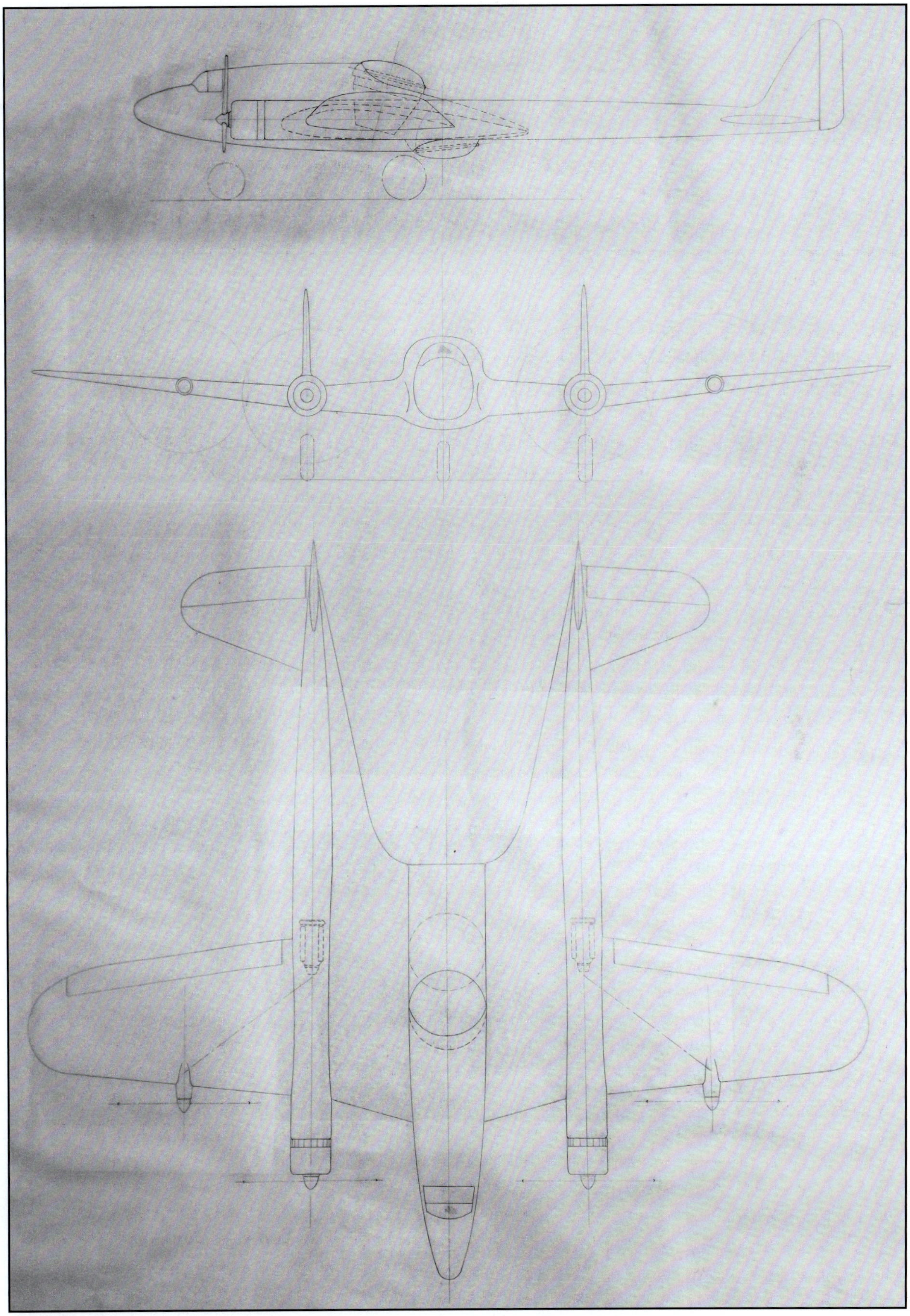

ABOVE **Parnall Type 384 bomber (31.8.38).** *Air-Britain*

ABOVE Model of the proposed Percival P.70 anti-submarine aircraft (late 1940s). *Peter Green*

PARNALL

Type 384 Heavy four-engine bomber with twin booms and no supporting tailplane or structure between booms, 31.8.38. Radial engines in larger inboard nacelles, outer propellers driven by shafts from second set of engines positioned in booms to rear of inboard units and level with wing trailing edge. Large dorsal and ventral defensive turrets at rear of fuselage 'pod', tricycle undercarriage. Span 91ft 0in (27.99m).

PERCIVAL

Percival was a company specialising in light aircraft and transports and primary trainer types.

P.26 Engine test-bed aircraft to Spec. 43/37, 1938. Single 2,000hp (1,491kW) Napier Sabre, span 64ft 0in (19.51m), length 42ft 9in (13.03m), gross weight 12,350lb (5,602kg), cruise speed 276mph (444km/h). Version fitted with 2,300hp (1,715kW) Bristol Centaurus had identical airframe and weight but cruise 278mph (447km/h).

P.37 Heavy bomber, 1943. Four 2,500hp (1,864kW) Bristol Centaurus, span 140ft 0in (42.67m), length 103ft 0in (31.39m), cruise speed apparently only 169mph (272km/h). Bomber version of 120,000lb (54,432kg) weight P.35 freighter. Both had all-wing 'Burnelli-type' layout with accommodation in aerofoil fuselage and twin tail booms. Bomber to have upper and lower remote-control gun barbettes.

P.38 Photo-reconnaissance monoplane, 1943. Two 1,500hp (1,119kW) Rolls-Royce Merlin, span 58ft 0in (17.68m), length 44ft 6in (13.56m), gross weight 23,300lb (10,569kg), maximum speed 451mph (726km/h). Unarmed. Similarity to Mosquito suggests could have been adapted as a bomber.

P.70 Naval anti-submarine aircraft, c1949.

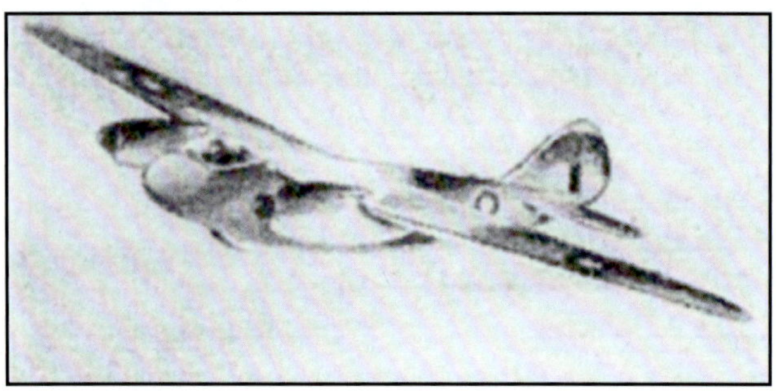

LEFT Artwork for the Percival P.38 reconnaissance aircraft (1943).

SAUNDERS-ROE

Saunders-Roe (Saro) was a flying boat specialist.

A.33 General purpose flying boat to R.2/33 begun as project P.937 and first flown 14.10.38. Damaged on take-off 25.10.38 and never flown again.

S.36 Lerwick flying boat to R.1/36 begun as project P.970 and first flown early 11.38.

P.1036 Single Bristol Mercury-engined flying boat amphibian monoplane with engine pod mounted above fuselage and extended aft to house gun turret and carry tail surfaces, 1939 to 1941. Weight 9,500lb (4,309kg); known as 'Scheme A'.

P.1037 'Scheme B' alternative to P.1036 with conventional central float, 1939 to 1940.

A.37 Shrimp scale model aircraft for S.38 design first flown early 10.39.

S.38 Large flying boat to R.5/39, mid-1939. Initial work to R.3/38, 1938. Later S.38A fitted with Centaurus engines, 4.40.

S.39 (P.1031) Flying boat project, 4.40. Revised to R.14/40, mid-1940. S.39A (P.1034) had retractable planing bottom.

S.41 Flying boat to R.14/40, 1.41 onwards.

S.42 Large flying boat, 1942 to 1943. Used wing of Avro Lancaster bomber and four Merlin XX engines. All-up-weight 70,000lb (31,752kg).

P.104 Maritime flying boat to R.2/48, 3.49. Addendum with design showing longer fuselage 6.49. Project became P.162. Work continued until about 1956 but never flown.

P.105 Military flying boat with pylon-mounted wing, 1951. Two Bristol Centaurus 171, weight 50,000lb (22,680kg).

P.106 Mixed powerplant military flying boat, 1949 to 1951. Two versions, both with four engines. First had V-tail, two compounded Griffon and two Nene jets – span 134ft (40.84m), weight 81,000lb (36,742kg). Second twin booms and tail floats, two Napier Nomad and two Armstrong Siddeley Sapphire – span 135ft (41.15m), weight 90,000lb (40,823kg).

P.110 Princess civil flying boat proposed as reconnaissance bomber, 1950.

P.162 Long-range reconnaissance and anti-submarine flying boat, 1952-56. Included work to R.2/48.

SHORT BROTHERS

(from 1943 Short Brothers & Harland)

Shorts had a strong reputation for building flying boats. Many pre-war and wartime Shorts project drawings were lost during the conflict so relatively little now survives on the company's project work from that period. The P.D-series relates to post-1947 projects from Belfast.

Flying Boat Design tendered to R.1/36, mid-1936.

S.25 Sunderland flying boat built to R.2/33 and first flown 16.10.37.

S.29 Bomber to B.12/36, became Stirling, first flown 14.5.39. Version proposed with cannon turrets, 1939.

Medium Bomber Project to B.13/36, 1.37.

Reconnaissance Torpedo Bomber Project believed proposed to S.30/37, 1938.

Composite Bomber Project for single-seat bomber to form upper component of composite arrangement. First proposed 27.4.38, enlarged design dated 6.7.38.

S.31 M.4 half-scale Stirling replica with Pobjoy engines flown 19.9.38.

S.34 Cannon-armed bomber to B.1/39, 4.39.

Flying Boat Design tendered to R.5/39, mid-1939.

High-Speed Bomber Unnumbered project for high-speed unarmed bomber, 2.40.

S.35 Flying boat to R.14/40, late 1940/early 1941. Shetland built to R.14/40 Issue II, first flown 14.12.44.

S.36 Super Stirling to B.8/41, 7.41 onwards.

'75 Ton Bomber' Three versions of basic design, 1.43.

S.38 Naval torpedo bomber and reconnaissance aircraft proposals to S.6/43, mid-1943. Specification amended to S.11/43, first flown as S.A.1 Sturgeon 7.6.46.

S.45 Seaford flying boat development of Sunderland built to R.8/42 and first flown 30.8.44.

P.D.2 Maritime flying boat to R.2/48, early 1949. Three designs proposed, one based on Shetland, one based on civil Solent, one all-new.

VICKERS-ARMSTRONGS

Vickers allocated project numbers to individual prototypes, to production runs and to unbuilt designs. All relevant numbers are included here for completeness.

249 Not allocated to a specific type. The '249' series of Vickers drawings (24901 to 24999) embraced most of the company's unbuilt projects from the early 1930s to towards the end of WW2 and included fighters, bombers (B.12/36, P.13/36, B.1/39, 6-engine, etc.) and other types. Separate project numbers were still allocated to some of the designs.

271 Bomber to B.9/32. Prototype first flown 15.6.36 and aircraft entered service as Wellington.

BELOW Vickers 280 naval fighter/dive bomber (20.2.35).

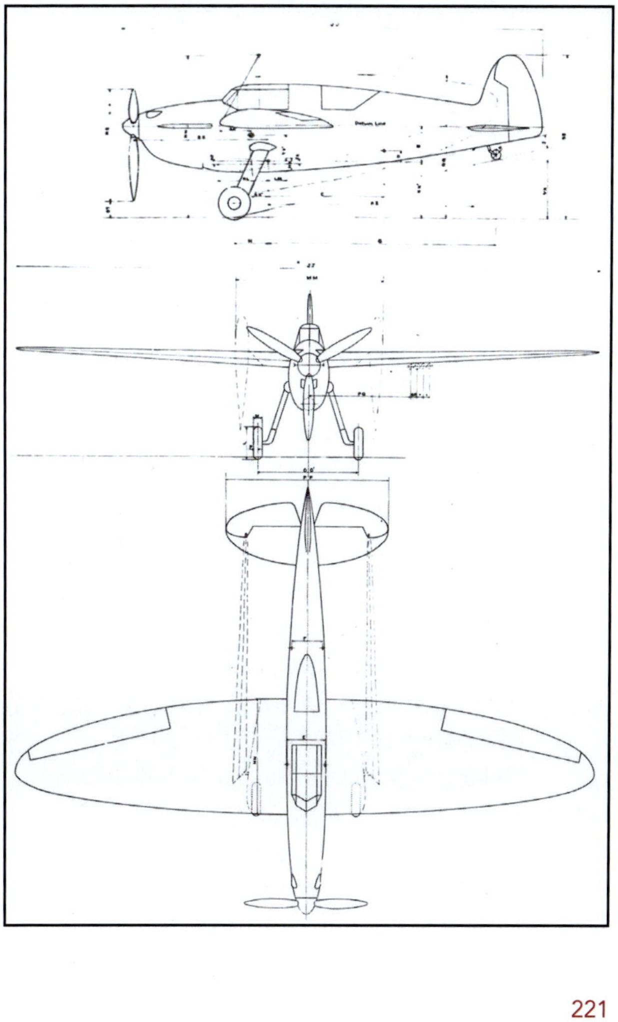

ABOVE **Vickers Wellington in flight.**

280 Mid-wing naval fighter/dive bomber to O.27/34, 20.2.35. Single Merlin I engine, span 33ft (10.06m), wing folding. Won design competition along with Blackburn Skua, single prototype ordered (serial K5177) but not built.

Torpedo Bomber Conversion of Type 271 to M.15/35, late 1935.

284 Bomber to B.1/35 with two Rolls-Royce Vulture, 6.35. Became Warwick prototype K8178 first flown 13.8.39.

285 Wellington Mk.I prototype L4212.

290 Wellington Mk.I production aircraft.

293 Heavy bomber to B.12/36, 9.36.

Medium Bomber Warwick development to P.13/36, late 1936.

298 Wellington Mk.II prototype L4250.

299 Wellington Mk.III prototype L4251.

400 B.1/35 (Warwick) proposal with Napier Sabre schemed for K8178, c1938.

401 B.1/35 (Warwick) with Bristol Centaurus CE.1.SM. Prototype L9704 first flown 5.4.40.

403 Wellington for New Zealand.

405 Heavy bomber to B.1/39, 4.39.

406 Wellington Mk.II production aircraft.

407 Wellington Mk.V prototype pressure cabin high-altitude second prototype.

408 Wellington Mk.IA production aircraft.

409 Wellington Mk.IB scheme for development.

410 Wellington Mk.IV serial R1220.

411 Production B.1/35 Warwick with RR Vulture II (design only), c1939.

412 Wellington Mk.IA production for New Zealand.

413 B.1/35 Warwick Mk.II with Centaurus IV, serial BV216.

415 Wellington Mk.IC production.

416 Wellington Mk.II L4250 with 40mm gun.

417 Wellington Mk.III production.

418 Wellington DWI Mk.I serial P2516.

419 Wellington DWI Mk.II L4356.

421 Wellington high-altitude Mk.V first prototype R3298 to B.23/39. First flown September 1940.

422 Proposed production of Warwick Mk.II with Pratt & Whitney R-2800 Double Wasp engines.

423 All marks of Wellington modified to carry 4,000lb (1,814kg) bomb.

424 Wellington Mk.IV production.

425 Special bomber with six Merlin HA engines.

High-Altitude Bomber Six-engine bomber project, 1.41 to 1.42.

426 Wellington Mk.V.

427 Warwick Mk.I conversion with Double Wasp engines, serial L9704 converted.

428 Wellington DWI Mk.III P9223.

429 Wellington Mk.XVIII production aircraft.

430 Wellington Mk.VII serial T2545 (cancelled).

431 Pressure cabin Wellington Mk.VI prototype W5795.

High-Speed Medium Bomber Several designs based on B.11/41 and Bristol Buckingham requirements, 4.42 onwards.

Unarmed Day Bomber Bomber development of Type 432 twin-engine fighter first flown late 1942, 6.5.42.

433 Pressure cabin Warwick Mk.III with four Merlin 60s to B.5/41, mid-1941.

434 Wellington with two Bristol Pegasus XVIII.

435 Wellington Turbinlite T2977.

436 Wellington Mk.V R3298 with Hercules XI engines and turbo-blowers.

439 Wellington Mk.II Z8416 with 40mm gun in nose.

ABOVE W5798 was an example of the high-altitude Mk.VIA variant of the Wellington. *Phil Butler*

440 Wellington Mk.X production.

441 Proposal to licence-produce American Boeing B-29 heavy bomber.

442 Pressure cabin Wellington Mk.VI production.

443 Wellington Mk.V W5816 engine testbed.

444 Warwick development.

445 Wellington Mk.II engine testbed Z8570 fitted with Whittle W.2B/23 jet engine.

447 Windsor prototype DW506 first flown 23.10.43.

448 Wellington HF616 fitted with single turbo-blower.

449 Wellington VIG – production Type 431 modified.

450 Wellington Mk.II W5518 to be fitted with Whittle W.2B/23 jet; cancelled.

451 Wellington Mk.IA testbed aircraft.

452 Wellington Mk.III minelayer serial BJ895.

453 Continuation of project drawing numbers after '249' series filled.

454 Wellington Mk.XI MP502 ASV.Mk.II.

455 Wellington Mk.XII Leigh light and ASV.Mk.III.

457 Windsor second prototype DW512.

458 Wellington Mk.XI (ASV.Mk.III) production.

459 Wellington Mk.XI MP545 trials aircraft.

461 Windsor Mk.III project with Merlin 85, c4.41 onwards.

'75 Ton Bomber' Five alternative designs submitted 14.1.43. Version of foreplane alternative drawn with six de Havilland jets 4.43.

463 de Havilland Mosquito converted to carry 'Highball' bouncing bomb – prototype DZ471.

464 Production Avro ('Dam Buster') Lancaster converted to carry 'Upkeep' bouncing bomb.

BELOW Another Wellington Mk.VI, photographed on 24 February 1942 during a flight from Boscombe Down.

465 Production Mosquito converted to carry 'Highball' bouncing bomb.

466 Wellington GR.Mk.XIII (ASV.Mk.II) production.

467 Wellington GR.Mk.XIV (ASV.Mk.III) production.

468 Warwick Mk.I L9704 fitted with nacelle guns.

469 Warwick GR.Mk.II production aircraft.

470 Wellington Mk.II W5389 fitted with Whittle jet.

471 Windsor Mk.IV serial NN670 (not completed).

473 Warwick GR.Mk.II daytime coastal patrol aircraft.

474 Warwick GR.Mk.V night-time coastal patrol aircraft.

475 Wellington engine testbed.

476 Windsor Mk.V NN673 with Merlin 100s.

478 Wellington Mk.X LN718.

479 Windsor variant with four Hercules.

480 Windsor Mk.IIA NK136.

481 Wellington variant.

483 Windsor B.Mk.I production aircraft; cancelled.

485 Warwick ASR.Mk.VI production.

486 Wellington Mk.II W5518 fitted with Whittle W2/700 jet.

487 Wellington Mk.XVII service conversions.

488 Mosquito 'Highball' aircraft DZ471 with air turbine.

489 Windsor 'L' special project for large bomber.

490 Wellington Mk.XVIII converted from Mk.XI.

492 Mosquito 'Highball' aircraft; special variant.

494 Windsor B.Mk.I long-range production aircraft; cancelled.

High-Altitude Heavy Bomber Designs with four or six RR Clyde engines, 11.44.

Windsor Development Variant fitted with four Griffon, 12.44.

600 Warwick HG341 and HG345 testbed aircraft.

601 Windsor B.Mk.II variant with Clyde. First brochure 1.45. Plans to convert prototype NN673 not completed.

602 Wellington testbed LN715 with two RR Dart turboprop engines.

603 Wellington testbed RP484 for Viking aircraft.

606 Warwick in-flight refuelling aircraft.

608 Wellington project with two Armstrong-Siddeley Mamba engines.

Jet Bomber Unnumbered high-altitude jet bomber project, 3.45.

VICKERS SUPERMARINE

Following Vickers' practice, many of the following relate to prototypes and production aircraft rather than projects but they are included to give a full list. Until the arrival of the Spitfire fighter, Supermarine had specialised in flying boats.

Heavy Bomber Studies made to B.1/35 but no official proposals to design competition, 1935.

314 Flying boat with two Vultures to R.1/36, 26.5.36.

316 Heavy bomber with four Bristol Hercules or RR Merlin and single fin to B.12/36, 30.9.36.

317 Heavy bomber with four Hercules and twin fins to B.12/36, 1.37. Mock-up built and prototypes ordered but destroyed by bombing raid before completed.

318 Heavy bomber with four Merlins and twin fins to B.12/36, 1.37.

322 'Dumbo' torpedo bomber and reconnaissance aircraft to S.24/37, 7.3.38. First flown 6.2.43.

328 Flying boat to R.5/39, 6.39. Initial scheme to R.3/38 (1938).

380 Design of second prototype 'Dumbo' torpedo bomber to S.24/37.

524 Maritime flying boat to R.2/48, early 1949.

WESTLAND

It is known that most of Westland's wartime project and design study brochures were still in existence after the war, but it appears that nearly all have now been destroyed. Fortunately a large 'chart' exists that outlines many of these projects together with brief details and a basic sketch.

Light Bomber General purpose bomber and reconnaissance aircraft to G.24/35, 1935.

P.10 Torpedo and reconnaissance aircraft to S.24/37, 3.38.

BELOW Sketch of the Westland ground attack aircraft (2.42). *Westland Archive*

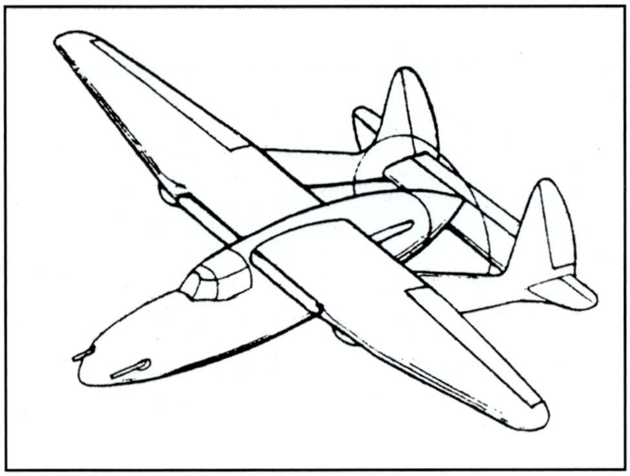

Light Bomber Short-range Delanne type project to B.7/40, 8.40.

Close-Support Aircraft Dive bomber and tactical reconnaissance aircraft to B.20/40, 6.41.

Heavy Bomber Delanne project believed designed to B.8/41, 10.41.

High-Altitude Bomber Design study based on Welkin, possibly to B.5/41, c1942. Extended nose for radar (to be used for precision bombing) and two 2,000lb (907kg) bombs in former gun bay; wing of 20% greater chord considered. Two Merlin 76/77, span 70ft 0in (21.34m), all-up-weight 19,000lb (8,618kg), maximum speed 380mph (612km/h). Mock-up only.

Ground Attack Aircraft Delanne type with tail booms, 2.42. One 1,400hp (1,044kW) Allison engine and two 40mm guns. Span 39ft (11.89m), wing area 200sq.ft (18.58sq.m), all-up-weight 8,000lb (3,629kg), maximum 300mph (483km/h) at ground level.

Heavy Bomber High-altitude design, 4.43. Sources suggest this was designed to B.3/42 but it had little in common with the requirement – was clearly intended to be a stratosphere bomber and as such appears to have lacked defensive guns. Powered by four Merlins intended to give 1,000hp (746kW) at 40,000ft (12,192m). Span 183ft (55.78m), wing area 2,800sq.ft (260.13sq.m), cruise speed 190mph (306km/h) at 50,000ft (15,240m), range 1,500 miles (2,414km), bomb load 4,000lb (1,814kg), all up weight 45,000lb (20,412kg).

Torpedo Bomber Bomber-reconnaissance type to S.6/43, 4.43.

Naval Bomber Combined piston/jet project to S.11/43, 8.43.

Jet-Powered Fighter-Bomber Studies for twin-engine designs in three different versions. No date but assumed around 1944.

P.1056 and P.1061 Fighter-bomber projects, 3.44 onwards. Similar configurations with twin Metro-Vick F.2/4 jets in centre fuselage.

W.34 Wyvern long-range naval strike to N.11/44. RR Eagle 24.H46 piston engine, first flown 12.12.46. De-navalised variant prepared to F.13/44 but discontinued.

W.35 Wyvern with RR Clyde or Armstrong Siddeley Python turboprop to N.12/45, first flown 18.1.49. Other proposed developments had Napier Nomad compound engine while S.Mk.5E of 3.54 had Napier E.141 Double Eland turboprop.

W.36 Wyvern development with 6,500lb (28.9kN) RR AJ.65 jet to N.12/45, 1946.

BELOW The Short Mayo *Maia* flying boat and *Mercury* seaplane combination in fight.

Appendix Two
British 'Wartime' Bomber Project Specifications

The Air Ministry has traditionally signalled to the British aircraft industry its expected future requirements via a series of specifications, against which tenders were usually invited.

Until the end of 1949 the sequential system used to issue these specifications was a letter/number/year arrangement. A typical example is B.1/35 which described a Heavy Bomber (in fact what became the Vickers Warwick): B stood for bomber; '1' indicated it was the 1st specification issued in that year, which was 1935. Alternative prefix letters included F (fighter), E (experimental), G (general purpose), M (torpedo bomber), N (naval) and P (light bomber); from about 1936 the lettering became more complex but the above description will suffice for this book. The reader should also note that specifications were not always put out to tender – for example there were a number of military types developed 'independently' during the period covered by this book and each would have had a specification written around it.

Specifications for an aircraft required for military service were usually accompanied by an Operational Requirement with its own 'OR' number, for example OR.19 for B.1/35. Further details of pre-1950 specifications can be found in *The British Aircraft Specifications File* by Meekcoms and Morgan.

B.1/35 (OR.19) Heavy Bomber: Armstrong Whitworth AW.39, Boulton Paul P.79 variant, Bristol project, Fairey project, Gloster project, Handley Page HP.55, Vickers 284 Warwick. Airspeed AS.29 later.

M.15/35 (OR.22) Torpedo Bomber: Avro 672, Blackburn project, Boulton Paul P.83, Bristol 150, Handley Page and Vickers projects.

G.24/35 (OR.25) General Purpose Aircraft: Avro 675, Blackburn project, Boulton Paul P.84, Bristol project, Gloster project, Westland project.

28/35 (OR.26) Heavy Bomber: Bristol 142 Blenheim.

R.1/36 (OR.32) Flying Boat: Blackburn B.20, Supermarine 314, Short project, Saro S.36 Lerwick.

M.7/36 Torpedo Reconnaissance Aircraft: Fairey Albacore.

10/36 (OR.28) General Purpose Aircraft (M.15/35 and G.24/35 combined): Avro, Blackburn B.26 Botha, Boulton Paul P.86, Bristol 152 Beaufort.

B.12/36 (OR.40) Heavy Bomber: Armstrong Whitworth AW.42, Boulton Paul P.90, Shorts S.29 Stirling, Supermarine 316, 317 and 318, Vickers 293. Bristol project later.

P.13/36 (OR.41) Medium Bomber: Avro 679 Manchester, Boulton Paul P.91, Bristol project, Fairey project, Handley Page HP.56, Hawker project, Shorts project, Vickers project.

S.30/37 (OR.53) Twin-engine Torpedo Bomber Reconnaissance Aircraft for FAA: Blackburn B.22, Fairey project, General Aircraft GAL.39A and 39B, Shorts project.

S.24/37 (OR.53) Torpedo Reconnaissance Aircraft: Blackburn B.21, B.29 and B.36, Bristol project, Fairey 100 (Barracuda), Hawker project, Supermarine 322 Dumbo, Westland P.10.

43/37 (OR.55) Engine Testbed: Folland Frightful, General GAL.43a, Percival P.26.

B.9/38 Twin-Engine Bomber: Armstrong Whitworth AW.41, Bristol 155.

B.17/38 Bomber: Bristol 155.

B.18/38 Bomber: Armstrong Whitworth AW.41 Albemarle.

B.1/39 Heavy Bomber: Armstrong Whitworth AW.48, Blackburn B.30, Avro 680, Bristol 159, Fairey and Gloster projects, Handley Page HP.60, Shorts S.34, Vickers 405.

R.5/39 (OR.69) Flying Boat: Blackburn B.32 and B.39, Saro S.38 and S.39, Shorts R.5/36, Supermarine 328.

1/40 (OR.78) Reconnaissance Bomber: de Havilland DH.98 Mosquito, Folland Fo.113.

B.3/40 (OR.80) High-Speed Bomber: Blackburn B.28, possibly Armstrong Whitworth AW.47.

B.6/40 (OR.83) Support Bomber: Bristol 160 Blenheim V (Bisley Mk.I).

B.7/40 (OR.84) Medium Bomber: Armstrong Whitworth project, Hawker P.1001, Westland project.

R.13/40 Flying Boat: Blackburn B.40

R.14/40 (OR.91) Flying Boat: Saro S.41, Shorts S.35 Shetland.

B.20/40 Support Bomber; Boulton Paul P.95, Fairey project, Hawker P.1006, Westland project.

E.28/40 (OR.101) 'Research Aircraft': Folland Fo.115 and Fo.116.

B.2/41 Medium Bomber: Bristol 163 Buckingham.

B.8/41 Heavy Bomber: Shorts S.36 Super Stirling, Westland project.

B.11/41 (OR.110) Bomber: de Havilland DH.99 (became DH.101), Hawker P.1005, Miles M.39.

B.3/42 (OR.115) Heavy Bomber: Vickers 447 Windsor.

B.4/42 Bomber: de Havilland DH.102 'Mosquito II'.

H.7/42 (OR.117) Torpedo Bomber: Bristol project and 164 Brigand.

R.8/42 (OR.118) Flying Boat: Shorts S.45 Seaford.

No Official Specification – '70/75 Ton Bomber': Two Avro projects, two Bristol projects, three Handley Page projects, three Shorts projects, five Vickers projects.

O.5/43 (OR.144) Torpedo Bomber: Blackburn B.47, Cunliffe-Owen project, Fairey single and twin-engine projects (including Spearfish), Folland Fo.119.

No Official Specification – Ground Attack Aircraft: Armstrong Whitworth AW.49, Boulton Paul P.99, P.100 and P.101, Cunliffe-Owen project, Martin-Baker project, Miles M.42, M.43 and M.44.

S.6/43 Torpedo Bomber: Armstrong Whitworth AW.53, Cunliffe-Owen project, Fairey project, Shorts project, Westland Project.

S.11/43 (OR.146) Naval Bomber: Armstrong Whitworth AW.54 and 54A, Blackburn project, Fairey project, Shorts S.38 Sturgeon, Westland project.

B.14/43 Heavy Bomber; Avro 694 Lincoln.

B.27/43 (OR.149) Heavy Bomber: Handley Page HP.66 Hastings.

E.9/44 Research Aircraft: Armstrong Whitworth AW.52.

O.21/44 Torpedo Bomber: Fairey Spearfish development.

N.11/44 (OR.174) Naval Fighter: Westland W.34 Wyvern.

N.12/45 (OR.213) Naval Fighter: Westland W.35 Wyvern.

N.16/45 Strike Aircraft: Fairey project.

R.5/46 (OR.200) Patrol Bomber: Avro 696 Shackleton.

R.2/48 (OR.231) Flying Boat: Saro P.104, Shorts P.D.2, Shorts modified Shetland, Shorts modified Seaford, Supermarine 524.

Appendix Three
British 'Wartime' Bomber Contracts

This list covers prototypes and unbuilt designs only; there are no production aircraft. The date gives the point where serials were allocated and comes from the Ministry's serial ledger. It should fall very close to the date of an ITP, which was the official authority to spend money, but some of the dates given fall after the start of work on their particular project, even to the point where preparations were under way for metalwork. In such cases the firm concerned may have begun its work as a private venture or short-term contracts may have proceeded the ITP.

Serial(s)	Type	Contract	Date	Comments
K4049	Vickers B.9/32	274142/33	12.12.33	Wellington
K4190	Fairey S.15/33 (TSR)	280480/33		Swordfish
K4240	Handley Page B.9/32	274141/33		Hampden
K4299	Armstrong Whitworth AW.29	321542/34	11.6.34	P.27/32
K4303	Fairey P.27/32	321541/34		Battle
K4586/K4587	Armstrong Whitworth AW.38	349065/34	9.6.34	Whitley
K4773	Saro A.33 (R.2/33)	351563/34		
K4774	Shorts S.25 (R.2/33)	351564/34		Sunderland
K7556	Vickers G.4/31 PV	436890/35		Wellesley
K8178	Vickers B.1/35	441973/35	7.10.35	Warwick
K8179	Armstrong Whitworth B.1/35	441974/35	7.10.35	Some sources quote as HP
K8180	Handley Page B.1/35	441975/35	7.10.35	Some sources quote as AW
L6889/6890	Supermarine B.12/36	605350/37		
L7244/7245	Handley Page P.13/36	624972/37	30.4.37	
L7246/7247	Avro P.13/36	624973/37	30.4.37	Manchester
L7269	Bristol 143	536795/36		
L7600/L7605	Shorts B.12/36	672299/37		Stirling
L7625/L7628	Fairey S.9/36	681749/37		
L9704	Vickers B.1/35	734772/38		See K8178
P1767/P1770	Fairey S.24/37	777067/38		Barracuda
R1810/R1815	Supermarine S.24/37	976687/39		'Dumbo'
R2659	Stirling with cannon turrets	2596/39		) Armament
R2665	Halifax with cannon turrets	10713/39		) development
R2671	Manchester with cannon turrets	7625/39		) aircraft (?)
T9124	Handley Page Halifax	987458/39		No details known
V8914	Blackburn R.1/36	498571/36		
X2871/X2875	Bristol B.1/39	B.62051/39	7.5.40	
X2880/X2885	Handley Page B.1/39	B.62052/39	7.5.40	
X8500	Blackburn B.3/40 (B.28)	B.81965/40	6.6.40	
AA276/AA279	Bristol Bisley (Rootes)	B.124276/40	28.6.40	Later became DJ702/DJ707
AD657/AD661	Bristol Bisley (Bristol)	B.69276/40		
BT308	Avro Manchester III	B.135521/40		
DG595	Avro Lancaster	B.135521/40		
DJ702/DJ707	Bristol Bisley (Rootes)	B.124276/40		See above
DT810	Avro Lancaster	B.135521/40		

Serial(s)	Type	Contract	Date	Comments
DW506/DW512	Vickers B.5/41	C/Acft/1153	15.7.41	
DX160/DX165	Folland E.28/40	C/Acft/741	15.8.41	
DX166/DX171	Saro/Shorts R.14/40	?		
DX249 to DX266	Bristol B.2/41	C/Acft/236		Buckingham
ES966/ES979	Blackburn R.13/40	C/Acft/1474	19.9.41	B.40
HV266/HV270	Hawker B.11/41	C/Acft/1712		P.1005
JR540/JR543	Shorts B.8/41	?	14.2.42	
MP478/MP481	de Havilland B.4/42	C/Acft/1955		DH.102
MP829/MP832	Vickers B.3/42	SB.24954	4.7.42	
MX988 to MX997	Bristol H.7/42	SB.25383		Brigand
MZ269/MZ271	Shorts R.8/42	C/Acft/2551		S.45 Seaford
NK136	Vickers B.3/42	C/Acft/1153		Windsor
NN670/NN673	Vickers B.3/42	C/Acft/1153	2.2.43	Windsor
PW925 to PW932	Avro Lancaster IV	C/Acft/3183	19.7.43	Lincoln
RA356 to RA363	Fairey O.5/43	SB.26862	13.8.43	Spearfish
RK787 to RK794	Shorts S.11/43	SB.27016	19.10.43	Sturgeon
RR910	Miles M.39	C/Acft/3461	12.11.43	
SR392	Miles M.39B	None given	12.2.44	See RR910
SR650 to SR657	Handley Page B.27/43	C/Acft/3401	24.2.44	HP.66
SX553	Handley Page B.27/43	C/A/3401	7.4.44	HP.66
TJ175 to TJ184	Fairey O.5/43	SB.26862	22.5.44	
TS371 to TS387	Westland N.11/44	C/Acft/4522	26.8.44	Wyvern
TS444 to TS455	de Hav. Sea Mosquito	C/A/4668	23.9.44	
TX374	Bristol Brigand	C/A/2903	16.2.45	
VD258 to VD269	Fairey O.21/44	C/Acft/5173	5.4.45	Spearfish development
VP109 to VP120	Westland N.12/45	C/Acft/5982	7.2.46	Wyvern turboprop
VP988 to VR123	Fairey N.16/45	6/Acft/378	20.6.46	
VW126 to VW135	Avro 696 (R.5/46)	6/Acft/1077		Shackleton

Glossary

A&AEE	Aeroplane and Armament Experimental Establishment, Martlesham Heath (pre-9 September 1939), Boscombe Down (post-9 September 1939).
ACAS(OR)	Assistant Chief of the Air Staff (Operational Requirements) [Air Ministry post].
ACAS(TR)	Assistant Chief of the Air Staff (Technical Requirements) [Air Ministry post].
ACM	Air Chief Marshal.
AD/RDT	Assistant Director/Research and Development (Technical).
AMDP	Air Member for Development and Production.
AMRD	Air Member for Research and Development.
anhedral	Downward slope of wing from root to tip.
AoA	Angle of attack, the angle at which the wing is inclined relative to the airflow.
AP	Armour piercing.
AS	Armstrong Siddeley.
A/S	Anti-submarine.
aspect ratio	Ratio of wingspan to mean chord, approximately calculated by dividing the square of the span by the wing area.
ASV	Anti-surface vessel (radar).
AVM	Air Vice Marshal.
AWA	Armstrong Whitworth Aircraft Ltd.
BP	Boulton Paul Aircraft.
c	Circa.
CAS	Chief of the Air Staff [Air Ministry post].
CinC	Commander-in-Chief.
chord	Distance between centres of curvature of a wing's leading and trailing edges when measured parallel to the longitudinal axis.
CNR	Chief Naval Representative (to MAP).
CofG	Centre of gravity.
CRD	Controller of Research and Development [MAP post].
DAMDP	Deputy Air Member for Development and Production.
DC	Depth charge.
DCAS	Deputy Chief of the Air Staff [Air Ministry post].
DDOR	Deputy Director of Operational Requirements.
DD/RDT	Deputy Director/Research and Development (Technical).
DDTD	Deputy Director of Technical Development [MAP post].
DGRD	Director General of Research and Development.
DH	de Havilland.
dihedral	Upward slope of wing from root to tip.
DOR(A)	Director of Operational Requirements (Air).
DSR	Director of Scientific Research
DTD	Director of Technical Development [MAP post].
EAS	Equivalent airspeed.
FAA	Fleet Air Arm.
HAL	Hawker Aircraft Limited.
HC	High capacity bomb.
HE	High explosive.
HMG	His Majesty's Government.
HP	Handley Page.
HSG	Hawker Siddeley Group.
IAS	Indicated airspeed.
incidence	Angle at which the wing (or tail) is set relative to the fuselage.
ITP	Instruction to Proceed.
Laminar flow wing	Specifically designed to ensure a smooth flow of air over its surfaces with uniform separation between the layers of air.
MAEE	Marine Aircraft Experimental Establishment.
MAP	Ministry of Aircraft Production – created in May 1940 to relieve the Air Ministry of its role of procuring aircraft and the equipment and supplies associated with them. Its functions were transferred to the Ministry of Supply in 1946.
MC	Medium capacity bomb.
Metro-Vick	Metropolitan-Vickers, a highly diversified company well known in particular for heavy industrial electrical equipment, but which also became involved with the first generation of jet engines.
MoS	Ministry of Supply – created August 1939 to provide stores used by the RAF (and the Army and Navy).
nm	Nautical mile.
OR	Operational Requirement.
OTU	Operational Training Unit.
PR	Photo reconnaissance.
R & D	Research and Development.
RAE	Royal Aircraft Establishment, Farnborough.
RDT	Research and Development (Technical).
RN	Royal Navy.
RNVR	Royal Naval Volunteer Reserve.
RP	Unguided rocket projectile.
RR	Rolls-Royce.
RTO	Resident Technical Officer.
TAS	True airspeed.
t/c	Thickness/chord ratio.
TRE	Telecommunications Research Establishment, Malvern.
TT	Torpedo.
USAAF	United States Army Air Force.
USN	United States Navy.
VCAS	Vice Chief of the Air Staff.

Bibliography and Source Notes

During research for this book a great deal of primary source material was consulted including original documents and project brochures held by the National Archives at Kew (AVIA 15, AVIA 53, AVIA 54, AIR 2 and AIR 20) and by Museums, Heritage Centres, groups and individuals, as noted in the Acknowledgements. Drawings and photographs are credited individually unless they came from the author's collection. Important secondary source material helped to get things started and to fill gaps:

Aircraft for the Royal Air Force: Michael J.F. Bowyer; Faber and Faber, 1980.

An Ill Fated Bird – The Avro Manchester: Twenty-First Profile Magazine No 6.

Armstrong Whitworth Aircraft since 1913: Oliver Tapper; Putnam, 1973.

Armstrong Whitworth Paper Planes: Ray Williams; *Air Enthusiast No 43*, 1991.

Avro Aircraft since 1908: A. J. Jackson; Putnam, 1965.

Before the V-Bombers: D. L. Brown; *Aeroplane,* 25 December 1959.

Beyond the Spitfire: The Unseen Designs of R. J. Mitchell: Ralph Pegram; History Press, 2016.

Blackburn Aircraft since 1909: A. J. Jackson; Putnam, 1968.

Boulton Paul Aircraft since 1915: Alec Brew; Putnam, 1993.

Bristol Aircraft since 1910: C. H. Barnes; Putnam, 1964.

Bristol – An Aircraft Album: James D. Oughton; Ian Allan, 1973.

The British Aircraft Specifications File: K. J. Meekcoms and Eric B. Morgan; Air-Britain, 1994.

De Havilland Aircraft since 1909: A. J. Jackson; Putnam, 1962.

Design and Development of Weapons – Studies in Government and Industrial Organisation: M M Postan, D. Hay and J. D. Scott, HMSO, 1964.

Fairey Aircraft since 1915: H. A. Taylor, Putnam, 1974.

Fairey Barracuda: Warpaint Series No 35: W. A. Harrison; Hall Park Books, 2001.

The Folland E.28/40: Torpedo Reconnaissance Bomber with Many Unusual Features: Author Unknown; *Flight* 3 January 1946.

From Sea to Air – the Heritage of Sam Saunders: A. E. Tagg and R. L. Wheeler; Crossprint, 1989.

Gloster Aircraft since 1917: Derek N. James; Putnam, 1971.

Hawker Aircraft since 1920: Francis K. Mason; Putnam, 1971.

Hawker's Light Bomber: Tony Buttler; *Air Enthusiast No 71*, 1997.

High Speed Bomber Design: H. P. Folland; *Aeronautics,* August 1939.

Industry and Air Power – The Expansion of British Aircraft Production 1935-1941: Sebastian Ritchie; Frank Cass, 1997.

Miles Aircraft since 1925: Don L. Brown; Putnam, 1970.

Miles Aircraft – the Wartime Years: Production, Research and Development During WWII: Peter Amos, Air-Britain, 2012.

Nimrod's Genesis: RAF Maritime Patrol Projects and Weapons since 1945: Chris Gibson; Crécy Publishing, 2014.

On the aerodynamics of the Miles Libellula tandem-wing aircraft concept, 1941 – 1947: Brian J. Brinkworth; *Journal of Aeronautical History*, 2016.

Operational Requirements: Ray Sturtivant; *Aeromilitaria* No 4 1996 and No 1 1997.

Percival Aircraft Limited: Potted History I: The Aeroplane Spotter, 7 February 1948.

Pre-War Bomber Composite Projects: Michael J. F. Bowyer; *Air Pictorial,* November 1974.

RAF Bomber Command and its Aircraft 1936-1940: James Goulding and Philip Moyes; Ian Allan, 1975.

RAF Bomber Command and its Aircraft 1941-1945: James Goulding and Philip Moyes; Ian Allan, 1978.

The Royal Air Force and Aircraft Design 1923-1939: Colin Sinnott; Frank Cass, 2001.

Saunders and Saro Aircraft since 1917: Peter London; Putnam, 1988.

Shorts Aircraft since 1900: C. H. Barnes; Putnam, 1967.

Sir James Martin: Sarah Sharman; Patrick Stephens, 1996.

Specification B.12/36: Twenty-First Profile Magazine No 6.

Spirit of Hamble: Folland Aircraft: Derek N. James; Tempus, 2000.

Supermarine Aircraft since 1914: C. F. Andrews and Eric B. Morgan; Putnam 1981.

Vickers Aircraft since 1908: C. F. Andrews and Eric B. Morgan; Putnam, 1969.

Westland Aircraft since 1915: Derek N. James; Putnam, 1991.

Wilfrid Freeman: Anthony Furse; Spellmount, 2000.

Index

INDEX OF HARDWARE

INDEX OF PEOPLE

BELOW Lancaster ED817 specially modified for the Dam Buster raid of May 1943, though the aircraft is not carrying the famous bouncing bomb.

ABOVE Short Sturgeon prototype RK747.

BELOW Avro Lancaster DV170 fitted out as the prototype Mk.VI with Merlin 85 engines in Lincoln-style nacelles and with annular radiators.

ABOVE Short Stirling W7530 of No. 218 Squadron.

BELOW Handley Page Halifax Mk.II W1245.

ABOVE The Short Shetland prototype in May 1945.

BELOW Boscombe Down photo of Bristol Buckingham KV335. *Crown Copyright*

British Secret Projects 3

Fighters 1935 to 1950

Tony Buttler

British Secret Projects 3 Fighters 1935 to 1950 describes the design and development of the British fighter from the end of the biplane fighter to the start of the jet era and through the crucial years of World War 2. The coverage of projects and programmes begins in the mid-1930s in the knowledge that war was coming, and goes through to some which appeared after the war had ended. During this period the art of fighter design took huge steps forward from fixed-gun and turret fighters, such as the Supermarine Spitfire and Boulton Paul Defiant programmes, to the first generation of jet fighters, the studies of which included the Gloster Rocket. In most cases these types were designed specifically to meet the requirements of the Royal Air Force and the Fleet Air Arm.

As with the companion volumes in the *British Secret Projects* series, author Tony Buttler has made full use of archive material, much of it never published before. Three-view drawings, photographs of models and original artist's impressions combine to show how these unbuilt designs would have appeared, and examples new to this volume include the Folland Fo.118 and the Westland P.13. Data and appendices summarise the projects, their contracts and specifications as part of a detailed insight into many fascinating aircraft designs.

This latest fully revised edition of *British Secret Projects 3 Fighters 1935 to 1950* provides a wealth of new information and many new photographs.

224 pages, hardback

ISBN: 9781910809174, £27.50